Calendar

OF

EARLY MAYOR'S COURT ROLLS

Calendar

OF

EARLY MAYOR'S COURT ROLLS

Preserved among the ARCHIVES of the CORPORATION
of the CITY OF LONDON at the GUILDHALL

a.d. 1298–1307

Edited by

A. H. THOMAS, M.A.

LATE OF ST CATHARINE'S COLLEGE, CAMBRIDGE,
CLERK OF THE RECORDS

PRINTED BY ORDER OF THE
CORPORATION UNDER THE DIRECTION
OF THE LIBRARY COMMITTEE

CAMBRIDGE : AT THE
UNIVERSITY PRESS
MCMXXIV

CAMBRIDGE
UNIVERSITY PRESS

University Printing House, Cambridge CB2 8BS, United Kingdom

Cambridge University Press is part of the University of Cambridge.

It furthers the University's mission by disseminating knowledge in the pursuit of education, learning and research at the highest international levels of excellence.

www.cambridge.org
Information on this title: www.cambridge.org/9781107463929

© Cambridge University Press 1924

First published 1924
First paperback edition 2014

A catalogue record for this publication is available from the British Library

ISBN 978-1-107-46392-9 Paperback

CONTENTS

CONTENTS

INTRODUCTION

THE NINE MAYOR'S COURT ROLLS, which are here set out in abstract, cover the period from 22 May 1298 to 2 August 1307, and are the only survivals, with the exception of a few fragmentary membranes belonging to 1377, of the original rolls of this Court. To some extent the loss is mitigated by the existence of other documents. Occasional proceedings of the Court are preserved in the series of Letter Books calendared by Dr R. R. Sharpe and published by the Corporation. A series of unpublished Plea and Memoranda Rolls, extending with a few gaps from 1327 to 1484, contain records of such actions in the Mayor's Court as seemed to the clerks worthy of remembrance either as legal precedents or as illustrations of the rights, privileges and pre-eminence of the City. In addition, from the reign of Edward III onwards, files of actions were kept, giving the declarations of plaintiffs, with short notes of the proceedings, judgments and executions. The latter records, especially numerous for the 16th and 17th centuries, are of interest owing to the full inventories of goods and chattels on which executions were made. But valuable as are these supplementary sources, the original rolls merit attention, because they were written at an early and important period of the City's development, and throw considerable light on ancient municipal law and legal custom.

It has been suggested that the system by which the records were created in mediaeval London was not conducive to their preservation. The enrolment of business done in the several administrative and judicial Courts of the Guildhall was in the hands of the four attorneys of the Mayor's Court, who frequently kept their documents in their own houses. Steps were taken by the authorities on more than one occasion to ensure that all records should be kept either in the Chamber or the City Treasury[1], but apparently with only partial success. Undoubtedly there was also serious loss during the Great Fire. Though no inventory of documents had recently been made, the Court of Aldermen was informed and believed that many records had perished[2]. Nevertheless the survival

---

[1] *Cal. of Letter Book L*, p. 17 (A.D. 1462); Letter Book X, fo. 156 *b*.
[2] Repertories of the Court of Aldermen, 75, fo. 331 *b*, 79, fo. 399.

in long unbroken series of the Charters, Custumals, Proceedings of the Courts of Aldermen and Common Council and the Rolls of the Court of Husting, which constitute probably the most complete collection of municipal archives now remaining, leads one to find other reasons for the absence of the Mayor's Court Rolls. It was the custom for the Sheriffs on completion of their years of office to retain in their own custody the rolls of their Courts, in case their administration of justice was called in question either by plaints of error, or by the King's Itinerant Justices[1] in their sessions at the Tower. In the latter case, any default would be visited primarily upon themselves—a cogent reason for regarding their rolls as private property[2]. The solitary roll of the early Sheriff's Court which has come down to us belongs to the year 1321, when the memorable Iter of the Justices took place at the Tower after an interval of forty-five years, and its preservation in the Guildhall was probably due in some way to that event. This custom would perhaps not apply at first to the Mayor's Court, which in its origin appears to have been an overflow court from the Husting of Common Pleas; hence the survival of the short run of original rolls. But there is reason to believe that as the court grew into distinctness, and the limits of its jurisdiction were more closely defined, the personal responsibility of the Mayor, as apart from that of the City, was accentuated. In the Plea and Memoranda Rolls there is mention of a "Mayor's Bag" for the year, in which his correspondence and legal documents were kept; and it is not unlikely that this bag, together with the roll, accompanied him on his retirement from office, after the permanent clerks had made such copies into the Letter Books and Plea and Memoranda Rolls as they deemed necessary for preservation.

[1] *Liber Custumarum* (*Munimenta Gildhallae Londoniensis*, Rolls Series), I, pp. 296-7.
[2] They were required, however, to hand over their Rolls of Novel Disseisin and Mort d'Ancestor on the expiration of their Shrievalties, since these actions did not fall within their private jurisdiction. *Liber Albus* (Rolls Series), I, p. 404.

IMPORTANCE OF THE MAYOR'S COURT

In later centuries, with the growth of London in wealth and population, the Mayor's Court far outshadowed the other City courts. Where citizens were concerned, no monetary limit excluded actions from its jurisdiction. Thus it remained an important court for personal actions long after the County Courts were confined to the recovery of small debts. In the 18th century a City writer, detailing the several actions which could be tried in the court, says proudly[1]: "In short, this is the most extensive court of the Kingdom, for all that is cognizable in the several courts of England, is the same in this"; and he is careful to explain one reason of its popularity: "Besides, a suit may be begun and ended here, within the space of fourteen days, for so small a charge as thirty shillings." Doubtless this was true of other ancient local courts. The mediaeval towns, jealous of the Common Law, and tenaciously clinging to borough customs, which had their origin in centuries before the emergence of the courts at Westminster, had this to justify them—that they were able to supply legal remedies as satisfactory as, and far cheaper and more speedy than, those of the royal courts.

GENERAL ADMINISTRATION OF JUSTICE IN THE CITY

In tracing the origin of the Mayor's Court, something should be said of the general administration of justice in the City. London shared the general desire of mediaeval towns to develop apart from the main current of national life, and to exclude both the law of the realm and the officers of royal justice. A special body of London law was already in existence before the Norman Conquest[2]: the citizens' anxiety for its preservation is shown in the charter obtained from William the Conqueror[3], which promises to the Bishop and Portreeve the law of King Edward's day. But they desire

[1] *Laws and Customs, Rights, Liberties and Privileges of the City of London*, A.D. 1765, p. 162.
[2] *Judicia Civitatis Lundonie, circa* A.D. 930–40, in Liebermann's *Gesetze der Angelsachsen*, I, pp. 173–83.
[3] *The Historical Charters and Constitutional Documents of the City of London* (W. de G. Birch), A.D. 1884, p. 1.

further that it shall be administered by their own officers, and that these officers shall hold and determine those pleas which the King regards as distinctively his own. Their wishes were temporarily fulfilled by the Charter of Henry I[1]. Among other concessions it was granted that no citizen henceforward was to plead outside the walls of the City in any plea; they might appoint from among themselves a Sheriff to keep, and a Justiciar to plead the Pleas of the Crown, and any man impleaded in a Plea of the Crown should defend himself by the oath adjudged to him in the City; there was to be no *miskenning* in the Husting, the Folkmoot and other pleas of the City; the Husting should sit weekly on Mondays; the citizens were to have their pledges, bonds and debts within and outside the City; the King will do them right by the law of the City concerning lands of which they make complaint to him. Except as regards the Folkmoot, about which, as a court of law, there is little evidence, the main features of civic jurisdiction are outlined in the above charter.

PLEAS OF THE CROWN

Already in the reign of Henry I that development, by which all serious crimes were regarded as offences primarily against the Crown, was well advanced. It was no small concession to the City that the King's administrative, financial and judicial servants should be appointed by the citizens, and that the process and proof in such pleas should follow the ancient law of London. Dr Round has traced the history of the several Justiciars who held office in the City during the twenty years which followed the Charter[2], and Mr W. Page has brought together much supplementary detail[3]. With the disappearance of this officer during the early years of Henry II[4], it would appear that the citizens lost all control

[1] The text of this Charter as given in *Liber Custumarum*, fo. 187 is the original source of the Inspeximus Charter of Henry IV, 25 May 1400. Mr W. Page has printed an accurate transcript of the latter in *London: its Origin and Early Development*, Appendix I. Mr Farrer in the *English Historical Review*, xxxiv (1919), p. 566, ascribes the Charter to the first half of 1132.

[2] J. H. Round, *Geoffrey de Mandeville, Commune of London.*

[3] *London: its Origin and Early Development*, pp. 186–206.

[4] *Ibid.* p. 206.

of serious criminal jurisdiction, except in so far as aggrieved
persons were content to sue for damages instead of proceeding
by an appeal of felony. The Justiciar's duties were possibly
undertaken by the Itinerant Justices or Justices in Eyre,
whose activity becomes more pronounced shortly after this
time[1].

INFANGENTHEF AND OUTFANGENTHEF

It has frequently been remarked that one object of the
Crown in centralizing criminal jurisdiction was to enjoy the
profits arising from it. This motive did not apply in the case
of common thieves, whose lack of property was generally the
origin of their crimes, and the right of hanging such thieves,
known as Infangenthef and Outfangenthef, was granted by
the Crown to many boroughs and lords of lands. Strangely
enough, there is very little evidence that the City enjoyed,
until comparatively late, this general right of executing summary jurisdiction over thieves caught with the mainour of
stolen goods upon them. Dr R. R. Sharpe was inclined to
think that the City possessed it[2], on the ground that Henry III,
when he granted this and other rights to Oxford in 1225[3],
declared that the citizens of Oxford are of one and the same
custom, law and liberty with the citizens of London. The only
contemporary testimony which would lend any support to
this view is found in the claim made by Robert FitzWalter[4] in
1303 to the right of drowning persons of his soke found guilty
of treason before the Mayor at the Guildhall, and of hanging
thieves similarly convicted. But the rights of the FitzWalters
as Bannerets and guardians of London can be traced far back[5]
—even before 1136[6], and the claim made in 1303 has all the
appearance of a traditional formula, repeated from a time when
as yet no Mayor sat in Guildhall. A solitary instance of justice
upon thieves in the 13th century is seen in 1264, when certain

[1] Petit-Dutaillis, "Studies supplementary to Stubbs' *Constitutional History*" (translated by W. E. Rhodes), p. 95.
[2] *Cal. of Letter Book E*, p. 275, n. 4.
[3] *Lib. Cust.* II, pp. 671–3.
[4] *Ibid.* I, p. 150; Introd. I, pp. lxxvi–lxxxiv.
[5] *Ibid.* p. lxxviii.
[6] Mary Bateson, "A London Municipal Collection of the Reign of John," *English Historical Review*, XVII (1902), p. 485.

persons who had followed the army of Simon de Montfort
to London, and had been convicted of robberies at Stepney
and Hackney, were hanged. We are told, however, that the
Commons of the City took such measures because of the
disturbed state of London[1]. In the latter part of this century,
it was undoubtedly the custom to send such thieves to
Newgate[2], there to await the Justices of Gaol Delivery[3], who
were already visiting the prison before 1216[4]. It should be
noted also that the King regarded Newgate as his own prison,
the repair of which was a charge upon his Exchequer[5]; and
the same was true of the City gallows[6]. Moreover, the many
rolls and books of the several London courts are silent as
to any such jurisdiction, until on 6 March 1327 the Charter
of Edward III[7] appointed every Mayor for the time being
a Justice of Gaol Delivery, and specifically granted Infangenthef and Outfangenthef. Concerning this grant, the
French Chronicle[8] says that Edward III gave to the citizens
franchises which no King had ever before granted to them,
to the effect that the Mayor should be Justice at the Guildhall, and that before him should be condemned those who
had been taken for felony or larceny within the Liberties.

[1] *Liber de Antiquis Legibus*, Camden Society (1846), p. 74. Similar
emergency measures were taken in 1303 and in 1326, see City's Plea and
Memoranda Rolls, A 1, membr. 16 (19): " . . . . homines suspensi ad furcas
domini Regis videlicet apud le Elmes prope Tybourne." Meanwhile in
1306, a woman was condemned at Guildhall by her enemies and hanged,
but no offence is mentioned. *Chronicles of Edward I and Edward II* (Rolls
Series), I, p. 146. These instances hardly justify us in assuming a regular
exercise of Infangenthef. In the composition made between the City and
the Bishop of London in 1228, it was agreed that thieves in the St Paul's
soke at Cornhill should be attached by the Bishop's bailiff. If they were
attached by the City bailiffs, they should be delivered to the Bishop's
Court for judgment, and one half of their chattels should go to the Bishop,
and the other half to the bailiffs of the City. While the right of the City
to felon's goods is thus recognised, the passage is not strong enough to
support the theory that the City gave judgment on other thieves. *Lib. de
Ant. Leg.* pp. 243–4.

[2] See below, p. 120.

[3] Brit. Mus. Add. Chart. 5153, membr. 14*b*. *Placita de Quo Warranto*
(Record Commission), p. 451. P.R.O. Assize Roll 547.

[4] *E.H.R.* XVII, pp. 719–20.

[5] *Great Roll of the Pipe*, 1189–90 (Rec. Comm.), p. 223.

[6] *Rot. Litt. Claus.* II, p. 9.

[7] *Historical Charters*, p. 53.

[8] *Chronicles of Old London*, H. T. Riley, p. 268; *The French Chronicle
of London*, Camden Society (1844), p. 59.

Three weeks later the first judgments on thieves are recorded in the City's books and rolls[1].

THE COURT OF HUSTING

The Court of Husting was the ancient and general court for the City, in which both legal and administrative business was transacted. It was already in existence in the 10th century[2], when Ethelgiva, wife of Earl Ethelwine of East Anglia, gave to Ramsey Abbey two silver cups of twelve marks of the standard of the London Husting. By the Charter of Henry I it was enjoined that the Court should meet every Monday, an extension till the next day for uncompleted pleas being allowed by Henry III[3]. All kinds of pleas except those of the Crown were pleaded. There is mention of deeds being enrolled as early as 1193–4[4]. Assizes of Novel Disseisin could be demanded[5] there, and in fact, all personal pleas[6], actions relating to land[7], and offences against the City ordinances[8], were within its competence in the early part of the 13th century. Signs of a division between its functions appear in 1244, when the Itinerant Justices directed that pleas of land should be held fortnightly[9], thus leaving alternate Mondays for common pleas. Such pleas of land were begun by a writ of Right and followed the old procedure, whereby the court determined the difficult question of intrinsic right, as contrasted with

[1] *Cal. of Letter Book E*, p. 276; Plea and Memoranda Rolls, A 1, membr. xvi (19). Infangenthef and Outfangenthef appear to have been claimed by several of the Sokes or private jurisdictions in London at the *Quo Warranto* inquiry in 1321. Most of the soke-owners, however, either disclaimed or resigned the right (*Plac. de Quo Warr.* pp. 460–1, 464, 470, 471, 473). The King's advocate, Geoffrey le Scrope, declared that in the Soke of St Martin's all felons taken had been delivered at Newgate by the Justices in the reigns of Edward I and Edward II (*ibid.* p.451), and though St Paul's claimed the right of hanging thieves at Stepney and Finsbury, Scrope objected that this Church had no gallows of its own, and that in any case the right was long obsolete (*ibid.* p. 456).
[2] *Chron. Abb. Ramesiensis* (Rolls Series), p. 38.
[3] City Records Office, Box 3, 26 March 1268.
[4] *Colchester Chart.* (Roxburghe Club), ii, p. 297.
[5] *Borough Customs* (Selden Society), i, p. 231; ii, p. cxx.
[6] *E.H.R.* xvii, p. 492 from Brit. Mus. Add. MS. 14,252.
[7] *Rot. Litt. Claus.* ii, p. 153; *Cal. Close Rolls*, 1237–42, p. 148.
[8] *Lib. Cust.* i, p. 39.
[9] City's *Liber Ordinacionum*, fo. 222; Iter Roll AA, membr. 6.

those actions instituted by Henry II, which merely protected possession. There were subsidiary actions relating to dower, and the payment of rents and services for tenements, which the Husting of Pleas of Land continued to entertain until 1260, when it was provided in full Husting that all pleas moved by writs of Dower and all pleas of Customs and Services should be heard on the same day on which the Common Pleas were held[1]. There were so many actions, says the annalist, moved by many kind of writs of the King, that they could not all be brought to a conclusion in one day between morning and vespers, or even compline. The effect of the order was to throw a great increase of work on the Common Plea division of the court, which already, we may imagine, was sufficiently burdened by a variety of actions there pleadable without royal writ. Relief was sought by the delegation of business to other courts.

THE SHERIFF'S COURT

The Sheriff's Court, as a separate entity, was probably of ancient origin, and its existence may be implied in the wording of the Charter of Henry I[2], which speaks of the Folkmoot, the Husting and *other pleas* of the City. Its jurisdiction seems to have been of a minor character, for there is no evidence that the Sheriffs of London in the 12th century ever held and determined the Pleas of the Crown, as their fellows did in the shires. The general policy of Henry II and his successors was to reduce the power of the Sheriffs. In less important pleas, however, one would expect the City Sheriffs to exercise over the Wardmotes that kind of jurisdiction, which characterised the Sheriff's Tourn elsewhere, though the exact relations of the Sheriff to the Wardmotes is still a matter of conjecture. They appear quite early to have heard actions for which no remedy was given in the courts of soke-owners, *i.e.* landlords possessing private jurisdiction in the City, for in a body of rules known as the *Libertas Londoniensis*, which Dr Liebermann ascribes to the first half of the 12th century[3], the Sheriffs are forbidden

[1] *Lib. de Ant. Leg.* p. 45.
[2] W. Page, *London: its Origin*, etc., Appendix I.
[3] *Leges Angl.* p. 72.

to bring an inhabitant of a soke to the King's Pleas, or to give judgment upon him, until the owner of the soke has failed to give redress[1]. There is proof again that before 1216 the Sheriffs were dealing with those offences of individuals against each other, for which the term *transgressio* or trespass became general in the 13th century. A collection of London laws of that date contains the following[2]: "If a man makes claim to the Sheriff of battery or affray, if there is blood or a wound, then the Sheriff ought to come and put the malefactor in pledge for the blood, and the aldermen shall say whether the king ought to have the plea or the sheriffs"—in other words, whether the offender should await the Itinerant Justices at the Tower, or be summarily dealt with by the Sheriff himself. Quite clearly, the Sheriff must not meddle with the recognised Pleas of the Crown. In 1244 the citizens told the Itinerant Justices that the Sheriffs held no pleas of the Crown, but afterwards confessed that they had dealt with such royal matters as weights and measures, whereupon the Sheriffs were amerced, and the Mayor and citizens were put to judgment for having concealed their actions[3]. But ordinary assaults and violence and minor wrong-doing were within their province. When in 1258 the King's Justices, Hugh Bigot and Roger de Turkelby, came to the Guildhall and there held pleas from day to day as to all those who wished to make plaint, the citizens persistently challenged them, on the ground that no one except the Sheriffs of London ought to hold pleadings in the City on trespasses there committed[4]. The Sheriffs held their courts in their houses during the greater part of the century[5], and it was not till its close that their sessions took place regularly in the Guildhall. The profits of jurisdiction, it must be remembered, were especially desirable to them, for only by such sources of revenue could they recoup themselves for the outlay of £300, paid to the Exchequer for their joint shrievalties of London and Middlesex.

[1] City's *Liber Horn.* fo. 230.
[2] Add. MS. 14,252; *E.H.R.* xvii, p. 493.
[3] City's Iter Roll AA, membr. 5.
[4] *Lib. de Ant. Leg.* p. 40.
[5] *Liber Ordinacionum*, fo. 173 (*circa* 1230); *Lib. Cust.* i, p. 280 (1285).

DELEGATION OF PLEAS FROM THE COURT OF HUSTING

While the Sheriffs' Courts were thus available for any surplus business from the Husting Court, a natural arrangement for the latter, which met by charter only on Monday and Tuesday, would be to postpone less important actions for the deliberation of the Mayor and Aldermen on other days of the week. But a meeting on Wednesday, though it might be held in full Husting, could not be described as a Court of Husting without offence to the charters. We have here, in short, the origin of a new Court. This development took place early in the 13th century in connection with the disputes of foreign merchants. Among the questions addressed by the Itinerant Justices to the City authorities in 1221 was the following[1]:

"Question: Whether the bailiffs of the City can terminate the pleas of persons called 'pepoudrous' passing through the City, who cannot make a stay there, concerning debts or injuries due to them, or ought they to await the Husting?"

"Answer: It was answered that these pleas are not wont to be held outside the Husting. But it was provided and granted that henceforth the Mayor and Sheriffs, associating with them two or three Aldermen, may hear such plaints immediately from day to day, if the Court (of Husting) shall not be sitting the same day; and justice shall be done without delay."

Henceforward the Husting ceased to settle the disputes of foreign merchants. No cases are recorded in the rolls of that Court, which survive from 1272 onwards, and the present Calendar shews that these actions were pleaded by the Law Merchant, both in the Mayor's Court and the Sheriffs' Court[2], either among the other actions or in sessions of the courts specially set apart for them[3]. Though in some mediaeval towns Piepowder Courts were held only in time of markets or fairs, the larger cities, through which foreign merchants were passing daily, included their actions among those of the citizens and entered both on the same plea rolls[4].

[1] *Lib. Alb.* I, p. 67. *Pepoudrous* and *piepowder* mean "dusty-footed," a name given to travelling merchants.
[2] See below, pp. 69–70, 101, 183. [3] p. 69.
[4] *Select Cases on the Law Merchant* (Selden Society), I, p. xx.

It would seem that the Sheriffs extended this permission to decide cases by the Law Merchant into a jurisdiction over similar cases of debt and covenant among citizens. In certain ancient ordinances in the City's *Liber Ordinacionum*, which appear to have been promulgated about 1230[1], mention is made that persistent complaints had arisen of delay in obtaining judgment for debts, which gave debtors the opportunity of escaping their obligations. Accordingly it was enacted that any debtor who was unwilling to plead before the Sheriffs on the ground that he was a freeman, should appear before the Mayor or his deputies, the amercement being paid to the Sheriffs. One is inclined to suspect some competition in this matter between the officials of the two Courts. Some thirty years later, in 1259, the Sheriffs received a distinct pronouncement in their favour, when a provision[2] was made that all pleas of debt as to the citizens of London should be held before the Sheriffs only, but at the end of the century, as will be seen in the following pages, pleas of debt were among the most common of the actions in the Mayor's Court. There are signs indeed that the Sheriff's Court was ready on occasion to challenge such actions[3], and that the jealousy of the Sheriffs' officials was shared by some of the citizens. In certain articles[4] conceded by Edward II in 1319 for the better government of the City, the Mayor was forbidden to draw to himself or to hear in the Chamber any plea belonging to the Sheriffs or any other pleas save those which by ancient custom of the City he ought, as Mayor, to hold.

[1] *Lib. Ord.* fo. 173. These ordinances were supposed by Miss Bateson to belong to the year 1300. The reasons for placing them some seventy years earlier are to be found in the facts that an annotator, writing about 1320, draws attention to the antiquity of the customs, and that the document concludes with an ordinance that moneys paid by the City to the Exchequer on behalf of Peter Newelyn, William Wite, and Roger le Burser should be collected from their rents. All three persons were Sheriffs before 1230. Roger le Burser is probably the same person as Roger le Duc, Sheriff 1225–7, Mayor 1227–30. See *Rot. Litt. Claus.* I, pp. 517 *a*, 569; Norman Moore, *Hist. of St Barthol. Hospital*, I, p. 358; *Ancient Deeds*, A. 1741; A. B. Beavan, *Aldermen of the City of London*, I, p. 366, citing *Great Rolls of the Exchequer*, 12 and 14 Henry III.

[2] *Lib. de Ant. Leg.* p. 41.

[3] See below, pp. 29–30.

[4] *Lib. Cust.* I, p. 268.

Meanwhile, however, in the middle of the 13th century the Mayor and Aldermen are meeting in a Mayor's Court on other days than Monday to hear actions between foreign merchants, and to some extent, between citizens. About the same time, the Court of Husting delegated to the new Court the conduct of actions arising out of disobedience to City ordinances. We are told that in 1263[1], when the City was in a disturbed condition, no Husting was held, and that only pleas of Intrusion were pleaded, and also pleas of plaint made which pertain to the Assizes. By pleas of Intrusion are meant the Assizes of Novel Disseisin and Mort d'Ancestor, which were taken before the Sheriffs and Coroner; the other so-called Assizes here mentioned were the City ordinances relating to victuals—bread, wine and beer, public order, and the regulation of trade. In later days a public prosecution will sometimes be made in the Husting, but the great majority of such actions are heard in the Mayor's and Sheriffs' Courts.

ACTIONS BY PLAINT AND WRIT

The reference to plaints bears witness to a change in the method of beginning actions which greatly affected the City courts, and was largely responsible for the development of the Mayor's Court. An aggrieved citizen in the 11th and 12th centuries would rarely think it necessary to invoke the aid of the King; he was content to carry his complaint either by word of mouth or in writing to the City authorities, and if he were granted access to the Husting, he explained his grievance in his declaration. Royal writs were few in the 12th century and covered but a small number of actions, and for some of these the City already had a sufficient remedy[2]. In the latter part of that century and the first half of the next the development of the King's Chancery and the Courts of Common Law resulted in an immense increase of Royal

---

[1] *Lib. de Ant. Leg.* p. 70.

[2] Notably the action for *freshforce* or novel disseisin, which was in existence before 1166, and met with the approval of Henry II. *E.H.R.* XVII, p. 708; Add. MS. 14,252, fos. 113 *a*–116 *b*; *Lib. Alb.* I, p. 114. It was begun by a plaint of Intrusion either in the Husting or in the Congregation of Mayor and Aldermen in the Chamber of the Guildhall. *Ibid.* pp. 195–8.

writs designed to cover every dispute. The principle became
established that no man need answer for his freehold
without a writ[1]. Even in such exclusive communities as
boroughs and manors, where the ancient customary law
held sway, litigants were occasionally glad to purchase
writs commanding the holders of the courts to afford a
speedy remedy, and this not only in direct claims to the
ownership of land but also in mixed actions relating to land,
such as claims for dower, the enforcement of covenants for
rents, and for the execution of wills, in accordance with the
City custom that a freeman could devise his lands. These
writs did not necessitate new actions—they became wedded
to the old forms of actions, and in many cases they merely
commanded the Mayor and Sheriffs to do justice according
to the law and custom of the City. We have already seen
how the Husting of Pleas of Land found it necessary to
transfer actions by writs of Dower and of Rents and Services
to the Common Plea side of the court. The latter division,
which decided cases begun both by writ and plaint, in its
turn was overwhelmed with business. The plaints of private
persons might admit of delay, but this was not the case with
an action by writ, which was speedily followed by other
writs more peremptory in tone. In consequence, actions by
plaint were crowded out of the Husting Court. By 1272—the
date from which a continuous series of Common Plea Rolls
has been preserved, practically the whole available time of the
Court is occupied by writ-actions. The Court still preserves
the theory that it entertains plaints[2], and very occasionally
it does so[3], but only rarely are such plaints heard to a conclusion. A careful examination of the thirty-two rolls from
1272 to 1307 reveals that behind almost every completed

[1] Glanvill says (I, I, 2) that no man need answer for his freehold without
a royal writ. This probably had its origin in some ordinance of Henry II.
In a writ of 1207, which John sent to the people of Ireland, he directed
that no one should be impleaded for his free tenement without writ of the
king or of his justiciar. *Rot. Litt. Pat.* (Rec. Comm.), p. 76. See Maitland,
Select Pleas in Manorial Courts (Selden Society), Introd. pp. liv–lv.

[2] Husting Rolls of Common Pleas, 5, membr. 3 (A.D. 1277).

[3] *Ibid.* Roll 25, membr. 6. Precept to the Sheriff to give execution of
a judgment in the Husting without writ "*de quodam cypho capto et injuste
detento*," *i.e.* an action "*de namiis injuste captis*." Similar precept in an
action of trespass not described.

action was a royal writ. Moreover, except as regards the action of account, the great majority of pleas concern lands and rents. Other personal actions must now be sought in the records of the Mayor's and Sheriffs' Courts.

FIRST RECORDED ACTIONS IN THE MAYOR'S COURT

The Mayor's Court Rolls here calendared begin only in 1298, though proceedings are mentioned in other City documents before this date. In a list of rules for counters and attorneys promulgated in 1280, these officials are forbidden to gainsay judgments, but if it seems to them that error has been made they must make plaint, according to the law and usage of the City, to the Mayor, who will redress such error[1]. We have here an action of error by plaint before the Mayor, in contrast to the similar actions by writ in the Husting. Next year[2] the Mayor's Court is busy with the punishment of tavern-brawlers, bullies, night-walkers, gamblers and other disorderly persons, who had offended against the ordinances of the City. Fraudulent bakers appeared before the Court in 1282 and were condemned to be drawn on hurdles through the streets[3]. There is record of actions for trespass and debt about the same time[4]. In 1285, when the King took the City into his hands, he strengthened the remedies for foreigners, by ordaining that either the Warden or Sheriffs should hear their plaints daily, and if on any day they were unable to do so, a deputy should act in their places[5]. An action against a monk of Westminster for impleading a citizen outside the City walls in a Church court was heard in 1292[6], and next year the keeper of the Winchester Seld was fined for

---

[1] *Lib. Cust.* I, p. 281. This was not a legal jurisdiction. The Provisions of Westminster, c. 16, say that no one but the King may hold pleas of false judgment, since a plea of this kind specially pertains to the King's dignity. The Statute of Marlborough, 1267, repeats the prohibition. At the *Iter* of 1321 no mention was made of the Mayor's Court practice in error, which was subsequently abandoned.

[2] *Cal. of Letter Book B*, pp. 1–12.

[3] *Ibid.* pp. 13–14; A, pp. 120–1.

[4] A, pp. 64, 213; *Lib. Cust.* I, pp. 282–3; *Lib. Ord.* fo. 231 b.

[5] *Lib. Alb.* I, pp. 295–6. For date, see *ibid.* p. 280.

[6] *Cal. of Letter Book A*, p. 144.

enhancing the price of goods and using an unlawful trone[1]. All these actions can be paralleled by others recorded in the rolls.

DISTINCTION BETWEEN THE HUSTING AND THE MAYOR'S COURT

As will be gathered from the foregoing remarks, the Husting of Common Pleas and the Mayor's Court were closely connected, though there were certain elemental differences. The former court sits only on Monday or by adjournment on Tuesdays, and the judges consist of the Mayor, Sheriffs and Aldermen. The latter sits on any day, and the Sheriffs are only present as servants of the court. The limits of their jurisdiction are beginning to be clearly marked. The Husting will only deal in the main with pleas by writ relating to lands and rents, and has devolved personal actions begun by plaint to the Mayor's Court. To some extent their jurisdictions overlap, and a confusion of phraseology is apt to mislead the reader. A brief comparison of the actions contained in the two series of Rolls may therefore not be out of place.

(a) *Actions common to both Courts.* The Court of Husting continued to entertain prosecutions for offences against the City ordinances. An action against the Keeper of the Winchester Seld was heard, but a day was afterwards given for the pleadings in the Mayor's Court[2]. Conversely, certain cases of the same nature begun and pleaded in the latter Court were remitted to the Husting for judgment[3]. Both Courts will hear actions against City officials or lax Sheriffs who have allowed debtor prisoners to escape, and will punish citizens who have resisted these officials or have used contumelious words against an alderman[4]. We find further that persons who had been sued to render account by a Writ of Monstravit, which provided for the summary arrest of a fugitive debtor, will turn upon the plaintiff in either Court,

[1] *Cal. of Letter Book C*, pp. 13–14. Trone, *sc.* a beam for weighing.
[2] *Lib. Cust.* I, pp. 115–6. See also the case of John de Ely, H.R.C.P. Roll 31, membr. 6, and p. 233 of the present Calendar.
[3] See below, pp. 30, 106, 137, 140, 254.
[4] H.R.C.P. Roll 24, membr. 14 *b*; 30, membr. 5; *Cal. of Letter Book A*, p. 192.

and claim damages on the ground that they possessed sufficient property in the City, by which they could have been brought to answer without personal arrest[1]. Both Courts again will summon guardians of orphans to render account of their wardship[2]. But whereas these actions are of constant occurrence in the Mayor's Court, on only four or five occasions can the Husting find time to deal with them within a space of thirty years.

(b) *Dissimilar actions bearing the same names.* In other actions apparently common to both Courts, there is a clear line of distinction. Actions of account by writ go to the Husting, by plaint to the Mayor's Court[3]. Debt in the former court relates to rents, in the latter to commercial transactions[4]. Detinue of deeds in the former is raised by the writ *de detencione cartarum*, in the latter it is raised by plaint and concerns pledges, recognisances and bonds[5]; detinue of chattels in the Husting touches distresses unjustly taken for rent, in the Mayor's Court the chattels detained were goods supplied in the way of trade[6]. Similarly actions of covenant begun by writ in the one Court denoted leases or sales of land unfulfilled, in the other breaches of commercial contract[7]. There is still loose mention of trespasses in the Husting. On examination they prove to relate to ordinary Husting actions, pledges unjustly taken, the diversion of rights appurtenant to a tenement, default of duty by City officials, waste and wardship of lands[8]. Even at the end of the 13th

[1] H.R.C.P. Roll 29, membr. 15. This action was by writ. For actions by plaint in the Mayor's Court, see below, pp. 104–5, 193–4, 205, 207, 240. A considerable battle was waged in the City round the writs of account. Debtors preferred to be sued on writs of *Justicies* and *Justicies inter Mercatores*, both of which allowed the debtor to be distrained, and to clear himself according to the law and custom of the City, *i.e.*, with a law, or oath-helpers. The writ of Monstravit, as was explained by the Sheriffs in 1302 (H.R.C.P. Roll 28, membr. 4 b), was a writ of the King's Council, which was terminated according to the Common Law by jury and was designed to meet cases where the debtor had no lands or tenements by which he could be distrained. See below, p. 105, note 1.
[2] H.R.C.P. 12, m. 8; 32, m. 14; and below, pp. 50, 232, 235–6.
[3] H.R.C.P. 17, m. 2; 18, m. 5 b, 11 b, etc.; and below, pp. 228, 239–40.
[4] H.R.C.P. 3, m. 4; and below, pp. 104, 105, etc.
[5] H.R.C.P. 2, m. 4; 3, m. 1; 4, m. 1; and below, pp. 128, 207.
[6] H.R.C.P. 24, m. 14; and below, pp. 113, 127.
[7] H.R.C.P. 10, m. 12; 11, m. 1; and below, pp. 55–6, 81, 93.
[8] H.R.C.P. 16, m. 10 b; 24, m. 7, 23 b; 25, m. 12 b; 34, m. 12.

century trespass was not very clearly defined, and on one occasion there was a debate in the Husting as to whether a Sheriff who had allowed a debtor to escape should be sued for trespass or debt[1]. On the other hand, the trespasses recorded in the Mayor's Court were true personal trespasses unrelated to land, and consisted of assaults, defamation, fraud and unjust interference with other people's rights, comfort or convenience. With the exception of a few writs ordering inquiry into affrays, reprisals for seizure of goods abroad, or the giving of more speedy justice[2], all actions in the Mayor's Court were begun by bill of complaint, and have so continued till the present day.

RELATIONS BETWEEN THE MAYOR'S AND SHERIFFS' COURTS

Although in many particulars, these Courts were exercising a concurrent jurisdiction at the close of the 13th century, there are already signs of the coming predominance of the former, especially in its control over City officers and in the matter of error. The Sheriffs were charged with the duty of making executions in private suits, and apparently they received the amercements of Court, both matters which would ensure their constant attendance. In addition they appeared frequently either as plaintiffs or defendants. The Sheriff's duties as collector of customs, murage, and other charges brought him into dispute with a population which resented all taxation, direct or indirect, and was obstinately convinced that the burden of taxation was unjustly distributed between rich and poor[3]. While the Sheriff had some power of hearing public prosecutions in his own Court, his position there as judge prevented him from being sued as a defendant. Thus he is frequently summoned to the Mayor's Court to answer charges of having made unjust sequestrations and distraints[4] in private suits and in the collection of customs. Occasionally the verdict of a jury is against him and he is amerced[5]. Citizens complained that he took unfair customs on salt and

---

[1] H.R.C.P. 24, m. B. dors.
[2] See below, pp. 21, 34, 42, 43, 113, 164, 178, 221.
[3] See complaints in *Rot. Hund.* (Rec. Comm.) London.
[4] See below, pp. 37, 172.   [5] pp. 184, 256–8.

had wrongfully forfeited poultry and fish[1]. Creditors sued him for returning attachments before they had recovered their debts[2], and for allowing debtors to escape. He has to answer for unjust discrimination against wharf owners[3]. On one occasion the Court greatly increased the damages against him which had been taxed by a jury[4]. The Sheriffs in their turn had frequent recourse to the Mayor's Court. They sued recalcitrant citizens who had resisted distraints or assaulted them, or had removed sequestration seals placed by the Sheriffs on their doors[5]. A frequent cause of offence was the smuggling of goods by water to Westminster, whereby the Sheriff lost his customs[6], the opening of bales of foreign goods and their sale before toll had been paid[7], and avowry by citizens of foreigners' goods in order to escape the duties[8].

The numerous pleas of error also tended to exalt the Mayor's Court. If a litigant before the Sheriff was aggrieved at the judgment recorded, the orthodox procedure was to present a Writ of Error in the Husting of Common Pleas, to the effect that there was manifest error in the record and process, or the giving of judgment. But in the early rolls of that Court, though several actions were entered, few appear to have reached the stage of pleading. We may imagine that the writ was allowed to lapse, and that plaintiffs were advised to seek their remedy in the Mayor's Court, in accordance with the ordinance of 1280 already mentioned[9]. Probably the action was regarded as equivalent to the ordinary actions against officials for default of duty, since the Sheriff appears as joint defendant with the other party. Meanwhile, however, the principle was gaining ground that error was a royal matter, and in course of time the old writ-action was revived in the Husting. All that remained to the Mayor's Court was the right of removing actions from the Sheriffs' Court before they had been submitted to a jury[10], records of which survive under the titles, "markments" and "querelae levatae."

Important as were the duties mentioned above, it should be noted that the Mayor's Court at this period appears to

[1] p. 241. [2] pp. 201, 241. [3] p. 184.
[4] p. 258. [5] pp. 159, 166.
[6] pp. 7, 12, 41, 42. [7] pp. 8, 85–6, 114. [8] pp. 8, 32, 40, 71–2, 161.
[9] *Lib. Cust.* I, p. 281. [10] *Lib. Alb.* I, p. 219.

have been less frequented than the Sheriffs' Court. A comparison of our rolls with such proceedings as were forwarded from the latter, shows that actions were entered in the Sheriffs' Court in far greater detail, and that the clerks of the Court were more careful and experienced lawyers. There is little mention of the Mayor's Court in the City Custumals which were compiled between 1310 and 1330. Probably the desire to extend jurisdiction would arise, not from the Mayor and Aldermen themselves, but from the Recorder, the Common Serjeant and the clerks and attorneys, who gained a living from the fees. At the great session of the Itinerant Justices at the Tower in 1321, when very full information was given about the other courts, there is no mention of the Mayor's Court as such, beyond a quotation of the Articles of 1319. Nevertheless the existence of the Court was known to the royal officers of justice, as is evidenced by the fact that in 1305 and 1309, special commissions of Justices were sent to St Martin's le Grand to review the judgments given in two at least of the actions decided in the Court[1].

DESCRIPTION OF THE MAYOR'S COURT IN RICART'S KALENDAR

The earliest general description of the Court is to be found in a document copied into one of the Custumals of Bristol, which was compiled by Robert Ricart[2], appointed Town Clerk of that City in 1479. Ricart tells us that the account of the ancient usages of London was "wretin oute of a boke that was maistir Henry Daarcy sometyme recorder of London in King Edward the thirdes daies"[3]. Henry Darcy was Mayor, not Recorder, of London in 1337 and 1338. Miss Toulmin Smith, who edited Ricart's Kalendar for the Camden Society, suggests that Darcy's book may have been one of those formerly belonging to the City and now lost—possibly the *Magnus Liber de Chartis et Libertatibus Civitatis*, which was

[1] The actions between John de Melan and John de Thotenham and Simon Beauflur, see p. 202, and *Cal. Pat. Rolls*, 1301–7, p. 403, and between Roger de Brunne and Avice la Haubergere, see p. 190 and *C.P.R.* pp. 538, 546.
[2] Camden Society (1872).
[3] *Ibid.* p. xx.

existing in 1327[1]. This may well be so, for the passages quoted
by Ricart have every appearance of belonging to the early
part of the 14th century. With the exception of the section
relating to the Mayor's Court, the material was also copied
by John Carpenter into the City's *Liber Albus* in 1419[2].
Darcy's book probably survived into the 16th century, since
no fewer than four manuscripts of that period are still surviving[3], which contain the section omitted by the *Liber Albus*.
An excellent translation appeared in 1647 under the title of
The City Law[4], the relevant portions of which are as follows:

Curia Majoris of the said City of *London*, is holden by the custome
of the same City before the Mayor and Aldermen for the time being in
the Chamber of the *Guild-Hall* or in *Husting* and that from day to day,
and there are treated, determined and discussed the Pleas, and matters
touching Orphans, Apprentices, and other businesses of the same City.
And there are redressed and corrected the faults and contempts of those
which do against the custome and ordinance of the City, as well at the
suit of the parties, as by Enquest of Office, and in other sort by suggestion
according as the causes require; and there they use to justifie Bakers,
Victuallers, and Trades-men, and to treat and ordain for the Government
of the City, and for keeping the Kings peace and other necessary points
of the City, and according as the time requireth.

Item, the Officers and Ministers of the said City being found faulty
are to be cleared before the Mayor and Aldermen as well at the Suit of
the parties by Process made, as otherwise, according to the discretion
of the said Mayor and Aldermen.

Item, the said Mayor and Aldermen use there to hold, and determine
Pleas of Debt and other Actions personal whatsoever, by Bill as well
among Merchants, and Merchants for Merchandize, as also between
others that will plead by Process made against the parties.

Item, the Mayor and Aldermen, or the Mayor and Chamberlain of
the said City take before them in the said Chamber Recognizances of
Debt of those that will, of what summes soever. And if the day of payment
be missed, then he to whom the Recognizance is made out of this Record,
shall have execution of all the Debtors Goods, and of the moyety of his
Lands within the said City, and it is taken as at the Common Lawes.

Item, Pleas of Debt according to the Ordinance called the Suit of
Smithfield, are determinable only before the Mayor and Aldermen according as is more plainly set down in the Ordinance thereupon made.

Item, the Assizes of Nusance are determinable by plaint before the
Mayor and Aldermen, and that plaint shall be served by the Sheriff the
Wednesday against the Friday; and then the Mayor and Aldermen ought
to proceed in Plea according to that which is set down in the Act of
Assize and Nusance in the said City.

[1] *Ibid.* p. xxi. Cf. *Lib. Alb.* introd., p. xvii. *Cal. of Letter Book E*, p. 215.
[2] *Lib. Alb.* pp. 181–90, 195–223, 260–80, 319–38, 364, 494.
[3] *Borough Customs* (Selden Society), 1, p. xxxviii.
[4] "The City Law or The Course & Practice in all manner of Juridicall
proceedings in the Hustings in Guild Hall, London. Englished out of
an ancient French Manuscript."

Item, the Mayor and Aldermen have alwayes used to set down penal Acts upon Victuals, and for other governance of the City and of the peace, according to their discretion and advice, and proclaim the same Ordinance within the said City openly to be kept in the Kings name, and of the City upon that penalty set down, and shall levie all those penalties of those which do contrary to the Ordinance aforesaid.

Item, the Mayor and Aldermen have alwayes used, and may by custome of the same City cause to come before them the offenders which are taken within the said City for Lies and false Nuses noised abroad in disturbance of the Peace Makers, and Counterfeiters of false Seales, and false Evidences, and for other notorious deceits known to them, which they shall find faulty of such malefactours by confession of the parties or by enquest, and then take them and punish them by the Pillory or other chastisement by imprisonment, according to their discretion.

Item, the Mayor and Aldermen have alwayes accustomed, and may by custome of the said City, change Process, abbridge delayes in actions personal as well before themselves, as in the Sheriffs Courts, and to make new Ordinances touching personal Pleas which Ordinances they under-stand to be reasonable and profitable for the people.

The cases set out in the following Calendar fall within the above description, shewing that the main outlines of the Mayor's Court were already established at the close of the 13th century. Later developments may be found in the City books, and several learned treatises of the 17th and 18th centuries illustrate the closer definition necessitated by decisions in particular cases[1].

PROCEDURE OF THE MAYOR'S COURT

PLAINTS. Much light on early borough procedure has been afforded by the two volumes of *Borough Customs* published by the Selden Society, and it will be sufficient here to note only new details or usages peculiar to London. The plaint by which actions were initiated was a written document delivered to the attorneys of the Court. In the 14th century there was little to distinguish it from the petitions which led to proceedings in equity[2], beyond the fact that the plaint contained pledges for prosecution at the foot, while the petition was marked *supplicacio*. Both were in French, and began with the customary formula: "As treshonorable & tresgracious seigneur le Mair de Loundres moustre & se

---

[1] Calthrop, *Reports of Special Cases*, 1670; *Lex Londinensis*, 1680; Strype's Stow, 1720; *The Priviledges of the Lord Mayor and Aldermen*, 1722; *The Laws and Customs of the City of London*, 1765; *A Concise Treatise of the Courts of Law of the City of London*, by Thomas Emerson, 1794.

[2] Mayor's Court Files, I, nos. 23, 29–32, 44, 76.

pleynt," etc. Sometimes the Aldermen and Recorder are mentioned and the terms of courtesy are varied. But in actions where a legal remedy could be applied, the original plaint was not produced in Court, being merely a preliminary for the summons of the defendant. The Court acted on a brief note handed in by the attorney[1], and the substance of the plaintiff's grievance was explained by him or his attorney in the declaration made in Court. In the next century it was no longer usual for the plaintiff to produce any actual plaint at all, except in actions relating to apprentices. Meanwhile the petitions for equitable remedies approximated to the common form known to students of Chancery proceedings.

MAINPRISE AND BAIL. The City rules as to mainprise, except in the case of persons charged or appealed for felony or grievous trespass in the Husting, were not elaborated according to any definite scale. As regards felony, the liberation of the accused person on mainprise was a dearly-prized City privilege. "If any man," says the Custumal of 1216[2], "be killed in London or the Portsoken the Sheriff ought to go thither and find out who killed him. If the neighbourhood names any one or suspects any one, or if the dead man himself has accused any one before he died, the Sheriffs ought to attach the accused and mainprise him by twelve good pledges—failing which he should take his body—for if the suspect were found elsewhere, he would not be let go in spite of finding pledges." This rule was recognised by the King's clerks, for in 1226 a Letter Close directed that a man accused of murder should be bailed by twelve good men to appear before the Itinerant Justices[3]. Though there was a disposition to confine the privilege to men who were found not guilty by juries on the ground of self-defence and were awaiting pardon[4], the City custom was generally allowed in

---

[1] An example is to be found sewn to membrane 3 of Roll I: *Johannes de Kent taillour queritur quod error interest Recordo & processu....quare petit quod predicta Recordum & processus veniant coram vobis.*

[2] Add. MS. 14,252, and *Lib. Horn*, fo. 255. A Latin version is given in *Liber Alb.* I, p. 113. See *E.H.R.* XVII, pp. 721–2.

[3] *Rot. Litt. Claus.* (Rec. Comm.), II, p. 160.

[4] *Cal. Close Rolls*, 1242–7, pp. 97, 278, 382.

the 13th century, notably in the case of Laurence Duket[1], who was suspected of the murder of Master William Lefremont, the physician. But as the disposition of the Crown to deal sternly with crime and to expend money on prisons became stronger, the City custom appeared to be an anachronism. The matter came to a head at the Session of the Justices at the Tower in 1321, when it was found that John de Gisors during his mayoralty had not only liberated a man indicted of felony, but had even admitted him to the freedom of the City by falsifying the date, in order that he should enjoy the citizen's right of mainprise. The Justices declared that the custom was contrary to the law and custom of the realm, tended to retard and suffocate justice and to encourage crime, and they adjudged that the Mayor and Commonalty should lose this liberty or custom for ever[2].

In less serious charges, the City seems to have been content to take sufficient mainprise, according to their view of sufficiency at the moment. A curious case in the Husting in 1278, where a man appealed for felony another who had thrust him in the left eye with a lance, shows that a single mainpernor was judged enough[3]. In the Mayor's Court, however, more substantial surety was generally required. Though one mainpernor might be allowed for the payment of a fine, the rendering of account, or even for keeping the peace in the case of responsible defendants[4], two was the usual number required for appearing to hear judgment, making proof by oaths, the payment of amercements or the restoration of goods[5]. Four or six were demanded in assaults and offences against civic ordinances, and such matters as charges of maintenance, and fines due to the King[6]. When a defendant appeared to be a source of disorder in the City, he might be

---

[1] *Rotuli Hundredorum* (Record Commission), 1, p. 410. The same custom held good in 1285. *Lib. Alb.* 1, p. 296.

[2] *Lib. Cust.* 1, pp. 373–4. This right of mainprise by twelve was not confined to citizens at the Iter of 1276. Add. Chart. 5153, membr. 13 *b*.

[3] *Cal. of Letter Book A*, p. 194. In 1302 nine persons who had been appealed in the Husting for the death of a man were each mainprised by a single mainpernor. H.R.C.P. Roll 27, m. 10 *b*. We may suspect that the Court attached little weight to this appeal.

[4] See below, pp. 30, 84, 144, 124.

[5] pp. 3, 28, 7, 258.   [6] pp. 190, 234, 233, 180.

called upon to find twelve mainpernors[1]—as for instance in the case of Roger de Lincoln, draper, who was bound over to keep the peace between himself and his following and the Sheriff and Alderman of the Ward. In one action of assault and defamation, the defendant needed no fewer than fifteen mainpernors[2]. In none of these cases does it appear that a man's mainpernors had any connection with the system of Frankpledge, as suggested by Miss Bateson.

PROOF BY OATH-HELPERS. When the plaintiff had declared his grievance and the defendant had denied or otherwise controverted the statement, the question of proof arose. The ancient method of proof in the City was by an oath, known as a *lex* or law, and the party which offered to prove his case by an oath was said to wage his law. It consisted of an oath denying the facts alleged, which might be supported by the oaths of a number of persons, who swore, not as to the facts, but as to the credibility and good faith of their principal[3]. A brief account of the different oaths waged in the City will illustrate those forms which survived in the Mayor's Court in our period.

(*a*) *The Great Law* was used in charges of murder and housebreaking before the Justiciar and the Itinerant Justices. A passage in the Custumal of 1216, which from its mention of the Justiciar may be dated before 1160, tells us that a citizen charged with murder, by hue and cry and witness, or with manifest housebreaking, with doors broken and hacked and obvious wounds, should be put to the Great Law at a time fixed by the Justiciar[4]. To support him, he must have thirty-six oath-helpers, eighteen from each side of Walbrook. He swore the oath once and was followed by his helpers. If a single one broke down in swearing or withdrew from the oath, the accused was liable to death or mutilation. There are several recorded cases of this method of trial. At the Iter of 1226 John Herlisun[5], accused of the death of Lambert de Legis, failed in his law, but was granted his life and limb at the prayer of the women of the City, and became a Hospitaller

---

[1] p. 154.   [2] See below, p. 20.   [3] *Lib. Alb.* I, p. 105.
[4] Add. MS. 14,252. For this passage see *Lib. Alb.* I, p. 111. *Borough Customs*, I, pp. 37–8.
[5] *Lib. de Ant. Leg.* p. 5. Cf. Iter Roll AA, membr. 4.

of the Hospital of Jerusalem. Before the Iter of 1244, the procedure had changed to six oaths by the accused, in each of which he was supported by six of his compurgators, making the total of thirty-six helping oaths. In this way, William Bertone cleared himself of a charge of having caused an abortion by assault[1]. At the Iter of 1251 there were several further instances of the Great Law performed both with success and failure[2]. But at the next Iter of 1276 only one accused person was submitted to the Great Law, namely a certain Christiana de Dunelmia who had been appealed of causing the death of her husband by administering poison to him. She was acquitted[3]. By this time, citizens who could not or would not find twelve mainpernors for their appearance before the Itinerant Justices were imprisoned and tried at Newgate, where there was a regular Gaol Delivery by Justices appointed for the purpose[4]. The City still claimed the Great Law at the Iter of 1321, but no one was submitted to it. The old method of proof had little to recommend it in comparison with the ordinary trial by jury[5].

(b) *The Middle Law of eighteen oath-helpers* mentioned in the Custumal of 1216[6] was applicable to charges of mayhem or maiming, as we learn from a later document in the *Liber Horn* written shortly before 1321[7]. We are told that the method of proof was a threefold oath by the accused " himself

---

[1] *Lib. Alb.* I, pp. 103–5. Iter Roll AA, membr. 4.

[2] *Lib. de Ant. Leg.* p. 18.

[3] Add. Chart 5153, membr. 10 b. Several citizens had been mainprised by twelve to appear before the Itinerant Justices. All of them, including the above Christiana, wished to put themselves on the verdict of juries. Ralph Parmenter was allowed to do so on payment of 20s.; others by the indulgence of the Justices, or because the suspicion against them was slight. The question was raised in Christiana's case as to whether a verdict of not guilty by a jury would be a sufficient acquittance, and it was decided that it would not be so.

[4] *Ibid. passim*; *Lib. de Ant. Leg.* p. 99; *Cal. Pat. Rolls*, 1266–1272, p. 537; *Rot. Hund.* I, p. 428; *C.P.R.* 1272–1281, p. 165.

[5] *Lib. Cust.* I, 321. The citizens said that a man could clear himself by twelve jurors according to the Common Law or by the Great Law of the City. All accused persons put themselves on juries. During the forty-four years preceding the majority of citizens indicted or appealed of murder appear to have been content to undergo an ordinary trial at Newgate. See P.R.O. Assize Roll 547, *passim*.

[6] *Borough Customs*, I, pp. 37–9, where the passage is considered to belong to the period 1131–1155. Cf. *Lib. Alb.* pp. 110–11.

[7] *Lib. Horn*, fos. 211–12.

the sixth hand," which would mean three oaths by himself, each supported by five oath-helpers. The only known case comes from the 12th century, when a certain John Bucquinte, accused of felony, was adjudged to the oath, himself the eighteenth, *i.e.* with seventeen oath-helpers[1]. In the *Liber Horn* it is said that the accused swore three times with six oath-helpers, eighteen in all. As there seems so little certainty as to the numbers, it may be concluded that the oath was seldom sworn, and even in 1216 was nothing but a dim memory. The same uncertainty is found with regard to an oath by twelve men. In 1257 in connection with a charge of unjust tallages against the Mayor and others, John Maunsel the King's Justice asked what was the custom of the City, and was told that for trespass against the King a citizen was wont to clear himself by twelve men[2]. But next day the populace at the Folkmoot was induced to deny this custom—a disavowal which the annalist records with indignation.

(c) *The Third Law of six oath-helpers* was applicable in several circumstances. In the early 12th century a citizen charged with having slain a man belonging to the Court of the King or of the barons, who had billeted himself upon the citizen by force, might swear with six of his kinsmen that he had killed the intruder on this account—and so clear himself[3]. A similar oath about the same period was adjudged where the king prosecuted a man in a plea of the crown, in which no private appellor accused him, and if the accused person failed in his sevenfold oath, he suffered loss of life or limb or a fine of 100s., as the seriousness of the crime warranted[4]. An illustrative case is found at the Iter of 1244. A woman had appealed a man for a violent assault, and afterwards died by her injuries. The crown took up the prosecution and desired information from the Mayor and citizens as to the custom of the City, which was reported as being

---

[1] *Lib. Alb.* p. 109. See *E.H.R.* XVII, p. 723.
[2] *Lib. de Ant. Leg.* pp. 33-4.
[3] Liebermann, *Gesetze der Angelsachsen*, p. 673; *Borough Customs*, I, p. 47, quoting from Add. MS. 14,252.
[4] *Ibid.* See also *Lib. Alb.* I, p. 112. A later section of the Add. MS. says that if an appellor is not of good character, the Justiciar can put a man to his oath with the seventh hand. *Borough Customs*, I, p. 25.

the sevenfold oath. The man was released on finding twelve mainpernors, and apparently the custom was then allowed[1].

The above forms of the Third Law in felony were clearly exceptional and the proper sphere of this comparatively easy method of proof was in the lesser forms of trespass and civil wrong, where it survived for several centuries.

(d) *The Third Law in Trespass* was claimed in 1257, when the citizens declared that a man could clear himself of trespass against any other person by making oath, himself the seventh hand[2]. All trespass, it should be noted, had two aspects. It was a wrong done by one man to another; it was also a breach of the King's Peace. According to the so-called Laws of Edward the Confessor, probably representing the law of the early 12th century[3], the King's Peace covered, among other times, the eight days of each of the three great festivals of Christmas, Easter and Pentecost. Doubtless trespasses committed at such periods were regarded as within the province of the King's Justices; and the compiler of the *Liber Horn*, writing just before the Iter of 1321[4], had this in mind when he tells us that the Third Law was used in charges of assaults, batteries, tolts, wounds, blows, bloodshed and other injuries committed during the above three festivals. But long before this time, the conception had taken root that all trespasses, committed at any time, involved some breach of the King's Peace, and although the local Courts continued to deal with them, the Crown keeps a close watch over them. By the Statute of Wales, c. 11, 1280[5], it was enacted that men should no longer wage their law either in felonies or in personal trespass, but go to juries in accordance with the law of England. In 1285, when the City of London was in the King's hands, he took the opportunity of abolishing the wager of law in trespasses where there was bloodshed or battery except by consent of the plaintiff[6].

---

[1] Iter Roll AA, membr. 2, which contains a fuller account than *Lib. Alb.* I, pp. 91–2.
[2] *Lib. de Ant. Leg.* pp. 33–4.
[3] Maitland, *Const. Hist.* pp. 108–9.
[4] *Lib. Horn*, fos. 210–11; *Lib. Alb.* I, pp. 58–9.
[5] *Statutes of the Realm*, I, pp. 66, 68.
[6] *Lib. Alb.* I, pp. 294–5.

(e) *The Third Law in Trespass in the Mayor's Court.* In our rolls we see this principle exemplified on several occasions. A plaintiff who complained of two assaults was willing to allow the defendant to clear himself by his law, but the latter refused on the ground that he acknowledged having pushed the plaintiff away, and thus having used battery[1]. Probably he intended to shelter himself under an exception that the assault was in self-defence. All other assaults were submitted to juries, except in an action where the plaintiff was a foreigner, and the Court adjudged that the defendant make his law, possibly because the assault was merely technical[2]. On the other hand, wager of law was frequently granted in non-violent forms of trespass, as for instance in defamation, disrespect to the Mayor, enhancing prices, and unjust attachment[3]. Occasionally a plaintiff would be required to make his law on some allegation contained in the defence. A poulterer charged the Sheriff with unjust forfeiture of his geese, and was ordered to make his law on the Sheriff's reply that the plaintiff was selling them unlawfully to retailers (p. 18). A Guildhall official complained that a man had slandered him by saying that he had taken bribes, and when the defendant answered that he believed the charge, the plaintiff was adjudged to clear himself by his law (p. 147). Where a law was refused, the offences were probably statutory. Certain defendants charged with forestalling were refused their law; and an assault on the King's bailiffs without battery was treated in the same fashion[4]. A plaintiff in an action for fraud objected to the defendant's law on the ground that he could prove the facts by a jury, and after consideration, the Court allowed the objection[5]. There appears to have been a feeling that a law was applicable only where damages were claimed, and as the punishment for fraud was the pillory, a jury was necessary. The same idea may have been in the mind of a plaintiff who objected to the defendant's law, because the offence, if proved, involved imprisonment[6]. But, generally speaking, wager of law

---

[1] See below, pp. 138–9.   [2] p. 235.
[3] pp. 97–8, 146–7, 73.   [4] pp. 229, 145.
[5] p. 173.   [6] p. 175.

in trespass was on the decline at this period. In 1301, the King's Justices, sitting under a special commission at the Leadenhall refused to allow a wager of law[1] to two prominent citizens, who had been accused of wounding John le Chaucer to the risk of his life, because such a defence was contrary to the Common Law of England. Again in 1329, another commission at Guildhall would not admit oath-helpers in a charge of conspiracy[2].

(f) *Wager of Law in Civil Actions* had a long history in the City, being found as early as the 10th century. In the Laws of Aethelred it was provided that a man, who had been charged by the Portreeve or Tunreeve or other reeve with withholding toll, could swear with the seventh hand that he withheld no toll which he was bound to pay[3]. Further mention of the custom in the 12th century shows that the foreigner in London enjoyed the privilege in pleas of debt and trespass[4]. It was defined in 1285 as applicable to breach of contract and debt, where the party plaintiff had no writing or tally to prove his claim[5]. The custom was not peculiar to London: it was a favourite method of proof in the Law Merchant at this period, and numerous instances are to be found in the proceedings of the Piepowder Courts[6]. Both in London and elsewhere it was tolerated by the common law in civil actions till long after the close of the Middle Ages, and was not abolished till the Act of 3 & 4 William IV, c. 42, s. 13.

(g) *Wager of Law in Civil Actions in the Mayor's Court.* Before dealing with the ordinary seventh-hand oath, mention should be made of two other oaths used in the City.

(i) *The Peremptory Oath.* According to the *Liber Albus*[7], if any person makes demand of a certain debt or other contract, and the party defendant says that his demand or

---

[1] *Lib. de Ant. Leg.* p. 249; *Chron. of Reigns of Edward I and Edward II* (Rolls Series), I, p. 128.
[2] *Ibid.* I, p. 244.
[3] Liebermann, *Gesetze*, I, p. 234.
[4] *Borough Customs*, I, p. 177.
[5] *Lib. Alb.* I, p. 294.
[6] *Select Cases on the Law Merchant* (Selden Society).
[7] *Lib. Alb.* I, p. 521. See also p. 217 for a rule that where the defendant raises a dilatory exception, the plaintiff can put him on his peremptory oath that the plea or exception was a true one.

his suit is not a true one, and thereupon puts himself on
the oath of the plaintiff forthwith, with his single hand, in
case the plaintiff will not make oath that his demand is a
true one, then the party defendant is adjudged to go quit,
and the plaintiff is amerced. Several cases in the Mayor's
Court illustrate the custom. A plaintiff in an action of debt
who had no tally to support his plea, offered to verify his
claim by his corporal oath and by consent of the defendant
did so successfully[1]. In another case of debt, where the plaintiff
had a tally, the defendant alleged a condition in the sale and
put himself on the oath of the plaintiff, who accepted the
challenge and won his case[2]. In all other cases, including one
where the plaintiff put himself on the oath of the defendant[3],
a deadlock seems to have arisen, neither party having evidence
beyond his bare word.

(ii) *Verification of Goods*. A single oath was also occasionally
allowed where a man's goods had been attached in the hands
of another person for a debt owed by the latter[4]. Possibly
the single oath was a concession to citizens only, since the
general rule both in London and elsewhere seems to have
been an oath with the third hand, and even a sixth hand was
not unknown[5]. The custom was analogous to that of identi-
fying waifs and strays[6], where a third-hand verification was
allowed. Somewhat similar was the usage in Foreign Attachment. A plaintiff might cause money or goods to be attached
in the hands of a third person, on the ground that they
belonged or were owed to his debtor. The third person's
remedy, if he had any grievance, was to appear in Court and
swear with the third hand that the goods and moneys
attached were not the property of the debtor to the value
of fourpence[7].

The ordinary seventh-hand oath is illustrated in many
cases in our Rolls, in such actions as breach of contract,
covenant, debt and detinue, where the plaintiff had no writing
or tally, or where the writing did not cover the matter in

---

[1] See below, pp. 13–14.   [2] pp. 122–3.
[3] pp. 66–7.   [4] pp. 95, 112–3.
[5] p. 68; *Select Cases on the Law Merchant*, 45, 5, 8, liv.
[6] *Borough Customs*, II, pp. 163–4.
[7] See below, pp. 17–8.

dispute[1]. Citizens were generally given an interval of a fortnight in which to produce their oath-helpers, while foreigners were expected to have them ready and to take the oath *incontinenti*—a provision probably intended to prevent delays in doing justice to passing merchants[2]. Already, as in the peremptory oath, the seventh-hand oath was beginning to be regarded as a proof *faute de mieux*. Plaintiffs could forbar a defendant's oath by producing witnesses, or a bond or deed[3]. At its best a law was merely a sworn testimonial to a litigant's credibility by one whose own credibility might not be above question. Mediaeval men made the oath as intricate and formal as possible in the hope that the divine powers would cause a perjured oath-helper to make some slip. Thus a defendant might fail in his law, because one of the oath-helpers called him Robert instead of Henry[4].

TRIAL BY WITNESSES. Another method of proof in use in the Mayor's Court has been called "trial by witnesses." Professor Maitland tells us that "for a moment it threatened to be a serious rival of trial by jury"[5], and that we should nowadays call it a trial by a judge without jury. Our rolls are particularly informative in certain details, of which little evidence is to be found in other borough records[6]—namely, the calling and examination of these witnesses. The custom was of ancient origin in London. In the 12th century[7] it was ruled that when a foreigner impleaded a citizen he could not prove against him by foreigners unless one of the two witnesses was of the city, and conversely a citizen could not prove against a foreigner unless one of his witnesses was of the country in which the foreigner dwelt. We may imagine this rule proved difficult in working, for it is not repeated. At the end of the 13th century either party could call witnesses, in such actions as debt, detinue and covenant, but apparently not both parties. The plaintiff after hearing the defendant deny the accusation,

---

[1] pp. 68, 121, 169, 170, 100, 105, 66, 113, 114, 187. See also *Lib. Alb.* 1, pp. 203, 294–5.
[2] *Ibid.* 1, pp. 295–6. For an instance, see below, p. 74.
[3] pp. 56, 123, 248.
[4] *Select Cases on the Law Merchant*, p. 20.
[5] *History of English Law*, 11, p. 637.
[6] *Borough Customs*, 11, pp. xxx–xxxii.   [7] *Ibid.* 1, pp. 165–6.

proffered his witnesses, by saying that the defendant defended unjustly and that he had good and lawful men, John and John, who were present, etc. On the rarer occasions when a defendant produced witnesses, it was usually to support some issue which had arisen in the pleadings[1]. Citing of witnesses would debar a defendant from his law. If the Court agreed to accept them, the party must take an oath immediately in Court that he would not call others than those he had named, nor suborn them[2]. The requisite qualifications for witnesses were that they had not suffered judgment for perjury, or been excommunicated, or put in the pillory[3]. In the case of foreigners vouching witnesses, the latter must be produced *incontinenti* —a rule which foreigners sometimes found to be a hindrance rather than a help, as in the case of a foreign defendant who produced one witness and caused the other to be essoined (excused) for his appearance, and lost his action for so doing[4]. The witnesses were examined by two aldermen, who put questions to them to ascertain whether their testimony agreed on all points[5]. In an action where one witness said that a bond was given at Paris, and the other at Nogente, the hearing was adjourned in order that the parties might come to an agreement meanwhile[6]. In another case heard on appeal in the Mayor's Court, the proof of the witnesses was annulled owing to a divergence of testimony[7]. A slight divergence might be passed over, as when one witness testified that a hawk was entrusted to the defendant, and the other witness called the bird a goshawk[8]. But in actions of debt, they were expected to testify and agree as to the contract out of which the debt arose, and if their testimony showed that a different sum was owed than what was claimed, the action was null[9]. The testimony of witnesses must be fully recorded by the aldermen who examined them, otherwise the record and process of the action would be found faulty[10]. In none of these actions was rebutting evidence called, or the testimony submitted to a jury. From the point of view of the unsuccessful litigant, trial by witnesses must have been

[1] See below, p. 134. [2] p. 125. [3] p. 118.
[4] pp. 248–9. [5] pp. 117, 120. [6] p. 138.
[7] pp. 181–4. [8] pp. 127–8. [9] pp. 141, 183. [10] *Ibid.*

unsatisfactory at the best of times. The matter was worse when witnessing became a trade. An ordinance was passed in 1345[1] to ensure that witnesses should be "men of good fame and not common suitors or provers before the Ordinaries of St Paul's or elsewhere, or suspected of evil." A few years later it was complained that witnesses were proved false in their examination, to the great slander of the City, and that others had been so well primed, selected and bribed that it was impossible to get at the truth. In future such witnesses must not be received[2].

Nevertheless, there were signs that a system more in consonance with modern ideas was in the making. When a rector was charged with avowing four putrid wolves in a cask, and pleaded that he bought them as medicine for lupus, all the physicians and surgeons of the City were summoned and gave evidence that in none of their medical and surgical writings was any disease mentioned for which the flesh of wolves could be used[3]. A man whose goods had been wrongfully attached abroad brought forward six witnesses who, in answer to the Mayor and Aldermen, declared that no one except the plaintiff had any property in those goods[4]. A City collector, charged with having uttered disrespectful words about the King, put himself on a jury and called to witness four persons who were present, and who were added to the jury for their information[5].

THE JURY IN THE MAYOR'S COURT. The commonest method of proof in the City at our period was the Jury, which, though not a native growth, was soon recognised to have great advantages. An early example of its use was the jury of forty-two persons by which a foreigner accused of murder could clear himself. Two Middlesex men at the Iter of 1244, being accused of murder by a man's widow, put themselves on a jury drawn from the three Aldermanries nearest to the place where the body was found, and were acquitted[6]. At the same Iter two citizens were also tried by juries for deaths

[1] *Lib. Alb.* I, p. 475.
[2] Letter Book G, fo. 92.
[3] See below, p. 51.
[4] p. 97.   [5] p. 58.
[6] Iter Roll AA, membr. 4 *b*; *Lib. Alb.* I, p. 102.

caused by violent blows. In the one case, the appellor's accusation was so flimsy that the Justices would not order the accused to the law of thirty-six, but for their own satisfaction ordered a jury of the Mayor and citizens to inquire and give a verdict, as the result of which the man was found not guilty[1]. In the other, the appellors having died and the Crown taking up the prosecution, the accused person voluntarily put himself on the oath of the Mayor and citizens and was acquitted[2]. A Grand Assize or a jury was the normal procedure in the Husting in 1272; our rolls show that the latter was equally general in the Mayor's Court.

In dealing with the other forms of proof, the law and witnesses, we have seen that a law was possible in the majority of actions except trespass with bloodshed or battery, or where there were deeds or witnesses, and that when witnesses were called there was no jury. On what principle then could a jury be summoned? Apparently all serious assaults, all offences against the King and his bailiffs, and all public prosecutions were jury-actions. But in many other actions, where it would seem that they were entitled to their law, defendants were content to go to a jury. In no case was a man who wanted a jury forced to make his law. It has been said that the consent of both parties was necessary before a jury could be called[3], and perhaps for this reason the clerk is generally careful to say, when one party demanded a jury, that the other did likewise. But in case of disagreement between the litigants as to the method of proof, the Court gave judgment on this point[4], and the parties had no choice but to accept it. The main idea which guided the Court seems to have been a desire to arrive at the facts of the case by the best possible means. In an action of fraud, the defendant wished to wage his law, and the plaintiffs objected on the ground that they were ready to prove the alleged receipt and sale by a jury[5]—an objection which was upheld by the Court. In another action[6] where the alleged wrong, i.e. delay

---

[1] Iter Roll AA, membr. 2 b.   [2] Ibid.
[3] Pollock and Maitland, History Engl. Law, II, p. 623. For an illustrative case, see Select Pleas on the Law Merchant, I, pp. 44–5, and the rules of Leicester in 1277, Borough Customs, I, p. 164.
[4] See below, p. 133.   [5] p. 173.   [6] pp. 168–9.

in the delivery of a consignment of wine from Bordeaux, was done on a voyage, and the plaintiffs objected to the defendant's law, the Court gave judgment against the former, because they had no power to summon any jury from which the facts could be better elicited than by the defendant's law.

It has been said that originally, when a defendant gave a direct denial to the plaintiff's story, proof by oath was the most appropriate course[1]. But when a defendant admitted the whole or part of the facts alleged, and then gave reasons to show that the plaintiff had no real grievance, or that the facts provided no ground of action, then the pleading was more properly submitted to a jury[2]. This kind of defence was called an exception, and the defendant who raised it might desire either to delay the action by a dilatory exception, or altogether to exclude the plaintiff from his plea. Undoubtedly pleading by exception played a great part in the general history of law, as regards the development of the jury. It will be noticed that it was very frequently used in the Mayor's Court, and that sometimes the parties continued to plead against each other until they reached an issue, which seemed to them, but not perhaps to us, to touch the heart of the matter, after which they went to a jury.

Although these may have been the original reasons which led to the one or the other method of proof, they do not appear to have swayed the Mayor's Court in its decisions. A defendant will bluntly deny the plaintiff's declaration and, without more ado, the parties are allowed a jury[3]. Or the defendant will admit the facts, and then raise his exception to show that the plaintiff suffered no wrong, or was not entitled to sue him. In so doing he lays himself open to the retort of the plaintiff that he has not denied the facts, and that the action is undefended[4]. But though such a retort might be dangerous in other Courts, the Mayor's Court is not greatly influenced by it. They continue the hearing, and where we might expect that they would submit an exception or issue to a jury, they adjudge that either the plaintiff or the defendant shall prove his case by making his law[5]. Doubt-

[1] P. and M. II, pp. 609-10; *Borough Customs*, I, p. 164.
[2] P. and M. II, pp. 616, 620.
[3] See below, p. 14, etc.   [4] p. 90.   [5] p. 18.

less, where either a law or a jury was admissible, the Court had definite rules on which to act, but it is not easy to deduce any rule, further than a desire to learn the truth and a predilection in favour of the jury. These two feelings had a close correspondence in the 13th century.

An examination of the several actions brings out at once a radical difference between the ancient and the modern jury. To-day the Court submits the facts to a jury for its verdict: in the 14th century the Court was doubtful about the facts and expected the jury to supply them. Professor Maitland has warned us of the danger of saying that the early jury was merely a body of witnesses[1], for if so, they would have been examined separately and would have given, not one but twelve verdicts. Nevertheless the statement is nearly correct. Elsewhere Professor Maitland, speaking of the Middle Ages[2], says: "A man who had been summoned as a juror and who sought to escape on the ground that he already knew something of the facts in question would have been told that he had given a very good reason for his being placed in the jury-box." Knowledge of the facts was in the City highly desirable in a jury. When a man was charged with assaulting another person in Court at the Guildhall, a jury was impanelled of persons who were actually present and saw the dispute[3]. Another complained that the Sheriff had not done him justice on a royal writ in his Court, to which the Sheriff replied that he had heard the action and the present plaintiff had lost his case. A jury was summoned of persons living round and frequenting the Guildhall[4]. Similarly in maritime and commercial disputes, mixed juries of merchants, travellers, masters of ships and waterside men from Billingsgate were summoned[5]. We find other juries of woodmongers, dyers and butchers[6], and juries of parishes, streets, and of people living round houses where assaults were said to have taken place. In the Plea and Memoranda Rolls, in an action against an unjust gaoler of Newgate, the duty of giving a verdict was entrusted to a jury of discharged prisoners, who would have the best of reasons for knowing the facts. But a jury must

[1] P. and M. II, p. 622.   [2] *Social England*, I, p. 291.   [3] See below, p. 15.
[4] p. 181.   [5] pp. 21, 39, 119, 193, 221.   [6] pp. 216, 230.

be not only well-informed but also impartial. Persons of the affinity of the plaintiff and defendant are excluded. On one occasion it is ordered that no skinner shall be impanelled[1]. Either of the parties might challenge the jury—in which case a committee of four persons was chosen to examine the challenge and report on oath. So anxious is the Court for full and reliable information that, in an action where the plaintiff and defendant each demanded a jury from his own neighbourhood, the Court summoned both[2].

To what extent the Court directed the jury, as to the matters on which a verdict was required, is not clear. In many instances a single issue was before them, and their task was simple. Often, however, they appear to have had a general commission to tell all they knew, with the result that the verdicts occupy more space than the pleadings. The jury will say that a defendant did not expose putrid meat for sale, but that another person named had done so[3]. In a dispute about a wardship they expatiate on the evil conduct of the plaintiff, acts of kindness by the defendant, and conclude by giving a description of the orphan's property[4]. Where a special inquest was ordered as to affrays an informative report might be expected, but the ordinary juries were sometimes fully as communicative. On occasion they will say that they do not know and have no means of finding out[5]; and sometimes when various allegations are made in Court, they will state in their verdict one fact only, which does not always seem to have a close connection with the dispute. In such a case, the Court asks the jury questions, and perhaps elicits further and valuable information[6]. The jury was expected to know its own mind; and one which gave a verdict and afterwards repudiated it was amerced[7]. On the other hand, they must be treated with respect. An angry woman who had lost her action, and said in the presence of the Mayor and Aldermen that the jury were lying was forthwith committed to prison[8]; on two occasions the jury themselves appeared as prosecutors to vindicate their honour and impartiality[9].

[1] p. 95. [2] p. 97. [3] See below, p. 56; cf. p. 14.
[4] pp. 171–2. [5] pp. 13, 41. [6] pp. 16, 31, 40.
[7] p. 13. [8] p. 199. [9] pp. 237, 252.

IMPARTIALITY OF THE CITY COURTS. A final word may be said about the quality of the justice dispensed in the City Courts. That there should be occasional irregularities, as in other Courts of the period, might be expected. Walter Hervy, who is regarded by some writers as a democratic reformer, is said by the compiler of the *Liber de Antiquis Legibus*, to have allowed very few pleadings in the Husting during his Mayoralty, the reason being that he himself was impleaded as to a certain tenement[1]. As Hervy was afterwards found guilty in the Husting, on the evidence of the King's Chancellor, of a piece of dishonest practice in the appointment of an attorney, it is not unlikely that his administration of justice was faulty[2]. He and his Sheriffs are charged with receiving bribes from fraudulent bakers[3]. Peter Cusin, Sheriff in 1273, was proved guilty of a like charge and dismissed[4]. In the presentments of the Ward Inquests of 1276, preserved in the Hundred Rolls, bitter complaints were made of the conduct of Ralph Crepyn, described as the Mayor's Clerk or Clerk of the Husting[5]. As will be seen from the following pages, unsuccessful litigants were not always satisfied with the judgments given. William de Leyre, an Alderman who served on several occasions as the Mayor's deputy, was charged by one impatient plaintiff with retarding justice in the interests of the defendant[6]. Another person, who seems to have been a pleader, contrasted the diligence of the Court under the then Mayor and under the King's Warden, to the disadvantage of the former[7]. In the Patent Rolls, as the result of the complaints of parties, there are recorded several appointments of justices to co-operate with the Mayor and Sheriffs in terminating actions which had been grievously delayed[8]. The custom of giving gratuities to judges and lesser officials, which survived for several centuries, was not conducive to justice. At the session of the Itinerant Justices in

[1] *Lib. de Ant. Leg.* p. 159.
[2] H.R.C.P. 2, membr. 6.
[3] *Lib. de Ant. Leg.*, p. 159.
[4] *Ibid.* p. 162.
[5] *Rot. Hund.* 1, pp. 415, 416, 419, 427, 429.
[6] See below, pp. 187-8.
[7] pp. 146-7.
[8] *Cal. Pat. Rolls*, 1272-81, pp. 239, 246, 285, 406, 409, etc.

1321 opportunity was taken to prefer a large number of complaints against City officials, which it is fair to remember were found on examination to have little substance[1].

It would, perhaps, be unreasonable to expect that the Rolls of the Husting and Mayor's Court should give direct evidence to confirm or deny the occasional accusations of injustice. But as far as one can judge, the pleadings are recorded quite fairly in these matter-of-fact documents, and the judgments which followed on the verdicts of juries and other methods of proof seem to represent an honest desire to do right. London citizens at this time were particularly vocal in their grievances. There is abundance of evidence to show that Edward I was deeply interested in the administration of justice, and that his Justices kept a close oversight on the proceedings of such important local courts as those of London. Moreover there was a continuous feud between the officials on either side—the royal and the civic clerks and lawyers. Thus the City authorities, subjected to constant criticism, had every motive to do their work well. The evidence of their Rolls would appear to show that their efforts had considerable success.

[1] P.R.O. Assize Roll 547.

A. H. T.

The Guildhall, London,
May, 1924.

CALENDAR OF THE EARLY MAYOR'S COURT ROLLS *of the* CITY OF LONDON

ROLL A

Court of H. le Galeys, *Mayor of London, Thursday* Membrane 1
after the Feast of St *Dunstan* [19 *May*] *A^o* 26 *Edw.* 22 *May* 1298
[1298]

John de Holebourne, Walter de Walebroc and Ralph de Dowegate, coopers of London, were attached at the instance of Adam Snow, cooper, to answer the King for contempt, in having sued the said Adam in the Court Christian[1] before the Official of the Archdeacon of London in a plea of covenant relating to certain ordinances of the Coopers, the cognizance of which pertained to the King, to the King's damage—£100. The defendants appeared and admitted that they had sued Adam on a contract between him and John, a cooper of London deceased, whose executors they were, and this they did in the matter of the execution of John's will, and not in other matters pertaining to the King, and thereon they put themselves on their country (*patria*)[2]. The Serjeant was ordered to summon a jury for the next Court. Afterwards on Monday the Vigil of the Nativity of St John the Baptist [24 June], the jury brought in a verdict that the defendants impleaded Adam Snow in the Court Christian in a plea pertaining to the King, against his Proclamation, and to the damage of the said Adam half a mark. Judgment that the defendants be committed to prison. Afterwards they came and paid the damages by the hand of Thomas de Wynton, Serjeant, and went quit.

John de Holebourne, Walter the cooper of St Nicholas Lane, William Styward, John le Tanckardmaker, and other coopers were summoned at the instance of Adam Snow, cooper, for

---

[1] The Church Courts claimed jurisdiction over the laity in cases arising out of breach of faith, which could be interpreted to include all contracts between laymen, especially if confirmed by an oath. These pretensions were resisted by the Crown, and by the City authorities, whose Courts lost business thereby. See Pollock and Maitland, *History of English Law*, II, pp. 199–200.

[2] *Patria*, i.e. a jury of the neighbourhood, street, parish, ward, or trade.

contempt of the King and Mayor, in that they made an ordinance that no one should sell a hoop (*circulus*), formerly sold at ½d and ¾d, for less than 1d, and so concerning other hoops, under a penalty, which ordinance was against the dignity of the Crown and to the grave damage of the Commonalty of the City—£100. The defendants denied that they made this ordinance, and put themselves on their country. Afterwards at a Court held on the Vigil of Sᵗ John the Baptist [24 June] a jury brought in a verdict that the coopers made the ordinance, required oaths of obedience, and had observed it then for a year and more. Judgment that they be committed to gaol[1].

6 June 1298   An inquest was held on Friday after the Feast of Holy Trinity [1 June] before John de Storteford, Sheriff of London, by good and lawful men of the Wards of William le Mazerer[2], Nicholas de Farndon[3] and Walter de Fynchyngfeld[4], viz. by Walter de Anbresbury, goldsmith, William Fitz Laurence, Robert de Notingham, John de Croydon, William de Notingham, William de Chigewell, Walter de Frenigham, John de Notingham, William de Asshendon, goldsmith, Henry de Keyle, Nicholas le Brun, Gerard le Peleter, Walter le Gardiner, Robert Gauge, William le Chaundeler, Robert de Donmawe, Richard Daniel, Thomas de Chygewell, William Alysaundre, Gylottus de Clopham, William de la Heylaund, John le Geldere and William de Gloucestre, cobbler, as to the malefactors and disturbers of the peace who came by night to the house of Master Henry de Derby, clerk, in Stanig Lane, and assaulted him and his men. The jury found that Alan, apprentice of Richard de Chigewell, Geoffrey son of Geoffrey Scot, Robert his brother, Thomas de Bromleye, John, apprentice of Geoffrey Scot, Richard de London, and Nicholas, journeyman of Joan de Dyrham, on the 4ᵗʰ June after vespers came with swords, misericords and knives, and attacked Master Henry and wounded his servant John Bryon, breaking his door and threatening him, and that they set a watch upon his house the night after, until they were driven away by good men of the neighbourhood. Being asked where

---

[1] See p. 16.   [2] Aldersgate.   [3] Farringdon.   [4] Cripplegate.

they went afterwards, the jurors answered that they all fled except the above Alan, who was arrested with his misericord in his hand by the neighbours and attached by the Sheriff's clerks, whereupon he and others threatened the lives and limbs of those who had arrested them. Precept was issued to the Sheriffs to attach the other malefactors.

Friday before the Feast of St Barnabas the Apostle [11 *June*]   *6 June 1298*

Richard Horn was summoned by Thomas de Wynthon, the Serjeant of the Mayor, to answer Adam de Harewe in a plea of trespass, but did not appear. He was summoned again before the Mayor and Aldermen on Wednesday, and told the Serjeant that he would not come. He afterwards appeared and defended his contempt against the King and the Mayor and Aldermen, admitting that he had received the summons but that he had refused to come because the Mayor had no cognizance of such trespasses except by default of the Sheriffs. Afterwards on Thursday following, he admitted the contempt and found mainpernors, viz. John de Mockyng and James le Vineter, to submit to the judgment (*quod stabit judicio*) of the Mayor and Aldermen when summoned[1].

Friday after the above Feast   *13 June 1298*

Richard Horn was summoned to answer Adam de Harewe   Membr. 1 *b* in a plea of trespass, wherein the latter complained that the defendant seized his cart, with two quarters of sea-coal in it, and had it driven to the house of Simon de St Martin, as though he were a bailiff, to the damage of the plaintiff and in contempt of the King. This cart, the plaintiff declared, he had himself hired from William le Wallere, servant of Hugh Curteys of Stibbenheth, to carry to his house in Bredstrade two loads of coal which he had bought from Geoffrey le Clerk of Northflete at Retheresgate[2], and the

---

[1] Cf. p. 16.

[2] Identified with Pudding Lane, Eastcheap. Dr R. R. Sharpe suggests that Retheresgate is derived from "rother," a horned beast, from the beasts brought by butchers to Eastcheap, and points out that the cattle-market at Stratford-on-Avon is called "Rother Market." Calendar of

coal had been measured, and the Coal Meter duly paid. The defendant admitted seizing the coal, but denied that he had committed any trespass in so doing, and he put himself on his country. Afterwards on Saturday, a jury of the venue of Retheresgate brought in a verdict that the two quarters of coal belonged to the defendant, who had bought them from Stephen le Chaundeler at Retheresgate, and that the plaintiff did not buy them from Geoffrey le Clerk, or hire the cart from William Walere (*sic*), as he averred. Judgment that the defendant go quit and the plaintiff be in mercy for a false claim.

14 June 1298 **Saturday after the above Feast**

Recognizance by Richard Horn of a debt of 5 marks of silver, payable to John de Donestaple, former Sheriff of London.

John le Noreys was summoned to answer John de Donestaple and Adam de Halingebury, former Sheriffs of London, in a plea of detinue of 20s in arrears of his farm of the Wardenship of Billingesgate, which he had by lease from them for £20 during their Shrievalty. The defendant acknowledged 14s in arrears, which he promised to pay within the Quinzime[1]. Thereupon the plaintiffs acknowledged satisfaction for the whole farm for the time when he was their bailiff.

18 June 1298 **Wednesday after the above Feast**

Information having been received that the Cordwainers and Cobblers had been guilty of bad work in mixing cordwain[2] with bazon[3], and bazon with cowhide, Thomas de Derby, Robert de Frowyk, Roger de Bristoll, Thomas de Norwych, Thomas de Chygewell, Godwyn le Cordewaner, and John de Lincoln, cordwainer, were sworn to make a scrutiny throughout the City and bring the names of offenders, to-

Letter Book I, p. 22, note. Apparently the wharf at the south end was at this time used as a coal-wharf.

[1] Fifteen days, including the day on which the promise was made.
[2] Cordwain: originally goat-leather made at Cordova; used generally for superior leather.
[3] Bazon, bazaine, basil: sheepskin.

gether with fraudulent goods, into Court on the above day. They presented on oath Roger de St Antolin, John de Becles, Thomas de Londoneston, Richard Page, John Dissot, Alan de Cycestre, Robert de Notingham, Ralph de St Edmunds, Stephen de Strode, Henry de Farnham, John de St Albans, John de Paris, Richard de Dounegate, William de Nornt (Northampton?), Roger de Greenwich, Richard de Ely in the Mercery, Adam de Gilingham, Robert de Assh, Roger de Bredstrate, Peter de Sauecompe, William de Norht, Richard de Crepelgate, John de Chobham, Richard de Hereford and Adam de Guillingham as being accustomed to do this fraudulent work, and they produced in Court such work found in their possession. The defendants admitted their offence. Judgment was given that the goods be burnt.

They likewise presented that John de. . . . removed his work and would not allow them to execute their office at his house, that Daniel Chyltren and John de Renham broke the sequestration which they placed on three of their chests full of such work, that Thomas le Coffer would not allow them to view his work, and that Thomas de Lodelawe broke the sequestration which Thomas Juvenal, the Mayor's Serjeant, placed on a certain chest, denied them a view of his work and carried it away forcibly. The defendant Daniel pleaded that the seals of the sequestration fell off his chests without his touching them, and that he opened a chest and took away a pair of boots (*heuses*). He was ordered to be kept in custody. The defendant Thomas said he did not know that Thomas de Derby and the others had orders to view. He was ordered to receive judgment on his confession. He also pleaded that when the Serjeant told him of their commission, he submitted, and removed nothing from his house afterwards, and he put himself on his country. Thomas de Lodelawe admitted that he was not a freeman, but denied the other offence and put himself on his country. John de Notingham did likewise. Afterwards a jury found Thomas le Coffer and the others not guilty, and they were acquitted. Precept was issued to the Sheriff to bring Thomas de Lodelawe to hear judgment on his confession that he was a foreigner engaged in buying and selling.

Membr. 2
19 June 1298 *Thursday before the Feast of the Nativity of St John the Baptist* [24 June]

Richard de Hacumby was attached to answer the Lady Blaunche, Queen of Navarre, executrix of the will of her husband Lord Edmund, brother of the present King, in a plea that he render account of the time he was her late husband's Receiver. She complained by her attorney John de Dyicton that the defendant received on several occasions the sum of £1500 and bound himself to render an account thereof, and that on Friday seven days after Pentecost in the new Abbey of St Clare near London he undertook to give an account, but afterwards refused to do so, to her damage £100. The defendant denied that he was receiver of any of the moneys of Lord Edmund for which he ought to render account to the plaintiff, or that he undertook to do so before anyone acting on her behalf, and he put himself on his country. A jury of the venue of Allegate was summoned against the next Court

20 June 1298 *Friday before the above Feast*

Geoffrey de Staunton was attached to answer Adam de Rokesle, Alderman, in a plea of trespass, wherein the latter complained that he came upon the defendant in Thames Street by the door of John de Storteford, Sheriff, fighting with a drawn sword against certain unknown persons, and as an official of the peace (*tanquam minister pacis*), he commanded him to surrender to the King's Peace, whereupon the defendant took him by the throat and tore his clothes and did other enormities in contempt of the King and the whole City. The defendant admitted the offence. Judgment was given that on the morrow he should come from the place of the offence to Guildhall, with bare head and feet, and clothed only in his tunic, in charge of two Serjeants, carrying in his hand an axe[1], and in the presence of the Mayor and Aldermen, hold up the axe with the hand which he had laid on the alderman, in order to expiate his offence to the alderman as a Justice and Guardian of the vill[2] (*tamquam*

[1] To show that he had rendered himself liable to the loss of his hand—the ancient penalty for striking an Alderman.

[2] The word *villa* here probably means the Ward. It is not used in the City Records to denote the City as a whole.

Justic⁹ & Custodi ville), or else receive judgment according to the custom of the City in such cases. On the morrow the defendant did as enjoined, and the plaintiff condoned the offence so far as he was concerned. The defendant was amerced for his contempt against the King, his pledges being John le Clerk, Coroner of the City of London, and Eustace Malebranche.

Monday the Vigil of Sᵗ John the Baptist [24 *June*]

23 June 1298

Richard de Hacumby offered himself against the executors of Lord Edmund, brother of the King, plaintiffs in a plea of account, and they did not prosecute. He goes quit and the executors and their pledges are in mercy.

John Peyure[1], who was confined in the prison of Crepelgate at the suit of Thomas Box for a debt of £18 due on a Statute, came before the Mayor and Aldermen and said he had paid the amount and had acquittances from the above Thomas. The latter was ordered to show cause why the petitioner should not be released, and did not come. Precept was given to the Sheriff to release him under security for his appearance when necessary, and the security was reported as follows:— Robert de Beregholte, Ralph le Marun, William May, "peleter"[2], Peter Berneval, Simon de Warewyk and others.

Membr. 2 b

Saturday before the above Feast

21 June 1298

The Commonalty of London complained of Alan de Newebery that he, as a lodging-house keeper, and Keeper of the Seld of Winchester and weigher of merchandise, acted as a broker and weighed the goods of foreigners and citizens both within and without the City, whereas no one ought so to weigh except the sworn weigher of the King, and was guilty of forestalling. They also complained that Mabel Rolaund, John le Haut, Everard de Wylnotht, Margaret Skof, William Marysone, Rabot de Warloys, Walter Coosyn and John Symbelpany were foreign[3] lodging-house keepers and

Hospites Flandr⁹ & Braund⁹

---

[1] Peyure *sc.* Pepper. Cf. p. 13.   [2] Skinner.
[3] *Forinsecus* denoted "foreigner" in the old sense: one who was not free of the City.

allowed foreign merchants to trade with other foreign merchants in their houses in all kinds of merchandise, which the defendants sent out of the City secretly by night, so that the King lost his customs; and whereas foreign merchants on departure left with them their unsold goods, which ought to remain bound up until their return, the defendants sold those goods for the benefit of the merchants both to citizens and foreigners, against the Liberty of the City; and further the defendants acted as brokers both for their own goods as well as for the goods of foreign merchants, and thus obtained the profits which the sworn brokers of the City ought to receive; they also avowed foreign goods, which was against their oath if they were freemen, and they sold their goods retail by small weights and measures both to foreigners and citizens. The defendants Alan de Newebery, William Marysone, Rabot de Warloys and Walter Coosyn pleaded that they were citizens and had done nothing which was not lawful for citizens to do. The others admitted that they were foreign lodging-house keepers; John Haut and John Shymbelpany confessed that they were not sworn brokers; Margaret Skof admitted that she allowed foreigners to sell wine in small measures in her house, and she and Shymbelpany also admitted selling the goods of foreign merchants after their departure and after quarantine to any one who would buy. But all the foreigners pleaded that they did not know that these things were forbidden in the City, and they denied committing the other trespasses alleged against them, and put themselves on their country. Afterwards a jury brought in a verdict that Alan de Newebery weighed wool and other goods of foreigners and citizens at Westminster with the King's Trone both during and outside the Fairs against his oath, that he was a broker between foreigners and retained a small profit therefrom, thus defrauding the Sheriff of his customs, that he forestalled goods whereby trade was disturbed and could not come to the City, that he gave lodging to foreign merchants and allowed them to trade with each other in his house and avowed their goods as his own, and that at the Winchester Seld he acted as a broker between foreigners and avowed as his own the kind of foreign goods they use at the Winchester Seld. They found the other defendants guilty of selling cloth in cords and sending it over the water by night, whereby the Sheriffs were defrauded of their customs, and of the other offences with which they were charged.

The Commonalty complained that Francis Rotelouth, *Lumbard⁹* Colouth Ballard, Tote de Mounteclare, Reymund de la *& Pro-* Browe, James Betely and William Pynnett were also guilty *vincial⁹* of the above offences. The defendant Francis admitted selling retail, and Friscote[1] admitted that he had received foreigners, but all denied the other offences. A jury brought in a verdict that Francis and Colouth were guilty, that Totte de Monte Claro and James Betely were foreign lodging-house keepers, but at present did not sell retail, and that Reymund de la Browe and William Pynnett were not lodging-house keepers but lived at the house of Thomas Godard, and did no trade now because of the war, though four years ago, when they were lodging with William Servatt, they dealt with foreigners in their lodgings.

The Commonalty complained that John le Rous, Henry *Alemann* Coupman, Teostardus le Estreys, Ecbryth de Werle, Ralph de Atterderne, Henry Hoppe, Hardmot, and Hyldebraund, merchants of Almaine, received foreigners and traded with them, and although they were free of customs for goods coming from their own parts in Almaine[2], they had become wholesale merchants (*grossores*) in "*aver de poys*," drapers and woolmen, and had meddled with merchandise belonging to those trades, without paying custom, and thus the Sheriffs were defrauded of their customs. The defendants claimed freedom from tolls on all goods of this kind, whencesoever they came. A day was given them to argue their claim, and a jury was summoned on the other charges against them.

Ralph de Abbehale, draper of London, was attached to *Membr. 3* answer John de Boclaund, knight, in a plea of trespass wherein

---

[1] Tottus and Frisottus de Monte Claro, whose names appear in various forms, were brothers, and Italian merchants of Lucca. See p. 24.

[2] As merchants of the Hanse of Almaine or Germany, which held a privileged position in the City. *Liber Custumarum* (Rolls Series), i, p. 196; Introd. pp. xlv–xlvi; *Liber Albus* (Rolls Series), i, pp. 485–8.

the latter complained that having bought cloth to the value
of 63s 4d from the defendant, he gave him certain pledges
for payment, viz. one gilded "coylter"[1], three garments
(*garnamenta*), one hood of medley, two supertunics furred
with bys[2], one coat and one hood furred with miniver[3], six
ells and a quarter of medley cloth, and one serge, value £10,
and the defendant had neither delivered the cloth nor returned the pledges. The latter admitted the sale and pledges,
but pleaded an agreement that if the purchase price was not
paid on a certain date he should retain the pledges, and he
produced an unsealed deed to that effect. The plaintiff denied
any such agreement and declared that the deed was not of his
making, whereupon the defendant offered to produce at his
own risk witnesses, who were present in Tamys Strete at
the handing over of the pledges. A day was given on the
morrow.

Afterwards the parties came to an agreement on terms
that the defendant pay the plaintiff 20s.

Robert le Treyere, Richard Godesname, Robert de
Thorneye, John de Ware, "batour"[4], Geoffrey de Cavendyssh, and Ralph Manyman, "ceynturer"[5], were acquitted
of harbouring foreigners &c.

Membr. 3 b
5 July 1298

Saturday after the Feast of the Apostles Peter and Paul [29 June]

Thomas Box agreed that his debtor, John Peper, should
be delivered from prison, on condition that the latter rendered
an account at Guildhall, of the moneys in dispute between
them.

Maykin le Chaundeler was acquitted of a charge of allowing
foreigners to trade in his Seld in Candelwykstrate, thus defrauding the Customs.

[1] Coylter: probably for *coulter*, a knife.
[2] Bys, bis, bisses: the brownish back of the squirrel in winter. Cf.
J. Hodgkin, *Notes and Queries*, II, s.v., March 2, 1912.
[3] Miniver: the belly of the squirrel in winter. *Ibid.*
[4] A maker or seller of *baterie*, i.e. copper and brass ware.
[5] Girdler.

Saturday before the Feast of St Margaret [13 *July*]

Alan de Newebery appeared for judgment on the verdict of a jury against him[1]. He was deprived of the freedom, but subsequently was readmitted on paying 60s fine to the Commonalty, on condition that if he were convicted again he should lose the freedom for ever.

Mabel Rolaund was amerced for harbouring foreigners &c., and John Haut, Margaret Scof and John Shybelpani were also amerced, and forbidden to act in future as unsworn brokers between foreigners, under penalty of forfeiture of all their goods.

The same day William Marysone and Walter Coosyn were deprived of the freedom, and subsequently readmitted on payment of 40s and 26s 8d respectively. Colouthe Ballard, Reymund de la Browe and Walter Pynett, foreigners, were amerced.

Monday following

Robert Jordan was attached to answer William de Alegate in a plea of trespass wherein the latter complained that when, as an official of the City, he summoned the good and lawful men of his bailiwick of Portsokne Ward to attend the Court of Common Pleas[2] at Guildhall, the defendant assaulted him, though he was doing what his Alderman commanded, and wounded him with a knife in the left side of his back to the depth of four inches—to his damage 100s. The defendant pleaded that he came quietly into the street within Allegate, when the plaintiff abused him and took him by the throat, and if the plaintiff suffered any harm, it was own fault; and he put himself on his country. A "good" jury was summoned for Wednesday.

On that day the parties came to an agreement by permission of the Court on terms that the defendant pay the plaintiff 20s and be amerced, and the plaintiff quitclaim all future actions. As regards the contempt against the King,

---

[1] See p. 7.
[2] The Husting of Common Pleas held on alternate Mondays for mixed actions mainly relating to land.

the defendant was mainprised by his brother Jordan de Alegate and Philip Somer to come before the Mayor next day.

Margery, widow of Richard le Fethermongere and Nicholas Hauteyn, executor of his will, came to an agreement with John de Oxonford, who complained that they had sued him in the Court Christian before the Official, in spite of the fact that the Mayor had sent his Serjeant, John de Wynthon, to forbid Master Stephen the Official to deal with the case. The plaintiff quitclaimed the trespass and the Court condoned the amercements.

17 July 1298 ## Thursday before the Feast of St Margaret[1]

The Commonalty brought a plaint against Estmer le Bouler of Candelwykstrate that he had bought and sold with foreigners, harboured foreigners, and avowed their goods, against his oath as a freeman. The defendant admitted buying three bales from foreigners to the use of some merchants of Bristol, because he understood that they were free of customs. He was fined half-a-mark on condition of his future good conduct. He denied the charge of harbouring and avowry, and put himself on a jury, which found him not guilty.

Membr. 5   Arnald Vylote, a foreigner, was forbidden to sell wine retail and to act as a lodging-house keeper for foreigners, unless he received special permission.

Aveswote was attached to answer the Commonalty on charges of being a foreign lodging-house keeper, buying Ryns wine from foreigners and selling it retail to foreigners and citizens, and allowing foreigners in her house to deal in ginger, woad, cloth and other merchandise, which they sent over the water by night, thus defrauding the Sheriffs of their customs. The defendant admitting buying and selling the wine, but pleaded a licence from Sir Ralph de Sandwych, then Warden of London, and Elyas Russel, then Sheriff[2],

---

[1] Query: St Margaret Virgin and Martyr, i.e. July 20?
[2] Sheriff, A.D. 1293-4. Assizes of wine had been set up in the City long before this date. Among the Ordinances made by the King "when he took the City into his hands" (A.D. 1285), is one that the Assize of Wine

who gave her leave to do so because there was no Assize of such wine at the time. She denied harbouring foreigners except her brother and the son of her uncle, or that she allowed buying and selling in her house. A jury of the venue of Ebbegate brought in a verdict that she had bought and sold wines, as she admitted, and that she harboured many more foreigners than her brother and her uncle's son, but whether they were kinsmen the jurors did not know; and also that she sold foreign woad retail to foreigners in her house. She was mainprised by Thomas Juvenal and John de Wengrave to come up for judgment on Wednesday. As the jurors afterwards repudiated their first verdict that she sold woad retail, and acquitted her of this charge, judgment was given that all the jurors be amerced for a false verdict, viz. William de Paris and his fellows as appears on the panel.

Saturday before the Feast of St Mary Magdalene [22 July]

19 July 1298

Clays Careman, merchant of Brabant, who was charged with the above offences, was found guilty by a jury.

Wednesday after the above Feast

Membr. 5 b
23 July 1298

Thomas Box and John Peper[1] came to an agreement on terms that the latter bind himself to pay 100s in satisfaction of all claims against him, and that the former undertake to acquit the Sheriff for delivering the above John from Newegate.

John de Trillawe, parson of St Dunstan, Thomas de Asshewell of St Anthony, and Roger de Appelby, deputed by the Archbishop of Canterbury to execute the will of Henry Box, and William Lambyn, Edward de Wycumbe, parson of St Botulph, Margery widow of Thomas Cros, and Thomas Cros her son, who were executors of Thomas Cros senior, an executor of Henry Box, were attached to answer John Beauflour in a plea of debt wherein he claimed from

be kept as before ordained, at the setting of the Warden. See *Lib. Cust.* fo. 219 b. It is possible that Sir Ralph de Sandwich set another Assize *after* 1293, but it is not recorded. ¹ Pepper *alias* Peyure. Cf. p. 7.

them £8 12d, for 1200 boards for the King's galley at 18s
the hundred, a perch (*una pertica*) value 2s, and 30 boards
value 15s, for which the late Henry Box had paid 54s,
leaving the total above claimed in arrears. The defendants
pleaded that they were not bound to answer because the
plaintiff had produced no tally in Court. The plaintiff then
offered to verify his claim by his corporal oath[1] at the discretion of the Court, and to this the defendants agreed. On
the day given the plaintiff made his law successfully to the
effect that on the day of his death Henry Box owed the
plaintiff £8 12d, not one penny of which had been paid.
Judgment was given that the plaintiff recover the amount
from Henry's goods and chattels. Afterwards on his own
behalf and that of the executors, the plaintiff presented the
money to the purposes of London Bridge, and also, as a
mark of charity, entered into a recognizance to pay the sum
of 40s to the same.

30 July 1298 *Wednesday after the Feast of St James the Apostle
[25 July]*

Cristina de Gravesende was attached to answer Richard le
Peleter in a plea of trespass, wherein he complained that when
he went with another of the Mayor's Serjeants to summon
the defendant and other common prostitutes living in the
City to appear before the Mayor and Aldermen at the
Guildhall, she and other unknown persons assaulted him and
struck him on the lip. The defendant denied the charge and
put herself on her country. Afterwards a jury of Garscherch
brought in a verdict that the defendant did not beat the
plaintiff, but was a party to an attack made on him by a certain
Robert de Bonevil her paramour (*specialis*). Judgment for
40d damages taxed by the jury, and that Cristina be taken
into custody till the damages be paid. A precept to take
the above Robert was issued.

[1] In breach of contract a defendant could put himself on the decisory
oath of the plaintiff, and if the latter refused to swear his claim, the
defendant went quit. Here the plaintiff offered the oath, which the Court
and the defendant accepted. Cf. *Lib. Alb.* I, p. 521.

Saturday the Vigil of St Laurence [10 *Aug.*]

Geoffrey de Taleworth was attached to answer John de Northon in a plea of trespass wherein the latter complained that the defendant attacked and beat him in the presence of the Mayor and Aldermen, when he was attending Guildhall, on business relating to certain trespasses done against him, in order to receive the judgment of right adjudged to him. The defendant denied that he was guilty of the trespass. A jury was summoned forthwith of good and discreet men then present, and came on the same day, consisting of William de Trimilingham, Roger de Wytham and others on the panel, who gave a verdict that the defendant was guilty. Judgment that he be committed to prison and pay the plaintiff 5s damages taxed by the jury. The defendant paid this sum on the Monday, and on Thursday half a mark for the trespass done against the King.

Richard de Laufare and Isabella his wife, executors of the will of Edith de Warners, brought a plaint against John de Storteford, Sheriff, of an error in the latter's Court with regard to the process and giving of judgment in an action between the plaintiffs and Henry Fitz Ancher, who was sued for 40 quarters of corn and 16 quarters of oats in arrear of an annual rent due to the plaintiffs. The Sheriff was summoned to appear on the morrow with the record and process to answer the plaintiffs in the plea of error, together with the above Henry Fitz Ancher.

Monday the morrow of the above Feast

Richard Hauteyn in mercy for default against Stephen de Coventre.

The above Richard was attached to answer Stephen de Coventre in a plea of trespass wherein the latter complained that as he was walking peacefully in Chepe on Friday before the Feast of St Margaret [13 July], the defendant assaulted him. The latter denied the assault and said that if the plaintiff received any harm it was due to his own insults, and he demanded an inquest thereon.

Afterwards a jury of Chepe brought in a verdict that the

defendant was sitting quietly on a seat in the shop of Ralph Godchep, when the plaintiff came in and would have beaten him, if a rescue had not been made by Geoffrey le Clerk and Richard Beaufiz, so that if the plaintiff received any hurt, it was his own fault. Judgment against the plaintiff, who was put in mercy for his false plaint.

The Commonalty complained of John le Launterner and Alice his wife in a plea of trespass, to the effect that the defendants dwelt in the city as foreigners and bought and sold merchandise, viz. lanterns, glass cups and mirrors, both to foreigners and citizens, to the damage of the City &c. 100s. The defendants admitted that they were foreigners, but denied such selling, and put themselves on a jury of the venue of St Augustine, where they dwelt. Afterwards on Wednesday the jury gave a verdict that the defendants were foreigners, and that they came into the City with their merchandise, which they offered for sale to the citizens, paying custom to the King according to the usage of the City, and that they offered both to foreigners and citizens what remained of their goods. Being asked if they thereby deprived the King of customs, the jury answered "No." Judgment was respited.

Membr. 6 b
12 Aug. 1298

Tuesday before the Assumption of the Blessed Mary [15 Aug.]

John de Holebourne, cooper, and other coopers paid fines, varying from 5s to 6d for trespass against the King[1].

Richard Horn came and pledged to the Mayor and Aldermen 20 casks of wine for a trespass done against them. Afterwards the latter, by special favour, condoned ten of the above twenty casks under the following arrangement:—that of the ten casks nine should be payable if the above Richard be convicted in future of ill-behaviour against the Mayor and Aldermen. He was fined 40s for his trespass against the King, to be paid on the following Thursday.

[1] See p. 1 for the pleadings.

Mabel, relict of John de Lodelawe, demanded against John
Gamel a debt of £163 4s. She had already prosecuted before
the Mayor and Aldermen an attachment of 30 sacks of wool,
belonging to the defendant, and sealed with his seal, which
were found in the City of London in the hand and seisin of
Robert Poleyn, the journeyman and trader of the defendant[1],
and had given the Sheriff security that she would prosecute
her claim. Thereupon the Mayor had ordered the Sheriff to
attach all wool and other merchandise belonging to the defendant in whosesoever hands they might be, in accordance
with the custom of the City, and to report thereon to the
Court. This was done, and on the above date Robert Poleyn
appeared and claimed the wool, on the ground that he had
bought it from the defendant at Shrewsbury and had paid
for it, and that it was thus his own, and he said further that
the defendant, on the day of the plaint being levied in the
Mayor's Court and the attachment made, had no property
in the wool, and if it had been lost by land or sea, he alone
would have suffered, and he offered to make whatever proof
was required of him as a foreigner. The plaintiff pleaded
that this testimony ought not to be accepted, because the
defendant had caused the wool to be taken from Shrewsbury
to London at his own expense, under his own seal and at
his own risk in the custody of Robert, who was his journeyman
and trader, and she demanded judgment whether Robert
could make a just claim to the wool. The latter said that the
wool had been carried to London at his (Robert's) expense

---

[1] By the City custom of Foreign Attachment the goods of a debtor
might be attached in the hands of a third person, called the garnishee.
If the debtor appeared and put in bail within a year and a day, the
garnishee was discharged. A garnishee was entitled to prove that the
debtor had no property in the goods attached to the value of fourpence,
so long as he appeared before the debtor had made a fourth default and
execution had not been sued. See *Lib. Alb.* I, pp. 208–9. The *Lib. Alb.*
does not clearly state how such proof was made. From this case and
another in Roll C, membr. 6 *b*, it appears that the foreign garnishee
swore with the third hand, i.e. he took an oath and two other persons
supported his oath with their own. It is interesting to notice that this
method of proving claims to property was used in the case of waifs and
strays in the fourteenth century. Mary Bateson, *Borough Custom* (Selden
Society), II, pp. 163–4.

and risk. Judgment was given that Robert make his proof, himself the third hand. He appeared on the day assigned and failed in his "law," admitting that he had only paid for £10 worth of the wool, and was under bond to John for the rest, and he altered his claim accordingly. The Sheriff was ordered to hold the attachment of the 30 sacks until the defendant, John Gamel, should be willing to submit himself to justice to answer the plaintiff for the above debt.

Membr. 7
16 Oct. 1298 *Thursday before the Feast of St Luke* [18 Oct.]

John de Sabriteswrth, "poleter," complained that Richer de Refham, Sheriff, in the market against Cordewanerestrate[1] took from him and unjustly detained four geese. The Sheriff defended the seizure on the ground that the plaintiff had bought the geese in order to sell them to the regrators against the proclamation of the City. The plaintiff denied that he bought them for this purpose. Judgment was given that he wage his law[2] for the Quinzime. Memorandum that the plaintiff was also adjudged to make his law for contempt alleged against him by the Sheriff. He was afterwards pardoned by the Mayor.

7 Nov. 1298 *Friday before the Feast of St Martin* [11 Nov.]

Roger de Bosco, beadle of Nicholas of Farndon without, John de Burgo, beadle of the same Nicholas of Farndon within, John beadle of William le Mazerer, and John le Clerk of Bredstrate appeared before the Mayor and were sworn to answer separately by what warrant they summoned the honest men of their Wards to the Church of the Brothers of the Sack[3] on the morrow of All Souls, and whether they themselves were there. The above Roger said that he was present, and at the instance of certain neighbours unnamed

---

[1] If the north end of Cordwainer Street or Bow Lane is meant, this would seem to be an early reference to a Poultry Market in Honey Lane.
[2] As a defendant, a position into which he has been thrown by the Sheriff's accusation.
[3] Stow (ed. Kingsford), I, p. 278, places the church or chapel of the Penitential Friars at the north corner of Old Jewry.

he had summoned Robert de Romeseye, John Gerlaund, Benedict le Sporier and William Ediman, but did not know the occasion thereof, except that the said men of the Ward drew up a petition to the Mayor concerning themselves. John de Burgo admitted that he was present and at the instance of Roger Hosebond and Roger de Asshendon he had summoned several brewers of his Ward but did not know the occasion thereof. John the beadle of William le Mazerer admitted the same, and said that the summons was at the instance of Peter de Hungrie. John le Clerk said that at the instance of John de Burgo he had summoned several holders of brew-houses viz. Nicholas le Convers, Richard le Barber, William le Fruter and Stephen de Haregwe. Richard le Barber of Douuegate did not appear and was summoned for Wednesday after the Feast of St Martin. The same day was given to the others.

Friday after the above Feast *14 Nov. 1298*

Gocelin le Serjant and Thomas ate Welle, Serjeants of Richer de Refham, Sheriff, were summoned to answer Peter de Ratlesdene, baker, in a plea of trespass wherein he complained that the defendants came to his house near Allegate and, on behalf of the Sheriff, attached his paste (*pastum*), which was worked and ready for baking, and carried it away from his house against his will, the value thereof being 10s for four quarters of corn. The defendants admitted going to the plaintiff's house, but denied that they arrested or attached his bread to hinder his profiting thereby. Richer the Sheriff also appeared and said that by virtue of his office he sent his Serjeants, on the ground that the plaintiff sold to regrators, to carry the bread to the Guyhald to be weighed and judged by the Aldermen as to whether it was of good weight, and that he did not take it or carry it away (so as to deprive him of it). The plaintiff pleaded that he did not sell his bread to regrators, except as other bakers did, and put himself on his country. Richer and the Serjeants did the same.

Afterwards an agreement was made, on terms that Peter released and quitclaimed all actions against the defendants and Richer, receiving 10s payable within the Quinzime. The defendants were amerced by the Court.

Wednesday before the Feast of St Andrew the Apostle [30 Nov.] A° 27 Edw. [1298]

William de Hereford, armourer, was attached to answer Thomas Romeyn and Juliana his wife in a plea of trespass, wherein they complained that the defendant came to Thomas's house in the Parish of St Mary Aldremarycherche at Vespers and used abusive words against Juliana, calling her false and double-tongued. When she ordered him to leave the house, he refused and took her by the bosom and shouted for the master (*post dominum suum*). Thereupon Thomas left his chamber and demanded the defendant's name and attached him for breaking the peace, and on this William violently ejected him and used opprobrious words. The latter now defended the force and tort, but subsequently admitted the accusation and put himself on the mercy of the Court. Damages were taxed by a jury at 20 marks. Judgment was given for that amount and the defendant was committed to prison. Afterwards he found pledges for keeping the peace viz. John de Basing, John de Hereford, Manekin le Armurer, Roger Brune, Adam le . . . ., Laurence Flambard, Peter de Waltham, John le Blound son of Walter, Adam le Fourbeur, William Bray, John de Rippelawe, Walter Hauteyn of Lincoln, Richard de Meldebourne, William de Gaytone and Richard Hautein, for the payment of the 20 marks damages in case of a second offence.

ROLL B

Court of H. le Galeys, *Mayor, and* Richer *the Sheriff* [1]
on Tuesday before the Feast of St Thomas the Apostle
[21 *Dec.*] *A° 27 Edw.* [1298]

Membr. 1
16 Dec. 1298

Writ, dated at Abbercorn, 15 Aug. 1298, directed to H. le
Galeys and the Sheriffs of London and Middlesex, stating
that the kings "valet," Nicholas de Montpelers, was robbed
in Zeland of a ship by men of that country, when the King
was in Flanders, and bidding the Mayor and Sheriffs give
him redress as best they can.

In accordance with the above, Lambinus Modersone was
attached to answer Nicholas de Monte Pessulano in a plea
that, when the plaintiff in the Quinzime of St Martin (11 Nov.)
A° 26 Edw. [1297] was crossing to Flanders in a ship of
Sandwich with goods belonging to the King and to himself,
i.e. cloth and other merchandise, the defendant with other
malefactors attacked him and took away the ship and the
goods in it, against the peace and to his damage 200 marks.

The defendant denied that he was guilty and put himself
on a jury of merchants and masters of ships who were accustomed to cross the seas, and the plaintiff did the like. The
Serjeant was ordered to summon a good jury for the Friday
following. Afterwards at a Court held on Wednesday before
the Feast of St Valentine (14 Feb.) the same year [1298–9], the
jury brought in a verdict that the defendant was not guilty
of the trespass or of the act, or of assenting thereto, or of
partnership with those who robbed the plaintiff. Judgment
that the latter recover nothing and the defendant go quit.

Court of the same Mayor on the Friday following

19 Dec. 1298

Nicholas de Monte Pessulano and Lambinus Modersone
appeared and a jury also. As Nicholas challenged all the
jurors in the panel, a day was given till the Octave of S^t
Hillary to hear the verdict. The Sheriff was ordered to bring

---

[1] The Sheriffs had no official standing in the Mayor's Court except as
servants of the Court; their presence on this and other occasions was
due to the fact that the writ was addressed to them as well as to the
Mayor.

the body of the above Lambinus on that day to receive the verdict of the jury.

John de Trillawe, parson of the Church of St Dunstan, appeared and on behalf of the executors of the will of Henry Box paid £4 6d, in part payment of £8 12d due on a Recognizance to the Wardens of the Bridge. He demanded on behalf of himself and his co-executors, that the executors of Thomas Cros, who was the other executor of Henry Box, should be distrained for £4 6d in arrears, which they owed to the above Wardens on a Recognizance, as appears in the Pleas held[1]....

Membr. 1 b   An Inquest, *ex officio* without writ, consisting of Adam Braz and others on the panel, was held at the Priory of St Bartholomew Westsmethfeld, before H. le Galeys and the Sheriffs of the City and Middlesex, on Friday before the Feast of St Andrew the Apostle [30 Nov.], to return a verdict as to the malefactors who dragged John de Stonham, a servant of the Earl of Lincoln, from the door of Clerekenwell, imprisoned him and did other enormities to him to his damage and in contempt of the said Earl. They gave a verdict that on the Friday evening before Michaelmas, John de Stonham and William de Dodington, servants of the above Earl, entered the house of John le Keu in Westsmethfeld to drink, and a certain Stephen, servant of Brother William de Ringeland, drank with them in turns, and words having arisen between them, Stephen struck John on the jaw with his hand, whereupon John le Keu turned them out of the house. Immediately Stephen followed John de Stonham with two knives in his hands to kill him, and seeing this, William knocked him down opposite the house of Richard ate Hole, while John fled towards the monastery church. Nevertheless Stephen pursued John to a bridge called Kaytifbreg, so that John in fear of his life drew a knife and struck Stephen in the left side, while they were in the kennel, and then fled into the church. Afterwards Stephen with a certain Walter de la . . . . and other unknown persons of the household of the Hospital of Clerekenwell followed John to the High Altar in the church, dragged

[1] 25 July, 1298. Cf. p. 13.

him out and took him to the house of Stephen de Weresdal, chief tithingman[1] (*decennarius*), to keep him till the morrow; and since Stephen was in danger of death from the blow, the tithingman asked Brother William de Ringeland to lend him the shackles of the Hospital to keep John safely. The jurors also said that these people put John de Stonham's feet higher than his head. Next day Roger de Appelby, Undersheriff of Middlesex, came and carried him off to Neugate, as Stephen's life was despaired off, until he could have sure information on the point from the physicians (*medici*). He remained in prison for three days, and was afterwards mainprised to stand his trial against anyone who should accuse him.

Whereas Matilda, wife of Robert le Barber of Garscherch, who is in the service of Sir H. le Despenser, Forest Justiciar for this side of Trent, brought a petition to the said Sir Hugh at his last coming to London, in which she alleged that Saer le Barber had said that Sir Hugh was unworthy of praise (*esse benedictus*) and that it was a great wonder that he had not lost his hood (?; *quin ipse non amissiset capitum suum*) in Gant in going into Flanders, and other enormities in contempt of the said Hugh, and also that he kept more robbers with him than any man in England—the above Hugh le Despenser summoned the Mayor and ordered him on the King's behalf to cause the said Saer le Barber to be attached by his body, and to send him to Neugate, in order that he might appear before him to answer for the trespass.

Tuesday before the Nativity of the Lord [25 *Dec.*]   *23 Dec. 1298*

Whereas it had been presented before Adam de Halling (beri), Alderman of the Ward of Allgate, in his Wardmote, that Roger le Rous makes a great roistering (*rigolagiam*) with unknown minstrels, tabor-players and trumpeters to the grave damage and tumult of the whole neighbourhood and against the prohibition; and that Peter Portehors is a receiver by

---

[1] Probably head of the Chief Pledges of the Ward. The system of Frankpledge, whereby groups of ten or twelve men were compulsory sureties of each other is frequently mentioned in the City Records: Iter Roll AA, membr. 2 *b*, 3 *b*, A.D. 1233 and 1241; *Lib. Alb.* I, pp. 99, 315, 332.

night of unknown depraved men and prostitutes; and that in the Rent of Ralph le Chapeleyn there is a low haunt of prostitutes and depraved men who go about the City by night; and that Alice la Clerekes harboured Robert le Ceinturer after she had forsworn the Ward, against the prohibition of the Alderman; and that Adam le Botoner is a receiver of evildoers—the above persons were summoned before the Mayor to answer &c. Roger, Peter, Adam and Ralph pleaded not guilty and put themselves on their country. Afterwards a jury brought in a verdict of not guilty for Roger, Peter and Adam, but said that Ralph knowingly harboured loose women against repeated warnings by his Alderman. He was put in mercy. Alice, who did not appear, was ordered to be attached.

Membr. 2
29 Jan.
1298–9
Thursday before the Feast of the Purification of the Blessed Mary [2 Feb.] A° 27 Edw. [1298–9]

Fulk de St Edmunds was summoned to answer Friscus de Monte Claro and Tottus his brother, merchants of Lucca, and John le Grant of London, in a plea of debt of 50 marks, due for a horse which the defendants bought, together with Hugh Bardolf and John le Brettoun late Warden of London, the amount being payable on Jan. 5 1294, as appeared by a deed in which Hugh, John and Fulk were severally responsible for payment. The defendant appeared by his attorney, Walter Woleward, and admited the deed and his seal. Judgment that he be in mercy and satisfy the plaintiffs at the Quinzime. The defendant appeared in Court on the Monday following and paid the plaintiffs 30 marks, for which he received an acquittance, the remaining 20 marks being respited till the Vigil of Easter. Afterwards the deed was delivered to him in the presence of the Mayor, G. de Northon, R. de Refham, Th. Sely and others.

Roger de Len, taverner, was attached to answer William de Leyre in a plea of trespass, wherein the latter complained that the defendant had abused him as he was walking harmlessly along Tamys Street, and had charged him with having procured the publication of an Assize of Wine by the Mayor

and Aldermen against the common good, in which Assize
the price of better wine was fixed at 1½d the gallon. The
defendant denied the offence and put himself on his country
and was mainprised by John Vigerous and Geoffrey de
Conductu. Afterwards he admitted the trespass and pledged
to the Mayor and the plaintiff two casks of wine. As he
could not find pledges for the same he was committed to
prison until &c.

Saturday before the above Feast

Richard de Pelham was charged by the Mayor and Aldermen that, being a freeman sworn to maintain the freedom,
he associated himself with a certain William de Wilton, a
foreigner, and bought merchandise with him at Bristol, which
ought to have been dealt with to the advantage of the merchants of the Liberty, but after William had bought the goods
at Bristol with his own and Richard's money, the latter met
them at Brainford, and forestalled and avowed them as his
own, whereby the Sheriffs were defrauded. The defendant
denied that he did as alleged at Bristol and Brainford and
demanded an inquest thereon. A jury of men of his trade
of the venue of Bridge, who were not connected with him
by affinity, was summoned and brought in a verdict of not
guilty. The defendant was acquitted and was told that he
might use the freedom as before.

Walter de Maydenestan, carpenter, was charged by the
Mayor and Aldermen with gathering together a parliament
of carpenters at Milehende, where they bound themselves by
a corporal oath not to observe a certain ordinance[1] or provision made by the Mayor and Aldermen touching their craft
and their daily wages, which was enrolled in the "paper" of
the Guildhall. The defendant admitted that he was at Milehende, but said that he never held a parliament there, or
took an oath or made any one else take one against the
ordinances, and he demanded an inquest. A jury was
summoned.

31 Jan.
1298–9

Membr. 2 *b*

[1] *Temp.* Gregory de Rokesle, Mayor. Cf. *Lib. Cust.* I, p. 99; Letter
Book A, fo. 88 *b*.

Thursday the Feast of St Agatha [5 Feb.]

Robert le Treyere was summoned to answer for certain trespasses against the City whereof he was deraigned by the Mayor and Aldermen, to wit, that as Warden of the Thames at Billingsgate, to which various goods came by water, which ought to be dealt with to the profit of the City, and other goods by land and water, which ought not to be allowed to go outside the City, the defendant allowed divers goods to go abroad, such as corn, bacon and other victuals. The defendant admitted that he allowed goods to go by the hands of foreigners over the sea, but pleaded that he never knew of the prohibition. Afterwards he made a full acknowledgment. A day was given till the next Court to hear judgment.

Wednesday before the Feast of St Valentine [14 Feb.]

Writ, dated at Loweder 9 July A° 26 Edw. (1298) to Henry le Galeys, mayor, reciting a Recognizance of £32 by Ralph Hardel to Reymund de Nevile and Arnald de Squinetta, and ordering the Mayor to liberate the above Ralph from Newgate if it appeared from an acquittance produced by him, which was to be examined in the presence of Ralph de Sandwich and John de Bauquell, that he had paid the amount due.

The above Reymund, Arnald and Ralph were summoned before the Mayor, when Ralph asked for a respite on the ground that he could not at the moment produce his acquittances, which were in the custody of Sir Hugh de Hengham, clerk. A day was given and he was remanded to prison. The other parties appointed as their attorney Oto, a merchant of Toulouse.

Afterwards Ralph showed three acquittances making mention of £7 10s, whereof one was a Release and Quitclaim of all actions relating to the whole of the above debt, and he demanded that these acquittances be allowed to him and that he be delivered from prison. Oto, as attorney of the other parties, said that he did not know whether the acquittances were the deed of Reymund and Arnald, who were now abroad, and he asked that the documents be kept in custody

till their return. Ralph offered to verify the acquittances;
but as the Court held that no verification could take place
in the absence of Reymund and Arnald, he willingly granted
that the deeds remain in the custody of the Mayor till their
return. Meanwhile his delivery from prison was allowed on
condition of his finding mainpernors to answer for the debt
if necessary.

Writ, dated at Ely 16 Jan. A° 27 Edw. [1298–9] to H. le
Galeys, mayor, reciting a complaint of Richard de Wyt that
he had entered into a Recognizance of £22 to Ralph Abbehal,
payable at Michaelmas 1298, before the above Mayor and
John de Bauquell, the clerk deputed to receive Recognizances,
and though he had paid the debt and received an acquittance,
the above Ralph had procured his imprisonment in Newgate.
The Mayor is ordered to hear the parties and inspect the
acquittance, and if it appeared that the complainant had paid
the sum due in accordance with the Statute[1], and was imprisoned for no other cause, the Mayor is to deliver him
from prison.

In accordance with the above, the parties were summoned,
when the complainant produced a tally under the seal of
Ralph concerning £20 2s, which he demanded should be
allowed. Ralph acknowledged the tally, but said that he gave
it to the plaintiff, blank and sealed, under condition that
Richard and his servant Reginald should meet to make account
and that the tally should be marked for sums received, but
that he never received more than 42s of the above debt. He
called to witness Reginald, who was not present in Court.

Afterwards the latter appeared on summons, and said that
he never received more than 42s on his master's behalf, and
that he and the plaintiff accounted together at Croyndon and
agreed about everything as regards 42s, which they placed
on the tally, but that he had never marked the tally for any

[1] A Statute Merchant was a bond of record. The Statute of Acton
Burnel, 11 Edw., enacts that the merchant was to cause his debtor to
come before the Mayor of London, etc., to acknowledge the debt due
and the day of payment. This Recognizance was entered on the Rolls of
Recognizances. The clerk then made out a Bill Obligatory, on which the
debtor's seal was affixed as well as the King's Seal, which was in the
custody of the Mayor.

other moneys beyond the 42s, and that the said tally (for £20 2s) was not the deed of his master.

Wednesday before the Feast of St Valentine [14 Feb.]

Jordan de Wytzand, broker, was attached to answer the Commonalty of London in a plea that, whereas the said Jordan was a sworn broker for ships only, he acted as a common broker in all kinds of merchandise against the custom, forestalled merchandise and procured it for others not of the Liberty, thus buying against his oath, to the damage of the City. The said Jordan defended &c. and said he was not guilty thereof, and put himself on his country. A jury of Walter le Fuller and others, as appears by the Panel, brought in a verdict of guilty, and said that he had done this all the time he had been in the City, and that he was not fit to remain in the City as a broker, because in the late war between the kings of France and England he informed the King's enemies abroad of English news (*rumores Anglicos*); and that he was an associate of Frenchmen at that time and more favourable to them than to Englishmen. Judgment that he abjure the City, that he engage in no trade (*officium*) in the same henceforth, and that he do not remain in the City more than one night, except by special permission of the Commonalty, under penalty of imprisonment.

John Gumbard was summoned to answer John de Worcestre and Gunora his wife in a plea of trespass, wherein they complained that he impleaded them in the Court Christian in lay pleas, against a prohibition[1] of the King directed to him and against a precept of the Mayor communicated by his Serjeant, in contempt &c. The defendant denied that he impleaded them as alleged, and waged his law. He was ordered to come with his law on the Quinzime. Pledges:— Robert de Keleshull and Walter Portehors.

Afterwards on Thursday after the Feast of St Peter in Cathedra [22 Feb.] the said John Gumbard made his law.

---

[1] This was an Original Writ obtainable from the Chancery. *Registrum Omnium Brevium*, A.D. 1634, p. 34.

Judgment that he go quit, and that the plaintiff be in mercy for a false claim.

Wednesday after the Feast of S[t] Matthew [Query: Mathias, 24 Feb.?]

Membr. 4
25 Feb.
1298–9

John Gumbard was attached to answer the King and the Mayor, on the grievous complaint of John de Worcestre and Gunora his wife, for having impleaded the latter in a lay plea before the Court Christian and for having sued against them a sentence of excommunication. The defendant pleaded not guilty and put himself on his country. A jury was summoned from the venue of Billingesgate.

Saturday after the above Feast

28 Feb.
1298–9

Peregrine de Orte, John de Ramus, John de Sataly and Ernald de Sere were attached to answer the King and John Juvenal, Serjeant[1], in a plea that whereas the plaintiff John, by precept of the Mayor and Sheriffs, had attached Bernard du Pyn for breaking a sequestration made upon him in an action of trespass, in which Peter Adrian was plaintiff, the defendants rescued him and assaulted the Serjeant. The defendants pleaded not guilty and put themselves on their country. A jury was summoned and they were accepted as pledges for each other to hear the verdict. Afterwards a jury from Bredstrate brought in a verdict that the defendants rescued the above Bernard, but did no other harm to the Serjeant. Judgment that they be committed to prison until &c.

Ash Wednesday following [4 March]

4 March
1298–9

The action (*loquela*) between Robert le Bedel, plaintiff, and Martin de Dollingham in a plea of debt was removed into the Court of Richard de Refham, Sheriff, as pertaining to the Shrievalty. A day given by the Sheriff on the Quinzime.

---

[1] Serjeant of the Chamber, cf. p. 35.

Gilbert le Barber confessed that he bought 5 casks of wine for the use of a foreigner against his oath as a freeman, i.e. from Simon de Salerne, a foreigner, to the use of Juliana de Carlisle, a foreigner, receiving 2s from the latter for brokerage. The Sheriff was ordered to bring him to the next Husteng, where judgment was given that he be deprived of the freedom.

Afterwards he was readmitted on a fine of 20s to the Commonalty, by mainprise of R. de Monte Pessulano for the payment thereof on the morrow.

5 March 1298–9 *The morrow of Ash Wednesday* [4 *March*]

Bernard du Pyn was attached to answer the King and John Juvenal in a plea that, whereas the above John, by precept of the Mayor and Sheriffs, sequestrated certain of his goods in a room in the house of William le Surrygien[1] and sealed them as an attachment, the defendant broke the seal and carried away the goods in contempt &c. Peregrine de Orde, John de Rames, John de Sataly, and Arnald de Sere were attached to answer a charge that they ordered him to do so and consented thereto. All defendants pleaded not guilty and put themselves on their country. Afterwards at a Court held on the above date, a jury brought in a verdict against them. Judgment that they be committed to prison, except the defendant Bernard, who was under age.

7 March 1298–9 *Saturday before the First Sunday* [*in Lent:*—8 *March*]

Thomas Juvenal and Alice his wife essoined[2] against Robert de Aldresgate, fishmonger, and Juliana his wife in a plea of trespass by R. de Leycestre.

---

[1] Surgeon.

[2] "Signifies an excuse for him that is summoned to appear and answer to an action, by reason of sickness or infirmity or other just cause of absence." Sickness was the common essoin. Other causes were: absence overseas or in the Holy Land, sickness whereby a man was bedridden, the King's service, constraint of enemies, falling among thieves, floods, the breaking down of bridges, etc. Jacob's *Law Dictionary.* An immense amount of definition took place as regards essoins, and constituted "the bulkiest chapter of our old law, the chapter on essoins." Pollock and

John le Gros, clerk, was attached to answer Francis de Vilers, knight, in a plea that, whereas the plaintiff was lodging, by precept of the Sheriff, in the house of a certain Agnes de la Cornere in Bredstrate until the King's arrival and until the King could provide for his lodging elsewhere, the defendant drew his sword against him, arrested his horses in the said house and would not let him take them away, and wounded his squire John in the face with a misericord in contempt of the plaintiff and to his damage 100s. The defendant pleaded not guilty and put himself on his country.

Afterwards, on the same day, a jury of Bredstrate brought in a verdict that the defendant was not guilty and did not prevent the plaintiff from taking away his horses. Being asked who prevented him, they answered that the men of Sir Walter de Beauchamp, Steward of the King, whose horses were stabled in that inn, would not allow any stranger's horse to enter. Judgment that the defendant go quit, and the plaintiff be in mercy for a false claim.

John le Leche, "mouner"[1], was attached to answer John le Wayer in a plea that, whereas the plaintiff was a servant of the King appointed by the Mayor to take the King's customs for the pesage[2] of corn on London Bridge, the defendant on Monday last came on to the Bridge leading a quarter of wheat belonging to a certain Henry le Cupere, baker, and as the said Henry was in arrears for the pesage of 4 quarters of wheat, which amounted to $4\frac{1}{2}$d, the plaintiff attempted to distrain the miller's horse, but the defendant would not allow him, and removed the horse and the custom due, and took him by the throat and snatched his cap, and drew his knife against him, in contempt of the King and the Mayor and to his damage 100s. The defendant admitted that

Maitland, *Hist. Eng. Law*, ii, pp. 562–3. Essoins in borough courts are illustrated in *Borough Customs* by Mary Bateson (Selden Society), vol. i. Special London rules on the subject are to be found in *Lib. Alb.* (Rolls Series), i, pp. 63, 64, 67, 77, 202, 471, and will be noted in the index to the present Calendar.

[1] Miller.

[2] Pesage was a custom for the weighing of corn and other commodities. The whole question of the City's right to exact this custom by its Sheriffs was discussed at the session of the Itinerant Justices at the Tower in A.D. 1321. *Lib. Cust.* i, pp. 326–333, 380.

he came with a quarter of wheat, but denied resisting the distraint, and said that Henry le Cupere did not owe more than ½d for pesage, which he was only bound to pay at the end of the week according to agreement; and as regards the other charges he pleaded not guilty and put himself on his country.

Afterwards on the same day a jury brought in a verdict that the plaintiff attached the wheat for the arrears of pesage, and that when he would have attached the miller's horse also, the defendant took the plaintiff's cap and wanted to blind him with it, whereupon the plaintiff struck him in the face with his hand, and they both drew their knives, but that the defendant did not strike the other or take away either the custom or the horse; the latter escaped by himself and ran to his stable while they were engaged in the mêlée. Judgment [breaks off].

Saturday before the Feast of St Gregory [12 March]

Membr. 5
7 March
1298–9

Elyas de Bristoll was summoned to answer the King and the Commonalty of London in a plea that whereas no freeman could lawfully avow contracts between foreigners or buy for foreigners, whereby the King lost his forfeitures, nevertheless the defendant avowed 24 sacks of wool which the Society of the Bardi[1] bought from a certain John de Lodelawe, a foreigner, in fraud and deceit of the Liberty, and to the damage of the citizens. The defendant said that he himself bought the wool from the above John and sold it to the Society, but that at the time of the first purchase he did not know the second purchasers, and thereon he puts himself on his country[2]. Afterwards at a Court, held on the Monday following, a jury brought in a verdict that the defendant bought the wool for

[1] Italian merchants of Florence.
[2] The defendant was charged with acting as an unlicensed broker between foreigners. He pleaded that two genuine sales took place, but the jury did not take this view. A long succession of ordinances was passed to prevent foreign merchants dealing with each other, selling retail, and remaining in the City more than a month. Additional MS. 14,252, Brit. Mus. fo. 123; *Lib. Cust.* I, pp. 68–71; *Lib. Alb.* I, pp. 492, 493; and the Letter Books *passim*.

the Society's use and at their risk and that he received nothing from the Society except brokerage. A day was given to the defendant to hear judgment and the same day given to the merchants. Afterwards, on the Tuesday following, the Court considering that the contract of sale and purchase was the fraud and deception of the defendant alone, and not the fault of the merchants, the attachment made upon the latter was delivered to them, and judgment was given that the defendant be deprived of the freedom.

Subsequently, at the instance of common friends, the defendant was readmitted to the freedom and sworn, on payment of 10 marks of silver to the Commonalty.

John de Elsingham, Andrew de Stibbenheth, Nicholas de Totenham, John ate Holte, Laurence de Wymbysh, Michael de Wymbysh, John May, Milo le Fevre, John le Simple, Roger de Wodestrate, John de Guyppewyco[1], Richard de Chigewell, John de Sholane, William de Sholane, Robert de Sholane, Robert de Sandwich and Stephen de Holte were attached to answer the City and the Commonalty of London in a plea that, whereas according to the custom of the realm of England no Parliament (*parlaymentum*) can take place relating to the aforesaid kingdom without the King and his Council, nevertheless the said John &c., privily by the imposition of a corporal oath, taken by all, made a parliament and confederacy in contempt of the King and to the harm of the City; and the confederacy was such that if any one offended against any citizen, the others would support him, and that no one was allowed to work with others than themselves, and for this purpose they had a casket (*pixis*) for their contributions, which casket was seen in Court; and also that they impleaded persons who had offended them before the Ecclesiastical Courts in lay pleas, and made several other provisions against the Liberty of the City; and that they drew up a charter for the confederacy, which was in the custody of John de Elsingham, in contempt &c. and to the damage of the city £100. The defendant John acknowledged that he had the charter and craved permission to bring it into Court.

[1] Ipswich.

Afterwards he said he could not find it. Since he had contra-
dicted his admission, judgment was given that he be taken
into custody. Precept was given to the Sheriff to bring him
to Court on Thursday with the charter. Afterwards, at a
Court held on Saturday the defendant John came, but produced no charter. Thereupon the Court ordered that a jury
be summoned to say whether the said John had maliciously
eloigned it. The other defendants then defended, and admitted that they made unanimously an ordinance to the effect
that none should work at night on account of the unhealthiness of coal (*propter putridinem carbonis marine*), and damage
to their neighbours; that their doors should be closed all the
year at the first stroke of Curfew at St Martins le Grand, and
that none of their households should wander through the
streets against the Proclamation; and that they made the
casket so that each master of the trade of smiths could put
a farthing a week therein to maintain a wax-taper [*cirgeam*]
to the honour of the Blessed Mary and St Laudus, and also
for the relief of any of the trade who should fall into poverty.
And as regards the trespass they put themselves on their
country. A jury was summoned for the Wednesday following.
Afterwards, at a Court held on Saturday before the Feast of
the Annunciation B.M. [25 March], the jury brought in a
verdict that the said John and the others were not guilty of
the trespass, and that the said John did not have any charter
in his custody contrary to the City. As it seemed to the
Court that the acknowledgments made were not prejudicial
to the King or the Liberty, judgment was given that the
defendants go quit.

Membr. 5 *b*   Frissottus de Monte Claro granted an acquittance, on behalf of himself and his brother Tottus, to Fulk de St Edmunds,
Sir John le Bretun and Sir Hugh Bardolf, the latter having
paid them fifty marks of silver due on the purchase of a horse.

William de Storteford, charged with resisting a sequestration upon his goods for a debt to Edmund, Earl of Cornwall,
incurred by him during his Shrievalty, put himself on the
favour of the Mayor and pledged himself in five casks of
wine, to be taken at the Mayor's pleasure.

Further writ dated at Bernes 22 Feb. 1298–9 on behalf of
Ralph Hardel, who complained that he had been kept in prison
for a debt of £32 due to Reymund de Nevill and Arnald
de Skynat, though he had paid the money and received
acquittances.

Return; to the effect that Ralph had produced his acquittances, which were deposited in court until the above Reymund
and Arnald returned from abroad. He remained in prison,
because he could not find mainpernors to answer for the
debt if necessary.

Thursday before the Feast of St Benedict [21 March]

19 March
1298–9

John Andreu was attached to answer the Mayor and Commonalty and Walter le Hethereve, bailiff of Queenhithe, in
a plea that, whereas it was unlawful for a foreigner to make
any contract of merchandise with another foreigner, nevertheless the defendant sold a fish called "moscles" by retail
to a certain William Purchaz, a foreigner, at Queenhithe, and
would not allow the above Walter to attach his ship and goods
for the offence, but drew his knife upon him in contempt &c.
and to his damage £20. The defendant admitted the sale of
fish, and said that he hired the above William to sell the fish
because he did not understand the selling of fish himself,
and thus his fish was sold to divers persons, but William
bought none of it by retail; and thereon he put himself on
his country. Precept was given to summon a jury and to
attach the ship and goods meanwhile.

Afterwards, at a Court held on Saturday, the defendant
admitted the offence. Judgment that his ship and goods be
forfeited to the King, and that the bailiff retain them in his
custody till the defendant satisfy the Sheriff for the forfeiture.

William de Broughton, skinner, was summoned to answer
William de Leyre[1] on a charge that, when the defendant was
distrained by John Juvenal, Serjeant of the Chamber, for
2 marks which he promised (*tendebat*) to the Commonalty
for the purchase of the freedom, he came to the plaintiff's
house and used opprobrious words to him, declaring that
the distraint was unjust and that William was plotting to drive

[1] Alderman of Castle Baynard Ward.

him and others from the Liberty of the City. The defendant denied the charge and put himself on his country.

Monday after the Feast of the Annunciation B.M. [25 March] A° 27 Edw. [1299]

Stephen de Uptone was attached to answer the King and Thomas Sely, Sheriff of London, in a plea of trespass, wherein the latter complained that, having been ordered by Sir Walter de Beauchamp, the Steward of the King's Household, to bring the defendant to Westminster to answer Julia, relict of Henry Box, in a plea of trespass, he sent his clerk, John de Fridaie-strate, to the defendant's house to carry out the order, but the latter closed his doors and gate against him, and also against the plaintiff himself and his clerks and Serjeants, so that the King's commands could not be fulfilled. The defendant admitted that John the clerk came to his house, but said he was in bed because it was late at night, and that he did nothing to hinder them from executing their orders. He demanded that inquest be made by a jury of the venue. A jury was summoned for Wednesday.

Writ dated at Westminster 28 March A° 27 Edw. [1299] to the Mayor and Sheriffs, to the effect that Richard de Burdegale, whom R., bishop of London, claimed as a clerk by letters patent, had been taken and detained in Newgate for a Recognizance of debt to Andrew Payne, although by the Statute[1] relating to Recognizances of debts to merchants, it had been laid down that clerks should not be so taken and imprisoned. They are to deliver him without delay.

Afterwards the Mayor sent this Original Writ to the Sheriff, Thomas Sely, by Philip de Mardel, for execution thereof, which writ remains with the Sheriff as his warrant.

Saturday before the Feast of the Translation of St Thomas the Martyr [7 July]

Thomas Sely, Sheriff, was summoned to answer Sabina Malemeins in a plea of trespass, wherein she complained that

---

[1] The Statute of Acton Burnel, 11 Edw. I.

he came to her house in the parish of Holy Trinity the Less, and unjustly distrained and sequestrated all her goods, and sealed the doors of her chamber, in connection with a claim of 40s by William Overton, though she did not owe that sum; and that he dragged her out of bed and did other enormities. The defendant pleaded that he went to the house of Michael de Carlisle, Sabina's husband, in obedience to a writ from the Exchequer, in order to distrain him for 40s, in which he had been condemned before the Barons of the Exchequer in an action of trespass at the suit of William Overton, and that he (the defendant) made no other distraint upon her, than this upon her husband, and he demanded a jury. The plaintiff answered that the above Michael was not her husband and had no goods in her house on which the Sheriff could distrain for 40s, nor even to the value of 2s; and thereon she put herself on her country. Afterwards a jury found a verdict for her on these issues. Judgment that the distraint be delivered to her, and the defendant be in mercy.

Thursday after the above Feast 9 *July 1299*

Hanekin Yacopp brought a plaint against Thomas Sely, Sheriff, to the effect that the latter distrained him by 25 pounds of copper. Afterwards he abandoned his plaint, saying that he had previously sold the copper to a certain Thomas de Doddeford. He was in mercy for withdrawing from his plea.

Thomas de Doddele (*sic*) was summoned to answer the King and the Commonalty of London in a plea that, whereas by the custom of London no freeman was allowed to avow contracts by foreigners or buy for the use of foreigners, whereby the king lost his forfeitures, nevertheless the defendant bought 25 pounds of copper from a certain Hanekin le Rede for the use of Robert Craumpe, a foreigner of Coventry, thus acting as an unsworn broker, and that he avowed the goods to be his own, whereby the sheriffs were defrauded of their customs. The defendant acknowledged that he bought the copper, but declared that it was for his own use and that he was not a broker, and that he did not know of any other merchant as a purchaser for the copper at the time he bought it; and thereon he put himself on his country. Afterwards, on the Monday following, a jury brought in a verdict that the defendant was not a broker, and that he bought the copper from Henekin le Rede for the use of Robert Craumpe, and that at the time of the purchase he knew the latter as his prospective buyer. Judgment that he be deprived of the freedom[1], and be precluded from trading within the same, under penalty of forfeiting all his goods as a foreigner.

Membr. 7
10 July 1299

Friday after the above Feast

Geoffrey David, butcher, was attached to answer the King and the Mayor in a plea that, whereas a common tallage of 2000 marks was granted to the King for renewing the Liberties of the City, and Richer de Refham, Sheriff, by precept of the Mayor and in the person of Hugh de Waltham[2], his sworn clerk, entered the defendant's house in the Parish of St Leonard, together with the Collectors of Bridge Ward, to sequestrate his goods and chattels in order to levy therefrom his portion, being a fourth, for the use of the King, the defendant would not allow the clerk and the collectors to carry out their duty, but refused the money, and broke the sequestration, which was placed on his chattels by the clerk in the presence of the collectors, and abused them. The defendant denied the charge and put himself on his country. He was committed to the Sheriff to produce him at the next Court to hear the verdict.

Letters Patent (French) from H. le Galeys, Mayor of London, to John de Claus of the Honour of Seguis, to the effect that he had received in London from Bernard de la Gane, burgess of Leyburn[3], by the hand of John des Claus of the Honour of Segur (sic), the sum of £17 in part payment of a debt of 250 tuns of wine, in which Bernard was indebted

[1] Here *libertas* denotes both the freedom, and the Liberties or boundaries of the City.
[2] Appointed Town Clerk before A.D. 1311. To his industry the City owes most of the information copied into the early Custumals.
[3] Libourne, in Gascony.

to him by his bond. In default of payment of the wine in time of peace before the war, he had caused the aforesaid £17 to be arrested, wherefore he quitclaims this amount to Bernard and his heirs. Dated at London 27 Aug. 1298. Witnesses:—Bernard Johann de la Rue Maior *dakes*[1], Peres Normand, Peres Simon, Renaud le Barber, Elys Gerard, Robert de Cornedale, clerk, and others.

Court of William de Leyre, *locumtenens of the Mayor, Friday before the Feast of S*[t] *James the Apostle* [*25 July*]

Membr. 7 *b*
24 *July* 1299

Henry Hoppe was attached to answer the King in a plea that, whereas according to the custom of the City merchandise coming from overseas to London, to be sold there to the profit of the citizens, ought not to be opened until it had arrived there, nevertheless the defendant, by his servant, met merchandise at Grenewych and took 25 pieces of wax from a ship of William le Mariner, and had them secretly carried away against the King's Proclamation and to the prejudice of the Liberties of the City, whereby the Sheriffs were defrauded of their customs; and also, together with the wax, he opened and carried away several bundles and false money[2], before they had arrived at the quay, and this he did in the absence of the Sheriff. The defendant admitted that he carried away the wax. Judgment that it be forfeited to the Sheriff. But as regards the money, he denied that he took it, and put himself on his country. A jury of sailors, travellers and good men of the venue of Billingesgate was summoned, and the defendant was mainprised on good security to hear the verdict. Afterwards, the jury returned a verdict that the defendant and his men had no money in the ship and carried none away. Judgment that he go quit.

Richard de Swerre was attached to answer a similar charge

[1] Cf. Letter Book B, fo. 99, "*de vico Maiori*." "*dakes*," of Arques or Aix? Bernard Johan was a Gascon. Cf. Cal. Close Rolls, 1296–1302, pp. 552–3.

[2] The *Statutum de Falsa Moneta* took the form of a writ dated 15 May, 1299, addressed to the various Sheriffs, forbidding the importation of base coin, and prescribing the penalty of death. See Cal. of Letter Book C, Introd. p. xiii; Statutes at Large, I, 145.

of removing six pieces of wax. He denied that they were unloaded by him, or by his means, or that he had any money in the ship, but he did not deny that the pieces were carried into his house, though without his knowledge. A jury of Thames Street was summoned for Wednesday.

Adam le Palmer, a freeman, was attached to answer a charge of avowing certain battery (*bateriam*) viz., a pan, a brass pot and other merchandise, value £8, for the use of a foreigner of Almaine. He admitted the offence; but as witness was borne by good and lawful men that he did not know the custom of the Liberty, his amercement was remitted. The battery was forfeited to the Sheriffs, who were asked by the Court to mitigate the forfeiture, which they afterwards did, at the instance of G. de Northon, to the extent of 40s.

Edmund le Coteler was attached to answer William Mokelyn and Roger de Derby in a plea that, whereas they had been ordered by the Mayor and Aldermen to guard the streets of their Ward against ordure, nevertheless the defendant late on Wednesday night relieved himself in the street, and when they went to take amends of him, he drew his knife on them, against the peace and despite the Proclamation. The defendant denied the charge and put himself on his country. Afterwards the defendant made default, and the jury gave a verdict of guilty in his absence. Judgment that he be in mercy. Being asked whether he drew his knife, the jury answered that he did not. Judgment that the plaintiffs be in mercy for a false charge.

Membr. 8
8 Aug. 1299

Saturday before the Feast of St Laurence [10 Aug.]

Walter Bareth was summoned to answer William le Pavour in a plea that, an agreement having been made between them that Walter should tile William's houses in Westsmethfield at a daily wage, and remain in his service till the work was done, nevertheless the defendant withdrew from his work, from Thursday the day of the agreement till the Tuesday following; and whereas the plaintiff needed journeymen tilers, defendant went about in Westsmethfield and elsewhere preventing workmen from entering his employment, by slandering him and saying that he would never pay his workmen any equivalent for their labour (*quod nunquam aliquod servicium aliquibus operariis suis redderet pro suo labore*)—to the damage of the plaintiff 100s. The defendant denied the trespass and put himself on his country. Afterwards, a jury brought in a verdict that the defendant left the service of the plaintiff contrary to the agreement, and that he prevented others from serving him, but they had no means of knowing whether he was in the habit of doing this. They taxed damages at 10s. Judgment that the plaintiff recover his damages and the defendant be kept in custody, till he find security for paying the damages and the amercement.

Tuesday after the Feast of the Assumption B.M. *18 Aug. 1299*
[15 *Aug.*]

John le Paumer was summoned to answer Richer de Refham, Sheriff, in a plea that, whereas the defendant and his Society of Bermen[1] (*Barmannorum*) in the City were sworn not to carry any wine, by land or water, for the use of citizens or others, without the Sheriff's mark, nor lead nor cause it to be led, whereby the Sheriff might be defrauded of his customs, nevertheless he caused four casks of wine belonging to Ralph le Mazun of Westminster to be carried from the City to Westminster without the Sheriff's mark, thus defrauding the latter of his customs in contempt of the King &c. The defendant acknowledged the trespass. Judgment that he remain in custody of the Sheriff till he satisfy the King and the Court for his offence.

Wednesday after the above Feast *19 Aug. 1299*

Adam de Shepeye, merchant of Coventre, complained of Thomas Sely, Sheriff of London, that whereas he came to London on Sunday [16 Aug.] after the Feast of the Assumption B.M. with his woolfells, the defendant on the Tuesday following [18 Aug.] unjustly distrained upon them to his damage of their value. The defendant claimed that the distraint was just, and said that after the plaintiff had

---

[1] Porters, carriers.

unbound the skins at the house which formerly belonged to Geoffrey de Cavendyssh in the street of St Lawrence Jewry, and had offered them for sale to certain merchants of the City, he afterwards refused to sell them and had them bound up again, intending to send them overseas for sale, to the prejudice of the Liberty. The plaintiff denied that he unbound the skins for sale, and said that Richer de Refham, one of the Sheriffs, had them unbound by his clerk, David, in order to make a scrutiny for false and counterfeit money, as ordered by the King throughout the ports, and that he never intended to send the skins abroad; and he demands that inquest be made. Afterwards, at a Court held on Thursday[1], the defendant remitted his action against the plaintiff (i.e. the distraint). Judgment that Adam recover his woolfells, and Thomas be in mercy for his false distraint.

Richard le Barber of Fletestrete was charged by the Mayor and Aldermen with allowing four casks of wine belonging to Ralph le Mazun of Westminster to pass through Ludgate without the Sheriff's mark, in prejudice of the Liberty, and contrary to the oath which he had sworn in the presence of the Mayor and Sheriffs. He acknowledged the trespass. Judgment that he be kept in custody till he had made due satisfaction to the Mayor and Sheriffs, according to the custom.

Membr. 8 *b*   Writ dated at Canterbury 17 July A° 27 Edw. [1299] to the Mayor and Sheriffs, ordering them to inquire by the oath of good and lawful men as to the malefactors who beat and wounded Walter de Berton at London, and to return the finding under the seals of themselves and the jurors.

Inquest taken on Tuesday after the Feast of St James the Apostle [25 July] A° 27 Edw. [1299] by oath of Adam Bernard, John de Folleham, Jordan le Ceynturer, Robert de Doddeford, Laurence le Coteler, Gilbert le Barber, John le Barber, William le Clerc, William de Sandwich, Richard Syward, Thomas le Poleter and Saer le Barber, who said that a certain William ate Wode committed the assault. Sealed as directed.

[1] This case is an illustration of that speedy justice for foreigners which the Mayor's Court was intended to supply. The offence took place on Tuesday, the case was argued on Wednesday, and judgment was given on Thursday.

Writ dated at Kenyton 7 Aug. A° 27 Edw. [1299] to the
Mayor and Sheriffs reciting that King Henry, the king's father,
by his letters patent at the instance of Richard, King of the
Romans[1], had granted to the merchants of Almaine, who had
a house in the City commonly called "*Gyhalde Teutonicorum*,"
that he would maintain them in the liberties and free customs
which they had enjoyed under his predecessors; and this
grant the present king had inspected and reissued under his
letters patent. Nevertheless the citizens had not allowed
those rights. Wherefore they are commanded to permit the
merchants to enjoy their liberties, or else appear *coram nobis*
to explain their disobedience.

Return; that the citizens had not interfered with the liberties
of the merchants of the Guild and of the Hanse of Almaine,
and as regards their complaints, these merchants when summoned had no charge to make against any one.

Wednesday after the Feast of the Exaltation of the Membr. 9
Holy Cross [14 *Sept.*]   *16 Sept. 1299*

Further writ, dated at Canterbury 11 July 1299, on behalf
of Ralph Hardel, who complained that he was kept in prison
for a debt of £32 to Remund de Nevile and Arnald de
Squinat, though he had paid the debt and had acquittances.

Proceedings in Court by virtue of the above writ. The
above Arnald denied that the acquittances were his deed and
claimed a jury of merchants, both citizens and foreigners.
Subsequently the parties submitted to the arbitration of
John le Clerk, Coroner of the City, Robert Hardel, Geoffrey

---

[1] Cal. of Letter Book C, p. 41. Printed in Rymer's *Foedera*, vol. 1, part ii,
p. 588. The Teutonic merchants or merchants of Almaine are said to
have coalesced with the Colognese merchants towards the close of the
thirteenth century. Riley, *Lib. Alb.* 1, p. xlii, tells us that both had
Guildhalls near Dowgate Dock. But though we read of the Guildhall of
the Colognese, and the Guildhall of the Teutonics in separate passages,
no document appears to mention them both in juxtaposition. See Harbin,
Dictionary of London, under "Steelyard," where a list of authorities is
given. Mr C. L. Kingsford in his edition of Stow's *Survey*, 11, pp. 278,
319, considers that the house of the Colognese merchants was "probably
identical with the *Gildehalda Teutonicorum*." But see *Placita de Quo
Warranto*, pp. 455, 468, where the Teutonic and Colognese merchants
make mention of their Guildhalls.

de Brakele and Reginald le Barber of Vintry, with power to add Richer de Refham, Sheriff, in case of disagreement. They awarded that Ralph pay Remund and Arnald 10 marks in full settlement.

Wednesday after the above Feast

Michael de Wymbyssh, smith, was summoned to answer the King, the Mayor, and Richard de Chigewell in a plea that, by means of Stephen del Holt, he caused the said Richard to be impleaded in the Court Christian &c. Afterwards the parties came to an agreement, on terms that if either were in future convicted of trespass against the other, he should pay one mark to the fabric of the new Chapel at Guildhall.

Friday before the Feast of St Mathias[1] the Apostle

Gregory le Botoner, defendant, essoined against Jordan le Seler in a plea of trespass by David de Candelwykstrate. The essoin does not lie, as Gregory was afterwards seen in Court.

Gregory Botoner was attached to answer Jordan le Seler in a plea of trespass, wherein the latter complained that the defendant used opprobrious words to him at his house in Wodestrate, and then followed him to the Saddlery[2], and there beat and wounded him to his damage £20. The defendant pleaded that the plaintiff had previously assaulted him, by striking him on the head and right arm, in his own house in Wodestrate at vespers, to his damage 20 marks, and that if the plaintiff suffered anything, it was owing to his own assault. A jury of Chepe and Wodestrate, together with reputable and lawful men living nearby in the Ward[3] of W. le Mazener, was summoned for Tuesday.

A jury of the venue of Wodestrate was also summoned in an action for assault brought by the above Gregory against Alexander de Chigewell and Michael his brother.

---

[1] Query: St Matthew, i.e. 21 September?

[2] The quarter of the City occupied by the saddlers in Westcheap near St Vedast Church. R. R. Sharpe, Calendar of Wills enrolled in the Court of Husting, I, p. 49.

[3] Aldersgate. Cf. Cal. of Letter Book A, p. 209; C, p. 12.

Tuesday before the Feast of St Michael [29 *Sept.*]

Ralph FitzPeter was summoned to answer William de Leyre in a plea of trespass, wherein the latter complained that the defendant came to his house in Colmanestrate to distrain for a certain rent which he was unjustly demanding, whereupon the plaintiff, as soon as he knew of it, had the distraint delivered by giving pledge and security to the Sheriff in the "Husteng," and the further consideration of the matter had been adjourned to the next Husting. Nevertheless the defendant, while the plea was still pending, had again distrained the plaintiff's tenants in the tenement, and although the plaintiff then obtained from the Mayor a prohibition against further distraint, the defendant had distrained him grievously for the third time in contempt of the Mayor. The defendant admitted that he had distrained the plaintiff for a certain rent charged on the tenement—as was lawful to him, but denied that he did so after the Mayor's prohibition. A jury from Colmanstrate was summoned for the Saturday following.

ROLL C

Court of the Chamberlain held on Saturday after the Feast of the Purification B.M. [2 Feb.] A° 27 Edw. [1298-9]

Thomas Brun(i)ng and John Elys were attached to answer the Commonalty in a plea of forestalling, whereof they were deraigned by John of the Chamber, clerk of the Commonalty, to the effect that the defendant Thomas was accustomed to avow the defendant John in buying and forestalling goods from foreigners outside the City, to the damage of the men of their trade. The defendant Thomas pleaded that John became his apprentice for a term of seven years, but only remained for four and three quarters years, when he arranged with him for the remainder of the term on payment of half a mark, and that afterwards John traded with his own property. And since the defendant Thomas admitted the receipt of money and the remission of the remainder of the apprenticeship, together with the avowry of merchandise, a day was given him till the Wednesday following to hear judgment.

John de Totenham, junior, was attached to answer Philip Dode, his apprentice, in a plea of covenant of apprenticeship, wherein the latter complained that he was apprenticed to the defendant by indentures for a term of ten years, and that he was dismissed after six and a half years, to his damage £10. The defendant admitted the covenant, but pleaded that Philip after many offences withdrew from the apprenticeship of his own accord, and that afterwards it was agreed that they should submit to the arbitration of reputable men chosen from either party, and as for himself he was prepared to stand by their award, but Philip refused to do so. The latter pleaded that the defendant was not able to maintain him in his service in a fitting manner and gave him permission to leave, and that he was always prepared to stand by the award, but that the defendant would not; and he demanded an inquest by the country. A jury of Sᵗ Mary de Conhope was summoned for Wednesday. Afterwards the defendant admitted the covenant, and that Philip had served him well and faithfully, and that he himself had not kept the covenant.

Judgment that he be amerced. The parties quitclaimed all actions against each other, after which the defendant paid a fine of 40d for the amercement.

Walter Parrok and John de Eston were attached to answer the Commonalty in a plea of trespass, it being alleged that the defendant Walter was accustomed to avow purchases by the said John from divers foreigners under cover of the freedom of his apprentice (*advocare predictum Johannem emere mercandisas diversas a diversis extraneis sub quopertura libertatis sui apprenticii*), whereas the defendant John on his own behalf and by purchase had bought from his master the unexpired portion of his apprenticeship; by which avowry the men of the trade had damage £10. The defendants admitted the trading, but Walter pleaded that John had been and was still his apprentice, and traded with his master's goods and not with the goods of foreigners, and he denied that John had bought from him the remainder of his term of apprenticeship. The defendants demanded that inquest be made by the country. And John of the Chamber who sued for the Commonalty did likewise. A jury from Cheap summoned for Wednesday.

Court of the Chamberlain held on Wednesday before the Feast of St Valentine [14 Feb.]   11 Feb. 1298–9

A loveday between Jordan de Langele and Katherine Atthecherch and Thomas her son.

Adam de Wytton was attached to answer Henry de Merlawe in a plea of covenant of apprenticeship, wherein the latter complained that Adam became his apprentice in accordance with the Will of Ralph le Cuteler, and afterwards left his service without leave, to his damage &c. The defendant admitted that his apprenticeship would not be completed till Easter next, but said that the above Ralph, late his master, had released one year of his term, and that he had left Henry's service through fear, but he was prepared to serve the remainder of his term. The plaintiff pleaded that the defendant ought not to be allowed to return to his service till he had done satisfaction for his trespasses, because the defendant had married within his term. Adam admitted marrying. A day was given to the parties till next Wednesday to come to an agreement.

A jury from Cheap and of " Cissehers " [1] brought in a verdict that John de Heston and Walter Parrok did not trade as partners for loss and gain; that Walter released to John the remainder of his apprenticeship; and that the latter did not forestall within the City or without, but that he had certain dealings with citizens and foreigners. Judgment was given that John's goods be taken into the hands of the City until &c., and that Walter be in mercy for avowing the said John and remitting his term.

Membr. 1 b
19 Feb.
1298–9

Court of the Mayor held on Thursday before the Feast of St Peter in Cathedra [22 Feb.] A° 27 Edw. [1298–9]

Adam de Fulham, junior, was attached to answer Nicholas Picot in a plea of debt, wherein the latter complained that the defendant, in obedience to a writ of the King's Steward and Marshal[2], attached Geoffrey le Power at the plaintiff's suit for 17 marks, and that the above Geoffrey admitted the debt, whereupon he was delivered to the defendant to keep him in custody till he satisfied the plaintiff for the debt, and that nevertheless the defendant allowed him to escape, to the plaintiff's damage £20. The defendant defended the words of Court, and admitted the arrest and imprisonment of Geoffrey, but alleged that Sir William de Apperle, acting as deputy of the Steward, sent a billet to him ordering him to send Geoffrey to his household, which billet was shown in Court, and that Master William afterwards sent Geoffrey back, but that the latter did not return to the defendant's

---

[1] *Et de Cissehers*. The meaning of this word is not clear. The Sheriff had power to summon a jury from a craft or a district of the City or of foreign merchants passing through the City, and I am unable to find that the word falls within any of these categories, unless it can be translated "and of tailors."

[2] A Court dealing with matters arising within the King's Household and the verge thereof. Its jurisdiction was limited by the *Articuli super Cartas*, § 3, A.D. 1300. *Statutes of the Realm* (Record Commission, A.D. 1810), p. 136. Cf. *Lib. Cust.* I, pp. 109, 111. *Liber de Antiquis Legibus*, fo. 82 a.

custody, which he was prepared to prove. The plaintiff maintained that it was from the defendant's custody that the above Geoffrey escaped. As the plea had its origin in the Court of the Steward and Marshal, a day was given to the parties until the arrival of the King at Westminster.

Wednesday the morrow of St Mathias the Apostle [24 Feb.] *25 Feb. 1298–9*

William de la Foreste, smith, was attached to answer the Commonalty by John of the Chamber, who sued for the same, in a plea of trespass, wherein the latter complained that, although it was the ancient custom that no one should remain within the City to trade with foreigners unless he was a freeman, nevertheless the defendant stayed ten years, trading like a freeman with foreigners, to the damage of the reputable men of that trade £40. The defendant defended the words of Court and admitted that he was not a freeman, but declared that he did not trade except with freemen, and that he was a handicraftsman (*operarius*), and not a merchant. The prosecutor alleged that the defendant and his men traded with both foreigners and denizens, even though he was a handicraftsman, and he demanded that inquest be made by lawful men of the craft of smiths, as also did the defendant. A jury summoned against Friday.

Thursday after the Octave of St Mathias the Apostle [24 Feb.] *5 March 1298–9*

Richard Horn was attached to acquit the Commonalty against the King for 300 marks, wherein John Horn, his father, was responsible to the Commonalty as regards his Receipt as their Sheriff. The defendant pleaded that he was not his father's executor, had inherited nothing from him, and had none of his goods and chattels, and he demanded an inquest thereon. Good men of the Wards of Bridge and Billingsgate were summoned against the first Monday in Lent.

An inquest was held on Sunday before the Feast of the Annunciation B.M. [25 March] before Mayor and Aldermen, as to what malefactors beat and wounded the men of the *22 March 1298–9* household of the Bishop of Durham, by Walter de Herlested, Adam de Arcubus, Symon de Oxon, Richard de Stanford, Geoffrey de Conductu, Alexander de Causton, Andrew Mele, Robert Frer, Gregory Lorimer, Robert de Donmawe, John Scharpe and William le Caundeler, who said on oath that a certain Richard le Lacer, on Wednesday before the Feast of St Peter in Cathedra [22 Feb.] A° 27 Edw. [1298–9], in a certain tavern, procured some of the bishop's men to go to the house of Richard le Cordewaner in Wdestret, where they threatened Richard, and one of them struck him on the head with a stick and threw after him (*post ipsum prostravit*) a big knife with which he was cutting leather, and not content therewith, entered his house and broke the door of his chamber and beat him, whereupon his wife raised the hue and cry. On this, Henry de Gloucestre and Elias de Suffolk came to the house to stop the affair, and the Bishop's men, letting go the above Richard, and drawing their swords, pursued them as far as the house of Elias. Meanwhile the neighbours, roused by the hue and cry, came to the place to restrain the men from doing further harm, and strangers and unknown persons joined in the fray, so that if the Bishop's men received any hurt there, it was done by unknown persons.

Membr. 2
20 Nov. 1299

Court of Elyas Russel, *Mayor, on Friday the Feast of St Edmund, King and Martyr, A° 28 Edw.* [1299]

Guy Bertand, Remund de la Bro and Hugelin Sampe were attached at the suit of Brachius de la Bro to produce their award in a dispute between the plaintiff and William Servat.

26 Nov. 1299

Thursday after the Feast of St Katherine [25 Nov.]

Thomas de Basinges was summoned to render an account to his late ward, Stephen, son of Richard de Abbendon, of his lands, tenements and rents, during his minority.

5 Jan.
1299–1300

Tuesday the Vigil of the Epiphany [6 Jan.] *A° 28 Edw.* [1299–1300]

Robert Wodhock, poulterer, and Brian the poulterer were attached to answer the Mayor for forestalling poultry in

Suthwerk, and all through the year. The defendants admitted the first charge, but denied the second and put themselves on their country. A jury was summoned for Thursday, and the defendants were committed to prison on their confession.

William, rector of the Church of Sᵗ Margaret Lothebury, was attached for avowing four putrid wolves sent from abroad in a cask. The defendant said that he bought the wolves because of a certain disease called "*Le Lou*." And as the defendant was examined by the Mayor and Aldermen concerning the disease, and admitted that he was not suffering from it, or knew anybody who was, and that he was not a physician or a surgeon, he was committed to the Sheriffs, for having first of all said falsely that he had the disease, until the truth of the matter could be elicited. The Sheriffs were ordered to summon all the physicians and surgeons of the City for Thursday. On that day the latter came into Court and said that they could not find in any of their medical or surgical writings any disease against which the flesh of wolves could be used. Accordingly the defendant was delivered to the Official[1].

Thursday after the above Feast

John de Kent, John de Paris, Agnes Godman, Laurence Schail, Richard le Barber, William Gorre, Peter le Blunt, William Crel, Hugelyn of Sᵗ Magnus, John de Reigat, Edmund Sket, John Bussard, Nicholas Sket, Robert the cook of Foxle, William de Waledon, John de Mardenheth and many other cooks were attached to answer the Mayor and Commonalty on a charge of forestalling capons, hens, geese and other victuals, before they reached the City and also within the City, before the hour of Prime and before the freemen could buy their necessaries. The defendants denied the charge and put themselves on their country. A jury, summoned from Cornhill[2] and from each Ward within the Gates and from the suburbs, consisting of William le Lou,

Membr. 2 *b*
7 *Jan.*
1299–1300

---

[1] Of the Archdeacon of London.
[2] I.e. the neighbourhood of Leadenhall, where the foreign poulterers had their stands.

4–2

Nicholas le Long, John Plot, Nicholas Brun, William Poyntel, Edmund Trentemars, Walter de Bredstrate, Richard Horn and others, brought in a verdict that certain of the cooks were guilty of forestalling poultry, and that the rest bought victuals and poultry outside their doors and elsewhere in the City from persons known and unknown, against the Proclamation. Judgment that each be mainprised by the other until &c.

Nicholas Beaublet, Adam Dalleye, Robert de Dalleie, John de Cherteseie, William le Hernesemaker, William de Chestehonte, Richard Rok, John Hamond and Walter his man, Robert de Cheleshuch, Geoffrey le Meuner, Ralph le Sporier and other spurriers were attached to answer the Mayor and Commonalty at the suit of Hugh Stroby, on a charge of having made an ordinance, confirmed by touching the Gospels, that no one of their trade of spurriers should do any work between sunset and sunrise, in consequence of which they had summoned Richard, the prosecutor's servant, before the Official of the Archdeacon, and charged him with working against the ordinance, and the said Richard, after being three times warned by the Official, had been expelled from the church and excommunicated, until he would swear to keep the ordinance. The prosecutor also alleged that the spurriers had made Clement and Robert le Rouwlmakere swear not to sell any of their goods to him; that they had ordained that no one should take an apprentice for less than 10 years and 40s; and that, if any one was injured by a person outside the trade, the defendant Nicholas promised to do him justice without any other servant of the king; and that no one of that trade would do anything for anyone dwelling within or without the City unless he were sworn to the ordinance [*et quod nullus officio predicto aliquid faciet alicui comoranti infra civitatem seu extra nisi fuerit juratus ordinacioni predicte*]. The defendants declared that they were not guilty, and put themselves on their country, and the prosecutor likewise. A jury of the venue of Fletebruge was summoned. Afterwards, the parties made agreement on terms that the prosecutor quitclaim all actions, and the confederacy was condoned because nothing of it had yet been put into operation [?—*eo quod nondum aliquid ex ea positum erat in factum*].

Saturday after the above Feast

William de Wolcherchehawe, taverner, was attached to answer Sir John Botetourte in a plea of trespass, wherein the latter complained that William beat one of his carters and tore his clothes[1] [? *delaniavit pannos suos*] and did other enormities &c. The defendant came and defended the force &c. and put himself on the mercy of the said Sir John, and pledged to him a cask of wine, which cask Sir John gave to the officers (*ministris*) of the Chamber of the Guildhall.

Sir Richard de Scolaund, knight, in the name of Sir William de Grandisone, offered to pay Tote de Monte Claro £21 pollard, which the latter refused, saying that Sir William owed sterling.

Monday before the Feast of St Hilary [13 *Jan.*]

Adam de Ely, fishmonger, put himself on the mercy of the Mayor and Aldermen for having sold his goods too dear, in contempt of the King's Proclamation, and of that of the Mayor and Aldermen.

The morrow of St Hilary [13 *Jan.*]

Walter Payn and John de Canefeld, bailiffs of the Guild of Weavers, and others of the same craft were attached to answer the Mayor and Commonalty at the suit of Henry le Jevene and others of the craft of burellers[2], in a plea of trespass, wherein the latter complained that the weavers, yearly on the day of St Edmund King in their Guild (*Gilla*) in the Church of St Nicholas Akonn, choose two bailiffs to hold their Courts and to hear and determine pleas of trespass, whereas the bailiffs ought to be under the jurisdiction and power of the Mayor, and be presented to him yearly and be sworn by him, and the Mayor ought to attend their Courts as often as he pleased, and any cloth which was found to be

---

[1] Possibly this is the meaning intended. It would appear to mean literally "took the nap off his cloths."

[2] The burellers are said by Riley, *Lib. Cust.* Gloss, to have been makers of *borel*, a coarse woollen cloth. Here they appear as middlemen employing weavers.

against the Assize should be burnt by the Mayor and not by
the bailiffs. Further the burellers complained that the weavers
ordained that no one of their craft should weave any cloth
from Christmas until the Purification under any circumstances; moreover they had destroyed many hand-looms after
the death of workmen, when they ought to have maintained
them by right and custom of the trade; and whereas the
burellers and others who had cloths to weave were able to
have them woven formerly for 16d or 18d, the defendants
by an agreement among themselves ordained, first, that none
of their craft should weave a cloth for less than 2s, secondly,
for less than 2s 6d, and thirdly, for less than 40d; and when
a certain Stoldus, a Lombard, who was a freeman, wished
to make sale of cloths for the common profit of citizens and
foreigners, the defendants would not allow him to do so,
until he had promised to pay two marks a year, and nevertheless they charged him 20s for the weaving of each cloth,
whereas the price should have been 4s at most; moreover
they ordained that if any bureller should injure any of their
trade his work should be put in defence, until he had been
corrected by them, thus defrauding the Sheriff and the King's
farm; further, the weavers put in defence the cloths of the
burellers and others at the instance of any of their craft who
was plaintiff in any plea, so that he to whom the cloth belonged could not have it, although their bailiffs had no power
to make any attachment on persons, who were not of their
Guild, without the Sheriffs. All the aforesaid ordinances, the
burellers complained, were to the prejudice of the Mayor
and Commonalty and Liberty of the City and to their own
damage £100.

The defendants denied that their bailiffs were accustomed
to be presented to, or sworn and admitted by, the Mayor.
Thereupon the plaintiffs alleged that in the time of G. de
Rokesle[1], Thomas Jordan and Reginald le Blount were so
presented. The defendants could not deny this, and a day
was given them on the Tuesday following to hear judgment
thereon, and to answer the other charges. The defendants
appeared on the day given and asked for the appointment of

[1] Mayor A.D. 1275 and 1285.

twelve men, chosen from each side. This was granted; and the twelve, being sworn and examined by William de Leyre and Thomas Romeyn, aldermen, ordained certain articles[1] for all time which are enrolled in the Chamber of the Guildhall. The weavers were amerced.

Monday before the Feast of SS. Fabian and Sebastian [20 Jan.]

18 Jan. 1299–1300

Charter of Henry II to the Weavers. [The membrane is incomplete and closes with "*contumeliam faciat.*" See *Lib. Cust.* (Rolls Series), vol. I, pp. 33, 418. Cal. of Letter Book D, pp. 221–2. The original Charter is preserved among the Archives of the Weavers' Company.]

Tuesday before the above Feast

Membr. 3 b
19 Jan.
1299–1300

John le Botonner[2], junior, was summoned to answer John Danesty in a plea of covenant, wherein the latter complained that he was bound to the defendant in a bond of £50 of common money ["sterling" obliterated] payable in portions of 100s, the last term being the Feast of the Nativity last, and that he duly offered to pay before that term the sum of £10. The defendant pleaded that after the above Feast the plaintiff agreed to pay him 100s sterling at Easter, and he,

---

[1] Letter Book C, fo. xlii. Printed with slight variations in *Lib. Cust.* I, pp. 121–6.

[2] This case and several following arose out of a Proclamation, followed by a Writ to the Sheriffs of London of 25 November, ordering that from Christmas onwards "pollards" and "crocards," a base form of foreign money, should pass at two a penny instead of their nominal value of a penny. A proviso follows: "So nevertheless that debts which are due by contract and covenant made before the said Christmas shall be paid in such money and as large a number of pennies as the covenant and the contract and the bargain was before made for." The citizens of London were unwilling to receive the pollards in payment, though willing enough to pay them. In this case the defendant produced a deed which seemed to bar the plaintiff from the benefit of the proviso. Another Writ of 28 January, 1299–1300, ordered that pollards and crocards should not be refused at two a penny, and made no mention of the proviso. The City authorities apparently were not sure whether this Writ cancelled the proviso. For the derivation of "pollards" and "crocards", see Letter Book C, p. 39, n., where it is suggested that pollards were so called from their being polled or clipped, and "crocards" from their being made so thin as easily to become crooked.

the defendant, agreed to condone the rest until &c. The plaintiff defended (i.e. denied) this agreement, according to the custom of the City, and was ordered to make his law at the Quinzime, on which day he appeared with his law. But as the defendant produced a deed stating that the plaintiff was bound to him in good and lawful sterling according to a contract made prior to a proclamation, which enjoined that all such payments should be made according to the terms of the contract, and the Mayor and Aldermen wished to consult as to whether the money now current could be used in paying, a day was given a week hence to hear judgment. And the £10 proffered by the plaintiff was handed to the Chamberlain to keep. Afterwards a further day was given till the Saturday before Sunday in Midlent.

William de Creye and Isabel his wife and Richard Hutgoh were found guilty by a jury of having assaulted and torn the hoods of William, prior of St Mary Suthwerk, Ralph his Canon, and Walter le Potagier and William de Reygate, who had gone to the tenement of the defendants in Westchepe in order to distrain them for 72s rent in arrears.

Betin de Luca was attached to answer John, servant of Simon de Paris, in a plea of covenant, wherein the latter complained that the defendant sold him cindon[1] to the value of £14 5s in November, for which he paid 45s, and at Christmas he had offered to pay the rest, but the defendant refused it. The latter pleaded that he ought not to receive the money except in sterling of the King's money, by virtue of the contract between them. The plaintiff replied that he ought to receive the money in crocards according to the King's Proclamation. Subsequently, on Wednesday after the Purification, the defendant agreed to receive two pollards for the penny sterling. On so doing, he went quit and the plaintiff received no damages.

William Goldsmith was acquitted of a charge of exposing putrid veal for sale. The jury added that a certain John Carle was guilty of the offence, and an attachment was issued against the latter.

[1] Cindon sc. sindon: a fine thin fabric of linen.

Saturday after the Feast of SS. Fabian and Sebastian Membr. 4
[20 Jan.] before William de Leyre *and* William de 23 Jan.
1299–1300
Beton, *aldermen, deputies of the Mayor*

Giles le Forner, servant of Roger de Derby, was attached
to answer the Mayor in a plea of trespass at the suit of
Richard, beadle of Walebrok, who complained that in accordance with an ordinance enjoining that watch should be kept
at Christmas[1], the watchmen of Walebrok (*custodes wayte de
Walebrok*) were on Walebrok, when the defendant Giles,
together with Hugh le Forner and Walter le Fannere, came
without a light and with edged weapons, and refused to
surrender to the Peace and defended themselves, wounding
some of the Watch, and then, hiding in the shadows, made
their way to the Ryole, so that they could not be found, to
the damage of the Watch and in contempt of the City 100s.
The defendant pleaded that a certain William had been
supping at his master's house, and that by the latter's orders
he accompanied him homewards, when they met the Watch
on Walebrok, and that as soon as he understood that they
were watchmen, he was willing to surrender, but the Watch
wanted to kill him, so that if they suffered anything, it was
because he defended himself. A jury was summoned and an
attachment issued against the above Hugh and Walter. On
the Wednesday following, a jury from Walebrok, Douuegate
and Cordwanerestrette brought in a verdict of guilty, and
the defendants were committed to prison.

Friday after the Feast of Purification [2 Feb.] 5 Feb.
1299–1300

Geoffrey de Somerceste was attached to answer John Crane
in a plea of trespass, wherein the latter complained that,
whereas it was ordained that two loaves or four might be
sold in a fixed place, the defendant carried a loaf of *tourte*[2]
through the streets, which he would not sell for less than 3d,
to the damage of the plaintiff &c. The defendant admitted

---

[1] Cf. Cal. of Letter Book C, p. 20; and *Lib. Alb.* I, pp. 646–53, for a
list of the many ordinances on this subject.

[2] Tourte or trete: coarse brown bread. See Riley's Glossary in *Lib.
Cust.* II, and the City's *Liber de Assisa Panis*.

the manner of sale. Judgment that he be committed to Newegate.

Thursday before the Feast of St Valentine [14 Feb.]

Martin de Dulingham, William de Horsham, John Dachet, Luke de Ware, John le King, Boidinus de Grene, and William Fatting were summoned before the Mayor and Aldermen to inform them of certain persons who, after the Proclamation, had refused money, and they declared on oath that they knew no such persons.

Adam Brun, John de Sabrichesworth and Thomas Brun swore that Adam Russel, Geoffrey Geffard, William Haber, hostermongere[1], Robert le Rede, Henry Pride, Simon Mamyware, Alice Hardeye, Gilbert Hunger, William son of Robert le Taillour, William Curteys, Walter Sopere, Richard Love and his servant had not observed the Proclamation.

Saturday before the Feast of S^t "Walentine" [14 Feb.]

Ralph le Mason was attached to answer the Mayor for contempt at the suit of Adam de Derlington on behalf of the King and the Commonalty, who complained that in accordance with an ordinance requiring two collectors to be appointed for each Ward, he himself was chosen for Cordwanerstrete, and a certain John Partriche paid the defendant (the other collector?) 21s pollard, for which the defendant had John's pledges, but the defendant refused to return the pledges unless John paid double, and when the plaintiff ordered him to return them on behalf of the King, the defendant followed him into the street and threatened him, and said "*Jeo ay chie a vous & au Ray ausi.*" The defendant denied that he was guilty and put himself on his country, and on Adam Mulgas, Gerdo le Armerer, John Swyrel and John Parti who were present[2]. And the plaintiff did likewise. A jury together with the above were summoned against Wednesday.

---

[1] Probably an oyster-monger. Cf. Cal. of Letter Book E, p. 156.
[2] The persons named formed part of the jury, which at this time was chosen for its special knowledge of the matter in dispute. See Pollock and Maitland, *Hist. of Engl. Law*, II, p. 637.

John le Fundour, dwelling in St Lawrence Lane, was attached to answer Nicholas, carter of Sir John Botetourte, in a plea of trespass, wherein the latter complained that the defendant took his cart and loaded dung into it against his will. The defendant said he bargained with Nicholas to carry a load of dung for a farthing. The plaintiff denied this, and being ordered to make his law did so at once. The defendant was committed to prison.

Tuesday the morrow of St Peter in Cathedra [22 *Feb.*] Membr. 4 b
23 Feb.
Walter atte Belhous, William atte Belhous, Robert le Barber 1299–1300
dwelling at Ewelleshalle, John de Lewes, Gilbert le Gras, John his son, Roger le Mortimer, William Ballard atte Hole, Peter de Sheperton, John Brun and the wife of Thomas the pelterer, Stephen de Haddeham, William de Goryngg, Margery de Frydaiestrate, Mariot, who dwells in the house of William de Harwe, and William de Hendone were attached to answer for forestalling all kinds of grain and exposing it, together with putrid grain, on the pavement, for sale by the bushel, through their men and women servants; and for buying their own grain from their own servants in deception of the people. The defendants denied that they were guilty and put themselves on their country. A jury of Richard de Hockeleye and others brought in a verdict of guilty, and the defendants were committed to prison till the next Parliament.

John le Chaundeler dwelling near the house of Peter de Bolyngtone, William le Hay of Wodestrate, Richard atte Rothe, William de Manhale, Stephen le Oynter, John de Lyndeseye, Walter de Waldegrave dwelling at the Stockes, Henry le Chaundeler, beadle of John Wade, John de Dunninghurst and other chandlers were attached to answer the King and the Mayor for selling the pound of tallow candles dearer after Christmas, in contempt of the King's Proclamation. The defendants admitted that they sold the pound at 4d before, and 5d after Christmas. They were committed to the Sheriff to take good security for their appearance at the next Parliament.

Roger de Acton dwelling at Clerkenwell, William his brother, dwelling without Altresgate, Geoffrey de Heston and James de Bury of the same place, Ralph le Frensche dwelling at Red Cross, Richard de Bernham dwelling without Crepelgate, Thomas Chese dwelling at Cherringe, John Fithele, Symon Fairman, dwelling without the Bar of Holleburne, and John Fairman, Henry Poer and William Eyrot of the same place, and other curriers were attached to answer the King and the Mayor for selling their leather dearer after the Proclamation about Pollards and Crocards, with the result that the cordwainers sold their shoes dearer. The defendants said that they did not sell their leather dearer after the Proclamation, but that the dearness was due to foreigners, for none of them had any hides at Christmas, and all the hides they worked afterwards had been bought from foreigners at double the price; and they asked for an inquest by the country. A jury was summoned against Thursday.

Membr. 5
17 Feb.
1299–1300

Wednesday after the Feast of St Valentine [14 Feb.]

John de Hadham, tanner, Geoffrey de Chelcheithe, John de Hormed, Ralph de Chelcheithe, Simon atte Spalebrige, Stephen de Hadham, Richard de Hadham, Richard le Hosker[1], Roger de Eddelmeton, William Balsham, Robert de Sellingdon, Philip de Hundesdiche, Gervasius his brother, John le Lunge, William, son of Geoffrey de Hundesdiche, Robert le Prest, Walter de Daginhale, Baudewin le Tannour, Richard le Bruys, Adam Baudri, Richard le Lung and John Baudri, tanners, were attached to answer the Mayor and Aldermen for selling more dearly after the Proclamation than before, and for concealing their goods and removing them from the City, and refusing payment in pollards. The defendants put themselves on their country. Afterwards, a jury of Nicholas le Brun and others brought in a verdict that certain of the defendants were not guilty, and that the

---

[1] The spelling of the names varies; Hosker appears in the same entry as Hoscher, Sellingdon as Schedlindon, and Daginhale as Haverhill, and Chabenham is given later as Chabeham, Canoun as Kanoun, Talifer as Taylefer and Elys as Helys.

rest sold more dearly for pollards than for sterling, but did not remove their goods or refuse money.

John Tilli, Walter de Bedefunte, William called le King, John Talifer, Hugh le Kisser[1], John de Sancto Salvatore, Adam de Hakeneye, Richard le Kisser, William Fleye, Robert Tilli, John Elys, Geoffrey Canoun, Thomas Bruing, Walter de Chabenham, Senn le Kisser and John de Bedefunte, kissers, were attached on a similar charge. A jury of William de Red and others brought in a verdict that some of the defendants were not guilty, and that the others had sold dearer for the pollard than the sterling, but had not concealed their goods or carried them out of the City to sell them dearer, with the exception of Walter de Bedefunte who had hidden his goods; and that John Tilli went out of the City and met carts bringing hides to Religious Houses and elsewhere and bought the hides against his oath as a freeman and sold them in the City. Judgment that John and Walter be committed to prison, and that the other guilty defendants be taken into custody to appear before the King (*coram Rege*) at the next Parliament.

On Friday after the Feast of S[t] Peter in Cathedra [22 Feb.] a jury of William de Red and others brought in a verdict that Walter Chese, William son of Clement, and Henry Puer, curriers, were not guilty of selling dearer after the Proclamation, but that Walter de Acton and William his brother concealed their goods and would not expose them for sale except in samples [*nisi per particulas*], and would not sell them except for sterling; that John le Fraunceys would not sell his goods at all; and that the other curriers sold dearer for pollards than sterling. Judgment that the Sheriffs take security from Walter de Acton and the rest to appear before the King and his Council at the next Parliament. *26 Feb. 1299–1300*

Eva la Callestere was attached to answer John Fuatard in a plea of trespass, wherein the latter complained that, when he *Membr. 5 b*

---

[1] "Kisser." Riley (*Memorials of London and London Life*, Introd. p. xxii) suggests a maker of "cushes" or armour for the thighs. In this passage we have a kisser forestalling hides and selling them, and on the next membrane a jury attributes the high prices of the cordwainers to the tanners, curriers and kissers. Probably the kissers were leatherdressers or dealers.

went, by the Mayor's command, with Thomas Sely, Alderman, into the Ward of Nicholas de Farndon to seize false
grain measures, the defendant assaulted him and bit his finger,
in contempt of the King and to his damage 100s. The
defendant pleaded that the plaintiff entered her house against
her will, for she did not know that he was a bailiff, and wanted
to lie with her, and if he received any damage, it was owing
to his own assault, and she demanded an inquest thereon.
A jury of Geoffrey de Finchinfeud and others found her
guilty of the assault and taxed damages at 12d, and she was
committed to prison.

Martin de Dullingham, butcher, was attached to answer
Roger Heved in a plea of trespass, wherein the latter complained that, when he went with Roger, Clerk of the King's
Wardrobe, to demand from the defendant a tally which he
had lent him, the defendant assaulted him. The latter pleaded
that the plaintiff assaulted him first. A jury of the venue of
the Stockes found him guilty and assessed damages at half a
mark, and the clerk's damages at 2s.

John de Wyncestre, cordwainer, William de Pelham,
Thomas de Derby, Robert de Frowyk, John de Laufer,
Stephen de Hollecote, John de Batricheseye, Henry Fitz
William, Geoffrey Bonmarche, Adam de Starteford, John de
Gildeford, Robert de Totenham, William atte Roche, Reginald
de Essex, Hankok le Cordewaner, William de Westminstre,
John de Wincestre junior, Philip de Luddelowe, Simon de
Kendale, John de Tissindon, John de Redinge, John Scot,
William de Sinngham, William Stanes, Hugh Stot, Andrew
de Lughteburgh, Simon de Norton, John de Soham, Henry
de Stanford, Walter de Norhamton, Robert de Webbele,
William de Redinge, Hugh de Esseburne, Roger de Bristow,
William de Norhamton, Thomas le Cofferer, William de
Treinlingham, John de Renham, William de Castle Barnard,
Peter de Sauescomb, Henry de Bury, Thomas Hasserwit,
John de Ware, Thomas de Norwich, John de Lincoln, John
de Chalham, Thomas de Luddelow, Alan de Reding, William
Wastell, Robert de Pampesworth, Robert de Norhamton,
Simon de Coundon, William de Sutton, John Wastell, Thomas

de Norwich, Richard Springefeld and Daniel de Chiltren, were attached to answer the Mayor and Aldermen for selling dearer after the Proclamation, concealing their goods, refusing money &c. A jury of John de Coffrerer and others brought in a verdict of not guilty, and said that if prices were higher in their trade (cordwainery) it was due to the tanners, curriers and kissers.

Adam de Fulham, senior, John le Benere, William Jurdan, Stephen Pykeman, Turgis Pykeman, William Pykeman, Robert Pykeman, John de Mockingge, William Sorweles, Salmon Borghard, Richard de Haddle, Robert de Folleham, John de Folham, John de Stebenhethe, Robert Sterre, John Bacheler, John Baldewene, Alan Aunore, Richard Pykeman, Robert Yvri, Thomas de Collingham, William Haunsard, William Rymond, William Greylaund, William Amys, Richard Horn, John de Colesdon, William Cros, Henry Cros, Stephen Lambin, Robert de Mockingge, Richard Swote, Walter Ragen, Giles Jurdon, Edmund Lambyn, Robert le Benere, Richard Aleyn, John Frochs, Geoffrey de Lyre, John Allyn, Robert Baudry, Symon Lambyn, John Moldefrey, Walter de Hakeneye, Richard Matefrey, John de Stratford, Richard Lichitfot, Peter de Bolinton, Adam de Ely, Bartholomew de Romberwe, Richard de Bernes, William de Barton, William Albyn, John de Tornham, Adam le Bakere, James Flinchard, William Flinchard and William Gubbe were attached to answer the Mayor and Aldermen for selling dearer after the Proclamation &c. A jury of Walter le Fullere and others brought in a verdict that the defendant Adam and the other fishmongers were not guilty.

Roger le Lenerd, John Gubbe, Walter Gubbe, John Scot[1], Membr. 6 Robert le Wolf, Robert Turck, John Elys, James le Reve, John de Romeneye[1], Adam Lutekyn[1], Adam Ballard[1], Richard le Barber, John de Ware, John de Brompton, Gilbert le Fevere of Fridaystrate, John de Coventre[1], John Makery, Richard de Watherby[1], Alan Wade of Quenehythe, John de Crepelgate, near Quenhithe, Robert Brangwayn at Castle Baynard, Geoffrey de Yarmouth[1], Henry de Bellehous,

[1] Mentioned in the Letter Books *passim* as bladers or cornmongers.

Laurence de Quenehithe, Richard Poterel[1] son of Richard Poterel, Geoffrey Godale at Flete, Henry de Cherringge, Thomas de Wrotham, Thomas de Leycestre, John de Stratford, William Gubbe, Thomas le Maderman, Geoffrey le Nayler of Sevethenelane, William le Brasour of Wolchurchehawe, John de Haveryngge[1], Stephen le Naylere, Adam Trug[1], John Page and Robert Atteloke were acquitted of a similar charge.

John Poyntel[2], Roger Poyntel[2], Peter de Helding, Stephen Dorgod, Thomas, brother of Roger Pointel, Raude de Borham, Robert de Bray, John Geryn, William Godale, William de Horsham[3], Gilbert de Bray, William Noger, John de Befald, Walter de Borham[3] and Richard atte Gate were likewise acquitted.

John Gilberd, John called le Longe, James de Bredstrate, Henry le Vocy, Yvo Balle, Robert le Longe, and Laurence le Saltmetere were attached to answer the Mayor and Aldermen for entering the boats of foreigners bringing salt, oysters and mussels, and taking a wage of 2d a day with expenses to sell the above goods at a higher price, to their own advantage, but to the damage of the City, since no foreigner can sell his goods retail either by himself or by another. A jury of Robert de Chalfhunte and others found the first three defendants not guilty, and said that the rest entered the boats of freemen, by their orders, and enabled foreigners to obtain part of their goods, selling them at a higher price than their employers would be able to charge if they were present (*intrant batellos liberorum hominum facientes forenses habere partem de bonis illis vendentes bona predicta carius quam domini facerent si presentes essent*). Judgment that Gilberd and the others go quit, and that Henry le Vocy &c. be mainprised to come up for judgment. Afterwards their offence was pardoned on condition that they did not occupy themselves with that trade any more.

---

[1] Mentioned in the Letter Books *passim* as bladers or cornmongers.
[2] Leathersellers.
[3] Curriers.

Friday the Feast of the Translation of St Edmund King[1] *18 March*
before William de Leyre *1299–1300*

John de Ware, "batour"[2], Alan Sprot, William de Ber-
hamstead, Adam Attecherch, Ralph le Batour, Nicholas
Sprot, John Baroun, Hugh le Batour, John Fraunk, William
Atteweld, William de Langele, John de London, William
Smart, Thomas Ailmer, Adam de Munden, William Sprot,
Robert de Hadham, Geoffrey Sewhat, William le Batour and
Walter le Delvere were attached to answer the Mayor and
Aldermen, for selling dearer after the Proclamation, refusing
pollards, selling more for four sterling than for seven pollards
doubled (*quam pro septem pollardis dupplicatis*), and further
with making a confederacy and appointing Geoffrey Suat (*sic*)
their bailiff and Walter le Delvere their beadle. The defendants admitted selling dearer, and pleaded that the pound
of metal which they bought at 2d before Christmas cost 4d
or 5d since, and they demanded a jury. The Court remitted
the jury because of the coming time (Easter) and allowed
them to choose four men from each mistery (*ministerium*) to
regulate prices according to the true value of the goods, viz.
from the craft of Girdlers[3]:—Adam Trug, Walter de Norwich,
John le Chamberleyn, and Ralph de Brawhing, and from the
craft of Batours:—John de Ware, Alan Sproth, John de
London, and Adam de Munden, who later came to an agreement that the pound of copper, which used to be sold for 8d,
should be sold for 7½d during the time that pollards were
current, and that what was sold for 7d should be sold for
6½d, and they were ordered to announce this to both crafts.

Richard de Stevenath, Richard Otgo, Richard Fatting, *Membr. 6 b*
Simon Tripasy, Thomas Dosswell, Boidinus de Grene,
Henry Palet, Maurice "*ad aquam*," Nicholas Sniggel, Roger
le Wynour, Maykin de Kent, and other butchers, were
summoned for selling dearer after the Proclamation &c. The
jury was remitted because of the imminence of the Passion,

[1] Query: Feast of St Edward K. and M. which fell that year on
a Friday?
[2] A coppersmith or dealer in *baterie*, i.e. beaten copper or brassware.
[3] Apparently this case arose on a complaint of the girdlers against the
batours.

and the butchers were warned to behave well in their sales, and to give such proper measure to their neighbours that it should not be necessary to summon them again.

Ralph Sporon was summoned to answer Robert le Boteler for detinue of a silver cup, with silver foot and covercle, value 5 marks, entrusted to the defendant to be remade at a cost of 40s. The latter admitted receiving the cup, and said that he delivered it to a certain Thomas de Linch, a journey-man (*vassel'*), to work on it. Thomas de Lynch appeared and said that the defendant agreed to give him two marks sterling for the work, which he had not paid. The defendant denied making this agreement with the journeyman and was ordered to make his law on the Quinzime, but meanwhile Ralph and Thomas agreed out of Court that the latter should receive 40s pollard for the work, which were deposited with the Chamberlain, and that he should condone to the defendant the making of his law. Both were amerced.

19 March 1299–1300 ## Saturday the morrow of the above Feast

Recognizance (*gongnovit se teneri*[1]) by Ralph de Honilane, alderman, to John de Petresdon of a debt of 40s payable on the morrow.

Katherine de Lincoln was summoned to answer William de Mount Seins in a plea that she return to him an iron horse-cuirass, and a pair of plates covered with cloth of gold and samite[2], which he pledged to her for 35s for cloth bought from Peter de Armenters, one of her household. The defendant said that the pledges were delivered to her servant, Peter de Armenters, and she demanded that he be summoned to answer with her. On the Tuesday following, the above Peter produced a deed to the effect that Sir William granted to Katherine that she might sell the pledges after Easter, paying to him any surplus over the 35s. The plaintiff admitted that this was the deed of a certain William de Monsens. The defendant further said that the pledges were sold for 22s 1d only. Thereupon the plaintiff offered to accept this

[1] A by no means extreme example of the clerk's Latinity.
[2] *Oxford English Dictionary*: A rich silk fabric worn in the Middle Ages.

statement if Peter would swear it with his single hand[1]. The latter did so and was acquitted, and Sir William was in mercy.

Thomas le Chaundeler was summoned to answer the Mayor and Aldermen in a plea that, whereas Matthew le Caundeler and his fellows were chosen to keep the Assize of Candles when Parliament was sitting, a certain Robert, servant of Sir John de Droknesford, wanted to buy a pound of candles for 3d, and the defendant refused the money; thereupon Robert had complained to Matthew, and the latter, in accordance with the ordinance made by the men of that craft, had caused the candles to be delivered to the servant for the above price, and afterwards the defendant had abused Matthew and struck him as he was standing in his shop. The defendant denied the offence, and a jury of Candel-wykestrate was summoned for Tuesday, on which day the parties made agreement on terms that the defendant pledge five casks of wine, to be forfeited if he were convicted in the future of any trespass against Matthew. He was mainprised by Richard Fiz, ceynturer, and John le Chaundeler of Ismongerelane to come up for judgment *quo et quando* &c. for his trespass against the officers of the craft, and the Mayor and Aldermen.

Richard Davy, baker, was attached to answer the Mayor and Aldermen on a charge that, whereas on Friday the Feast of the Translation of S[t] Edward, he was dragged on the hurdle because his bread was false, when he arrived home and descended from the hurdle and entered his house, he took a bone and threw it at the tabor-player and broke his tabor through the middle. Peter de Berneval undertook to produce him before the Mayor on the Tuesday, on which day the defendant did not come. Peter was summoned to hear judgment for failing to produce him, and order was given to distrain the defendant.

[1] An example of the decisory oath as sworn by the defendant. Cf. *Lib. Alb.* I, p. 521.

28 March
1300
**Monday after the Feast of the Annunciation B.M.
[25 March] A° 28 Edw. [1300]**

John le Poer appeared before the Mayor, and with the third hand[1] verified a foal (*unum equum fanum*) value 1 mark, as his property. This animal, being in the seisin of Peter de Annardestoun, knight, had been arrested as an attachment in a plea of the Forest in Parliament. It was now delivered to the above John.

29 March
1300
Tuesday after the above Feast

Sir Eustace Delehak claimed from John de Stanes two silver gilt cups, which had been put in his hands as security for a debt of 5 marks 10s 8d due to John de Dorking for a doublet (*pro una duploid°*) and gambeson. The latter acknowledged receipt of the money, but as the plaintiff did not prosecute his plea, the defendant went quit. He was amerced for previous defaults, and the plaintiff for non-appearance.

Membr. 7   John in the Lane was summoned to answer Brother John de Shorisdich of the Order of Friars Preachers in a plea that whereas the Friar bought from the defendant at Smethefeud a bay horse for 60s, which the defendant asserted to be healthy and sound in its limbs, nevertheless the said horse when it came into the Friar's possession and before that time was maimed in the shoulders (*maynatus in chapulis*). The defendant said that he did not warrant the horse (*ecum*) and he was prepared to prove &c. He was ordered to make his law on the Wednesday, but appeared without it; whereupon the Friar claimed judgment as in an undefended action. The defendant pleaded that he had not offered to make his law, but the Friar had done so. On Thursday judgment was given that the plaintiff recover the 60s with 40d expenses of the horse, and that the defendant have his horse back and be in mercy.

4 April 1300
Monday after the Octave of the above Feast

Ralph de Petypount was summoned to answer Thomas de Canvyle in a plea that he detained 5s, which the plaintiff's

[1] See p. 17 n.

servant handed to him under the plaintiff's seal to carry to a certain Peter of St Lawrence Lane. The defendant acknowledged receiving the money, but only as money owed to himself for work done; but he offered to repay it, if the plaintiff would swear with his single hand that the money was intended for Peter. When the plaintiff offered to do so, the defendant condoned the oath. Judgment for the plaintiff and that the defendant be in mercy.

Wednesday after Quasimodo [17 *April*]

Membr. 7 *b*
20 April 1300

Richard de Wellaund having complained of error in the record of a plea of debt by royal writ between himself and Walter de Mouncy in the Court of John de Armenters, Sheriff, the latter was ordered to produce the record and to summon the above Walter. On Tuesday after the Feast of St Mark the Evangelist [25 April] the plaintiff appeared, but the Sheriff reported that Walter could not be found in his bailiwick. John de Armenters produced the Record as follows.

Court of John de Armenters, Sheriff of London, held for foreigners on Tuesday before Easter [10 April] A° 28 Edw. [1300]. Walter de Munsy, knight, was attached by writ to answer Richard de Weylond, knight, in a plea of debt of 40 marks wherein the latter complained that he went with the army to Scotland in the 26th year of King Edward[1] as a follower of the defendant, and lost three horses value 80 marks, and that they made an account together about Christmas 1298 at Pulham, co. Norfolk, when the defendant entered into a bond to pay him 40 marks for the loss of the horses, which bond he had subsequently acknowledged in London before trustworthy persons, yet nevertheless he had failed to pay the money. The defendant pleaded that the bond was a foreign one, that the horses were not "merchandisable"[2], that he and the plaintiff were both foreigners,

---

[1] In 1298 Edward I invaded Scotland and defeated William Wallace at Falkirk.

[2] I.e. a mercantile matter, subject to the law merchant, in accordance with which the Court would take cognizance of disputes between foreigners.

and that the latter had his remedy at Common Law, since
he, the defendant, had sufficient property in the kingdom for
the purpose of distraint and attachment; and he asked the
Court to consider whether they would take cognizance of the
action. The Court informed him that he might answer further
if it was of any advantage to him. The defendant then
inspected the deed, and after comparing the seals and
examining it, denied that it was his own, and demanded an
inquest by the venue of Pulham, where the deed was alleged
to have been drawn up. And the plaintiff Richard answered
nothing against this. Accordingly on the ground that the
contract was a foreign one, that the action was not "merchandisable," and that the Court could not call in a jury of
the venue, the plaintiff was advised to seek his remedy at
Common Law. Afterwards the plaintiff wanted the defendant
to swear that the writing was not his deed, and demanded
that it should be enrolled.

Membr. 8
20 April 1300

Wednesday after Quasimodo [17 *April*]

Thomas de Wandelesworth, Robert de Eltham, Walter de
Wymbeldon, William de Roudon, William le Fraunceys,
Adam le Pestour, John Fuatard, John de Bedeford and John
Grigori were attached to answer Reginald the Chaplain,
Stephen le Fannere[1], Isabella his wife and Felicia their
daughter in a plea of trespass, wherein they complained that
on Sunday after Easter, when the plaintiff Reginald with his
clerk was in the plaintiff Stephen's house, the defendants
broke in the door, assaulted Reginald, and tried to get money
from him, and when they could not, handed him over to the
Beadle of Billingesgate Ward, and then returned and beat
the plaintiffs Isabella and Felicia. The defendants said they
were appointed to the Watch that night, and on a rumour
that Reginald was with Isabella as her paramour, they knocked
at the door, which was opened to them, and asked Reginald
what he was doing there at that time of night, but they did

---

[1] Subsequently spelt "Vannere" and "Wannere." The confusion of
v and w, which Charles Dickens noted as characteristic of the Londoner,
is frequently found in these Rolls, *sc.* Vaus, Waus; Vigerus, Wigerus;
Valentine, Walentine; Andevyle, Andewyle; etc. There are also numerous
instances of uncertainty in the matter of aspirates.

nothing further; and thereon they put themselves on their country. A jury of Billingesgate and the two neighbouring Wards was summoned.

Saturday next to (ad) *the Feast of St Mark the Evan-* 23 *April* 1300
gelist [25 *April*]

Robert le Treyere and Alan Wade were summoned to answer the Mayor and Aldermen on a charge of avowing the goods of Walter de Andewyle of Amiens and Ralph de Dovre, to the damage of those of Amyens, Nele and Corbie belonging to the Hanse, by concealing the King's customs. The defendants denied the avowry; but Alan said that the previous year he had sent 14 casks of woad overseas to the North to the above Ralph that he might sell them on his behalf, and that he owed £10, but that he had not avowed Ralph's goods, and he demanded an inquest thereon. The defendant Robert said that he had received from the above Walter Andevyne of Amyas (*sic*) 120 quarters of wheat, of which 60 remained to be sold, but said he received no other goods from Walter, nor any goods at all except for sale in the name of the said Walter; and he likewise demanded an inquest thereon. He was forbidden to pay Walter anything for the 60 quarters until the Court had come to an understanding (*posuerunt rationem cum*) with the men of Amiens[1]; and a jury was summoned for Monday. On that day, before William de Leyre and Geoffrey de Norton, deputies of the Mayor, a jury of John de Waus and others said that they could not among themselves find out whether Alan was guilty. He was acquitted. Adam de Ely was charged the same day with avowing the goods of Mauncel, a burgess of Amiens, and put himself on his country. On Friday a jury of Robert Sutel and others brought in a verdict that the above Robert le Treyere received and warehoused 120

---

[1] The citizens of Amiens, Corbie and Nesle had special privileges in the City of London in accordance with a treaty made in the Husting before the Mayor, Aldermen and citizens in A.D. 1237. They were allowed to unload, store and sell freely their woad, garlic, onions and other merchandise, wine and corn excepted, on payment of 50 marks annually to the Sheriffs. *Lib Alb.* 1, pp. 164–73 *et passim*.

quarters of wheat and sold it in his own name and kept the money by him, and that the above Adam avowed the woad of Maunsel of Amiens. Robert and Adam were committed to prison.

26 April 1300   *Tuesday after the above Feast*

John de Kirketon, John Bolychromp called "Byndere," Richard de Kirketon and Robert de Staunford, brokers of carts, were charged that they met foreign carters five leagues outside the City, and warned them that if they went to the City the carts would be seized by the King's officials, and then, after hiring the carts for a mark or 16s, they afterwards let them out to freemen and foreigners for two marks or 30s, in contempt of the King and to the damage of the citizens 100s. Robert admitted the offence and the other three were found guilty by a jury of William de Helweton and others. They were committed to prison.

Thomas de Rederesgate, keeper of the Quay of St Botolph's by Billingesgate, was found guilty by a jury of John de Wodeforde and others and committed to prison, for housing wood belonging to foreigners of Greenwich and other places, and avowing it and selling it retail.

11 May 1300   *Wednesday after the Feast of St John before the Latin Gate* [6 May]

Robert le Breton, who was attached in the house of John de Armenters, Sheriff, by a servant of Sir William de Middilton, clerk of the Household of the King's son, was found guilty by a jury of Henry le Pottere and others, of taking carts with the goods and ale of their owners, and making the latter pay him a fine for delivery, on the pretence that he was a member of the Prince's Household.

Membr. 8 *b*   William Sciphupe was attached to answer Walter Heyne, clerk to the King's son, for being possessed of a silver knife belonging to the Prince. The defendant admitted receiving the knife from John Gamel for 14s which the latter owed him for carrying the King's wines at Fulham, and said that he afterwards pledged it for 8s to William, servant of William Wigerus. The said servant admitted the receipt and said that he pledged it five years ago to a taverner of Sutwerk, who was now dead, and that he could not get the knife. Judgment that the plaintiff recover the knife or its value against William Sciphupe, and that the latter pay the plaintiff 8s, and recover the knife against the servant; and as the servant could neither produce the knife or find security for producing it, he was committed to prison until &c.

William de Insula was summoned to answer Reginald Denmars that whereas no toll should be taken except by the Sheriffs, nevertheless when the plaintiff came to the defendant's house to buy merchandise, the latter arrested the merchandise bought, and demanded from him for each dozen pennyworths a farthing more. The defendant was first ordered to make his law on the Quinzime; but as he would not allow the goods to be delivered by Thomas Juvenall, the Mayor's Serjeant, a jury was summoned for Monday.

Saturday the morrow of St Botulph [17 June]

18 June 1300

John de la Roche, Alan de Cressi, Geoffrey de Cressi, and John de Cressy of Pountif[1], foreign weavers, were attached to answer Silvester de Morton and others of the Guild of Weavers, for exercising that craft against the Charter of Henry III to the Weavers of London, in which it was laid down that no weaver should remain in the City or in Suthwerk to weave or make cloth unless he belonged to the Guild, under penalty of £10 forfeiture to the King. The defendants asked to hear the Charter read, and pleaded that they were not versed (*nec se cognoscunt in consuetudinibus*) in the customs of the City and the laws of the realm. As regards the penalty nothing at present. They were told not to meddle in that craft without the consent of the Weavers, to whom a charter had been granted, under penalty &c.

Henry de Farinham appeared to answer a complaint of *20 June 1300* Ralph de Arras. He was forbidden by the Mayor to lease out (*ne aliquam shopam locet*) any shop of any freeman of London.

[1] Pountif: probably Ponthieu.

Whereupon he said that he had a free tenement in a certain shop at St Botolphs[1] which the plaintiff claimed to be his for a term of years. The latter was directed to prosecute his claim before the Wardens of the Fair of St Botolph's in London, who would report their finding to the Mayor and Aldermen.

Ralph le Mortemer was attached to answer John Tilli in a plea of debt of 16s 8d, borrowed by him at Baldhok A° 25 Edw. [1296–7], and repayable on his next arrival in London. The defendant denied the loan, and was ordered to make his law on the spot as a foreigner, which he did with the seventh hand[2]. He was acquitted and the plaintiff was in mercy for a false claim.

An inquest was taken before Elias Russel, Mayor, on 23 June, 1300, by the oath of William Peter, Robert Joye and others from the Wards of Porthesocne and Alegate, who presented that Ralph the Chaplain, dwelling in the rent of Gilbert de la Marche, was a receiver of thieves and prostitutes by night, that Walter le Coupper was a night-walker who made disturbances in various inns in the Ward, and that a certain chaplain in Belleryteryslane in the rent of Matthew le Caundeler did the same, to the terror of the neighbourhood. Order was given to arrest them.

Membr. 9
30 May 1300 Plea of Reymund de Margoys held before Elyas Russel, Mayor, John de Armenters and Henry de Fingrie, Sheriffs[3], on Monday in the Feast of Pentecost [29 May] A° 28 Edw. in obedience to a Writ of 10 March, in which the Mayor and Sheriffs were bidden to give Reimund de Margoys,

[1] Boston, Lincolnshire. The City of London had chartered privileges in regard to citizens of London impleaded at the Fair of St Botulph's. See Lib. Cust. 1, 178–183; Lib. Alb. 1, p. 405. The Wardens here mentioned were London citizens chosen to demand jurisdiction over citizens impleaded at the Fair, and to settle their cases by law merchant. See Cal. of Letter Book C, p. 98; Lib. de Antiquis Legibus, fo. 142 b; and City's Charter of 26 March, A.D. 1268.

[2] He found six other people to take the oath with him. According to Lib. Alb. 1, p. 203, a foreigner in an action of debt could make his law with the third hand. This case confirms Miss Bateson's suggestion (Borough Customs, 1, p. 177) that the compiler of Lib. Alb. made a clerical error and should have written "seventh hand."

[3] The Sheriffs were present, because the action arose out of a writ addressed to them equally with the Mayor.

merchant of Bordeaux, execution of a Recognizance made before Henry le Galeys, Mayor, and John de Baukwell, whereby William le Splenere was bound to the above Reymund in a debt of £12.

Precept was issued to enquire what lands and tenements the above William had at the date of the Recognizance. A jury of twelve men of the City returned that he had in fee on Nov 23, 1286, a messuage and five shops, now in the tenure of Adam de Hallingbury, of 100s annual value, of which he paid 20s yearly to the New Temple, 20s to the Hospital of St John, 10s to the Bishop of Ely and 10s for repairs, thus leaving a net annual value of 40s. Thereupon the plaintiff demanded execution. As it was found that the above Adam now held the tenements in fee, he was summoned to appear before the Mayor the next day to show cause why execution should not be made. He appeared and resisted it, on the ground that the above-mentioned William le Splenere held the tenements from the Master of the Knights of the Temple and the Prior of St John of Jerusalem by the above services, as from the chief lords of the fee, and on default of those services the Master and Prior had sued out a Writ of Customs and Services and demanded the tenements as "Gavelet"[1], as they could not be distrained upon, and had finally recovered them as a "Schertford"; wherefore Adam claimed that by the custom of the City, the tenements could not be burdened any further for rent or any other service belonging to the time when the above William had them in demise from the chief lords. The Mayor and Sheriffs gave a day in order to consult the Rolls of Common Pleas, when it was found that the Master and Prior had sued out a Writ of Customs and Services against Beatrice, widow of William le Splenere, and had recovered the tenements against

[1] The action of Gavelet in London was begun by a writ of Customs and Services. If the demandant could find nothing on the premises on which to distrain, he was allowed to seize the land itself as a distraint. If the tenant paid double, together with a fine, within a year and a day, he might recover it; otherwise it remained to the demandant, being called "forshut." See *Lib. Alb.* 1, p. 62. Other forms of the word are forshard, shartford, shortford, foreschoke. Jacob, *Law Dictionary*, explains it as meaning forsake, i.e. the tenant as it were forsook the land. *O.E.D.* suggests a derivation from *foreclore*, to foreclose.

her as a Gavelet on the death of her husband. Accordingly a jury of the four neighbouring Wards was ordered to give a verdict as to whether the tenements ought to be burdened further by reason of any debt of the said William, under whose authority (*sub cuius virga*) she had entered into possession; and also whether the tenement was still in the hands of the said Beatrice, or of the Master and Prior, or of the present tenant through the Master and Prior who recovered it, whereby the tenement would be exonerated of all debts; and a day was given to the Wednesday following. On that day Adam de Hallingbery appeared and the plaintiff Reimund made default. Judgment was given that the former go quit and that the latter be in mercy.

Membr. 10
2 July 1300
Saturday after the Feast of the Apostles Peter and Paul [29 June] A° 28 Edw. [1300]

William May, clerk, was ordered to bring into Court on Monday, Jaketta[1], a minor and daughter of his sister, and to appear himself to answer the Mayor and Aldermen in charges against him. Walter de Dyry and Alice his wife were also warned to produce the will of Michael de Provincia[2].

A day was given to Richer de Refham and Gibert le Abrokur to make an account of the King's moneys, received by the said Wybert (*sic*), and not paid to Richer during the time when the latter was Sheriff.

5 July 1300
Tuesday after the above Feast

John le Benere was summoned to answer John le Frounceys in a plea of covenant, wherein the latter complained that the defendant bought fur from him to the value of £8 16s, and undertook to pay him that amount, and acquit him of a Recognizance, neither of which he had done. The defendant pleaded that he bought fur to the value of £5 8s. At this point came John de Armenters and demanded his Court, which was granted to him, and the parties were told to go into the Sheriff's Court.

[1] Otherwise "Jakemina"; see p. 77.
[2] Cf. Letter Book B, fo. 2 b, "Michael de Provins."

Wibert de Abbevile (see above, "Gibert le Abrokur") entered into a Recognizance of 8s 10d to Richer de Refham, payable at the Quinzime.

William May was summoned to answer Walter Diri and Alice his wife concerning Jakemina, daughter of Michael de Pountif, then in the defendant's wardship. The plaintiffs alleged that, though the wardship of minors ought not to be in the hands of a kinsman to whom her inheritance could descend[1], the defendant was the heir of Jakemina; and accordingly they demanded that the wardship be transferred to themselves, in accordance with the will of the above Michael which they produced in Court. The defendant answered that Jakemina was in the wardship of her aunt, the Prioress of Kelingburne, and that the plaintiff Alice ought not to have the wardship, because the girl's inheritance was derived from her mother, and that her father left her nothing, and could not devise her wardship, since her inheritance lay within the Liberty of the City. As it was found that the above Michael by his will left the girl nothing, judgment was given that the wardship remain with the Prioress.

John de Ely was summoned to answer Michael de Wonburn in a plea of debt of £9 due on a Recognizance to Henry de Winchester, knight, of whose will the plaintiff was executor. The defendant pleaded that the plaintiff was not an executor. Thereupon the latter produced the will, with a clause to the effect that the testator committed to his executors the distribution of the residue of his goods for the good of his soul, in accordance with the instructions of the Lady Idonea his wife

[1] According to the statement of London custom made before the Itinerant Justices in 1244 (*Lib. Alb.* 1, p. 108) the plaintiffs would be correct in saying that the wardship should not be in the hands of a kinsman who could inherit. But the City denied this in 1310 (Coram Rege Roll, Pasch. 3 Edw. II, rot. 74 (No. 200)), declaring that the matter lay within the disposal of the Mayor and Aldermen. The right of a freeman to devise the wardship of his child was reaffirmed about the middle of the fourteenth century (Ricart's *Calendar*, Camden Society, p. 99). In this particular case the Court laid down that a freeman could only devise a wardship when he left an inheritance. No question of the "orphan's portion" seems to have arisen, probably because the testator had no real or personal estate in the City.

and Brother Simon his son. On the back of the will was an
endorsement showing that it was proved before the Official of
London in 1299 as the nuncupative or last will of the deceased, but whereas the testator appointed Edmund Paske and
Hugh Petipas his executors, the Official had appointed Lady
Idonea in place of Edmund, who refused administration, and
Michael de Wonburn in place of Hugh, who was suspected of
"notorious delapidation." The defendant pleaded that he
need not answer the plaintiff as executor, and that it was not
a true will, since the seal of the Diocese was not appended nor
that of the testator, and that the plaintiff was not an executor,
except as a deputy, and then only under the supervision of
Brother Simon, who was not present, and the plaintiff had
produced no authorisation from him for recovering the debt.
After adjournments that the Mayor might take advice, the
parties appeared, and the defendant now pleaded that the
plaintiff could not have a better ground of action than the
testator, if he were alive, and that during the Shrievalty of
Thomas Romayn and William de Leyre (1290–1), he (the
defendant) had been imprisoned in Newgate at the suit of
the testator on the above Recognizance, and had been delivered from prison by him, a compromise having been made
by an indenture which he produced in Court. This indenture
was a covenant (French) to the effect that if the defendant
did not pay Sir Henry de Winchester £9 by Christmas 1291,
for which he had pledged his houses and appurtenances, then
the houses should belong to the said Sir Henry, who should
be recouped for his expenses, and the Recognizance should
stand; but if the money were paid, the houses should return
to the defendant and he should receive an acquittance. The
defendant now pleaded that he had already been imprisoned
on the Recognizance and delivered by the testator, and he demanded judgment whether he could be imprisoned again on
the same Recognizance or be molested for the said debt. The
plaintiff answered that he still had the Recognizance, which
had neither been disallowed nor cancelled, that he had the
same ground of action as the testator, and that the defendant
had produced no acquittance; on which grounds he claimed
judgment. As the Mayor wished advice as to the force of

the Recognizance, and the defendant had not his counsel ready, a day was given till Monday the morrow of All Souls[1].

Monday after the Translation of St Thomas the Martyr *[7 July]*

Membr. 10 b
11 July 1300

Walter de Frogwell, beadle of the Ward of Cordwanerstret, plaintiff in a plea of trespass, and William son of Richard de Mountpelers, Michael Pickard, John Silly and his servant Michael, defendants, came to an agreement by permission of the Court on terms that the defendants buy the plaintiff a gown, value half-a-mark, and the plaintiff be in mercy. The amercement was condoned because he was a "bailiff."

Walter the bailiff of Queenhithe was summoned to answer Salemann Michel, Robert the baker, and Salemann Fyges, boatmen of Serre[2], in a plea that, contrary to immemorial custom, he took from them a basin of salt as custom, to the prejudice of their liberties; and further on Thursday last, when they wanted to leave the Quay, having sold their goods, he arrested their boats. The defendant justified the arrest as having been made at the suit of Roger le Palmere and Roger de la Vyne; and as regards the salt, he claimed that he and his predecessors, acting on behalf of the Sheriffs, had always been seised of a basin of salt, and he demanded that inquest be made by the country. The plaintiffs answered that a basin of salt was due for wharfage only, and not for custom, and they never paid any custom on salt except 2d the sieve (*siva*). They claimed also that they could go by water to Westminster and beyond, on this side of the Bridge, to sell their wares without leave of any one; and they demanded an inquest thereon. The defendant pleaded that they could not sell their wares this side of the Bridge, except only in the Port of Queenhithe. The jury was respited till the coming of the Mayor, and the basin was delivered to the bailiff under mainprise of John de Brenkele and Robert de Gloucester.

[1] This action was not terminated till 4 July, 1301 (see p. 108), when the Court held that the subsequent covenant cancelled the Recognizance, and gave judgment for the defendant, John de Ely.

[2] Sarre, co. Kent?

Thursday after the Feast of St Margaret [20 *July*]

The Prior of Holy Trinity was summoned to answer the Mayor and Aldermen in a plea that, whereas it had been found by a jury of the Ward of Bradestrete and the three neighbouring Wards[1] that from time immemorial the Priors had been charged with the duty of building, covering and repairing a bridge by the Wall, where the Walebrok enters into Bradestret Ward, by virtue of holding the advowson of All Hallows on the Wall and certain rents near this bridge, and that likewise the Prior had a right of way for carts bringing wood and other necessaries from his manors— nevertheless the said bridge was so ruinous that no one on horse or foot could cross it without danger, owing to the default of the Prior in repairing it. The Prior appeared and pleaded that he was not bound to repair the bridge, and produced a Charter of King Henry[2], great-grandfather of the present King, granting that the Priors should be quit of such repairs, and he said further that he had no tenements or rents near the bridge, except the Church of All Hallows, which he held to his own uses, and the advowson of it, which he and his predecessors held before and since the granting of the above charter. Ralph Pecok, appearing for the Commonalty of the City, alleged that the Prior and his predecessors had always repaired the bridge when necessary since the granting of the charter, and accordingly he claimed that the Prior should not be quit of the duty by his charter. The latter said that this answer should not be allowed to nullify his charter, because in the Statute *de Waranto* it was enacted that when any one claimed a liberty by charter, he should be judged by the tenor of the charter, and accordingly he demanded judgment. He said further that in the Statute of Westminster it was enacted that no one should be distrained

---

[1] This was an inquest taken before the Mayor on the 8th July this year. A translation of the finding is given in Riley's *Memorials of London and London Life in the 13th, 14th and 15th Centuries*, p. 43, from Letter Book C, fo. 47 b.

[2] See Cal. of Letter Book C, p. 73; Dugdale, *Monasticon*, vol. VI, part i, p. 157. The dispute seems to have dragged on until the session of the Itinerant Justices in the Tower, A.D. 1321, when the Prior of Holy Trinity undertook to repair the bridge over Walbrook. *Lib. Cust.* I, p. 409.

for repairing bridges save those anciently accustomed to do it, and since his charter showed an ancient acquittance from so doing, he claimed judgment as to whether he ought to be distrained. To this Ralph Pecok answered that the Statute *de quo Waranto* only applied to liberties issuing from lords, and not to liberties of this kind, i.e. concerning the making of bridges, parks, and ponds, and he likewise demanded judgment.

Saturday the morrow of St Mary Magdalene [22 *July*]   23 *July 1300*

Alice la Blund offered herself against Walter de Flete. The Court of the Dean and Chapter of St Paul's was allowed to Richard Gladewyn, "sokenreve," and the parties were given a day to appear in that Court.

Wednesday after the Feast of St James the Apostle [25 *July*]   Membr. 11 *b* 27 *July 1300*

Peter the Surgeon acknowledged himself bound to Ralph de Mortimer, by Richard atte Hill his attorney, in the sum of 20s, payable at certain terms, the said Ralph undertaking to give Peter a letter of acquittance. This Recognizance arose out of a covenant between them with regard to the effecting of a cure. Both were amerced for coming to an agreement out of Court. A precept was issued to summon all the surgeons of the City for Friday, that an enquiry might be made as to whether the above Peter was fitted (*abilis*) to enjoy the profession of a surgeon.

Friday after the above Feast before William de Leyre, *the Mayor's deputy*   29 *July 1300*

Thomas Beauflur proved by the evidence of John de Buttertone and Jordon, a mariner, that at Calays on the 3rd Feb. John de Cesterton threatened to do him personal hurt and to burn his houses. The latter was attached, and mainprised by William Canoun, John de la Barre, John Harwe, clerk, Walter de Wenlok, Thomas de Salop, and Richard le Barber of Douegate.

Thomas de Frowyk, Roger de Frowyk and William Beynin were summoned to answer Agnes, widow of Reginald Frowyk, in a plea that they produce her late husband's will[1] which, she alleged, they had kept in their possession unproved. The defendants Roger and William pleaded that after the will had been proved before the Official of the Archdeacon of London, it was left in the possession of the defendant Thomas. The latter said that he entrusted it to the mother of the deceased, Isabella Frowyk, of whom he and Walter de Finchingfeud, alderman, were executors. Subsequently he produced the will, which was returned to him, to be brought into Court *quo et quando.*

John de Douwegate was mainprised to restore to the above Agnes five deeds needed by her in connection with her property outside the City of London, held by her in the name of her son Henry, because the lord of the fee was distraining her for services not due from that land.

Membr. 12
30 July 1300

Saturday after the Feast of St James the Apostle [25 July] before William de Leyre *and* Walter de Finchingfeud, *deputies of the Mayor*

Stephen de Colegate was summoned to answer Henry le Galeys in a plea of trespass, wherein the latter complained that he entrusted the defendant with lead for covering his Chapel, and the defendant substituted inferior lead, at half-a-mark the wey (*pondus*), and covered the Chapel with it. A jury from the venue of Candelwykstrate and of men of the defendant's craft was summoned. A jury of Vintry was also summoned to deal with a charge against Ralph Hardel of carrying away lead, value 20s, from the plaintiff's house in the parish of St Martin Vintry.

9 Aug. 1300

Richard le Keu, fishmonger, was summoned to answer Henry his apprentice for breach of covenant, in driving the plaintiff out of his house and service, though the latter had

---

[1] This will was enrolled in the Court of Husting (H.R. 29 (74)) on 17 October the same year. The testator left to Agnes his wife all his real property in London for life, including a tenement in Milk Street then in the seisin of his mother, which he had no power to devise, as was proved by the executors.

served him faithfully. The defendant pleaded that the plaintiff had left his service of his own free will, by going to a certain woman night and day with his master's possessions, for which he had rendered no account. A jury from this side of the Stocks was summoned for Wednesday.

Tuesday the morrow of the Assumption B.M. [15 *Aug.*]   *16 Aug. 1300*

Adam de Hidecroun and Richard le Gayoler of Newgate were attached to answer Geoffrey de la March in a plea of trespass, wherein he complained that after he had brought water in a "tyne"[1] from Ludegate for the use of his master Richard de Gloucestre, the defendant Adam took the water and filled his own pot with it, and when the plaintiff cursed (*blasfemavit*) about it, the defendant took the plaintiff's stick, and hit him on the head with it and upset the tyne. The defendants denied the assault. A jury of Ludegate was summoned, and the above Adam was mainprised for hearing the verdict by John Huberd, "flecher"[2], and John le Brun. Subsequently the parties came to an agreement on terms that the defendants pay the plaintiff 2s and put themselves in mercy. Richard's amercement was condoned by W. de Leyre.

John atte Selde (*de Senda*), William Kinesman, Thomas Wastel and John de Talworth were found not guilty of going out of the City to forestall wood and charcoal, by a jury of Vintry, Queenhithe and Castle Baynhard. Richard le Keu, Richard Baudechun, William Baudechun, William de Chalfhunt, Robert Orpedeman, James le Swayn, Robert le Clovier, Thomas le Norreys and Thomas le Rutur, being found guilty, were adjudged to lose their freedom, and to pay toll to the Sheriff in future as foreigners.

Wednesday after the above Feast before W. de Leyre   Membr. 12 *b*
                                                             17 Aug. 1300

Bernard Johan was attached to answer John de Cornibia in a plea of trespass, wherein the latter complained that he owed the defendant £80 on a bond payable at certain terms,

[1] A large water-vessel. Cf. Letter Book D, fo. 99 *b*.
[2] A maker of bows and arrows.

on security of his goods which might be distrained and retained by the Steward and Marshall, the Barons of the Exchequer, the Justices of the Bench, the Mayor and Sheriffs
&c., and that he had repaid £13 11s, when the defendant,
four days before the Feast of St Mary Magdalene, without
informing the Mayor and bailiffs that payment was in
arrears, and although the plaintiff was a freeman of the City
and had enough property in London whereby he might have
been forced to come to Court, followed him on his journey
to the Fair of Thoraud, and at Caleys had him arrested and
imprisoned by the bailiffs of that town for five days, until
William de Brouthton of London paid him £16 18s on the
plaintiff's behalf. On the Friday following the parties came
to an agreement by permission of the Court on terms that
the plaintiff withdraw his action, and the defendant enter
into a Recognizance to pay him or John de Brouthton the
sum of £11 on the Feast of St Bartholomew next (24 Aug.)
under mainprise of John de Dowegate. The plaintiff put
himself in mercy, which was condoned by William de Leyre.

27 Aug. 1300   *Saturday after the Feast of St Bartholomew [24 Aug.]*

Robert Derman was summoned to answer Ralph Ratspray
on a charge of avowing and "covering" the merchandise of
a certain Andrew de Berkyng. A jury of Bisopesgate, Stockes,
Eschep, and St Nicholas Shambles was summoned for
Wednesday.

John of the Seld was summoned to answer John de
Armenters, Sheriff, for avowing two casks of wine which he
bought from Peter de Pyne, a foreigner, for the use of
Julian de Cardoyl, a foreigner. The defendant pleaded that
the wine was bought for his own use, and that Julian had no
interest in it on the day of the arrest. A jury of Vintry consisting of Thomas Drinkwater and others brought in a verdict
that John knew that Julian would buy his wine before he purchased it himself. Judgment that he be deprived of the freedom.

Membr. 13   Record of Proceedings in the Sheriff's Court, 3 Sept. to
3 Sept. 1300   1 Oct. 1300, in an action of covenant between John Fraunceys,
"peleter," plaintiff, and John le Benere, defendant.

Saturday before the Feast of the Nativity B.M. [8 Sept.] Membr. 14
before W. de Leyre *and* Walter de Finchingfeud, *the* 3 *Sept. 1300*
Mayor's deputies

Simon de Paris was summoned to answer William Belebuch,
"cossur"[1], in a plea of covenant, wherein the latter complained that the defendant bought from him at Smethefeud
a bay horse, in exchange for another horse and four marks, to
be paid if both were satisfied with the horses; and that the
defendant rode the plaintiff's horse outside the Bar at Smeth-
feud and returned with it immediately, so that the plaintiff
could not examine the defendant's horse[2], and thus the defendant unjustly detained the plaintiff's horse, to his damage
&c. The defendant pleaded that the bargain was without
condition. Thereupon the plaintiff offered to acquit him of
his plea if he would swear that the bargain was unconditional.
On the defendant's agreeing to do so, the plaintiff asked leave
of the Court to come to terms, which was granted. An agreement was then made that the plaintiff should have his horse
back again if he paid six marks to the defendant before
Monday night. The plaintiff put himself in mercy, which
was condoned by William de Leyre.

Tuesday before the Exaltation of the Holy Cross [14 Sept.] 13 *Sept. 1300*

William de Donecastre appointed Thomas Juvenal his
attorney to sue, attach and distrain, at the suit of the Sheriff,
the merchants of Brabant, in order to recover 22 marks and
35 sacks of wool, value 420 marks, which John, Duke of
Brabant, had lately caused to be taken from the said William
at Andewerpe by arrest.

Saturday after the above Feast 17 *Sept. 1300*

Eustachius le Mercer was attached to answer that, whereas
it had been ordained by the King and his Council that all
bundles of goods coming from overseas should remain un-
opened until they were examined by the Sheriffs or other

[1] Cossur, *sc.* coser, cosser, corser: a horse-dealer.
[2] The plaintiff's argument seems to be that the defendant "rushed"
him into the exchange, but that the bargain was not valid until he was
satisfied with the defendant's horse.

good and lawful men elected and sworn to that office, nevertheless the defendant went to the house of Brachius Gerard
in his absence and, saying that he was a bailiff, had a bale of
goods opened. The defendant admitted that he went with
John, servant of Roger de Parys, to the above house, but said
that he had nothing to do with the opening of any bale, and
he demanded an inquest thereon. A jury from Langeburn
Ward, consisting of John de Shaftesbiry and others, gave a
verdict that the defendant went to the house in the presence
of Gydotty Gy, partner of Brachius, and found a bale bound
up, and asked if it contained goods for sale and if it could
be opened, and the said Guy (*sic*) assented. Thereupon the
defendant and another person opened the bale, and finding
nothing that they wanted, went away, and the said Guy
offered them money for the custom, and asked if they were
Customs Officers, to which they answered no, they were only
merchants. The jury could not find that false money or
anything else contrary to the Proclamation was in the bale,
nor that Eustace came there as a bailiff, but only as a broker.
Judgment was given that he go quit, and that Guy find
security to come before the Mayor and Aldermen on Thursday;
viz. Brachius Gerard and Ralph de Alegate. The Sheriff was
ordered to bring the Officers of the Scrutiny (*custodes dicti
scrutinii*) the same day.

Richard Tripaty and Laurence de Shirebourne were attached to answer a charge of having used insulting language
to Roger de Lenne, servant of John atte Gate, before dusk
in Thames Street in the parish of Allhallows the Great in
the Hay, and that afterwards they entered the house of
William Marisone, and asked William's wife to open the
door of a room, in which they wished to indulge in buckler-
play[1] [*ad bucularium ludere*], and when she refused, they drew
their swords and attacked her, and when, owing to the tumult,
Richard le Barber, beadle of the Ward, came with his rod
to keep the peace, they assaulted and beat him also. The
defendants denied that they did any harm to the woman or

---

[1] Buckler-play or fencing was frequently forbidden by ordinance.
Lib. Cust. I, pp. 282–3; *Lib. Alb.* I, p. 274.

the beadle, and the defendant Richard said that they found the beadle and the servant Richard fighting, and that the latter struck the beadle on the breast, but that neither he nor the other defendant did anything. A jury of Douegate was summoned, and Laurence was mainprised by Richard the Tailor of Langeburne Ward and Henry le Sauser, and Richard Tripaty by. . . . Thorp, John le Botoner, junior, and John Cendal, mercer.

William le Bracur and Thomas le Keu were summoned to answer the Mayor and Aldermen, on the complaint of persons living in Thames Street belonging to the craft of woodmongers (*buscariorum*), for buying and selling their goods at markets and fairs and in the City, though they were not freemen. The defendants denied that they were foreigners and called to warrant the Paper of the Chamber of Guildhall. The Chamberlain was ordered to search the Paper and report on Thursday.

Tuesday before the Feast of St Michael [*29 Sept.*]

Membr. 14 b
27 Sept. 1300

Stephen de Flete, Gerard de Hopstathe, Peter de Aske, John Teste, Gilbert Flemingg, John Fernus and Thomas de Dichefeld were summoned to answer Peter de Blakeneye, John de Dorking, John Beauflur and John Bussard in a complaint that John, Duke of Brabant, had taken part of the plaintiff's goods when they were exposed for sale in the Duchy of Brabant, for which reason the Sheriff had been ordered to attach the goods of all Brabantine merchants until the Duke made restitution, and that the defendants were under the dominion of the Duke. The defendants denied this, and said that they belonged to the City of Malynges and held of the Bishop of Leges, and that the Bishop held of the Church of St Lambert and had nothing to do with the Count of Brabant; and they demanded an inquest by foreign merchants who knew the said country. On Wednesday a jury of Theotard le Estreys, John de Eldchirk, Eylbrich, Henry Colle of Collon, Godelin de Colon, Tykimann the goldsmith, James Fisshe, Albridus de Dynaunt, Lambert Maulechyn, Peter de St Vincent, John Saunterre, Baldewyn Chapun and

Guy de Goly found a verdict for the defendants. Order was given to return their distraints, and the plaintiffs were told to sue distraints on men belonging to the Duke's dominions.

Thomas de Donecastre, Canon of the Church of Bedlehem, was attached to answer a charge of having sued a certain Richard de Keles, apprentice of William de York, for assault before the Official of the Archdeacon of London, against the King's prohibition of the citing of laymen in the Ecclesiastical Courts in matters belonging to the Crown. The defendant admitted having sued Richard as alleged, but only as allowed by ecclesiastical law. The plaintiff Richard pleaded that the defendant was suing him maliciously in order to extort money, and as the defendant had tacitly agreed that he acted against the King's prohibition, since he had neither denied it or confessed it, he demanded judgment as in an undefended action. As the Mayor wanted further information, a day was given that an inquest might be made by a jury of the venue.

The same day Robert, called " de Tylemount," produced Letters Patent (French) of Sir Arnald, Count de Los, to the effect that the above Robins (*sic*) was one of his servants and merchants, and that the horses in the possession of Robert and his servants belonged to and were under the protection of the said Arnald, who prayed that no harm be done to the said Robert. Dated A.D. 1291. As it appeared by this letter and the evidence of Peter de Edelmeton and other credible persons that the above Robert did not belong to the dominions of the Duke of Brabant, the attachment made upon him was returned to him.

William de Storteford was summoned to answer Geoffrey le Hurer, who complained that on Tuesday before Lent 1298 he went by the defendant's orders with Sir Geoffrey de Norton and William de Londonstone to the Earl of Cornwall, who was then staying at Asherugge, in order to prevail upon the latter to deliver an arrest which he had made at Henley on some citizens of London, in reprisal for a trespass done by the Sheriffs against his own men. The Earl had consented, and the plaintiff waited four days after the others had departed for the Earl's letter of delivery, and then coming home in great haste broke the shin of his horse, and accordingly he demanded from the defendant either the value of the horse, or a new one, which the defendant refused. The defendant pleaded that he could only be liable for the horse in three cases viz. if the plaintiff had gone to military service and remained from the beginning till the end of the war; or went by night under his orders at excessive speed; or went by day under his orders and was attacked by robbers and his horse was stolen; and he demanded judgment as to whether he was liable under any of these cases. A day was given till Monday after the Feast of St Michael.

On which day the parties came, and the plaintiff demanded judgment on the ground that the defendant tacitly admitted that he was the defendant's servant and went by his command. The defendant pleaded that he was at liberty to affirm or deny it, since it was not part of the plaintiff's case. The plaintiff then said that if the defendant denied it he was prepared to make it the issue. Whereupon the defendant denied that the plaintiff went in his service, and said he went in the service of good men of the City whose goods were attached at Henley; and thereon the parties put themselves on their country. A jury was summoned for Thursday, on which day the parties came to an agreement by permission of the Court, on terms that the defendant pay two marks and put himself in mercy. On the morrow the plaintiff appeared before Nicholas Picot, John de Donestaple, and Simon de Parys and acknowledged satisfaction. *Roll D. membr. 1 3 Oct. 1300*

Court of the Soke of the Prior of St Bartholomew, London, held in Honilane on Sunday before the Nativity of the Lord [25 Dec.] A° 28 Edw. [1299] *Membr. 15 20 Dec. 1299*

Adam Braz essoins concerning detinue of chattels against Geoffrey Trotter and William de Tolyndon by Stephen de Wethresfeud.

Sunday after the Feast of St Hilary [13 Jan.] adjourned till the next Sunday *17 Jan. 1299–1300*

Sunday after (? before) the Conversion of St Paul [25 Jan.]

Geoffrey de Trotter and William de Tolyndon offered themselves against Adam Brace in a plea of detinue of chattels, wherein they complained that they took four quarters of barley, value 29s 4d, to Adam's house, in mistake for the house of a certain Ramessey, and that Adam detained them. The latter defended, and demanded judgment as to whether he was bound to answer them, since they produced no cause of action, or any tally, by which they could bind him to answer them. The plaintiffs demanded judgment as in an undefended action, because they had said in their count that the grain arrived at his house and was received by him and his household, and he had not denied it. A day given till the Octave.

Sunday before the Feast of the Purification B.M. [2 Feb.]

Geoffrey le Trotter and William de Tolyndon offered themselves against Adam Brace in a plea of detinue of chattels, and again demanded judgment as in an undefended action. And because the Court held that they had alleged a sufficient ground of action, i.e. ignorance, judgment was given that the defendant answer further. Afterwards the defendant admitted that he had received three quarters, for which he acknowledged that he owed the plaintiffs at the rate of half a mark the quarter, but he pleaded that he did not receive the fourth quarter; and thereon he put himself on his country. The plaintiffs demanded judgment, because the defendant proffered another answer than what the Court could receive, and they pleaded further that the defendant did not owe the value alleged, but 7s 4d, the price at which the quarter was then being sold. A day was given till the Octave.

Sunday after the above Feast

Adam Braz essoins by Stephen de Wethresfeld. A day given till the Octave by the Canon of the said House, by consent of the parties.

Sunday the Feast of St Valentine

On that day the parties appeared and the Court could not make a jury. Accordingly a day was given till the first Court of Henry de Fingrie, to hear and determine the plea.

Court of Henry de Fingrie, *Sheriff of London, Wednes-day after the above Feast*

Adam Braz essoined by Stephen de Wethresfeud. And note that the Prior of St Bartholomew sent his record, and warranted the essoin till the Octave.

Wednesday after the Feast of St Mathias the Apostle [24 *Feb.*]

Geoffrey le Trottere and William de Tolindone offered themselves against Adam Braz in a plea of detinue of four quarters of barley, value 29s 4d, as appears in the Record of the pleas of the Court of the Prior of St Bartholomew sent to this Court. The defendant pleaded that he need not answer concerning four quarters, as he only received three, and these of the value of 20s, at half-a-mark the quarter, for which he was willing to give satisfaction. The plaintiffs declared that they carried four quarters, at 7s 4d the quarter, to Adam's house, and this they offered to prove as the Court should direct. The defendant agreed that the plaintiffs should swear, touching the holy Gospels, and if they did so, he would give satisfaction for the four quarters. The plaintiffs then took the oath, and judgment was given that they recover the barley, or its value, and that the defendant be in mercy.

Court of Elyas Russel, *Mayor of London, Friday the morrow of St Edward King*[1]

Adam Braz complained of error of judgment in a plea which was in the Court of Henry de Fingrie without writ &c. on account of which the Sheriff was ordered to bring his record on Wednesday last. The Sheriff produced the record, in which no error was found. Precept was issued to execute the judgment, and the above Adam was in mercy.

[1] Query: Translation of St Edward, King and Confessor, i.e. 13 Oct.?

ROLL D

Court of Elyas Russel, *Mayor, Saturday after the Feast of St Michael* [29 Sept.] *A^o 28 Edw.* [1300]

Martin le Tauier[1], Heyne de Holecote, John de Gaiateshal, Roger Taup, John Scot, Alexander le Tauier, Roger le Fraunceys, Roger Martre, Adam Cornys and John Alger were attached to answer the King and the men of the Craft of Skinners (*officii Peletrie*), for ordaining a new ordinance touching their craft, viz. that whereas of old they took 5s for the thousand of "Grysover"[2], they now took 6s, and 2s and 3s more than formerly for every thousand of work (*operis*), to the prejudice and damage of the King, the nobles, and their craft. The defendants pleaded that nowadays more good work was needed for the thousand, and double as much in other skins than formerly, and yet all necessaries for their work were dearer than before. They denied that they made a confederacy by oath or any other bond, and said that those who were willing to pay more were served more quickly, but otherwise they did not take more except on account of the dearness of necessaries; and thereon they put themselves on their country. A jury was summoned for Monday, on which day the parties came to an agreement on terms that for the work of each thousand of "Grysovere" 4s be charged, and 5s 6d for "stranglin"[3], "polan"[4], and every other kind of black work (*nigri operis*), 4s 6d for "Roskyn"[5], 12d for a hundred "Coninges"[6] of England, 8d for "Coninges" of

---

[1] The tawyers or white-tawyers were dressers of white leather, who prepared skins for the skinners or pelterers. The present dispute appears to have been between the skinners and the curriers, who dressed tanned leather. See *Lib. Cust.* I, p. 94.

[2] Grisover: grey-work, i.e. the dressing of the grey fur of the squirrel. Cf. *Liber Horn.* fo. cclix *b*: "*Md qe Gris et bis est le dos en yver desqirel & la ventre en yver est menever.*"

[3] Stranglin appears to have been the red fur of the squirrel with the grey hairs of his winter-coat showing through. Cf. *Lib. Horn. ibid.*: "*Strandling est squirel entre feste Seint Michel*"; probably between Michaelmas and Christmas. The derivation of *strandling* is uncertain; possibly from late Latin *stragulum* or *stragulatus*, meaning "varied in colour."

[4] Polan. *Lib. Horn. ibid.*: "*Polane est esquireux neirs,*" i.e. black squirrel.

[5] *Ibid.*: "*Roskyn est desquirel en este*"; the squirrel's red summer coat.

[6] Rabbit.

Spain, and 7d for "scrimpyn" [1]. The defendants agreed that
in case of contravention of this covenant, three men of the
Skinners, and one from the Curriers, elected on either side,
should affix penalties according to the offence.

Chynus de Burgo was attached to answer Silvester de
Morton, weigher of the King's Beam, on a charge of insti-
gating certain unknown persons to assault him, when he took
his beam to the house of Walter de Rokesle in Langburn
Ward to weigh goods. The defendant denied the offence and
said that the plaintiff wanted to set up his beam at a foul
door [*ad hostium putridum apponere*], and a servant of the
house prevented him, but this man was not the defendant's
servant. Afterwards a jury of the venue of St Mary de
Wolenoth found the defendant not guilty, and the plaintiff
was amerced for a false claim.

Tuesday after the above Feast

John le Benere was summoned to answer John le Fraunceys
in a plea of covenant, wherein the latter complained that the
defendant bought from him £8 16s worth of skins, and
promised to give him an acquittance for £8 recovered against
the plaintiff in the Sheriff's Court, and pay him the balance
of 16s, which he now refused to do. The defendant pleaded
that he bought skins to the value of £4 16s, and his wife
on her own account bought skins to the value of 7s, and
that he was always willing to give him an acquittance for
that amount. The plaintiff claimed that this defence was
unjust, because he had good and lawful men, John and
Gilbert, who were present at the sale; and thereupon by his
attorney Terricus de Enefeud he took a corporal oath that
he would not produce any others than these, and would not
suborn them. Afterwards at a Court held on the morrow of
All Souls he appeared with his witnesses, who were sworn
and examined by William de Leyre and Nicholas Picot,
aldermen, and gave evidence in support of his plea. Judg-

[1] Scrimpyn. Riley defines this as a skin of less value than rabbit. *Lib.
Cust.* Gloss.

ment that the defendant fulfil the covenant and be amerced. His amercement was condoned because he was poor.

Geoffrey Beble, chaplain, complained to the Mayor and Aldermen that Antony, rector of the Church of Hurtts[1] in the Archbishopric of Canterbury, who dwelt in his house as a member of his household, had stolen £17 out of his chamber and taken it to the house of Brachius Lumbard of the Society of Puche[2], to be paid out to him by the Society at Paris, and had received a letter addressed to the Society at Paris. The above Brachius was summoned and admitted the receipt of the money, and said that it had not been paid out in London or Paris, but that he did not know whether it had been paid by the Society elsewhere. As the said Antony was not in Court, and as the Society in Paris had written to the other Societies not to pay the money, and as it was not known whether any other Society had already paid, Brachius was forbidden to pay the money until further orders.

6 Oct. 1300   *Thursday the Feast of St Faith*

Hugh de Canterbury was attached to answer John de Hattefeud in a plea of trespass, wherein the latter complained that when he went to Smethefeud to buy a palfrey for Sir John de Ingham, Precentor of St Paul's, the defendant and Stephen de Skelton, his domestic (*manupastus*), and others beat him on the head and wounded him in two places. The defendant pleaded that he was not present on the occasion and had no part in the assault. A jury of Smethefeud was summoned for Wednesday, when the parties came to an agreement on terms that the defendant pay the plaintiff 20s on the morrow. The attachment on the defendant was to remain till he paid, and he put himself in mercy. The amercement was condoned at the instance of Sir John de Cham.

[1] Hurst, co. Kent?

[2] *Archaeologia*, XXVIII, p. 221. E. H. Bond, etc., "La compaignie de Pouche de Florenze," the *Pulci* of Florence. Cf. p. 116. On 20 February 1301, the plaintiff obtained a letter close directed to the Mayor and Sheriffs, ordering them to cause the Society to pay the plaintiff the money which had been stolen from him by Anthony de Burgundia. Cal. Close Rolls, A.D. 1296–1302, p. 431.

Friday the morrow of the Feast of St Edward King[1]

John Witffihe was summoned to answer Isabella sister of
Master John Bushe on a charge of beating her, tearing her
clothes, and striking her on the face with a handful of mud
(*cum taio*) in the parish of St Mildred Poultry. A jury was
summoned, and it was ordered that no skinner should be
included in the panel. Afterwards the parties came to an
agreement on terms that the defendant pay the plaintiff 4s,
and be in mercy.

Friday after the Feast of St Luke the Evangelist [18 Oct.]

Walter de Wetersfeud claimed ten sacks of wool which
were attached on Ralph de Brakele at the suit of William le
Riche, and demanded to be admitted to verify his goods.
John de Ware, William's attorney, was asked whether he had
anything to say against such admission, and said nothing.
Thereupon Walter swore[2] that the above Ralph, on the day
the attachment was made on him, had no wool to the value
of 4d of his own, so that if the wool had been lost, he himselt
would have suffered. Judgment was given that the wool be
delivered to the claimant.

Walter de la Quenhethe was attached to answer Henry
Mable in a plea of trespass wherein the latter complained
that on the previous Saturday he carried wood to the Quay
of Queenhithe and there exposed it for sale, and the defendant attached his boat and wood until he had paid 2s,
against the Liberty of his lord the Abbot of Wautham and
to his own damage. The defendant admitted attaching the
wood because the plaintiff, who was a foreigner, was selling
to a certain....le Clovier, but he denied that he received 2s,
and said that the boat came into his seisin only because of
the wood. A jury of Queenhithe was summoned for Wednesday. The defendant was ordered to take an oath from
Hugh le Fraunceys, Henry de Hanewell and the plaintiff

---

[1] Query: Translation of St Edward, King and Confessor, i.e. 13 Oct.?
[2] From this case it would appear that a garnishee who was a freeman
verified his goods with the "single hand." A foreigner was required to
find two oath-helpers. Cf. pp. 17, 66.

that the wood which was attached in their possession belonged either to the Abbot of Waltham or to themselves, and that they were not carriers [*traventarii*], and the wood would be delivered to them. On Wednesday the plaintiff made default, and he and his pledges were in mercy.

Membr. *2 b*
27 Oct. 1300

Thursday the Vigil of the Apostles Simon and Jude [*28 Oct.*]

The Court of the Weavers[1] in the action of Eustace, cook of the Earl of Lancaster, plaintiff against Walter Payn, Gilbert Payn and Andrew Payn for debt, was granted with the consent of the parties, and a day was given on Saturday.

3 Nov. 1300

Thursday the morrow of All Souls [*2 Nov.*] *before* William de Leyre, *deputy of the Mayor*

Mainprise of William le Bret of Wyntringham and Dyonisia his wife to render the account which John de Norton and Sibilla his wife demand of them, viz. Thomas de Hales, Robert le Moneour, Geoffrey de Talworth and William le Heymonger.

A jury of the venue of Castle Baynard, consisting of Nicholas de Cambridge and others, brought in a verdict that the house and quay formerly belonging to Nicholas le Moneyer were vacant and unlet from the twelfth to the fourteenth years of King Edward, and this not by default of William le Bret and Dyonisia his wife, as John de Norton and Sibilla his wife assert, and that the house and quay were then let until the latter recovered them by an Assize of Novel Disseysin, and that William and Dyonisia spent 15s 11d on the property, as they say. Judgment to be given on Tuesday.

4 Nov. 1300

Friday after the Feast of All Saints [*1 Nov.*]

William le Brasur was summoned to answer Thomas de Bray in a plea of covenant, wherein the latter complained

[1] In the ordinances relating to the Weavers granted this year, it was provided that the Weavers should have a weekly Court for business and pleas, to be held by the Mayor if he wished, and in his absence by four good men of the Mistery, and that a yearly meeting of the Guild should take place in the Minster of St Nicholas Acon. *Lib. Cust.* I, p. 122.

that in August at the defendant's request he became mainpernor with him of a certain John Bunting for half of £10
against Agnes Greyland, and that the defendant promised to
save him harmless, and afterwards refused to do so. The defendant denied asking or promising anything, and demanded
an inquest by the venue of Wollecherchehawe. The plaintiff
demanded an inquest by the venue of Vintry. The two
juries were summoned for Friday.

Saturday after the above Feast

Peter de Coumbe made proof by Edmund de Coumbe,
Elyas de Bristoll, Hugh Baudry, Andrew de Rothewell, John
de Northfolk and Reginald Auberkyn that the 9 sacks of wool
attached at Hardeburg at the suit of Margaret, daughter of
John de St Omer, belonged to him and Stephen de Blakeneye
his partner, and that no one else had to the value of 4d or
more in those sacks. The above Edmund &c. were asked by
the Mayor and Aldermen, on behalf of John de Trillowe,
Rector of the Church of St Dunstan, Thomasyn Gydechon
and John de Northfoulk, executors of John de St Omer,
whether the said John had anything in the sacks at the time
of the attachment. They answered no.

Wednesday before the Feast of St Martin [11 *Nov.*] 9 Nov. 1300
before William de Leyre *and* Geoffrey de Norton,
deputies of the Mayor

John de Rokeslee, Nicholas de Fonte, and Robert de
Blechinglee, were summoned to answer Elyas Russel, who
complained that on Monday at Douegate the defendants
assaulted his men and overturned his cart laden with Flemish
tiles, so that the tiles were broken on the pavement, to his
damage 100s. A jury was summoned for Saturday.

Stephen de Coventre was summoned to answer Richer de
Refham in a plea of trespass, wherein the latter complained
that on Tuesday, when Roysia de Coventre was suing the
plaintiff in the Husting for having occupied her seld in Cheap
against her will, the defendant abused him in Court, calling
him false and perjured and convicted of fraud, in contempt

of the King and his Court. The defendant denied having done so and offered to make his law. Afterwards the parties came to an agreement by permission of the Court.

Membr. 3 *b*
10 *Nov. 1300*

Thursday before the above Feast

William Koc, and Richard Treuchapeman, "fruters," took an oath to make a just scrutiny of cider-vinegar and sour wine, and concerning all of their trade who engage in saltery, and to do right therein.

12 *Nov. 1300*

Saturday after the above Feast

William le Ireys and Alice la Converse his wife were summoned to answer Nicholas Pycot in a plea of eloignment of a deed, wherein the latter complained that he entrusted a bond for 17 marks to Walter de Henlee, attorney at the Court of the Steward and Marshall, and that he came on Wednesday to Cornhulle, where he found the deed in the possession of the defendants, who refused to restore it. The defendants said they received the bond as a pledge from the above Walter for a loan of 6s; they offered to restore it to the plaintiff for 3s, if he would promise to help them to recover the debt from Walter when he came into those parts. The plaintiff agreed and judgment was given accordingly.

Membr. 4
19 *Nov. 1300*

Saturday before the Feast of St Edmund King and Martyr [20 Nov.]

Precept was issued to Henry de Fingrie, one of the Sheriffs, to produce the record of the judgment given in his Court between Ranulph Balle and Isabella his wife, plaintiffs, and Peter de Monte Pessulano and Agnes his wife, defendants, for a debt of £8. The record being produced, no error was found. Judgment that the Sheriff make execution, and that Peter and Agnes, who had complained of error, be in mercy.

The Prior of the New Hospital of the Blessed Mary without Bissopesgate offered himself against John Heyrun in a plea of trespass. The latter to be distrained.

The above Prior was summoned to answer Thomas Godard in a plea of covenant, wherein the latter complained that the Prior's predecessor, Roger, in March 1296 had leased to him for life two shops in Sopereslane at 104s annual rent, and as regards one shop the present Prior refused to fulfil the covenant. The defendant admitted the covenant and said that a certain John Heyron was occupying the shop, so that he could not obtain seisin until &c.

Saturday after the Feast of St Katherine [25 Nov.] A° 29 Edw. [1300] 26 Nov. 1300

John Heyrun, junior, was summoned to answer the above Prior in a plea of trespass, wherein the latter complained that he let to the defendant a shop in Sopereslane from Easter 1298 till the following Easter, and the defendant refused to surrender the shop on expiry of his term. The defendant said the shop was his own free tenement, and that the Prior on the day of his plaint had only a rent issuing from it; and he demanded judgment whether he need answer for his free tenement in this Court. Judgment was respited till Saturday.

Thursday after the Feast of St Andrew [30 Nov.]

Membr. 4 b
1 Dec. 1300

Precept was given to John de Armenters, one of the Sheriffs, to produce the record of the judgment in his Court in an action by writ between Elyas Corbel[1], who claimed 84 marks, and Robert Hardel, defendant, as regards which the above Elyas complained that error had been made. The record being produced, it was found that there was no error in the matter of two acquittances for £35 in the name of Elyas, and one acquittance of £4 10s in the name of Garsyas de Marsolano, servant and attorney of Elyas, or as regards four and a half marks allowed to Robert for gauging. Judgment therein was confirmed. Precept was issued to summon Robert's witnesses, Geoffrey and Walter, for the next Court concerning the sum of 20½ marks. Afterwards it was found

[1] See p. 101.

that there was no error in this particular also. Judgment that Elyas be in mercy.

9 Dec. 1300 *Friday after the Feast of the Conception of the Blessed Mary* [8 Dec.]

Adam de Hallingbiry[1] was summoned to answer Peter de Hungrie in a plea of debt, wherein the latter complained that in Adam's Court he obtained judgment for 100s against William de Kelvedene and John Spendelove, who had wounded him so that his life was despaired of, and that subsequently the defendant and his bailiffs had refused to execute the judgment. The defendant pleaded that he was a layman and asked for the help of his clerks, Richard de Wymburne and Peter the clerk, which was allowed to him at his own risk. Afterwards on 19 Dec. the defendant denied that he attached the above William and John, at the plaintiff's suit, or that he had seisin of their bodies, on account of which he would be responsible for any money, and he demanded to make his law. A day was given him on Monday after the Feast of S[t] Hilary.

Matthew le Chaundeler was summoned to answer William La Postle in a plea of trespass, wherein the latter complained that he hired a house from the said Maykin[2] in Candel-wikstrat &c. The defendant demanded judgment, on the ground that his name was Matthew, and the plaintiff had previously made his allegations against him in that name, and now under the name of Maykin, as to whether he need answer under the latter name. As this was found to be the case, judgment was given that the plaintiff recover nothing and be in mercy, and that the defendant go thence without a day.

John le Benere acknowledged receipt from John le Fraun-ceys, "peleter"[3], of £8 due on a Recognizance made in the Court of Richard le Botoner, Sheriff of London.

---

[1] Sheriff, 1296–7.

[2] This appears to be a case of "miskenning." By the Charter of Henry I it was laid down that there should be no fines exacted for such mistakes or variations in pleading. Nevertheless the plaintiff lost his action here and was fined for an unjust claim.

[3] Skinner.

[Record and process of an action in the Sheriff's Court.]

Court of John Darmenters, *Sheriff of London, on Saturday the morrow of St John the Baptist* [24 *June*] *A° 28 Edw.* [1300]

Robert Hardel[1] was summoned to answer Elyas Corbel in a plea of debt of 84 marks, due on a purchase of wines made at St Botolph's Fair by the defendant and Ernald Barage from the plaintiff and Guy Barlack, for the payment of which a Recognizance was made. The defendant produced acquittances for two sums of £20 and £15, and a letter from Garsyas de Marsolano, servant and attorney of the plaintiff, to whom he had paid £4 10s. He pleaded that he also paid 20½ marks to the plaintiff at the house of John the clerk of Vintry, for which he ought to have received an acquittance, and with regard to which an action was now pending between them. He claimed an allowance of 4½ marks for gauging the wine, as the casks were not of the right size, and demanded judgment as to whether he owed anything further. The plaintiff admitted receipt of the £35, but denied that Garsyas de Marsolano was his attorney. A jury of Vintry was summoned on these points. As regards the gauging, he pleaded that the Recognizance was final and the allowance for gauging, if any, ought to have been made beforehand. On this matter the parties put themselves on the arbitration of wine-merchants, citizens and foreign, viz. Reginald le Barber, William de Beverley, Matthew de Wodeham, Richard Hardel, Henry de St Osith, Alan de Suffolk, William Trent, Gerard Orgoyl, Reymund Margyz, George de Acre, Vitalus Manent and Bartholomew de Rivers, who awarded, according to the Law Merchant hitherto observed among them, that the gauging should be allowed to the defendant. Judgment was given that 4½ marks be allowed for the gauging of 59 sextars of wine which were deficient. Afterwards at a Court held on Tuesday the Vigil of the Apostles Peter and Paul, the plaintiff was adjudged to give an acquittance for the 20½ marks. Meanwhile a jury of Reginald le Barber and others brought in a verdict that the above-mentioned Garsyas de Marsolano

[1] See p. 99.

was the assignee of the plaintiff, and that he gave an acquittance for £4 10s, though they did not know whether at the
time he produced the bond. Judgment was given that the
defendant be quit of the debt, and the plaintiff be in mercy
for a false claim.

[Record and process of an action in the Sheriff's Court.]

Membr. 6
9 June 1300

Court of John de Armenters, *Sheriff of London, on
Thursday after the Feast of the Holy Trinity* [5 *June*]
A° 28 Edw. [1300]

Proceedings in a plea of covenant, wherein Robert Hardel
complained that Elyas Corbel refused to give him an acquittance for a payment of 20½ marks. The defendant pleaded
that the plaintiff had made no mention in his count of any
debt owed to him, but merely of a sum of 20½ marks, and he
demanded judgment whether he need answer such a plaint.
The plaintiff said he made mention in his count of a covenant
broken, and as the defendant was not willing to answer the
plaint according to the "words of Court," he claimed judgment as in an undefended action. At a later Court the
plaintiff was ordered to say to what debt the 20½ marks belonged, and did so, whereupon the defendant was directed
to answer further. The latter then denied that he received
the money or agreed to give an acquittance. To this the
plaintiff replied that he had witnesses, Geoffrey and William,
who were present, and he demanded that they be examined.
After an adjournment owing to lack of Aldermen, the above
witnesses were examined separately in the presence of William
de Betoyne and Thomas Romayn, aldermen, and agreed in
support of the plaintiff's pleading. Judgment was given that
the plaintiff receive an acquittance, and that the defendant
receive the money from John the clerk, Coroner, to whom
he had entrusted it, and be in mercy.

Membr. 7
10 Dec. 1300

Court of Elyas Russel, *Mayor, on Saturday after the
Feast of the Conception B.M.* [8 *Dec.*]

Thomas le Keu, Henry atte Mersshe, Thomas Crudde,
Walter de Brompleye, Symon de Hereford, Robert le

Gurdelere, Richard de Rocheford, and Thomas le Fox, Master Cornmeters at Queenhithe, and Thomas le Ram, John Sket, Nicholas le Couk, William le Fiz Saundre, Walter de Paris, Henry atte Mershe, Robert le Clerk, Robert Mikelman, Walter le Milneward, John le Smyth, Symon de Sabrichteworth, Richard Scheyl, Geoffrey Hodle, William de Tolyngdone, Richard le Brewere, William de Heytfeld, Robert Gous, Roger Crisp, Symon de Laitone, Geoffrey le Keu, William de Herppinge, David Caperiche and Walter Nekkeles, servants of the above Masters, were attached to answer Roger le Palmere and his friends, corndealers, in a plea of trespass, wherein the corndealers complained that, whereas according to ancient custom in London and the Suburbs, the bakers and brewers should pay for the metage, carriage and porterage to their houses of all corn bought at Queenhithe as follows:—from Queenhithe through all streets and alleys to Westchep, the Church of St Anthony, Horshobrigg and Wolsiesgate in the Ropery, $\frac{3}{4}$d; beyond to Flete Bridge, Neugate, Crepelgate, to the opposite side of Berchenereslane on Cornhulle, Estchep and Billingesgate, 1d; and from Queenhithe as far as the Barres of the Suburbs, 1$\frac{1}{4}$d— the Masters did not faithfully measure the corn according to their oath, or treat the people as of old, and the servants charged more than they did formerly for carriage and porterage against their oath. The defendants denied that they were guilty and put themselves on their country.

Monday after the Feast of St Nicholas [6 Dec.]   *12 Dec. 1300*

A jury of John de Stratford and others[1] brought in a verdict that the Master Cornmeters were not guilty, and they were acquitted. They said further that for the meting, carriage and porterage of corn no more ought to be taken for the quarter than as mentioned above, and that the servants demanded and took more, especially for carrying to the Ryole. Their offence was condoned, but they were warned not to repeat it under penalty of abjuring their craft.

[1] The verdict of the jury is set out at length in *Lib. Alb.* I, pp. 241–4.

14 *Dec. 1300*   *Wednesday after the Feast of St Lucia* [13 *Dec.*]

Alan le Pestur was summoned to answer Peter de Durdrich in a plea of debt of £14 due on a sale of handmills, value £18 as they lay in a heap, at 29s the last, with the condition that if there were more or less lasts than computed, the buyer should pay more or less, whereof the defendant had paid £4 and refused to pay the balance. The defendant admitted the purchase, but said it was agreed that the money should be paid if the handmills were satisfactory, which they were not. A jury of Billingesgate was summoned against the next Court.

Membr. 7 b   *Friday after the above Feast*
16 *Dec. 1300*

Ralph Hardel was summoned to answer Henry le Galeys, who complained that the defendant took away the gutter between their houses which had received the water from the plaintiff's roof for 20 years and more. A jury from Vintry was summoned for Monday.

19 *Dec. 1300*   *Monday before the Feast of St Thomas the Apostle* [21 *Dec.*]

John Heyron, junior, was attached to answer Peter Adrian in a plea that he render account for the time when he was the plaintiff's receiver and traded for their common profit, from Michaelmas 1296 to Michaelmas 1300, during which time he received £66 from the plaintiff. The defendant pleaded that he received £12 10s wherewith to trade abroad, solely to the profit and at the risk of the plaintiff, and these goods, together with his own, were lost at sea. He demanded judgment as to whether he was responsible, and offered to make his law that he received nothing further than the above sum. The plaintiff claimed that he ought not to be admitted to his law as this was a plea of account[1], which he wished to be settled by the judgment of the Court or by a jury, and a law was not a just method in that plea, and he demanded judgment as in an undefended action. Afterwards at a Court held on 27 Jan. the parties appeared, and the defendant

---

[1] Cf. p. 132; *Lib. Alb.* i, p. 215.

pleaded that the cognizance of the action belonged to the Husting[1] and not to that Court. A day was given for the next Husting of Common Pleas.

Tuesday after the Feast of S[t] Hilary [13 *Jan.*] *A[o]* 29 *Edw.* [1300–1]

Alan le Pestur and Peter de Durdrich came to an agreement out of Court. Both were amerced.

Coppe Cotenne appointed Ralph de Algate, clerk, his attorney to receive £47 15s due to his partner Stoldus[2] from the Sheriff of London for the ferm and issues of the bailiwick of London and the county of Middlesex, as appears more fully among the names of *Arogañ* contained in a certain Dividend of the King's Wardrobe.

Thursday after the Feast of the Conversion of St Paul [25 *Jan.*]

William le Mariner was summoned to answer Tedmar̃c, merchant of Almaine, in a plea of debt of 100s for merchandise sold to a certain Simon, servant and attorney of the defendant, for the use of the defendant. The latter denied that Simon was his servant on the date mentioned, or that he received the profit of the goods, and offered to wage his law. He came with his law on the morrow. The plaintiff condoned it, and put himself in mercy.

[1] Pleas of Account were heard in the Husting of Common Pleas on writs of *Monstravit* and *Justicies*. *Monstravit* was a Common Law action necessitating a jury. The *Justicies de computo* apparently admitted of a "law," while the *Justicies inter mercatores* was terminated according to the Law Merchant. Probably the present action was by the last-named writ, and would naturally belong to the Husting, since actions of account in the Mayor's Court were begun by plaint alone. By A.D. 1337 the old writ-action was obsolete in the Husting, and actions of account were heard by plaint in the Mayor's and Sheriff's Courts. Cf. *Lib. Alb.* I, pp. 184–9.

[2] Stoldus, who was presumably the same as Taldo Janiani [Cal. of Letter Book B, p. 94, and 94 n.; Cal. Close Rolls, 1296–1302, pp. 87, 271], and Coppus Cotenne were among the principal agents of the Frescobaldi. Apparently they had advanced money to the Wardrobe and had received an assignment on the Sheriff of London for the amount of the debt, which would be deducted from the farm paid by the City. The "dividend" was probably an indenture containing the names of creditors. The precise meaning of "*Arogañ*" is not clear. Neither of these persons, as far as is known, were Arragonese.

Friday after the above Feast.

A jury of Roger de Evere and others found Thomas Abraham, ironmonger, guilty of going to Southwark to meet merchants and smiths coming from the dales (*de Wallibus*[1]) to London with horsehoes, nails and other merchandise belonging to the trade of ironmongers, and of forestalling those goods, and also of avowing foreigners' goods. Judgment respited till the next Husting.

Saturday after the Purification B.M. [2 Feb.]

Geoffrey de Canefeud and Roger de Wandlesworth, weavers, were attached to answer Henry le Juven, "burler"[2], in a plea of trespass, wherein the latter complained that he delivered two cloths to the defendants to repair and weave the same between the Epiphany [6 Jan.] and the Purification [2 Feb.], and although there was an ordinance that men of that craft should work during that time, as at other times of the year, they refused to do so. The defendants denied that they ceased work maliciously and put themselves on their country. Segin the Weaver, Richard Salman, John Broud and Robert Moriz, weavers, who were likewise sued by Richard de Wrotham, William de Uggele, burler, Robert de Freston and Walter de Hallingbiry, respectively, also put themselves on their country.

Recognizance by Thomas de Brumleye of London to Walter de Hakeneye and Adam Simond, citizens, of a debt of £100 due at Michaelmas 1299.

Walter de Hackeneye produced the above Recognizance before the Mayor. Luke de Haveringe, one of the Sheriffs, through William de Londenston, his clerk, was ordered to attach the debtor, and returned that he could not be found in his bailiwick. Richard de Caumpes, his fellow-Sheriff, was then ordered to hold an inquest as to the lands and tenements of the debtor on the day of the Recognizance and return the

---

[1] *Sc. Vallibus.* This would appear to be the meaning. But in Cal. of Letter Book C, p. 88, there is mention of smiths of the Wealds (*de Waldis*) in connection with the ironmongers of the City.
[2] A middleman in the cloth trade. Cf. pp. 54 n., 107.

finding under the seals of the jurors, which was done as
follows:—the jurors, Nicholas de Cantebrig, Laurence Smith,
Geoffrey Scot, William Smith, Stephen Bernard, John
Fairhod, Henry de Somersete, John de Stratteford, William
de Heston, William Brett, goldsmith, Peter de Boligton and
Elyas Everard returned that the debtor had in fee and
inheritance in the City of London at the date of the Recognizance:—one house in Distavelane of an annual value
40s; two shops with a solar 36s, one house with two shops
33s 4d, and two other shops in Old Fish Street 28s; total
annual value, when they were let, £10 14s 4d, charged with
40s rent to the lords of the fees and 5 marks for the keep of
a chaplain, leaving a nett annual value of 107s 8d. The
documents having been examined, the Sheriff was directed
to give seisin to the creditor as a free tenement till his claim
was satisfied, which delivery of seisin was performed by
Richard de Crofton, the Sheriff's clerk. Afterwards at a Court
held on Saturday after the Octave of Easter, Walter de
Hackeneye was summoned to show cause why the execution
of the Recognizance should not take place.

Wednesday after the Purification B.M. [2 Feb.]

8 Feb.
1300-1

Henry le Juven, "burler," and the other burellers offered
themselves against Richard Salamon and the other weavers.
A jury of Matthew le Chaundeler and others said by their
faith to the King that the weavers ceased work by their own
malice and fraud to the damage of the burellers, 18s 11d, in
the following amounts:—Henry le Juven, 5s 6d; Richard de
Wrotham, 6s 3d; William de Uggele, 2s 6d; Robert de
Freston, 2s; Walter de Hallingbiry, 2s 8d. Judgment for
those damages.

Saturday before the Feast of S^t "Walentine" [14 Feb.]

11 Feb.
1300-1

John le Fraunceys, peleter, acknowledged himself bound
to Richard Sprot in 21s payable at Easter. The money was
stopped in John's hands, in order that it might be paid into
the Chamber, since the said Richard owed them that amount
for his freedom.

Thursday after Ash Wednesday [15 *Feb.*]

Nine silver spoons, weighing 8s 6d, and one mantle of "Bluett"[1] furred with "bisses"[2], attached from Robert de Rokesle in lieu of 20s, which was his portion towards raising the sum of £1048 due to the King for divers debts of the City, were delivered to the Chamberlain of the Guildhall, Nicholas Picot, and valued at 4s for the mantle and 8s for the spoons by the oath of good and lawful men. Paul le Botiller made the delivery to the Sheriff.

Pleas before Elyas Russel, *Mayor, on Tuesday after the Feast of the Apostles Peter and Paul*[3] [29 *June*] *A° 29 Edw.* [1301]

Michael de Wynborn[4], executor of the will of Henry de Wynton, knight, deceased, was summoned to answer John de Ely in a plea that whereas the plaintiff was bound to the above Henry in a statute of £9, and having failed to pay was committed to prison in the shrievalty of Thomas Romeyn and William de Leyre, A° 19 Edw., being subsequently liberated in accordance with an agreement made between them, nevertheless the defendant had caused him to be committed to prison again for the same debt. The defendant pleaded that he had been appointed executor and administrator by the Official of the Archdeacon of London, in place of Edmund Pask, and having found the Recognizance among the papers of the deceased, he had sued the plaintiff on it, and as the latter had not produced any acquittance he demanded judgment. The plaintiff then said that the above Henry had entered into possession of tenements belonging to the plaintiff, and he produced the agreement above mentioned. By this deed Henry de Wyncestre (*sic*), knight, had consented that if the money was paid by Christmas 1291, the Recognizance should be cancelled and certain houses pledged to him should be returned, but if not, the houses should remain his property. The agreement (French) was dated at London, 24 Aug. 1291, and witnessed by Sir Rauf de Sandwich, then Warden of

---

[1] Blue cloth.   [2] See p. 92, note 2.
[3] Query: Tuesday after F. of St Peter in Cathedra, i.e. 28 Feb.?
[4] For earlier proceedings in this dispute see p. 77.

London, Thomas Romeyn and Willyem de Leyre, Sheriffs, Willyem de Bettoyn, alderman, Richard de Hakene and Aleyn le Chandeler. The plaintiff pleaded that by this agreement the Recognizance lost its effect, and he demanded judgment as to whether he could be imprisoned or troubled further about the debt. The defendant said that, as the Recognizance remained uncancelled with the above Henry, and the plaintiff had not produced any acquittance, he demanded judgment on that ground (*precise*). The Court gave judgment that the plaintiff be quit of the Recognizance, and that the defendant be amerced.

Friday after the Feast of St Mathias the Apostle [24 Feb.] A° 29 Edw. [1300–1]

Membr. 10
3 March
1300–1

Peter de Leycestre, plaintiff in a plea of debt, offered himself against James de Brabazuns and Castellus his partner, merchants of the Society of Bonseingyurs[1], who had this day by their essoin and did not come. Order was given to distrain them.

On Monday before the Feast of St Gregory Pope [12 March] Edmund the tailor, Martin de Dullingham, Robert le Blund and Roger le Rous complained to the Mayor and Aldermen that Roger de Waltham had threatened them in life and limb, which threats they proved by William de Caxtone and Ralph de Thakstede. The Sheriff was ordered to take the body of the above Roger into his custody till he should find security for keeping the peace.

6 March
1300–1

Monday before the Feast of the Annunciation B.M. [25 March]

20 March
1300–1

An inquest to discover what malefactors and disturbers of the peace had beaten, wounded and ill-treated the men of Sir J. de Brytannia[2], was taken before Geoffrey de Norton,

---

[1] Cf. p. 124, where the Society is called "*de la gruntable*" of Sienna. Cf. Cal. Close Rolls, A.D. 1296–1302, p. 303, "Society of the Bonzcini," pp. 314, 589, "Society of the sons of Bonseignor of Siena."

[2] John de Dreux, son of the Duke of Brittany and of Beatrix, daughter of Henry III. In 1306, on the death of the Duke, he received a grant of the Earldom of Richmond held by his father. Cf. Roll G, membr. 12. Chron. Edw. I and Edw. II, I, p. 257 *et passim*.

deputy of the Mayor, by the oath of William Passemer, Hugh
le Armurer, Reginald le Feyver, Roger le Coteler, William
le Barber, John Garlaund, Stephen le Corriour, Reginald
Germin, Roger de Paris, Adam de Whiteby, John Sterre,
William le Spicer and Adam le Couper, who said that on
Thursday last about midnight two men, Credo and Falwey,
went with other unknown persons to a brothel close to the
house of Nicholas le Lockyer in Fletestrate, and there among
themselves raised the hue and cry, whereupon a certain
Adam le Coteler came to the door of the brothel and on
behalf of the King ordered Credo and Falwey and the others
to do no harm to anyone. The latter came out and with drawn
swords pursued Adam to his house, and broke the door of
his hall and entered. Adam resisted them and then took
refuge in his solar, closing the door on himself, but Credo
and the others broke down that door also. Seeing that he
was likely to be killed, Adam climbed out of the window and
so escaped. When the others found that he was gone, they
returned to Adam's chamber and pursued his servants, and
wounded and ill-treated them in the curtilage of a neighbour's
house. The jurors further said that Credo and the others had
received no harm from Adam or his servants or neighbours
so far as they could discover, but the same day they were
embroiled with the Bishop of Durham's men outside the Bar
of the Temple, and if they came by any harm they received
it there.

22 March
1300–1

Wednesday before the above Feast

The record and process of an action in the Sheriff's Court[1]
between Peter de Munkuc and Geoffrey Segyn was examined
on the complaint of Peter, and was confirmed. Judgment
was given that Geoffrey recover the £10 awarded to him in
the Sheriff's Court.

Membr. 10 b
23 March
1300–1

Thursday before the above Feast

Simon le Coteler and Katherine his wife were summoned
to answer William Jordan and John le Benere, Wardens of

[1] See p. 117.

London Bridge, in a plea of trespass wherein the latter complained that the defendants had been found guilty, by a jury, on a charge of abetting their sons John and William in ill-treating the neighbours, and had come before the Mayor's deputies on 5 Aug. last year, and had promised not to harbour or maintain their sons in future under penalty of forfeiting to the Bridge their house on the Bridge, and that nevertheless they had received and maintained their sons in assaulting the neighbours, and in threatening them that they would light such a fire that it would be seen by all the dwellers in London—to the grave damage and terror of these neighbours. The defendants pleaded not guilty. A jury was summoned for the next Court after Hokeday[1].

Saturday after the Octave of Easter [2 *April*] *A° 29* *15 April 1301* *Edw.* [1301]

Dignus Reyneri, Lombard, and Thomas Gydechoun[2] of Lucca came and acknowledged that they had received from Sir Eymer de Valence one silver cup with a gold foot and covercle weighing 12 marks, one silver basin weighing 4 marks, and four gold rings set with sapphires and one with topaz, which were to be returned to Sir Eymer on Saturday before Pentecost. Cancelled because Sir Eymer acknowledged receipt.

Thursday before the Feast of St George [23 *April*]   *20 April 1301*

An inquest came by William le Chaundeler and others in a panel, and said on their oath that William and Roger le Mirurers had prosecuted Cristine la Milnward in the Court Christian after the prohibition of the Mayor and bailiffs. Judgment that they be committed to prison until &c.

---

[1] Cf. Cal. of Letter Book C, p. 76, where further proceedings are given.
[2] Probably a partner of Ricardo Guidiccioni, who belonged to the Society of the Ricardi of Lucca. Cf. Cal. Close Rolls, 1302–1307, p. 357. Dignus or Dynus Reyneri of Lucca is several times mentioned in the Close Rolls as a creditor in Recognizances.

2 May 1301   *Tuesday before the Feast of the Invention of the Holy Cross* [3 *May*]

A jury of the venue of Ismongerlane was summoned to say on oath whether Gilbert de Sewar broke into a cupboard filled with the goods of John de Bittrele, the keys of which were under the King's sequestration, and whether John Stangne and Bartholomew le Chalaundrer, executors of the will of John de Bitterle (*sic*), carried away goods to the value of £100 as alleged by John de Combes, who prosecuted for the King. The defendants were mainprised by Thomas de Chykewell, "lorriner," John de Gay, John Michel, William Alisaundre, Henry de Gildeford, clerk, and Roger de Leycestre. They were found not guilty.

Membr. 11   *Friday after the above Feast*
5 May 1301

Robert de Uptone entered into a Recognizance to pay a debt of 20s to Katherine la Frаunceyse of the Ryole on the Quinzime. The said Katherine gave the money for the making of the Conduit.

10 May 1301   *Wednesday before the Ascension* [11 *May*]

James de Berners was attached to answer Richard de Gloucestre on a charge that he met the latter's servant William riding on his corn in St Christopher's Street, and had upset him and the corn by the door of St Christopher's Church, beating him and pursuing him to the plaintiff's house, where he assaulted another servant Walter de Whyteney, to the plaintiff's damage by lack of his men's services, £100. The defendant's attorney denied the trespass. Subsequently, 2 June, the plaintiff made default and the defendant was acquitted.

18 May 1301   *Thursday before the Feast of St Dunstan* [19 *May*]

Thomas Romayn and Simon Godard swore that the goods and chattels attached on William de Hebuthon for payment of £6 18s, which the latter owed to "John the Gote" and his partners on a Recognizance made in the Guildhall at Easter, were their own property, and that William had no interest in them at the time of the attachment.

Robert de Roquesle was summoned to answer Roger le Ferun in a plea of detinue of a horse, wherein he complained that the defendant came to his house in the parish of St Michael, Cornhill, and took away his bay horse, value 10 marks, to his damage 100s. A day was given to the defendant to make his law on the Quinzime. *Membr. 11 b*

Friday before the Feast of St Barnabas [11 June]
9 June 1301

Henry de Bustre was attached at the suit of William de Donecastre, as being a burgess of the Duchy of Brabant, on the ground that the Duke was indebted to the plaintiff in divers sums of money, as appears by the King's writ remaining with the Sheriff. A jury of Robert Hardel and others brought in a verdict that the defendant was not a burgess of the Duke, and had no goods and chattels in the Duchy. He was acquitted.

Godfrey de Alemain was acquitted of the like charge.

Monday after the Feast of St Botulph [17 June]
19 June 1301

Thomas de Donecastre[1] was attached to answer Ralph Pekoc, who sued for the City, in a plea of trespass, wherein the latter complained that he had made an inspection of the Common Moor outside Bishopsgate with his servants William Pointel, Richard de Hattefeld, Roger Sueting and Thomas Bruming in a boat belonging to William Pointel, and had found part of the meadow cut and the grass carried away. On

---

[1] The Bishop of Bethlehem, a bishop *in partibus*, owned a portion of the Moorfields, the remainder being common land belonging to the City. On 12 September 1298 (Letter Book B, fo. 34), the City let to William Pointel the reeds growing on the moor, on condition that he did not meddle with the grass or water. The bishop's attorney, Canon Thomas de Donecastre, otherwise known as Brother Thomas de Bedleem, had carried away the grass from the City's meadow, and was now sued by Ralph Pekoc, the City's Prosecutor, for so doing. Moorfields at this time consisted of swamp and water-meadow, with channels deep enough for boats. See article in *Archaeologia*, vol. LXXI, by Mr Frank Lambert, M.A., F.S.A., on "Some Recent Excavations in London."

tracing the grass to the close of the defendant, they had questioned him on this trespass done to the City, whereupon with his servants Ralph, Alexander, Robert le Gardiner and Roger le Messager, the defendant had assaulted him and taken the boat away. The defendant denied the trespass and declared that the boat was his own property, and put himself on his country. Afterwards on Monday after the Nativity of S[t] John the Baptist [24 June] he came and restored the boat and submitted to the judgment of the Court. He was committed to prison until &c.

Membr. 12
20 June 1301

Tuesday after the above Feast

William de Dalby, attorney of Peter de Leycestre, acknowledged receipt of 300 marks sterling from James le Brabazun of Scene and his partners[1]. The latter went quit.

A jury of the venue of S[t] Lawrence Lane in Jewry was summoned against the next Court to say on oath whether Walter de S[t] Omer unbound a certain bundle of mercery from foreign parts, in the house of John le Botoner, junior, and sold the goods against the prohibition of Richard de Caumpes, Sheriff, without paying toll, as the Sheriff avers, or whether the said John le Botoner paid a fine of 12d for customs for the bundle, saving to the Sheriff the customs on saffron and silk, if any were found in the bundle, whereas none were found, as the defendants say. Afterwards the parties came to an agreement by permission of the Court, and the penalty was condoned.

27 June 1301

Tuesday after the Feast of S[t] John the Baptist [24 June]

Roger le Ferun offered himself against Robert de Roquesle in a plea of debt, the latter having a day on Monday to make his law, which he had waged against the plaintiff concerning the detinue of a horse, value 10 marks. And as he did not come, he was ordered to appear on this day to hear judgment, when he again made default. Judgment was given for the plaintiff for 10 marks, and that the defendant be amerced.

[1] See p. 109.

Thursday before the Translation of St Thomas [7 July]   6 July 1301

Alexander de Scaylesworth of Northampton was attached by 10 casks of wine, because the Bailiffs of Northampton had arrested the goods and chattels, value 20s, of Richard Poterel, junior, of London, as a forfeit, which goods Richard had bought in Northampton market. The defendant found pledges, Walter de la Legh and Walter le Fuller, to restore Richard's goods within eight days, and to satisfy the City for the contempt and trespass. Afterwards he came and satisfied the plaintiff[1].

Tuesday before the Feast of St Margaret Virgin [20 July]   Membr. 12 b
                                                              18 July 1301

Walter Bullok, taverner, acknowledged that he owed to Peter de Paris, Spicer of our Lady the Queen, 20s payable on the Quinzime.

An inquest was taken before Elyas Russel, Mayor of London, on the above day by John de Cheswyk and other jurors of Langborne Ward, Candelwykstrate and Cornhull, as appears on the panel, with regard to the malefactors and disturbers of the King's peace &c. They said on oath that when Philip de Spine and his companions of the Society of Spine[2] on Saturday at the hour of vespers were sitting at supper in their lodging (*hospitium*), talking together about the war between the Kings of France and England, magnifying and praising the King of France and his baronage, and vituperating and despising the King of England, and calling him a wretched and captive King who had lost so much, vilely and miserably, in the war—on account of this abuse and contempt continually repeated against the King of England

---

[1] The City's right to take *Withernam* from the citizens or burgesses of other cities or boroughs, as a reprisal for toll taken from London citizens, was granted by the Charter of Henry I, and afterwards many times confirmed. It was a very general method of redress at this time. Mary Bateson, *Borough Customs*, I, pp. 119–25.

[2] The Society of the Merchants of Spina were a Florentine trading company. Philip de Spine was probably the same person as Philip Gerardini of that Society. Cf. Cal. Close Rolls, A.D. 1302–7, p. 5. He was alleged in A.D. 1302 to have procured the death of William Baman at the hands of Thouse le Lumbard. Cal. Close Rolls, A.D. 1296–1302, p. 546.

by Philip and his companions, a certain John le Lung, their
servant, an Englishman, began to murmur and contradict
them. Thereupon the said Philip, moved by anger, struck
him with his fist, and when the servant fled from their further
malice and harm, they pursued him with drawn swords and
misericords as far as St Edmund's Church, and would have
slain him in the church, if the neighbours had not arrived
on hearing his shouts, and questioned Philip and his companions as to why they made so great an uproar, terrifying
the neighbours and the whole neighbourhood. Philip and the
others, in reply, cursed them and called them "English-
oundes," and turning back home, threw down stones outside
their house and made a stronghold against the bailiffs of the
City, until the Mayor arrived. The jurors also said that Philip
and his companions of the above Society, Pouch Lumbard
and the members of his Society[1], John of the Society of the
Friscobaldi[2], Theobald Courter, Cose Lumbard[3] with his two
sons and his Society, Bonaventure and Bynde, dwelling at the
house of James de Cene on Cornhull, Rogaz, servant of
Burgensis Fulbard of Florence, and Simonetus de Sercle of
the Society "Sercle noyr"[4], were accustomed to raise up-
roars in the City of London by night and day to the terror
of the whole neighbourhood and the disturbance of the
King's peace, by abusing and afterwards beating, ill-treating,
wounding and maiming anyone who withstood them or re-
proved them for their evil words and deeds. The jurors said
further that the above Philip and all the others of the various
Societies were accustomed to drag the wives, daughters and
servants of good men of the City, and other girls passing by,

[1] Cf. p. 94: "The Society of Puche"; *Archaeologia*, xxviii, p. 243,
"The Pulci of Florence"; *ibid.* p. 283, "*Societas Pulicum.*" Cf. Cal. Close
Rolls, A.D. 1296–1302, p. 431; A.D. 1302–7, p. 87.

[2] *Arch.* xxviii, p. 221, "La Compaignie de sire Jon de Friscobald de
Florence." The Friscobaldi are frequently mentioned in the Close Rolls
as financial agents of Edward I.

[3] Possibly the same person as Francis Cose, a merchant of the Society
of the Bardi of Florence. Cf. Cal. Close Rolls, A.D. 1296–1302, p. 354.

[4] *Archaeologia*, xxviii, p. 221, "La compaignie du Cercle Neyr de
Florenze." Note: "The terms black and white have reference to the
two parties distinguished as 'Bianchi' and 'Neri,' which at this period
filled the cities of Pistoia, Florence and Lucca with tumult and bloodshed." *Ibid.* p. 241, "*Circuli Neri.*" Cf. Calendar of Close Rolls, *passim*.

into their lodgings and to violate them against their will, and if the women had any men in their company, they would detain the latter in their yard and beat them, until they had accomplished their purpose on the women thus violently dragged into their lodgings; and all this against the peace and to the damage and scandal of many women, and in contempt of the English.

[Record and Process of an action in the Sheriff's Court, Membr. 13 endorsed "*Recordum istud affirmatur*"[1].]

Court of Henry de Fingrie, *Sheriff of London, on* 17 June 1300 *Friday before the Feast of the Nativity of St John the Baptist* [24 *June*] *A° 28 Edw.* [1300]

Peter de Moncuk was attached to answer Geoffrey Sigyn in a plea of debt, wherein the latter complained that the defendant, on the eve of St Michael last, promised to pay him £20 on behalf of Gaillard de Gassak, being empowered by the latter to receive that sum in payment of a debt incurred by the King, and though the defendant received £10, he had not paid the plaintiff anything. The defendant defended the words of Court, and while admitting that he had received £10 of the King's debt, denied the promise to pay the plaintiff, and offered to make his law on this point. The plaintiff said that he defended unjustly, since he had witnesses Vitalus and John, who were present when the promise was made, and whom he asked leave to produce on the spot[2], as both parties were foreigners. Their examination was postponed for lack of aldermen till the next Court. The defendant then objected to John on the ground that as plaintiff in the Court of John Darmenters in a similar case concerning a debt of Gaillard, in which the present defendant was defendant, John had called Geoffrey Sigyn as witness, and it would be a hardship and against law that two plaintiffs should thus call each other alternately to witness. To this the plaintiff replied that John

---

[1] See p. 110.

[2] Foreigners were required to produce their witnesses "*incontinenti*," in order that passing litigants should not be inconvenienced by delays (*Lib. Alb.* I, p. 295). In the next case a citizen is granted fifteen days to bring his witnesses.

was a fit witness, because he had never suffered judgment for perjury or been excommunicated or put in the pillory, and therefore he claimed judgment. After several respites the Court gave judgment on 9 Sept. for the plaintiff for £10, on the ground that the witness could not be rejected in this case, and that the "exception" raised by the defendant was inadmissible.

Membr. 14 [Record and Process of an Action in the Sheriff's Court, endorsed "*judicium istud affirmatur.*"]

6 *July 1300* *Court of* Henry de Fingrie, *Sheriff of London, on Wednesday before the Feast of the Translation of S*ᵗ *Thomas the Martyr* [7 *July*] *A*° *28 Edw.* [1300]

Peter de Monte Pessulano and Agnes his wife were summoned to answer Ranulph Balle and Isabella his wife in a plea of debt, wherein the latter complained that Agnes bought from Isabella 20 quarters of barley at 7s 4d the quarter and 4 quarters of oats at 3s 4d the quarter, amounting to £8 silver, which she had not paid. The defendants denied the sale and receipt, whereupon the plaintiffs offered to produce witnesses, Robert and Roger. A day till the Quinzime was given them to do so. The witnesses, being sworn and examined in the presence of Salamon le Cotiller and Simon de Paris, aldermen, gave evidence that Peter and Agnes received the grain from Isabella in their house on Cornhull between prime and nones, they themselves and other persons unknown being present. A day was given for hearing judgment, and as the defendants made default and produced no warrant for their essoin "*de servicio regis,*" judgment was given for the plaintiffs.

ROLL E

Court of John le Blund, *Mayor of London, Monday the Feast of St Edmund King at the end of the 29th year of King Edward* [1301]

Colard de Wateresseye, Peter de St Trond, Simon Gaste, John Ascelyn, Henry Stable, and Andrew Gerste of the same, John Echelkerke of Thorpmond in Almaine, William de Herkestowe of Lincoln and Mabia (*sic*) Rouland were attached to answer William de Donecastre in a plea that whereas John, Duke of Brabant, was indebted to the plaintiff in £400 by a letter in which he bound himself and all his subjects and merchants for the payment of that sum, and had not paid it— the defendants by a conspiracy with the merchants of Brabant had avowed as their own property certain sacks, sarplars and pockets of wool, which had been attached as the property of Brabantine merchants, thus defrauding the plaintiff to the value of £100. The defendants pleaded severally; Colard that he was of Dinant and a subject of the Bishop of Liege; Peter, Simon, Andrew, Henry and John that they were of St Trond and subjects of the same Bishop, John Echelkerke that he was of Thorpmond in Germany, William de Herkestowe that he was a subject of the King of England, and Mabel that she was a subject of the King and a freewoman of the City of London; and all declared that the goods were their own, and put themselves on the verdict of merchants, native and foreign, travellers and sailors (*passaiores et nautas*). Afterwards the defendants were allowed to find mainprise to answer for the goods and produce them on the Quinzime of St Hilary, unless meanwhile they could prove by sealed letters from their several towns that they were not subjects of the Duke of Brabant, and that the aforesaid goods were their own.

Friday before the Feast of St Katherine [25 *Nov.*]

Recognizance of John de Red, "sauser"[1], and Alexander le Coffrer to Luke de Haveryng in 10 marks sterling payable at Easter.

---

[1] Sauser: salter.

Robert le Gardiner, of co. Lincoln, plaintiff in a plea of trespass, and Stephen de Upton, defendant, came to an agreement on the following terms, viz. that whereas the defendant had entered into a bond of 40s with regard to the trespass, that sum should be condoned for one mark, half of which should be paid at once, and the other half put in respite until it was apparent how Stephen intended to behave towards the plaintiff. The former was in mercy for the trespass, which was pardoned by the Mayor.

Membr. 1 b
13 Dec. 1301

Wednesday the Feast of St Lucia Virgin

Judgment in the action between Stephen de Larder and Thomas Abraham and Richard de Caumpes, Sheriff, was respited for a week through default of Walter de Finchingfeud[1], one of the examiners.

Thomas, son of Thomas de Oxford, offered himself against Thomas de Suffolk, William de Red and Henry de Bondon. The said Thomas and William pleaded that they were not bound to answer without Henry, who was their co-executor of the will of Thomas de Oxford and was absent. Order was given to distrain him. The executors were directed to bring into court the other children of the testator, Adam, Cecily and Joan.

20 Dec. 1301

Adam, beadle of Alegate Ward, reported to the Mayor and Aldermen on 20 Dec., that on the hue and cry being raised in the Ward the preceding night, he found a certain Robert, son of Robert de Lasshingdon of Gloucester, breaking a window and carrying away a bundle of cloth, as the neighbours testified, and took him to the Tun. The prisoner came before the Mayor the same day, and as he did not appear to be of good fame and could find no pledges, he was delivered to the Sheriffs to be committed to Neuwegate until &c.

12 Jan.
1301-2

Friday after the Feast of the Epiphany [6 Jan.] A^o 30 Edw. [1301-2]

A jury of Candelwykstrete opposite St Martin's Lane was summoned for Wednesday to say whether Gilbert Payn slandered the Mayor.

---

[1] Examinations of witnesses in the Sheriff's Court required the presence of two Aldermen at least.

[Record and process of an action in the Sheriff's Court, Membr. 2 with "*stet Recordum*" at foot.]

Court of Luke de Havering, *Sheriff of London,* *13 Dec. 1300* *Tuesday after the Feast of the Conception B.M.* [8 *Dec.*] *A° 29 Edw.* [1300]

Robert de Frowyk was summoned to answer Henry de Dunlee in a plea of covenant, wherein the latter complained that the defendant covenanted to buy from him 2 casks of wine for 9 marks, and 20 quarters of oats for £4, and to enter into a statute of the staple of Westminster for the payment, and that the defendant had done neither. The defendant denied the covenant and offered to make his law. He subsequently made a default, but again demanded to be allowed to make his law on the ground that he had waged his law and had afterwards essoined, whereby his default was purged. The plaintiff pleaded that the essoin was not admissible, and the Court, accepting this pleading, gave judgment for the plaintiff, on the ground that after the defendant's default he had been summoned to hear judgment, and though he had afterwards essoined, his essoin ought not to prejudice the plaintiff[1].

Court of John le Blund, *Mayor, Saturday after the* Membr. 3 *Feast of the Purification* [2 *Feb.*] *A° 30 Edw.* [1301–2] 3 *Feb.* *1301–2*

William Simond offered himself against Adam de Fulham, junior, in a plea of debt. The latter had requested the aid of clerks, and had essoined "*de communi*" and "*de servicio regis,*" and now did not come. He was summoned to hear judgment at the next Court.

Wednesday the Feast of St Valentine [14 *Feb.*] *14 Feb.* *1301–2*

Richard le Barber was summoned to answer Robert de Fyngrie in a plea of trespass, wherein the latter complained

---

[1] When the defendant made default, he lost his right of making his law and the case was set down for judgment. The decision of the Court seems to have been based on the rule in *Lib. Alb.* I, p. 202, "and if any parties appear and plead up to inquest or judgment, then they shall be ruled according to the usages of the City, without having any essoin in such personal actions either before or after."

that he had proved a debt of 12s 3d against the defendant in the Soke of the Bishop of London, of which the said Richard had paid 5s, his goods being sequestrated for the remainder by the Bishop's sokereve, and that the defendant broke the sequestration and removed the goods. A jury of the venue of Cornhull Tun was summoned against the next Court.

14 March 1301–2   Recognizance of Richard le Barber to Robert de Fingrie in 4s payable at the Quinzime.

Membr. 3 b 16 March 1301–2   *Friday after the Feast of St Gregory* [12 *March*]

A jury of the venue of St Leonard of Estchep was summoned to say on oath whether Roger de la Weyg assaulted Sir Bosoo de la Rokele[1], knight of the Lord King, and tore his clothes on Wednesday before the Feast of St Peter in Cathedra this year against the peace &c.

23 March 1301–2   *Friday before the Annunciation B.M.* [25 *March*]

Jakemin de Sessoln, attorney of John de Croily, offered himself against Robert Thurk in a plea of debt. Order was given to distrain the latter.

11 May 1302   *Friday after the Feast of St John before the Latin Gate* [6 *May*]

Robert Turk was amerced because he had no warrant for his essoin "*de servicio regis.*"

John de Crouly claimed from the above Robert £16, by one tally produced in Court, for woad sold and delivered to him. The defendant admitted the purchase, but said that it was on condition that he sold it under the plaintiff's name and not his own, and he put himself on the oath of the plaintiff. The latter appeared before Geoffrey de Norton and William de Leyre, deputies of the Mayor, and swore that the sale was without condition. Judgment was given for the plaintiff and that the defendant be in mercy.

[1] Probably the same person as Bru' de la Rokele mentioned in Cal. of Letter Book C, p. 47.

On Wednesday the eve of the Ascension, before *"dominus"*[1]
John le Blunt, Mayor, John de Croy appointed James de
Sysouln his attorney to sue execution of a debt of £16 which
he had proved against Robert Turk, and to receive the money
and give an acquittance in his name.

Friday, the morrow of the Ascension [31 *May*]

James de Wadencourt was summoned to answer Robert
Turk in a plea of covenant, wherein the latter complained that
he had bought a shipload of corn, viz. 300 quarters, at
41 quarters to count as 40, at a certain price from the above
James, and that the latter had received from him 20s as
earnest-money and God's silver, and ought to have delivered
the corn at the hythe of Billingesgate, and had refused to do
so. The defendant admitted the covenant and having received 1d as God's silver and 20s as earnest-money, but said
that he sold a shipload and not a certain number of quarters,
and that he was on his voyage when a sudden storm arose
and the sea grew so dangerous that he could not fulfil the
contract, nor was he bound to do so, because peril of the sea
was excepted in the covenant. The plaintiff denied this exception and offered to make his law on the point. Thereupon
the defendant said he had witnesses, Wybert and Adam, as to
the exception, and he took an oath that he would not produce
any other witnesses than these and would not suborn them.
Afterwards at a Court held on Friday before the Feast of
Pentecost he produced his witnesses. An agreement was then
arrived at by the intervention of friends and by permission
of the Court, the terms being that James should pay Robert
£4 to cover the 20s earnest-money and all other costs, and
be in mercy, while Robert should give him an acquittance as
regards the contract.

John Russel, plaintiff, appointed as his attorney Reymund
de Margeys or Bernard de Margeys or Bydau Manent against

---

[1] Aungier's French Chronicle (*Chronicles of Old London*, H. T. Riley,
p. 247) says that John le Blunt was knighted 22 May, 1306. *"Dominus"*
here is probably equivalent to "master."

James de Brabazon and his partners of the Society "*de la gruntable*" of Sene[1] in a plea of debt.

Thursday within seven days of Pentecost [10 *June*] *before Geoffrey de Norton, deputy of the Mayor*

John de Richemond, servant of Matthew le Peyntour, John de S[t] Omer, servant of William Leschild, sadler, Henry le Heumer, servant of Manekyn le Heumer, Manettus, son of William le Barber, John, son of Nicholas de Cambridge, and Robert Scot, fishmonger, who were captured and put in the Tun, were attached to answer William Mory, Geoffrey de Notingham, Robert Motoun, Henry de Hundesdich, Ralph le Cordwaner, Bartholomew le Botoner, John Baroun, John de Norfolk, and Richard le Barber, beadle of the Ward of Walebrok, in a plea of trespass, wherein the latter complained that while they were keeping watch on the night following Tuesday in the week after Pentecost, the defendants in the middle of the night assaulted and beat them. The defendants denied the charge and said that on Wednesday morning, when the light was quite clear, they were going towards Stratford, and in Candelwykstrate they met the Watch and surrendered to them without doing any harm; and they put themselves on a jury, which was summoned for Thursday. John de Richemond was mainprised by Matthew le Peyntour, John de S[t] Omer by William Leschild, sadler, and Henry le Heumer by Peter le Heumer, that no harm would be done to the Watch by them or their following. The son of William le Barber, John, son of Nicholas de Cambridge, and Robert Scot were mainprised to attend the Court and did not come. Accordingly they were attached and their mainpernors were summoned to answer why they had failed to produce them. Afterwards on Thursday a jury of John le Juvene and others from five Wards found on oath that the defendants committed the assault when midnight was striking at S[t] Paul's, and were captured after the hue and cry had been raised by

[1] Sienna. This society was also known as the *Bonseignours, Bonseignori* and *Bonzcini*. Cf. p. 109 n. 1. I have not been able to ascertain the meaning of "de la gruntable."

horn and voice, and the neighbouring wards had come to help, and that Manettus wounded William Mori to his damage, one mark, and that previously he and his companions and other unknown persons had filled an empty cask with stones on Monday midnight, and set it rolling through Graschirchestrate to London Bridge to the great terror of the neighbours. Judgment was given that Manettus go to prison till he had paid the mark, and that the others likewise go to prison.

Thursday before the Feast of St John the Baptist *21 June 1302*
[*24 June*]

William Cros was summoned to answer Gilbert de Schorne in a plea that he pay him £20, and deliver a bond for 20 marks, which had been entrusted to him by the hands of Geoffrey de Norton, Alderman of the Ward, on condition that if a Fine could not be levied in the Husting concerning certain houses demised to the plaintiff by Henry Cros and Joan his wife, the said £20 and the bond should be returned to him. The defendant denied the claim, and said that the £20 was paid as a debt owed to him by Henry Cros, in connection with which debt he had the houses from Henry Cros for a term of three years. The plaintiff then vouched to witness Edmund and Walter, who were present, and took an oath that he, would not produce any other than these witnesses or suborn them. Afterwards the witnesses gave evidence on oath, and judgment was given for the plaintiff.

A jury of the venue of Briggestrat came by John de Sutton and others in the panel, who said on oath that John Orpedeman did not lay violent hands on the Master of the Hospital of St Giles without London nor deny a distraint to him in the presence of Thomas Kent, Serjeant of the Mayor, as alleged, except in order to save the fish lying on his table from being thrown down into the mud, and for no other reason. The said John and the Master had a day to hear judgment.

A jury of the venue of Bredstrate and Cordwanerstrate, which was summoned to say on oath whether Roger de York, cordwainer, assaulted Richard Leving, beadle of the Ward of Bredstrate, to his damage 100s, came on Wednesday before the Feast of St Bartholomew the Apostle[1] [24 Aug.] by Richard le Chaundeler and others, and said that the defendant maliciously threw down the said Richard, so that he fell against the pavement and broke his head, to his damage half a mark. The defendant subsequently was distrained by 22 pairs of shoes, valued by oath of Thomas de Aldewych, Thomas de Douegate and Richard de London, cordwainers, at 8s to pay the half mark damages, and as he did not come

Membr. 4 b to acquit the pledges taken, the shoes were delivered to the plaintiff, who returned 1s 4d surplus to be repaid to the defendant.

10 July 1302 *Tuesday after the Feast of the Translation of S*^t *Thomas the Martyr* [7 *July*]

A jury of the venue around the house of Symon Bolimer of Castle Baynard was summoned to say on oath whether Symon broke a sequestration made on him by the Sheriff, for 20s owed by him on a tallage of 18d in the pound. Afterwards the said Symon paid the 20s, and proceedings were stayed.

12 July 1302 *Thursday after the above Feast*

Brother Thomas, Bishop of Rochester, appointed Richard Gladewyne his attorney against Robert Turk in a plea of debt.

Robert de Maundevile appointed Robert le Blunt his attorney against John Joce in a plea of debt, before the Mayor on Friday the Feast of St Margaret [20 July]. And the plea is in the Sheriff's Court.

28 July 1302 *Saturday after the Feast of S*^t *James the Apostle* [25 *July*]

The Sheriff was ordered to bring into Court, Roger de Springwell, "toundur"[2], and William Cros, fishmonger, executors of the will of John de Middelburgh, mercer, to do and receive what law (*jus*) shall dictate at the next Court.

---

[1] Query: Bartholomew the Confessor, i.e. 24 June?
[2] Shearman.

John de Pountoyse was summoned to answer Reginald de Frowyk in a plea of trespass wherein, the latter complained that he had leased to the defendant a house outside Alderiches-gate from Michaelmas 1300 for one year, for 40s, and the defendant held it till Easter 1302, and had damaged the locks, timber and other fixtures to the extent of 100s. The defendant craved a loveday. Subsequently the parties came to an agreement by permission of the Court.

[Record and process of an action in the Sheriff's Court, Membr. 5 endorsed "*Recordum affirmatur.*"]

Court of Richard de Campes, *Sheriff of London, on* 28 Oct. 1300
Friday before the Feast of All Saints [1 Nov.] *A° 28 Edw.* [1300]

Stephen de Larder was attached to answer Thomas Abraham in a plea of detinue of a goshawk (*ostorium*), which the latter alleged that he handed over to the custody of Stephen in Midlent until Michaelmas following, the value being £10, and that Stephen acknowledged receipt, but now unjustly detained it, to his damage 100s. The defendant denied that he had received the goshawk or acknowledged receipt, and offered to prove it by his law according to the custom of the City. The plaintiff declared that he could produce John and John as fit and lawful witnesses, who were present at the acknowledgment. A day was given to produce them at the Quinzime.

Wednesday after the Feast of St Edmund King [20 Nov.] 23 Nov. 1300

Stephen de Larder essoined against Thomas Abraham for hearing his suit (*de secta*[1] *sua audienda*), by William de Reyle. A day was given to him, through his essoiner, for Friday before the Feast of St Nicholas [Dec. 6], on which day the parties appeared. Thomas Abraham then offered himself against the defendant and demanded that his witnesses be examined. John, the first witness, being sworn and examined in the presence of the Sheriff and Walter de Fynchyngfeld and Henry de Gloucestre, aldermen, testified

---

[1] I.e. his witnesses.

that on Wednesday before the Feast of All Saints (Nov. 1) he was present when the defendant acknowledged the receipt of a goshawk (*Anglica lingua unum Goshauek*), i.e. between the hours of Prime and Tierce in the porch (*in atrio*) of the Guildhall between two doors, in the presence of John, the other witness, and others. John, the second witness, agreed with the above evidence, except that the defendant only acknowledged the receipt of a hawk (*Anglica lingua simpliciter unum hauek*). A day was given for the next Court that the Sheriff might consult with the Mayor and Aldermen. Afterwards at the Court held on Wednesday after the Feast of S[t] Gregory Pope [12 March] the parties came and demanded judgment. Whereupon judgment was given for the plaintiff for the goshawk[1] or its value, and that the defendant be in mercy.

Membr. 6 [Record and process of an action in the Sheriff's Court.]

4 May 1302 ## Court of Peter de Bosenho, *Friday before Hokeday [6 May] A° 30 Edw.* [1302]

Reimund de Sordes of Bayonne was attached to answer John de S[t] Pierre of the same in a plea of detinue of three deeds, wherein the latter alleged that on 26 May, 1301, he pledged to the defendant three deeds, sealed with the seal of the Earl of Lincoln, containing £300, for £701 5s small Tournois[2], due from him to Reimund at the fair of Bruges in the following month, which money the plaintiff paid by the hands of Ralph de Brakkelee, merchant, but though the said Ralph demanded the deeds in return, the defendant detained them to his damage £100. The defendant declared that he was not bound to return the deeds till the money was paid, and produced a bond under the seal of the plaintiff to that effect. The plaintiff did not deny this bond, but repeated

[1] The Court overlooked the difference in testimony.
[2] "*Turon parvorum*," small money of Tours in France. The *livre Tournois* is said to have been worth one-fourth of a pound sterling. Cf. Cal. of Letter Book C, p. 59, n. But according to Roquefort, *Glossaire de la Langue Romaine*, the *livre Tournois* was worth 20 *sols* and the *livre Parisis* 25 *sols*. We learn from an action on p. 193, that £17 Parisian was worth £4, which would give a value of about 4s 8½d for the *livre Parisis*, and about 3s 9¼d for the *livre Tournois*.

that he had paid his debt through Ralph de Brakkelee at the Fair of Turruk, and that the defendant had pretended that the deeds were in Bruges and had promised to restore them, but had not done so. The defendant pleaded that the plaintiff had no acquittance for the money, and that therefore the deeds remained with him according to the terms of the bond, and asked for judgment whether the plaintiff could recover on his bare word (*simplici verbo suo*). The plaintiff offered to verify the payment. Afterwards at a Court held on Thursday before the Feast of the Nativity of St John the Baptist [June 24] the parties appeared, and the plaintiff again offered to verify the payment and the detinue, by merchants and other good and lawful men, natives and foreigners. Judgment was given that as the plaintiff could not produce an acquittance and admitted the bond, which was not cancelled, he should recover nothing, and be in mercy for a false claim.

In dorso. John de Seint Pere did not prosecute[1], and was plaintiff. Therefore he and his pledges are in mercy.

Court of John le Blound, *Mayor of London, Friday after the Feast of St Peter ad Vincula* [1 *Aug.*] *A^o* 30 *Edw.* [1302]   Membr. 7   3 *Aug. 1302*

John Aldebrandyn of the Society "*Claren de Pistorye*"[2] acknowledged himself bound to Sir William Howard in an alms dish and a cup with foot and covercle of silver weighing 25 marks, to be returned on the morrow of the Exaltation of the Holy Cross (14 Sept.) on payment of 20 marks, the amount for which they were pledged.

Wednesday before the Feast of St Bartholomew [24 *Aug.*]   22 *Aug. 1302*

Reymund de Sordes[3], defendant, offered himself against John de St Peter, plaintiff, in a plea of error made in the Court of Peter de Bosenho, Sheriff, in an action of detinue of three

---

[1] The endorsement was made in the Mayor's Court, where the plaintiff withdrew from his plaint of error.

[2] The Chiarenti, a mercantile company of Pistoja in Tuscany. They were summoned, together with other Italian trading companies in the City of London, to confer with the King at York in A.D. 1303. Palgrave, *Parliamentary Writs*, I, p. 134; Cal. Close Rolls, A.D. 1302–7, p. 87.

[3] See p. 128 for the action in the Sheriff's Court.

deeds. The above John had essoined twice and did not appear now to prosecute his plaint. He was amerced, and the defendant went thence without a day. Execution of the judgment was ordered and the box of deeds was delivered to the defendant.

28 Aug. 1302 On Tuesday after the Feast of St Bartholomew the Apostle [24 Aug.] John, son of Geoffrey de Cavedihs, came before the Mayor and admitted that he opened with his foot the door of a certain sealed chamber[1]. He was committed to prison.

A jury was summoned from the venue of St Laurence and Cheap to declare on oath whether John le Botoner broke the sequestration made on him for the Queen's Gold, and counselled the neighbours and prevented them from paying more than the half of what was demanded from them, and thus hindered and delayed payment to the Queen.

Membr. 7 b
12 Sept. 1302
Wednesday after the Feast of the Nativity B.M. [8 Sept.], for foreigners

James le Reve[2] offered himself against Peter de Bosenho, Sheriff, and Nigel le Brun, executor of the will of Robert de Bree, in a plea of error, wherein he complained that the above Peter did him injury in a plea of account in which the above Nigel was plaintiff and he was defendant—by giving judgment that there should be auditors of his account. The Sheriff produced his record, in which it appeared that Nigel appointed Geoffrey de Morton or Richard Gladewyne and William de Reylee or one of them his attorney. The above James pleaded that he initiated the plea of error, and claimed that the attorneys appointed by Nigel in the Sheriff's Court, as appeared by the Sheriff's record, should not be admitted for the defence here, and therefore claimed judgment by default. Richard Gladewyne pleaded that the defendant could not make default, as he had appointed him, Richard, as his attorney till the case was ended; also that the plaintiff charged error against the Sheriff

---

[1] He broke the sequestration by opening the sealed door.
[2] See p. 132 for the action in the Sheriff's Court, and pp. 131, 135, 142–4 for further proceedings.

and could show no error in the record. He demanded that the judgment be confirmed and execution thereof allowed. A day was given till the next Court.

Precept was given that John de Sutton and other jurors of Bridge Ward appear this day and assess damages sustained when John Orpedman laid hands on the Master of the Hospital of St Giles without London and denied him a pledge. The Serjeant reported that summons had been made. As Robert de Mokking, John Freschfihs, John Baldewin and Elias Pykeman did not come, order was given to distrain them against next Tuesday.

John de Shaftisbiri, Brian de Mendham and other jurors of Langebourn Ward said on oath that Margery, relict of John de Twyford, clerk, and Henry de Schenefeld, goldsmith, executors of the will of the above John, came on Monday night after the Feast of the Nativity B.M. [8 Sept.] to the house which the above John rented from Brachius Lumbard in Langeborne Ward, and opened the door and took away a feather bed, two sheets, two coverlets and two andirons, value 8s, against the peace and the prohibition of Sir John le Blunt, then Mayor. Margery and Henry were summoned for Saturday to answer thereon.

Monday after the Feast of the Exaltation of the Holy Cross [14 Sept.] 17 Sept. 1302

James le Reve, plaintiff, offered himself against Nigel le Brun, executor of the will of Robert de Bree, and Peter de Bosenho, Sheriff of London, in a plea of error made in a plea of account between the above Nigel, as plaintiff, and himself, and demanded judgment by default. Richard Gladewyne and Geoffrey de Morton denied the default. The plaintiff declared the error to consist in the fact that the Sheriff adjudicated auditors of the account, whereas he was not bound to render account of the £74, which he received from Robert de Bree to trade therewith to their common profit, because he was robbed of those goods with others of his own on the coast of Brittany; and he alleged other errors in the record. The

Sheriff asked for a day to take counsel till the morrow, which was granted to him.

A jury of St Lawrence Lane in Cheap Ward was summoned to declare whether Philip le Viroler broke the sequestration on him for 16s, Queen's Gold, and whether he refused to allow Thomas de Kent, Serjeant, to make the sequestration on him.

[Record and process of an action in the Sheriff's Court.]

<table>
<tr><td>Membr. 8
27 Aug. 1302</td><td>Court of Peter de Bosenho, Sheriff, Monday after the Feast of St Bartholomew [24 Aug.] A° 30 Edw. [1302]</td></tr>
</table>

James le Reve of London was summoned to answer Nigel le Brun, executor of Robert de Bree of Dublin, merchant, in a plea that he render a reasonable account of moneys accruing to their common profit, in that the above Robert on Palm Sunday 1290 handed to him £100 to trade therewith in Ireland for two years, and the defendant had rendered no account. The latter admitted the receipt of £74, with which he bought goods, and said he was three times robbed on the coast of Brittany in 1290, and was imprisoned for twelve weeks, and demanded judgment whether he ought to render account. Nigel demanded judgment on his recognizance, and pleaded that the defendant should be forced to give an account on his receipt, and said that the defendant, at the time alleged, was in Ireland for a whole year trading and could not be robbed in Brittany, and this he was prepared to prove by the evidence of English and Irish merchants and of the Commonalties of Dublin and "Crakfergus," as well as by the Rolls of the King's Customs of Wools and Hides in that province. James repeated that he was robbed and was ready to prove it by sailors and merchants trading in that country. As regards the £30, he said he never received more than £74, and was ready to defend it by his law. Nigel pleaded that the defendant ought not to be admitted to his law, since actions of account ought to be settled by a jury[1], but in any case he was ready to answer him. A day was given till the next Court.

[1] Cf. p. 104; *Lib. Alb.* I, p. 215.

On Tuesday after the above feast the defendant appeared
by his attorney, Richard Scot. On Thursday the Court,
wishing for consultation, fixed the next hearing on Friday
before the Feast of the Nativity of the Blessed Mary [8 Sept.];
on which day the Court, on the ground that the defendant
acknowledged receipt of the £74 and showed no acquittance
for that sum, gave judgment that he should render an account,
and appointed Paul le Botiler and John Tilli as auditors, to
hear the account in the Guildhall on the Sunday. The
defendant was mainprised by John le Benere. A day was
given till the next Court in order that the Court might be
advised as to whether the defendant should make his law
about the £30, or the matter be inquired into by a jury.

Appended: writ *de computo inter mercatores*, witness the
King at Westminster 18 July A° 30 Edw. [1302]. Endorsed
"*Datus est dies partibus in quindena Pasche proxime sequenti.*"

[Record and process of an action in the Sheriff's Court.]

Court of Robert le Caller, *Thursday after Midlent*   Membr. 9
[1 *April*] *A° 30 Edw.* [1302]   5 *April 1302*

Bartholomew Bynau was attached to answer Walter le
Bokeler in a plea of detinue of a horse value 40s, which he
had hired to take him from London to York for 7s, on
condition that the horse be returned within a month. The
defendant said that he hired the horse, which was only worth
a mark, to take him to the King in Scotland, and that the
plaintiff sent his servant John to look after the horse, which
fell sick on the way, and that he returned it to the servant
within the month to take it back to his master. The plaintiff
replied that he was ready to prove that the horse was worth
more than a mark; and the servant John, who joined himself
with his master in the plea, denied that it was returned to
him. The defendant said that he had witnesses, Fortanus
and Bernard, who were present, and craved leave to produce
them in accordance with the custom of the City. Having
taken an oath not to produce witnesses other than the above,
he demanded a day. Thereupon the servant John said that he

was himself a foreigner, and that when a suit concerning foreigners was called, the party producing witnesses should produce them at once in Court, and as the witnesses were not there, he demanded judgment. The defendant pleaded that he had been summoned to answer the above Walter, who was a freeman, and that John had only joined his master to support him, and he said further that if he lost the case, the plaintiff would retain the whole profits[1] of the action; and he demanded judgment.

After two adjournments, the defendant made default, and did not produce his witnesses; whereupon on 12 May, judgment was given against him. As the value of the horse was at issue between the parties, a jury was summoned to inquire as to the value of the horse and assess damages. On 19 June a jury of the Conduit and Bredstrate brought in a verdict that the horse was worth two marks on the day it was hired, and they assessed the damages, by reason of the detinue of the horse from the Feast of the Purification [25 March] till the present day, at 23s 2d, or 2d a day. Judgment was given accordingly, and that the defendant be kept in custody till he paid or found security for payment, since he was a foreigner and had no goods in the bailiwick.

Note. Bartholomew did not prosecute (his plaint of error). The defendant went thence without a day[2].

Membr. 10   [Record and process of an action in the Sheriff's Court endorsed " *Recordum istud infirmatur.*"]

Court of Peter de Bosenho *on Friday after the Feast of St Faith* [6 *Oct.*][3]

John le Barber essoined against John de Laufare, cordwainer, in a plea of trespass, by Stephen de Wetherfeld.

On 11 Oct. judgment in the above case was respited till the next Court from lack of jurors. On 20 Oct. John de

[1] I.e. that John had no real part in the action, and therefore the action was between a foreigner and a citizen, in which case the rule about the immediate production of witnesses would not apply.

[2] See p. 135.

[3] Query: Friday the Feast of St Faith, i.e. 6 October? The next Court took place on 11 October.

Laufare, the defendant, essoined, and again on 25 Oct. On 27 Oct. a jury of the venue of Wodestrate between John le Barber, plaintiff, and John de Laufare, defendant, gave a verdict for the plaintiff with 40s damages. Judgment for that amount and that the defendant be committed to prison.

[Note by the writer of the Mayor's Court Roll]:—They claim error, first, because the Sheriff did not send the original plea; secondly, because he makes mention of judgment being put in respite, whereas no judgment appears in the record; thirdly, because the defendant essoined twice "*de communi*" without an intervening appearance; fourthly, because judgment was given for 40s damages, and that the defendant's body be committed to prison, without the principal plea preceding.

[The above mentioned original or principal plea subsequently produced and sewn on the foot of the membrane]:— Court of Richard de Campes, Sheriff, on Wednesday before the Feast of St Michael [29 Sept.]. John de Laufare, cordwainer, was attached to answer John le Barber on a charge of assaulting him in Wodestrate. The defendant pleaded that the plaintiff assaulted him first in his house, and that any damage he received was on this account. A jury was summoned against the next Court.

Court of John le Blund, *Mayor of London, Wednesday after the Feast of the Exaltation of the Holy Cross* [14 *Sept.*] *A°* 30 *Edw.* [1302]   Membr. 11   *19 Sept. 1302*

Bartholomew Bynaw[1], who complained of error in the Court of Robert le Callere, Sheriff of London, in an action between himself and Walter le Boceler, had this day and did not come. Judgment that he and his pledges be in mercy, and that Walter go thence without a day. The Sheriff was ordered to make execution.

James le Reve[2], plaintiff, offered himself against Peter de Bosenho, Sheriff of London, and Nigel le Brun, executor of

[1] See p. 133 for the action in the Sheriff's Court.
[2] Cf. p. 142, 2 May, 1303, when the defendant produced his proof and the plaintiff made default.

the will of Robert de Bree, in a plea of error made in the Sheriff's Court in an action of account wherein the plaintiff was defendant. The plaintiff said that the error consisted in the fact that he was ordered to render account before auditors, and that the Court took no notice of his offer to prove that he had lost the money on the coast of Brittany by the evidence of sailors and merchants trading there. The present defendants pleaded that the plaintiff should be precluded from this verification, on the ground that they were ready to prove that the plaintiff could not have been robbed as alleged, since he was in Ireland, and they claimed judgment because he had admitted receipt of the money and had produced no acquittance. The Court decided that as neither party had evidence to support their allegations, a day should be given in the Quinzime of Easter for them to produce their evidence, and that meanwhile execution of the judgment given in the Sheriff's Court should be stayed.

Three dishes and one cup taken from Bartholomew Bynau for 49s 10d, which Walter le Bokeler was awarded against him in the Court of Robert le Callere, were valued by oath of Michael de Wymbourne and John de Lutegreshale, goldsmiths, at 48s 2d, and they weighed 50s 8d. A day was given to the said Bartholomew to satisfy the plaintiff within eight days, otherwise the pledges would be sold.

5 Oct. 1302 *Friday after the Feast of St Michael [29 Sept.]*

Richard de Bolingtone and Alice his wife, Emma her sister, and Geoffrey, clerk of the Church of St Nicholas Coldabbey, were summoned to answer a charge of assaulting Agnes de Norhamptone in the highway by the Gate of St Augustine. Subsequently the parties came to an agreement, and the amercement was condoned because they were poor.

Membr. 11 b *Thursday before the Feast of the Apostles Simon and*
25 Oct. 1302 *Jude [28 Oct.] A° 30 Edw. [1302]*

William de Bray was summoned to answer Thomas Abraham in a plea of trespass, wherein the latter complained that though he was a citizen and had not offended against the above William, the defendant caused him to be attached on Wednesday the Feast of the Assumption [15 Aug.] at Luton Fair, by the goods which he had taken there for trading, and had kept these goods for three days, till the plaintiff answered him before the bailiffs of the town of Luton in a plea of trespass, and that by means of a jury procured by the defendant and of his affinity, damages of 20s were awarded against the plaintiff, for which his goods were still under arrest; and afterwards the defendant caused his goods, which were going to London, to be attached in St Albans by the bailiffs of the Abbot, to the value of £8, on Monday after the Feast of the Assumption, which goods still remained attached, in prejudice of the Liberty of the City of London and to his damage £20. The defendant pleaded that the plaintiff had assaulted him on the above Wednesday [15 Aug.] at Luton and for this reason he had had his goods attached, and also that he had assaulted him on Tuesday [14 Aug.], the eve of the Assumption, after dinner at Luton Fair, within the authority and Liberty of the Abbot of St Albans, and that therefore he had caused him to be attached in the town of St Albans within the same Liberty, as was lawful to him, and he demanded judgment. The plaintiff also demanded judgment on the confession of the defendant, and said that even if he had offended against the defendant, which he had not, the latter had done prejudice to the Liberty of London in causing him to appear before other judges than those of the Liberty of London, and outside the walls, and in having him attached at St Albans on the Monday for an alleged offence on the Tuesday preceding. A day was given at the next Husting to hear judgment. Afterwards at a Court held on Monday after the Feast of St Edmund [16 Nov.], the above Thomas offered himself against the above William, who did not come. Order was given to distrain him.

Friday before the Feast of the Apostles Simon and Jude 26 Oct. 1302 [28 Oct.] *before* William de Leyre

Thomas Abraham essoins against William de Bray by Robert de St Gervas.

Roger de Shorne was summoned to answer William le Poleter in a plea of debt, wherein the latter complained that by request of the above Roger he lent to the latter's son Robert £9 18s 5½d at Nogente in Artoys, and afterwards came to Roger's house in London and showed him Robert's bond, whereupon Roger paid him 24s pollard for 12s sterling and promised to pay the rest within the Quinzime, thus becoming debtor for his son; but though the plaintiff gave him the bond, the defendant had subsequently refused payment. The defendant denied that he had asked the plaintiff to lend the money to his son or that he had assumed his son's debt. The plaintiff produced witnesses, Nicholas and John, of whom the former said that he was present when the plaintiff lent the money at Paris and Nogente, that Robert gave a bond at Paris, and that he was present when Roger, in his house opposite "*les Escanz*"[1], thanked William for the loan, and paid 24s pollard; the parties, he said, were sitting in Roger's hall on a bench facing the road and drinking, and Roger's wife was present. The second witness, John, agreed with the above, except that he said the bond was given at Nogente. A day was given to hear judgment on Wednesday, unless the parties were able to agree meanwhile.

7 Nov. 1302   *Wednesday after the Feast of All Saints* [1 *Nov.*] *A° 30 Edw.* [1302]

Thomas Abram was summoned to answer William de Braye in a plea of trespass, wherein the latter complained that the defendant had him attached by his horse in the town of Luton to answer him in a plea of trespass, in prejudice of his freedom of London. The defendant denied it, and had a day at the Quinzime to make his law, when judgment was given against the plaintiff on his making default.

Membr. 12   *Saturday after the Feast of St Martin* [11 *Nov.*]
17 Nov. 1302

John de Brekesheved, servant of Terricus le Vileyn, was attached to answer Adam de Berlee in a plea of trespass,

---

[1] The Exchange.

wherein the latter complained that the defendant assaulted him on two separate occasions. The defendant put himself on a jury. The plaintiff said that the custom of the City in pleas of trespass was for a man to acquit himself by his law[1], and he was willing to allow the defendant his law. The latter refused, because he admitted that he laid hands on him and pushed him away. Judgment was respited till Wednesday, and the defendant was delivered to the Sheriff for his appearance on that day.

Peter Maupyn came before John le Blunt, Mayor of London, and acknowledged that he owed to Sir Eble Mounz, knight, £6 14s 8d, that sum being due to Sir William de Mounz or his attorney on the Octave of St Andrew [30 Nov.].

Tuesday before the Feast of St Lucia Virgin [13 Dec.] *II Dec. 1302*
A^o 31 Edw. [1302]

A jury of the venue of Manionelane was summoned for Friday to say whether the house of William de Basinge was burnt on Monday after Michaelmas, by fire issuing from the house of Maud le Lou, due to carelessness on her part, as the above William alleged.

John de Laufare offered himself against John le Barber, in a plea of error made in the Court of Peter de Bosenho, then Sheriff, in an action of trespass[2], in which John le Barber was plaintiff. The Sheriff sent his record, and an error was found therein. The judgment of the Sheriff's Court was annulled, and the present plaintiff went thence without a day.

Henry de Mora waged his law to John de Laufare, clerk, on the charge that he assaulted the latter. He is to make his law on Thursday next.

---

[1] This was the case until A.D. 1285, when the King ordained that in pleas of trespass where there was bloodshed or battery the matter be determined by inquest, unless the party plaintiff assents that the defendant clear himself by his law. *Lib. Alb.* I, p. 294. Wager of law continued in trespass where there was no battery or bloodshed. *Ibid.* p. 204.

[2] For proceedings in the Sheriff's Court see p. 134.

Saturday after the Feast of St Lucia Virgin [*13 Dec.*]

Paul le Potter was in mercy for default against Robert de Alegate.

The same Paul was attached to answer Robert de Alegate in a plea of trespass, wherein the latter complained that Paul, who was a freeman like himself, caused his goods to be attached by the bailiffs of Luton at Luton Fair, in prejudice of the Liberty of London. The defendant denied that he caused the goods of Robert to be attached, but instead those of a certain Robert Rose, "poter," who owed him £20, which he was prepared to prove. Thereupon Robert said that a certain Thomas Rose was his journeyman[1], and had charge of his goods which were attached, and this he was willing to prove, and to prove the custom of the City. A day was given on Tuesday.

Afterwards on Tuesday the plaintiff demanded permission to verify his plea. The defendant said the plaintiff could not be admitted to his law, as the question was reserved for a jury at the last court, and he called the Mayor's record to witness. Afterwards a jury of Gilbert le Mareschal and others said on oath that the goods, on which the attachment was made, belonged to Robert de Alegate. Judgment was given that Paul make delivery of the goods, and be at the next Husting to hear judgment concerning this attachment made against the Liberty of the City, and concerning the damages of Robert, which were taxed at 20s.

Membr. 12 *b*   Alan de Maldon was summoned to answer Egbrith de Werpe of Almaine in a plea of error made in the Court of Symon de Paris, Sheriff of London, in an action of debt in which Alan was plaintiff[2]. The above Egbrith complained that the error made was in the process, and that whereas "Detard," Alderman of the free merchants of the Hanse of Almaine, came and demanded his Court concerning the above Egbrith as a free man of the Hanse, which Court he claimed to have by Charters from the Kings of England as well as

[1] "*Vallettus*," meaning an employee who had served his apprenticeship, but had not yet set up as a master.
[2] For the action in the Sheriff's Court see p. 181.

by Charters of the City of London, the above Sheriff, not challenging that claim, nevertheless unjustly proceeded with the plea. He said further that the Sheriff condemned him in £33 11s 2d, whereas the plaintiff claimed £34 13s, and failed to prove the whole of that amount. Moreover the witnesses were insufficient, since they could not say out of what contract the debt of £33 11s 2d had its origin, as they ought to have done. Thus the error consisted in saying that a faulty proof was good, and in proceeding to judgment. Afterwards at a Court held on Friday after the Purification [2 Feb.] a day was given to the parties to hear judgment at the next Husting.

Thursday the Vigil of St Thomas the Apostle [21 Dec.]   *20 Dec. 1302*

Master Geoffrey de Hengham was attached to answer Richard Hauteyn for prosecuting pleas against him in the Court Christian at Norwich as regards goods and chattels which did not concern a will or matrimony, but related to tithes from lands which were not in the plaintiff's possession —and this he had done, in spite of the fact that he had acknowledged before the Mayor that he had no ground for such actions except as a means of vexation, and the Mayor, in accordance with the ancient Liberties of the City, had inhibited him from bringing such actions to impoverish the plaintiff. The defendant pleaded that he had no need to answer this charge, as the plaintiff had already sued him in the Mayor's Court, and he had been acquitted, to which he called the Mayor's record as witness. Moreover he pleaded that this present action was pending in the Sheriff's Court, and demanded judgment as to whether he need answer it now. The plaintiff denied that the defendant had been acquitted, and as regards his assertion that the case was pending in the Sheriff's Court, pleaded that this "*excepcio*" was a dilatory one, and that his first answer to the action should be dealt with first. Accordingly he demanded judgment whether he was bound to answer this dilatory exception. A day was given to hear judgment at the next Court.

ROLL F

Court of John de Blunt *on Thursday the morrow of the Apostles Philip and James* [1 *May*] *A°* 31 *Edw.* [1303]

Nigel le Brun[1], executor of Robert de Bree of Dublin, offered himself by Geoffrey de Morton, his attorney, against James le Reve in a plea of account, and produced a letter close under the seal of the Commonalty of Dublin, and a letter patent under that of Cragfergus, and a letter of Richard (?) de Bereford, the King's Treasurer in Ireland, testifying that the above James was in Ireland, during the twentieth and twenty-first years of King Edward till Pentecost, trading with the goods of Robert de Bree, deceased. The plaintiff did not come, and did not certify in any Court as regards the robbery upon him and his imprisonment on the coast of Brittany during the above twentieth year. Judgment that he and his pledges be in mercy. Simon de Paris, Sheriff, was ordered to execute the judgment given in the Court of Peter de Bosenho, late Sheriff.

10 May 1303 *Friday after the Feast of St John before the Latin Gate* [6 *May*]

Elias Russell offered himself against Robert de Rummesseye in a plea that the latter acquit him of five marks, which he undertook to pay on his behalf, against Andrew de Sakevile, groom of the Prince of Wales, for a horse which Robert had of Andrew. And Robert came and acknowledged that he had received the horse, and showed no reason why he should not acquit him. Judgment that he be distrained to acquit him.

A jury of the venue without Bisshopesgate was summoned for Monday to say on oath whether John le Hornere had made a malicious error in proving the will of William le Hornere, which he said was made on Thursday before the Feast of the Ascension, whereas he acknowledged before the

---

[1] For earlier proceedings in this action see pp. 130, 132, 135. See also pp. 143, 144.

Mayor that it was made on the Wednesday preceding, as was alleged by Walter Osekin, or had merely erred from simplicity, as he himself pleaded. The defendant was mainprised by William Poyntel and William le Hornere to come on Monday to hear the verdict.

A jury of the venue next to the Friars of the Cross[1] was summoned to say whether Walter at Waye, John Scot, "gaunter"[2], and Henry atte Stufhous made an assault on Juwecta Wenge, by beating her doors and windows with sticks and other arms on Sunday night.

Thursday before the Feast of Pentecost [26 *May*]   *23 May 1303*

Simon de Paris, Sheriff, was summoned to answer Geoffrey de Morton, attorney of Nigel le Brun, executor of the will of Robert de Bree, for his delay in making execution of the judgment in the Court of Peter de Bosenho, Sheriff. The defendant answered that the defendant in that action, James le Reve, had been mainprised by John le Benere to render account of £74, and as John had not produced the defendant, he had distrained him by goods, value 20s, either to produce him or to render account for him, and the said John had declared that he was not willing either to render an account, or to give satisfaction for the above money.

On Monday the Vigil of S[t] *Barnabas the Apostle*   Membr. 1 b
[11 *June*]   *10 June 1303*

Guydo Bonaventure was attached to answer Thomas atte Velle[3], serjeant of the Sheriff, in a plea of trespass, wherein the latter complained that when he went by precept of the Mayor to Guydo's house in Langeburne Ward to distrain[4]

---

[1] The House of the Crutched Friars, and not the street, appears to be meant.   [2] Glover.

[3] Otherwise Thomas atte Welle.

[4] No clear rules are given in the City Custumals with regard to the taking of distresses or distraining. Both City officials and private persons are shown in these actions as actually taking and removing articles of value to compel the appearance in Court of a debtor, or to secure the payment of rents. But as regards private persons, distraining exposed them to the danger of an action of trespass by the distrained person, in which the sympathies of juries were often with the latter. An action also lay in the Husting of Common Pleas, called *Replegiare* for distresses

him for money owed to the Commonalty, and had put his seal on his door, the defendant took the seal away, threw it in the street and assaulted him. The defendant denied the charge, and put himself on his country, and the plaintiff also. A jury of the venue was summoned against Wednesday.

2 Aug. 1303   *Friday after the Feast of St Peter ad Vincula* [1 *Aug.*]

Gilbert Payn was summoned to answer the Mayor and Commonalty and Nicholas Pikot, guardian of John and Thomas, sons of Walter Hauteyn, being under age, in a plea of trespass. Order was given to distrain him against the next Court.

Robert de Molton came and acknowledged that he covered his house, and that he laboured in it in the Parish of St Benedict Shorhogge, against the Mayor's prohibition. A day was given on Monday to hear judgment.

12 Aug. 1303   *Monday after the Feast of St Laurence* [10 *Aug.*]

Simon de Paris, Sheriff, was summoned to answer Nigel le Brun, executor of the will of Robert de Bree, in a plea of error, in that he gave judgment that James le Reve, defendant in a plea of account, should acquit himself as regards £30 by his law. Also he complained that the Sheriff would not make execution of the judgment against the above James as regard £74, but delayed it till James and his mainpernor had withdrawn from his jurisdiction, to the plaintiff's damage £80. The Sheriff said that the plaintiff had not prosecuted his suit, and he claimed judgment. Geoffrey de Morton

unjustly taken (*Lib. Alb.* I, p. 188), and in the Sheriff's Court "*de Placito capcionis et detencionis catallorum.*" In the present case a distraint was taken in the manner of a sequestration. By the later custom of London, on an action of debt being entered, the officer of the Court went to the house or warehouse of the defendant and hung a padlock on the door, which he sealed. On the fifth Court day following, the plaintiff might have judgment to open the door to have the goods appraised, unless the defendant put in bail to have the sequestration dissolved (Jacob's *Law Dict.*: Sequestration in London). At this period, however, sequestration appears to have been used principally for the collection of arrears due to tallages.

pleaded that the plaintiff had not made default, because he, Geoffrey, was Nigel's attorney in the principal plea in the Court of Peter de Bosenho, late Sheriff, and was accepted as such in the Court of Simon himself, and that his present action was accessory and dependent on the principal plea, and therefore he demanded judgment. The Sheriff pleaded that the action was a new one, and as Nigel had not appeared himself or appointed Geoffrey as his attorney in this action, he demanded judgment precisely whether he need answer him therein. A day was given on Friday to hear judgment.

Monday after the Feast of the Assumption [15 *Aug.*]   Membr. 2
                                                            19 Aug. 1303

Roger de Lincoln, draper, was attached to answer Hugh Pourte, Sheriff of London, in a plea of trespass, wherein the latter complained that when he went into Thames Street opposite the house of Katherine de Lincoln to attach the defendant to answer Katherine in a plea of trespass, Roger would not allow himself to be attached by the Sheriff and bailiff of the King, but laid violent hands on him, seized him by the chest and tore his clothes in contempt of the King and to his damage £20; and as he would not find pledges, the plaintiff had sent him to prison. The defendant denied the charges of unwillingness and put himself on a jury. As regards the assault he demanded to acquit himself by his law. The plaintiff pleaded that as the offence was one against the King and his bailiffs, the defendant was not entitled to make his law[1]. This contention was upheld by the Court

---

[1] By the Statute of Wales, A.D. 1284, c. 11, it was enacted that men should no longer wage their law in the King's court by way of answer to a charge of breaking his peace. The King took the opportunity in 1285, when the City was in his hands, of abolishing the wager of law in cases of trespass where there was bloodshed or battery, except by consent of the plaintiff. *Lib. Alb.* 1, p. 294. In this case we have a further limitation apparently made by the City authorities in support of their officers. The previous year a trial took place at Leadenhall before John Botetourte and other Justices, of Elias Russel and others for an assault upon John le Chaucer. The defendants claimed to clear themselves in a simple trespass by wager of law, but their claim was not allowed as being contrary to the law of England. *Chron. Edw. I and Edw. II*, Rolls Series, 1, pp. 127–8. Nevertheless wager of law still continued to be allowed in the City courts in cases of trespass where there was no bloodshed and battery, and even in trespasses alleged to be against the peace. *Lib. Alb.* 1, p. 204.

on Monday, when Roger was mainprised by Thomas de
Frowyk, goldsmith, Thomas de Staundon, goldsmith, John
le Amayler, goldsmith, Ralph de la Bare, goldsmith, Walter
de Walepol, goldsmith, Richard de Burdeus, John Walsheman,
"fevere," Manekyn le Heumer, Henry de Faveresham, cordwainer, Richard Bullok, taverner, John de Luttegreshale,
goldsmith, and Walter Conestable, goldsmith, for his appearance in Court to hear the verdict of the jury, and for keeping
the peace between himself and his following, and Hugh
Pourte and Adam de Foleham, alderman, and the above
Katherine. A jury was also summoned to say whether the
defendant broke the sequestration made upon him by Thomas
atte Welle, Serjeant of the Sheriff, for his arrears of the
present tallage of £1100. Afterwards, on Monday after the
Feast of St Bartholomew, a jury of Gilbert de Mordone and
others found the defendant guilty of the charges against him,
but was unwilling to undertake the matter of the sequestration, on which another inquest was ordered. Judgment
that he go to prison.

Richard de Luda, tailor, was attached to answer Hugh
Pourte, Sheriff of London, on similar charges. The same
jury found that the defendant allowed himself to be attached,
but would not find pledges, for which reason the Sheriff had
committed him to prison.

9 Sept. 1303 **Monday after the Feast of the Nativity B.M.
[8 *Sept.*]**

Geoffrey Hubertyn of Lucca, plaintiff, appointed Nicholas
Teste his attorney against the Abbot of Tylteye in a plea of
debt.

14 Sept.1303 **Saturday before the Feast of St Matthew the Apostle
[21 *Sept.*]**

Peter Berneval was summoned to answer the Mayor for
lack of respect to him, and because he said in the presence
of Sir Ralph de Sandwich that he wished to God that the
latter was still Warden of the City as he used to be, because

business was dealt with speedily under him, and; this he said out of disrespect to the Mayor. The defendant waged his law that he was not guilty. He was permitted to make his law on the Octave.

The same Peter was summoned to answer William, clerk of the Chamber, for saying that the latter received money from the executors of Simon Godard to support unjustly their side in the action between them and Peter, and that the Commonalty had lost 200 marks and more through him. On being asked how he wished to acquit himself, the defendant admitted that he had spoken thus, and that he believed it. The plaintiff denied that he had received anything or that the Commonalty had suffered any loss through him. He was adjudged to make his law on the Quinzime. Afterwards the plaintiff appeared to make his law, and Alice, relict of Simon Godard, and Richard Costantyn, executors of Simon Godard's will, Roger de Linton, Robert le Convers, goldsmith, Robert de Pipehirst, Richard de Shordich, William de Harewe, Thomas de Farndon, ... Jordan, "paternosterer"[1], William de Pelham, and Gilbert le Bole, cordwainers, Mark le Draper and Richard Anesty came likewise, and offered themselves to make the law for him and acquit him of the charge against him. The Mayor and Aldermen condoned the law. The above Peter did not come. Judgment was given that William be acquitted[2].

Tuesday after the Feast of St Matthew the Apostle [21 Sept.], before Nicholas Pycot

Membr. 2 b
24 Sept. 1303

Two posnets, one small basin, two coverlets (*chalones*), and one new saddle-bow (*arzoun*) taken on John de Waledene, saddler, for 10s owed to John de Nony, were valued by oath of William de Stebenhethe, "batour," Roger le Batour, and

---

[1] A maker of paternosters or rosaries.

[2] The King's court at this time and long afterwards gave no action for defamation, which was usually dealt with in the ecclesiastical courts, though actions for defamation were common in the manorial and other local courts. The defendant here alleged that his words were true on the principle *veritas non est defamatio*, and the Court threw on the plaintiff the onus of disproving them. He was "acquitted" because the defendant absented himself, but apparently no damages were awarded to him. See Pollock and Maitland, *Hist. Eng. Law*, II, pp. 536–8.

Thomas le Taillour of St Lawrence Lane, at 22d for the posnets and basin, 20d for the coverlets and 6d for the saddle-bow. A day was given till to-morrow to John de Waledene to acquit them; otherwise they would be sold. As he failed to do so, they were given to the above John de Nony on Thursday in part payment of his debt—also a screen (*scrinea*).

19 Oct. 1303   On Saturday the morrow of St Luke the Evangelist, John de Tynerval constituted John le Fauchor his attorney by a letter, which the Mayor sealed for him with the Mayoralty seal. This document appointed John le Faucheur and Roger le Graunt to receive debts owed to him in France, and especially to obtain from the executors of Margaret, late Queen of France, £100 Parisian[1], due to him partly in payment of a debt and partly as a legacy from the above Queen. Dated 15 Oct. 1303.

23 Oct. 1303   *Wednesday after the above Feast*

William de Pelham, Robert de Frowyk, John de Wynton, John de Laufare, William de Singham, Thomas de Derby, and other master cordwainers of London were summoned to answer William, called "Cok," de Laufare, John de Bristol, William de Walthom, John de Paris, Andrew Scot, Roger Monkessone, John de Kent, and John de Bechesworthe, and others their companions, being journeymen workers of "Cordwanerye"[2], in a plea of trespass, wherein the latter complained that the above masters compelled and bound by an oath other masters, to lower, by common consent of all the master cordwainers, the wages of the journeymen cordwainers, viz. 1d for the making of a dozen pairs of shoes, and $\frac{1}{2}$d for each pair of top-boots (*ocrearum*), and $\frac{1}{2}$d for each pair of ankle-boots (*botorum*), against the ordinance and custom of the trade of immemorial usage, and to the impoverishment of the same journeymen. The masters of the cordwainers came and said that the custom

---

[1] The *livre Parisis* was worth about 4s 8$\frac{1}{2}$d. Cf. pp. 128, 193.
[2] *Servientibus Cordwanerye operariis* (*famulis* crossed out).

of the trade, before the circulation of the "*cokedonii*"[1] and crocards, was to give for the repair of 12 pairs of shoes not more than 5d, and for one pair of top-boots 1d, and one pair of ankle-boots 1d; but on account of the high price of food and the decreased value of money, they had increased these amounts by 1d for the shoes and ½d for the top- and ankle-boots, until the money should be improved and there should be a greater abundance of food; and they asked that a jury should be called on the matter. And the journeymen likewise. A jury consisting of Roger de Lintone and others said that the masters, before the coming of the "*cokedeni*" and crocards, used to pay 5d, 1d and 1d, as they said, for the above classes of work, but they could not find out among themselves about the alleged oath. Accordingly the journeymen were told to work well and faithfully, and serve their masters and the people, and that they should not demand more than the above amounts, and that they were in mercy for their false claim.

Thursday the Vigil of All Saints [1 *Nov.*]   *31 Oct. 1303*

Margaret atte Blakeloft was summoned to answer John le Botoner in a plea that she restore to him £7, which she owed him of the goods of Adam and Margery, children of John de Storteford, to whom he was appointed guardian by the Mayor and Aldermen. Margaret came and said she had a husband John who was not mentioned in the plaint, and she demanded judgment [as to whether she need answer without him]. Judgment that he be summoned against the next Court.

William de Spersholt was summoned to answer Alice de Sutton in a plea of estrepement[2], wherein she complained that William removed and carried away a cistern, three handmills, and a lead receptacle [*alveum*] from her house in Lothebury, which house she had recovered against him— against the prohibition of the Mayor in the Husting. The defendant admitted that he moved the cistern and other

[1] *Sc. cocodones*, a kind of base French money, like the pollards and crocards.

[2] An action of waste against a tenant.

utensils as being his own goods, and demanded judgment. The plaintiff said that the cistern &c. were fixed with nails, and had been put in position by her father and belonged to her house, and she put herself on a jury. Afterwards a jury of Thomas Eylmere and others gave a verdict in her favour and fixed the damages at 20s. Judgment for that amount.

Membr. 3
9 Nov. 1303

Saturday before the Feast of St Martin [11 Nov.]

Richard de Wetherbe, bailiff of Queenhithe, was summoned to answer John de Brinkele, Roger le Palmere, Roger Husbonde and other cornmongers of London in a plea that the above Richard did not allow any of the cornmongers to measure their corn before they had paid 1d the quarter for the Hithe; and although before dinner they paid this 1d, nevertheless after dinner he compelled them to pay another penny the quarter, unjustly and against the liberty of the City of London, and to the damage of the cornmongers £20. The above Richard said he only took the penny which his predecessors had taken, and thereof he found the King was seised. The plaintiffs said that he and his predecessors took the 1d before dinner and after, unjustly. Richard answered that he found the King seised of this custom, and that it was not his business to determine the King's seisin. The plaintiffs and the other cornmongers said that the custom was never applied to the King's benefit, and that he took it unjustly, and they asked for an inquiry by a jury. Afterwards the parties came on Wednesday after the Feast of St Katherine [25 Nov.], when the defendant declared that he was the servant and attorney of William de Combe Martin and John de Burreford, Sheriffs of London, and that he collected the said custom in their name and by their authority. The Sheriffs came also and acknowledged him as their servant, and the taking of the penny as just, because they found their predecessors had taken it for a long time, and that the King and their bailiwick were seised of it. The plaintiffs again declared that both they and their predecessors had taken it unjustly, and demanded an inquiry by a jury. A day was given, and the Sheriffs were ordered to produce all customs relating to Queenhithe. Subsequently at a Court held on Tuesday after the Octave of St Hilary [13 Jan.], before the Mayor, Aldermen, and four men from each Ward summoned for the purpose, the parties came. And since the Sheriffs did not produce their customs, the Mayor and Aldermen delivered to them certain customs[1], which they were not to transgress.

Friday after the Feast of St Martin [11 *Nov.*]

Richard de Wolchirchhawe and Olive his wife, relict of William de Wolchirche and executrix of the latter's will, were summoned to answer Sir Thomas, Rector of the Church of St Mary de Wolchirch, and John atte Gate, her co-executor, in a plea that the defendants return to them and the Commonalty of London £256, which they had in their custody by delivery of the executors of the goods of the testator, from which sum 120 marks were assigned by agreement of the executors for constructing the pavement of Bishopsgate Within, as far as the money would go, and for the good of the testator's soul. For this sum of £256, the above Richard had given to the executors a bond which had been put in the hands of Thomas Perceval as common friend, and now they detained this sum to the damage of the plaintiffs. The defendants admitted that they had £89 of the testator's goods, which he wished to be expended on the repair of the above road, by direction of the Mayor and Aldermen and the executors, but the remainder they had paid to the use and profit of the testator; and this they were ready to prove by an acquittance. Walter de Wanlok, one of the executors, did not come, and order was given to distrain him. The Bailiff was also ordered to warn Thomas Perceval to come on the morrow with the bond. A day was subsequently given at the request of William de Braye, Official of the Bishop of London, and other adjournments took place. Meanwhile the defendants were ordered by the Mayor to keep safely the £89 which they admitted having in hand.

[1] These customs are not set out in any of the City books.

Saturday the Feast of St Clement [23 Nov.] A° 32 Edw. [1303]

James Ponchinus was summoned to answer John de Burreford, Sheriff of London, in a plea of trespass, wherein the latter complained that the defendant struck a certain Henry de Lobiere, in his Court in the Guildhall.

Precept was given to Peter de Bosenho, late Sheriff, to be here on Tuesday with his clerks and rolls, in order to render account of his receipt of the Queen's Gold[1].

Membr. 3 *b*
12 Dec. 1303
Thursday after the Feast of St Nicholas [6 Dec.]

A jury of the venue of St Clement's Lane, consisting of Thomas de Wynton and others, said on oath that Stephen de Wynton did not make the brown bread (*panem bissum*) which was seized in the bakehouse of Thomas de Wrotham in St Clement's Lane, for which he was arrested on the ground that the bread weighed 20s 8d less than it ought to do, but that a certain Thomas de Bedeford, oven-man (*furnator*) of Thomas de Wrotham, made it and sealed it with the seal belonging to the house of his master, to his master's profit. Judgment that Stephen go quit, and that Thomas de Wrotham be distrained to answer concerning what may be charged against him.

[1] The Queen's Gold was a percentage of one mark of gold to every hundred marks of silver paid by the City to the King by way of grant or fine. It was unpopular in the City, and in the reign of Henry III a dispute on the subject was carried before the King and his Council, with the result that on 23 December, 1255, Queen Eleanour issued a charter quitclaiming the Queen's Gold on all fines during her lifetime, saving the rights of her successors (*Lib. Cust.* I, pp. 38, 39). The matter arose again in 1342, when the Exchequer claimed Queen's Gold, which should have been paid to Queen Philippa on a composition of £2000 for the twentieth granted by Parliament to Edward I in 1306. The City pleaded that Queen's Gold was due only on fines, and that the £2000 was a matter of liberality and goodwill. On the Rolls and Memoranda of the Exchequer being searched, it was found that the Queens had received their Gold on all grants as well as fines whatsoever. The City had no further argument to offer and precept was issued for levying the money (Cal. of Letter Book F, pp. 68–72). A month later, however, in connection with another claim for Queen's Gold, the City reiterated its objection, but was forced to raise the money. (*Ibid.* pp. 85–6, 90; City's Plea and Memoranda Rolls A 4, membr. 6).

Alan de Sutton, called "Ballard," saddler, was summoned to answer Manekin le Heumer and his fellows, collectors of the tallage of £1000, for the Ward of Cordewanerstrete, and John Juvenal, Serjeant of the Commonalty, for contempt of the King and the Mayor and Commonalty, in that he violently snatched away from the plaintiffs a woman's supertunic of green furred with squirrel, which they had taken from him by way of distraint for the 10s which he owed to the tallage. The defendant denied that he snatched it away violently, as they complained, and put himself on his country. A day was given to hear the verdict.

Monday after the Feast of St Lucia Virgin [13 Dec.]   *16 Dec. 1303*

A jury was summoned from the venue of St Clement's Lane by Candelwykstrete to say whether Thomas de Wrotham made a certain brown loaf &c. The defendant was mainprised by John de Brynkele, Roger atte Vine, Roger Hosebonde, and Adam Wade to hear the verdict and receive &c. The case was subsequently postponed owing to the absence of Aldermen, and the defendant was again mainprised by John Baunber, Thomas le Maderman, Edmund Lambyn, Paul le Potter, Robert Box and John de Shaftesbiry. Finally a jury consisting of Stephen le Potter and others said on oath that the above Thomas had no profit from bread made in his bakehouse, except 4d the quarter, which was the rent for the use of the bakehouse and utensils, and that a certain Thomas de Bedeford made the bread and sustained judgment for the same. Judgment that the defendant be acquitted.

Tuesday after the Octave of St Hilary [13 *Jan.*] *A° 32*   Membr. 4
Edw. [1303–4]   *21 Jan.*
    1303–4

As it was testified by good and faithful men, and by Sir William de Bereforth, King's Justice[1], that Thomas de Saleford, goldsmith, had threatened Adam de Warwick and Edward his son in their lives and limbs, the Sheriff was

---

[1] *D.N.B.*, Chief-Justice of the Common Bench, A.D. 1309.

ordered to keep the above Thomas in custody till he found twelve pledges for keeping the King's Peace.

Since Geoffrey de Notingham, skinner, admitted that he had struck William de Prestwod, skinner, who had accused him of agreeing to a confederacy of journeymen skinners [*familiorum peletrie*], and of paying money into their box, he was committed to prison, &c.

22 *Jan.* *Wednesday before the Feast of the Conversion of*
1303–4 *St Paul* [25 *Jan.*]

A jury of the venue of London Bridge was summoned to say on oath whether Richard le Schethere, Stephen his son, Roger de Warewyk, cobbler (*sutor*), John his son, Richard Hagyn, Gunnora his wife, John de Sandwich, cobbler, Robert, apprentice of Robert le Fourbur, William his mate, and Richard his mate assaulted the Watch in the above Ward on the eve of the Epiphany [6 Jan.]. Afterwards on Wednesday after the Feast of the Conversion of St Paul [25 Jan.], a jury consisting of Henry le Blund and others found that the defendants assaulted John de Berking, William le Wite and Walter, the servant of Henry Bod. They were fined 8d each for damages; and for breaking the peace at night-time to the terror of the neighbours and the scandal of the City they were sent to prison.

Simon de Canterbury, skinner, was summoned to answer Geoffrey le Lacer in a plea of trespass, wherein the latter complained that he had bought from the defendant five dozen lambskins for 10s, of which eleven were false and counterfeited out of old skins, being newly sheared again. The defendant denied the fraud and said that he bought the skins at St Botulph's Fair in their present condition and sold them as such, and thereon he put himself on his country. And Geoffrey said he bought them as lambskins, and that the defendant, knowing they were false, deceived him, and he also demanded a jury. A jury of Walebrok was summoned for the morrow.

The Sheriffs were ordered to bring before the Mayor on Membr. 4 *b* Friday twelve bakers from each side of Walebrok, to say on oath how many men hired their bakehouses for 4d the quarter. The jury of Roger de Derby and others presented the names of twenty-six bakers of tourte-bread[1] who hired bakehouses, and six who owned their own, and twenty bakers of white bread who hired, and one who owned bakehouses. [The rents varied from 1 mark to 11 marks per annum, and from 2d the quarter baked to 4d, with or without utensils. Among the places mentioned were the Parish of St Mary atte Hull, opposite the King's former Wardrobe, Ebbegate, Sivethe-strete, Kironlane, the Church of St Tauntellin[2], Basingelane, and St Clement's Lane. The lessors included William le Micere, Alfred le Weyder, Juliana Aubyn, Gautrinus le Fraunceis, the Rector of the Church of St Werburg, and the Brothers of the House of St John.]

Wednesday after the Feast of the Conversion of St Paul 29 *Jan.*
[25 Jan.], by the Mayor and John de Wengrave[3] and *13.03–4*
other Aldermen

The Sheriffs were ordered to be present on that day to say, and also to do, whatever the Mayor and Aldermen should enjoin upon them for keeping the King's Peace. And they did not come.

A jury of the Venue of Alegate consisting of Robert Lorchon and others said on oath that John Sampson came on Thursday night, the morrow of the Circumcision [1 Jan.], and joined the Watch and Ward in Alegate, and went with them till he arrived between Alegate Gate and the House of the Brothers of the Cross[4], where he entered into the house of a certain imbecile [*fatue*] woman, who raised the hue and cry, and when the men of Sir John de Sandale, who were coming from the house of Roger de Frowyk with a light in front of them, heard the noise and entered the house of the above woman, the defendant assaulted Giles Peche, John de

---

[1] Bakers of *tourte*, a coarse brown bread.   [2] St Antholin.
[3] Cf. p. 164.   [4] The Crutched Friars.

Sandale, junior, and William le Reve, to their damage half a mark each. They said also that the above John is a regular nightwalker who goes out to do harm, and has been three times indicted by the Wardmote for the same. Judgment that he be delivered to the Sheriff for safe custody until &c.

A jury from the venue of Walebrok were summoned to say whether Reginald de Holcote, currier, was a dealer in skins and other things belonging to peltry, against the ordinance and rights of that trade.

4 March
1303–4   *Wednesday after the Octave of St Mathias the Apostle* [24 Feb.]

William de Wautham was attached to answer the Mayor &c. for prosecuting a plea in the Court Christian relating to rents and tenements, which plea belongs to the King's Court, and especially concerning certain rents devised in his will by John de Export for the provision of a chaplain to pray for his soul in the Church of St Mary le Bow—which will was not enrolled in the Husting of London as it ought to have been[1]. The defendant said that he had sued no plea in the Court Christian relating to a lay fee, and he put himself

---

[1] The claim of the City to the probate or enrolment of wills in the Husting probably goes back to the early thirteenth century. Already in 1193 deeds were so enrolled (Page, *London, its Origin and Early Development*, p. 112). A document in the City's *Liber Ordinationum*, fo. 173, which is dated by Miss Bateson (*Borough Customs*, II, p. cxxxix) as of A.D. 1300, but from internal evidence is clearly *circa* 1230, lays down that no one could be secure of a tenement devised, unless the will were enrolled. In 1268 the Bishop of London's deputy endeavoured to deprive the City of its right of probate, but the case was taken to the King, who decided in the City's favour (*Lib. de Ant. Leg.* fos. 110 *b*, 111). Ultimately a compromise seems to have come into force, whereby wills of lands were taken first before the Ordinary of the Archdeacon of London, and then proved in the Husting. This was already an old custom by A.D. 1357 (*Cal. of Letter Book G*, pp. 88–9), though there is little in the wills enrolled in the Court of Husting to show that they had already been before the Ordinary, and, on the other hand, many wills proved before the Ordinary never came to the Husting. But the City never varied from its contention that all wills ought to be so enrolled, and a method of compulsion was adopted, whereby any beneficiary under a testament within the City could cause the same to be enrolled in the Husting by writ of *ex gravi querela* to the Mayor (Fitzherbert, *New Natura Brevium*, 1794, p. 199). Cf. Sharpe, *Cal. of Wills enrolled in Court of Husting*, I, pp. xlii, xliii.

on his country. A jury was summoned against the next Court
of Common Pleas after Hokeday, and the same day was
given to the defendant to hear the verdict.

A jury of Castle Baynard Ward, consisting of Adam
Absolon and others, declared that the two quarters of wheat
which were attached from Thomas atte Loke for 13s 4d,
being his fifteenth due to the Queen's Gold, were the property of Robert atte Loke, and that the above Thomas had
no interest in them to the value of 4d. They said also that
Robert did not trade with any goods of Thomas nor avow
them, as was charged against him. Robert now mainprised
Thomas to appear in Court at Easter to satisfy the Commonalty as regards the mark claimed from him.

Friday before the Feast of the Conversion of St Paul Membr. 5
[25 Jan.]   24 Jan.
                                                          1303–4

Roger de Derby and others said on oath that certain persons
hired bakehouses &c. [Note. The list is identical with that
on Membr. 4. See p. 155.]

Wednesday after the Feast of the Purification B.M. Membr. 5 b
[2 Feb.]   5 Feb.
                                                          1303–4

Gerard le Fruter, John Oki, William de Writele, Richard
de Bermingham, Robert le Skynnere, Terry de Dudlee,
William de Meleforthe, Robert de Meleforthe, Geoffrey
Trentemars, Adam Knith, Stephen atte Losue, Richard
Treuchappman, Henry Pride, Walter de Aldresgate, and
other "fruters" were summoned to answer the Mayor and
Aldermen for having made a confederacy between them,
strengthened by an oath, that none of them would buy the
fruit of any garden within London or without before the
Feast of the Nativity of St John the Baptist [24 June], so that
they might then have their fruit as it were for nothing—
and this they did without the King's warrant and in contempt
of him, and to the great loss and hardship of the people.
William de Writele, fruiterer, came and said that the above

Gerard came to him soon after Easter last, saying that the fruiterers were all poor and captives on account of their own simplicity, and if they would act on his advice they would be rich and powerful, namely, if they would bind themselves by an oath not to buy before the Nativity of St John the Baptist, when they could buy and sell all fruits according to their will. He himself agreed, and took a book in his bosom to the meeting of fruiterers, whereupon they all took their corporal oath as above; but afterwards, reflecting that the confederacy was not good, lawful, or to be advocated, he repented of his oath, and bought his fruit as he was wont to do. As regards his trespass he puts himself on the mercy of the Court. A day was given to him at the next Husting of Common Pleas to hear judgment.

And as regards the accusation made against him that he bought and forestalled fruit to the damage and scarcity of the King and his people, he demanded a jury.

And the above Gerard, John Oky, Richard de Bermingham and the others demanded a day to answer the charges, which was granted to them. But on the day given the Mayor and Aldermen could not find time to deal with the case, and another day was given.

Membr. 6
26 Feb.
1303–4

Wednesday after the Feast of St Mathias the Apostle [24 Feb.]

Adam de Benetele was attached to answer William de Fridaystrete and Philip de Merdele, Serjeants of John de Burreforthe, for slandering them, calling them thieves and robbers, and raising the hue against them in contempt of the King and to their damage 100s, when they distrained him by a small maser-cup for his arrears due to the 2000 marks and the Queen's Gold, which distraint they were ordered to make by the Mayor and Aldermen in accordance with the record submitted by the Chamberlain. The defendant denied the charge and demanded a jury. A jury from the venue of Friday Street was summoned against the Friday.

Philip le Cotiller was summoned to answer Richard Edward, butcher, in a plea of covenant, wherein the latter complained that Philip apprenticed his brother Walter to him for seven years, and became surety and principal debtor for Walter's faithful service as an apprentice, and that the latter had left him without permission and carried away £4 16s of his goods, and though he claimed that sum from the defendant Philip, as surety, the defendant refused to pay it. Philip pleaded that Richard committed the goods to Walter on the arrangement that he give an account within the first half year, and this before the apprentice had any knowledge of the business, and against the defendant's wish; and he demanded judgment whether he ought to answer for goods so committed, and a jury to say whether Walter carried away the goods. A jury was summoned for Wednesday after Hokeday. Afterwards at a Court held on Friday after the Quinzime of Easter, a jury of Richard Sharp and others said on oath that the above Richard committed his money to Walter the apprentice to trade therewith, before the latter had learnt the business, and that Walter, having lost them to the value of 20s, took fright and fled. Judgment that the plaintiff recover nothing and be in mercy, and that Philip go thence without a day.

John de Madefrey was attached to answer the Mayor and Commonalty because, when William de Fridaystrete and John Juvenal, Serjeants of the Commonalty and of the Sheriffs, distrained him by a piece of cloth for his arrears of his fifteenth due to the Queen's Gold, he snatched the pledge away. The defendant admitted that he would not let them take it away, because it seemed to him unjust. As it was found from the Chamberlain's Record that the distraint was just, judgment was given that the defendant go to prison &c. Afterwards he was mainprised by Gilbert Cros and Adam "*de villa Sancti Johannis*"[1], tailor, to appear on Friday to hear judgment and to receive and do what the Court should consider.

A jury of the venue of Vintry, consisting of John de Salisbiry, cordwainer, and others, said on oath that Garsias de Sanetere is not a nightwalker and evildoer, as indicted by the Inquest *de officio* taken by the Mayor and Sheriffs with

[1] Perth.

regard to nightwalkers and evildoers, on account of which indictment he had been imprisoned. Judgment that Garsias be acquitted; and he was enjoined to stay within doors after curfew so long as he remained in the City, and forbidden to do any harm to anyone either by night or day, under penalty of imprisonment.

. . . . . was found armed with iron corset and cap and a sword in the Guildhall in the presence of the Mayor, Aldermen, and many citizens. He was adjudged to forfeit his arms and be committed to prison.

Membr. 6 b
18 March
1303–4

Wednesday after the Feast of St Gregory [12 March]

A jury of the venue of Vintry was summoned against Wednesday after the Quinzime of Easter, to say on oath whether Gylenzon de Genue weighed any merchandise or mercery in the City of London between citizens and strangers by the beam produced in Court, as he was accused of doing.

The jury between Reymon Momace of Gascony, plaintiff, and Philip Burgy de More was respited till Saturday for lack of jurors. Afterwards, on Monday before the Annunciation B.M. [25 March], a jury of Roger le Ferrour and others said on oath that the two horses, whereof one was black and the other "baustan"[1], which were attached from Philip Burgy, merchant of the Society of the Mosi[2], at the suit of Reymon Momace of Gascony, belonged to the said Philip on the Saturday after the Feast of St Gregory Pope [12 March], and not to Master Walter de Ipre or any other man of Flanders, as Reymon alleged. Judgment that Philip have his two horses.

24 March
1304

Tuesday the Vigil of the Annunciation [25 March]

Gydo Bonaventure appointed John Tyle his attorney against John le Engleys, Serjeant[3] of the Fair of Champenoise Brie and attorney of the same, in a plea of debt.

[1] O.E.D.: having white spots on a black or bay ground.
[2] The Mozze, or Mozzi, were a rich trading company of Florence. Archaeologia, xxviii, pp. 221, 243; Cal. Close Rolls, passim.
[3] Serviens, used indiscriminately in the City Records for a Serjeant of the Court, a journeyman workman, and the beadle of a Ward.

Letters of attorney and recommendation, addressed to all justices and justiciars, ecclesiastical and lay, to the effect that Hugh de Calvomonte and John Cayn of St Manehuld, Wardens of the Fair of Champenoise Brie, had appointed John the Englishman to do certain business on behalf of the Fair; and on behalf of Philip, King of France and Navarre and Lord of Champenoise Brie, they pray that the above John may be well treated on his journeys by the justices &c., as they would wish their own servants to be treated. Sealed with the Seal of the Fair, January, 1303. R. de Monte Calvulo.

Wednesday after the Quinzime of Easter [29 *March*]

Simon de Graham was attached to answer John de Burreforth, Sheriff, that whereas he was a foreigner, and not of the Liberty of the City, he bought much merchandise, such as spicery and other things, from certain foreign merchants and especially from . . . . Durand who was dwelling in the house of William Servat, through the instrumentality of Henry de Farnham, spicer, hired by Simon for the purpose, thus defrauding the King and his bailiffs of the customs due. The defendant denied that he bought merchandise except from a freeman of the City, and this he was prepared to prove in such manner as the Court adjudged. A jury was summoned from the venue round Bokerelesbury for Friday.

Richard de Houndeslowe was summoned to answer the Prior and Brothers of the Order of St Augustine for killing horses and burying their carcasses within the Walls of London against the ordinance of the citizens, thus corrupting the air to the danger of the Brethren and citizens dwelling around. The defendant did not deny killing and skinning the horses &c., but said that the men of his trade had always been accustomed to do so and had never been prohibited. He was mainprised by John Baudry and John Note, tanners[1] of the

---

[1] Tanning was extensively carried on in Moorfields, as may be seen from the masses of leather cuttings exposed during excavations. *Archaeologia*, vol. LXXI, iii. "Some Recent Excavations in London," Frank Lambert, M.A., F.S.A.

Moor, for his appearance on Friday to hear judgment. Afterwards, on Friday after the Quinzime of Easter, he came before the Mayor and Aldermen and swore on the Gospels that he would not henceforth skin any carcasses within the City or bury them within the City or cast them in the ditches either within or outside the City, and if he knew of any one else doing so he would inform the Mayor and Chamberlain[1].

17 April 1304 *Friday after the Quinzime of Easter* [29 March]

Thomas le Palmere offered himself against William de Fridaistrete, late clerk of Peter de Bosenho, Sheriff, in a plea that whereas the above William was charged by Peter to collect the Queen's Gold, and received 16s from the plaintiff, he only acquitted him against the Mayor and Chamberlain for 13s, so that the plaintiff was wrongfully distrained for 3s. The above William, who had this day, did not come. The Court ordered that the Sheriff be distrained to attend on Monday to show cause &c.

John le Barber, plaintiff, and John de Laufare, cordwainer, defendant in a plea of trespass, made agreement by permission of Court, on terms that the latter pay the former one silver mark.

2 May 1304 *Saturday the morrow of the Apostles Philip and James* [1 May]

A jury of the venue of Billingesgate, consisting of John de Romeneye and others, said on oath that the ship of William Clayssone called the "Pelerim," which was attached at the suit of Henry de Lincoln, burgess of Gernemue[2], belonged to Durdrich in Holland, and not to Almaine. Judgment that the ship remain attached till Henry receive satisfaction for his damages in Friseland.

[1] The Chamberlain was responsible during the Middle Ages for such sanitary and "Public Health" measures as were undertaken by the City.
[2] Yarmouth.

Saturday after the Feast of the Apostles Peter and *4 July 1304*
Paul [29 *June*]

William Smert, "shippewrith," was attached to answer Adam de Foleham, alderman, for claiming to be free of the City.

Walter de Wanlok was attached to answer Jordan Moraunt and the bailiffs of the City in a plea of trespass, wherein they complained that when John Juvenal went to distrain him for £20, which he acknowledged as owing to Jordan in the Paper of the Guildhall[1], the defendant would not permit the distraint, and removed the distraint made on him and the sequestrated goods, in contempt of the King. The defendant admitted that he would not allow the Serjeant to make a sequestration upon him. Judgment that he go to prison. He denied that he broke the sequestration or carried away the goods, and claimed a jury. Afterwards a jury, consisting of William de Cantebrig and others, said that he removed the sealed door from the hinges, and carried away sequestrated goods to the value of 20s. Judgment that he go to prison till he satisfy Jurdan for the goods removed. At a subsequent Court a day was given him, at the instance of Gilbert, son of Thomas de Clare, to appear in Court and satisfy Master Jurdan for the 20s, and the King for his contempt.

Saturday after the Feast of St Thomas the Martyr *11 July 1304*
[7 *July*] *A^o* 32 *Edw.* [1304]

A jury of the venue of Bradestret by the Church of St Bartholomew the Less was summoned to say on oath whether David the clerk, Gocelyn, and Thomas de Kent received from Richard le Clerk 6s 8d, Queen's Gold, as he avers, or 4s, as they say.

[1] Refers to the Rolls of Recognizances on vellum. *Papera* is used generally of a register. The above Rolls have survived for the period A.D. 1285–1392.

25 July 1304   *Saturday after the Feast of St Margaret Virgin [20 July]*

John le Wyttawyere skinned a black horse[1] in the week before the Feast of the Invention of the Holy Cross. To be distrained.

Membr. 8   *Monday after the Feast of St James [25 July] before*
27 July 1304   John de Wengrave[2], *deputy of the Mayor*

Robert de la Bourse de Brugges who was distrained by 6 tuns of woad, and Eustace Liene de . . . . , who was distrained by 17 tuns of woad, by the King's writ at the suit of Remund de la Bruwe, offered themselves against the latter, and demanded return of the distraints in accordance with another writ which they produced. The Sheriff gave evidence that Remund was not in town and could not be warned. He was ordered to warn him to come on Friday to hear verification of the above goods.

Writ, dated at Strivelyn 22 July A° 32 Edw. [1304], to the effect that Adam de Fulham had complained that Robert, son of Walter le . . . . , had entered his chamber by night, broken open his chests and carried away rolls and memoranda relating to his Aldermanry, charters, writings obligatory, tallies, jewels and other chattels, and that the Mayor and Aldermen had delayed giving him a remedy, and had allowed the above Robert to wander about the City consuming the above goods. The Mayor &c. were ordered to make amends to the above Adam and do justice in the matter.

In accordance with the above writ, Robert was attached to answer Adam in a plea of trespass, wherein the plaintiff claimed damages £300. The defendant pleaded not guilty and demanded a jury. A jury of the venue of London Bridge

---

[1] I.e. within the City. Cf. p. 161.

[2] John de Wangrave, Alderman, was sworn on Monday after the Feast of the Conversion of St Paul (25 January) A° 32 Edw. [1303–4], to render all judgments in the Husting well and truly after the Mayor and Aldermen have come from consultation and have arrived at an agreement, and also all other judgments touching the Commonalty of London, and to set in order and cause to be enrolled all pleas in the Husting. Cal. of Letter Book C, pp. 132–3 and note.

was summoned for Thursday, and the defendant was main-prised by Henry le Blound, "stokfihsmongere," and Peter Berneval to hear the verdict. Afterwards the parties came, and another day was given them.

Saturday after the Feast of the Nativity [8 Sept.] *12 Sept. 1304*

Beringer Aulyn, Matthew de Corbins and many companions were attached to answer John de Burreforth[1], for selling dates and several kinds of spices to citizens and foreigners by their own measures against the Liberty of the City. The defendants denied the charge and demanded a jury. A jury of the venue of the Ryole was summoned for Tuesday.

Court of J. Blound, *Mayor, held by him and* John de Wangrave *on Saturday before the Feast of St Andrew the Apostle* [30 Nov.] *at the beginning of the 33rd year of King Edward*

Membr. 8 b
28 Nov. 1304

Bartholomew de Fihsbourne, Thomas de Meles, Henry de Melingg, Peter de Somersete, Roger de Raby, Geoffrey de St Cross, Robert de la Marche, Simon FitzWarin, and "Adinettus" of Gascony were attached to answer John le Blound, Mayor, John de Lincoln and Roger de Paris, Sheriffs, for assaulting them with bows and arrows on Friday night after the Feast of All Souls [1 Nov.]. They denied the charge and put themselves on their country. A jury of the venue of Cheap between the Church of St Mary le Bow and Friday Street was summoned, and the defendants were mainprised by Hugh de Oxford, Peter le Hireys, and Roger de Redingge. Afterwards the jury, consisting of William de Wyncestre and others, brought a verdict of not guilty, and they were acquitted.

On this day judgment was given by the Mayor and Aldermen that the two casks of new wine which John le Botoner, junior, admitted having harboured [*hospitasse*] among his old wines be forfeited.

2 Dec. 1304

---

[1] Sheriff, A.D. 1303–4. This was an action against foreigners for trading retail.

18 Dec. 1304 *Friday after the Feast of St Lucia Virgin* [13 Dec.]

A jury of the venue of Wodestrete around St Alban's Church was summoned to say whether Gregory le Botoner and John de Wynton, "fuster"[1], hindered William de Carletone, Serjeant of the Sheriff, from making a distraint on John for a debt acknowledged in the Sheriff's Court.

20 Jan.
1304-5
Wednesday the Feast of SS. Fabian and Sebastian [20 Jan.] *A^o 33 Edw.* [1304-5]

Thomas de Kydemenstre, "chaucer"[2], was summoned to answer William de Beverlee, because he did not clothe, feed and instruct his apprentice Thomas, William's son, but drove him away. The defendant said that the apprentice lent his master's goods to others and promised to restore them or their value, but went away against his wish; and he demanded a jury. Subsequently a jury of William de Upton and others said the apprentice lent two pairs of shoes belonging to his master and was told to restore them, but, frightened by the beating which he received, ran away; further that the master did not feed and clothe his apprentice as he ought, being unable to do so, to the apprentice's damage 40d, but that he was now in a position to look after his apprentice. Thereupon Thomas de Kydemenstre said he was willing to have the apprentice back and provide for him, and the father agreed. Judgment that the master take back the apprentice and feed and instruct him, or that he repay to the father the money paid by the latter, and that he pay the father the 40d and be in mercy.

26 Jan.
1304-5
Tuesday the morrow of the Conversion of St Paul [25 Jan.]

Philip Hodde appointed William de Toulouse his attorney against Remund Geraundon, Remund de Vile Fraunk, Peter Fanne, and Donan de Ponte in a plea of debt.

[1] Saddle-bow maker. Cf. Cal. of Letter Book C, p. 167, n.
[2] Shoemaker.

Wednesday after the above Feast.

Philip Hodde offered himself against Remund Geraundon, plaintiff, in a plea of covenant. The latter did not prosecute his plaint[1]. He and his pledges in mercy. And the Sheriff brought his record.

Bernard de la Rochele was attached to answer Arnold de Teler of Gascony in a plea of trespass, wherein the latter complained that Bernard bought from him five casks of wine for £10 in London, and took him to a tavern and paid him 20s in part payment, and while they were sitting in the tavern, caused the casks to be loaded on carts and taken away from his custody against his will, to his damage £10. The defendant said he was a broker to a certain Adam le Brocher as regards the five casks, and that the latter paid him 20s in part payment, and that Arnold himself made delivery of the wine to Adam. Afterwards a jury of Vintry, consisting of Alan de Suffolk and others, said that the plaintiff delivered the wine to Adam and not to the defendant. Judgment that Arnold gain nothing by his plaint and Bernard be acquitted.

A jury of the venue of the Conduit, consisting of Ralph Godchep and others, said that a certain boy carrying water in a tankard came on Saturday last opposite the shop of Adam de Boctone, "cofferer"[2], and there came also a cook and a clerk called William de Radendene, both then unknown, and ill-treated the boy, so that the neighbours thought he would be killed. Thereupon a certain Adam de St Albans, fearing this would happen, asked the cook and the clerk why they were beating the boy so maliciously. And the clerk replied that they would beat him as they liked in spite of Adam. And when Adam took the boy from their hands, the clerk bit Adam, and Adam took the clerk by the hood and tore it. And the cook struck Adam, who struck him back. They said further that several foreigners unknown to them were round them; and if the cook and the clerk received any harm, they had no cause of complaint.

---

[1] This was a plea of error made in the Sheriff's Court. See p. 168.
[2] Maker of coffers or chests.

Friday after the Purification B.M. [2 Feb.]

Alan de Suffolch and other jurors said that Bernard de la Rochele, broker and citizen of London, was host to foreign merchants dealing in woad &c., but did not trade with them. Bernard admitted that he had charge of the wines and the wife[1] of Gerard de Orgoyl, who was then abroad. And because the use and custom of the City do not allow a broker to be a host or a merchant, the said Bernard was mainprised by Alan de Suffolch and Henry le Gaugeour to come on Wednesday to receive judgment.

Hugh de Strubbi was summoned to answer Nicholas Beaubelet in a plea of trespass, wherein the latter complained that the defendant took away the plaintiff's apprentice, Robert le Fraunceys of Malteby, and detained him in his service. The defendant denied the charge, and said that Hugh drove the apprentice away, and that he, the defendant, often asked him to take the apprentice back, but the plaintiff refused, whereupon he took the apprentice into his service lest he should perish of hunger; and he demanded a jury. A jury of the venue of Fletestrete was summoned against Wednesday.

[Record and process of an action in the Sheriff's Court.]

Court held on Tuesday before the Feast of St Hilary [13 Jan.]

Philip Hudde, master of the ship called "le Messager" of Lym, was attached to answer Reymund Gerardoun in a plea of covenant, wherein the latter complained that he and other merchants freighted the above ship from Bordeaux to the Pool of London, and put on board 134 casks of wine, so that the ship should go directly from Bordeaux to the Pool, as appears in an indenture dated at Bordeaux 15 Oct. A°33[2] Edw.

---

[1] The defendant seems to have pleaded that the wines and the wife were merely chattels deposited in his charge. The Court considered that the wife was her husband's agent.

[2] An error for A° 32 Edw., i.e. 15 Oct. 1304. Cf. p. 166, where the case came up on appeal.

between the parties. The said Philip, however, on his journey perceiving certain casks of wine floating in the sea and being moved by cupidity, made a delay and got together part of the casks, and overloaded his ship with them knowingly and maliciously, and when he came to Portesmeuwe[1], he tied [*applicuit*] up there, and wickedly remained six weeks, whereas he ought to have gone direct to London; and afterwards when he came to London and ought to have tied up in the Pool, he maliciously grounded his ship on a sandbank, whereby the plaintiff lost two casks on the voyage and also the sale of his wines. The defendant denied the charges, or that he did any of the matters alleged knowingly and maliciously, and said he was ready to defend himself by his law according to the custom of the City. The plaintiff pleaded that the defendant ought not to be admitted to his law, because he charged him with certain matters touching a covenant contained in a deed, and if the defendant was unwilling to answer otherwise, he claimed judgment as in an undefended action. The defendant pleaded that he had done none of the things the plaintiff alleged, and as he had handed over the wine, he demanded judgment as to how he ought to defend himself. A day was given at the next Court for judgment. Afterwards the parties came and added nothing to their pleadings. And since the plaintiff did not deny that he had received the wine, which he had consigned at Bordeaux, and since the defendant was ready to defend himself by his law in the matter touching the covenant, and as the Court had no power to summon any jury by which the truth of the matter could be better or more safely investigated than by the defendant's law, which law the plaintiff refused to admit, judgment was given that Reymund gain nothing by his plaint, and be in mercy, and that the said Philip go thence without a day.

[1] Portsmouth.

ROLL G

Further proceedings of the Court of J. le Blound, *Mayor, Friday after the Feast of the Purification B.M.* [2 *Feb.*] *A° 33 Edw.* [1304–5]

Nicholas Beaubelot was summoned to answer Hugh de Strubby[1] for retaining Robert Fraunceys of Maltby, his apprentice, in his service for six years, and not having him enrolled in the Paper of the Chamber of Guildhall[2] according to the use and custom of the City. The defendant admitted that he kept him unenrolled, but said that it was the plaintiff's fault, as the latter did not pay for the enrolment according to the covenant between them. The plaintiff said no money ought to be paid for enrolment—only 20s for his teaching and sustenance, and this he had paid; and he demanded to acquit himself thereof by his law. A day was given at the Quinzime.

Adam le Brochere was summoned to answer Arnold de Teler in a plea that he pay him £9 owed for five casks of wine, which the plaintiff sold him, and which he fraudulently took away on payment of 20s, promising to pay the rest when the plaintiff came to his house; but before the latter's arrival he sent the casks to Coventry, and when the plaintiff came and asked for his money, he did not pay it, but only said he would do his best to pay. The defendant admitted buying the wine, but said he had not the money to pay at present. He admitted also that he promised to pay and had

---

[1] Cf. p. 168.

[2] The Ordinances of the Cordwainers, granted in Walter Hervey's Mayoralty, A.D. 1271, enjoined that none of that trade should receive an apprentice except by consent of the Mayor and Commune, and that the apprentice, among other fees, should pay 2s to the Commune—a provision which would imply some entry in the City books (City's *Liber Horn.* fo. 340). According to the *Chronicles of Edward I and Edward II* (Rolls Series), p. 85, "a certain liberty was provided in London in A.D. 1275, namely that the names of apprentices should be enrolled in the Paper of the Guildhall, as well as of those who wished to purchase the freedom, and that anyone whose name was not to be found in the Paper, should be deprived of the freedom." The reason given was that many pretended to the freedom who were not entitled to it. Three methods of obtaining the freedom are mentioned: patrimony, apprenticeship and purchase. In 1300 definite ordinance was made to enforce the enrolment of apprentices in the Paper within a year of their indentures, by prosecuting those masters who failed in this duty (*Lib. Cust.* I, p. 93).

sent the wine to Coventry. Judgment that the defendant for his fraud be committed to prison till he satisfy the plaintiff for the money. Afterwards, on Thursday following, Robert de Dodeford and Peter de Byri, skinners, entered into a Recognizance to pay the £9 on the Quinzime.

Saturday after the Feast of St Valentine the Martyr [14 Feb.]
20 Feb. 1304–5

A jury of Adam Wade and others said on oath that if a foreign merchant discharged wines or woad upon the quay of a citizen without the latter's knowledge, he ought to pay, for the first day and night, 1½d for each tun of wine or woad.

Wednesday the Vigil of the Annunciation B.M. [25 March]
24 March 1304–5

Margery de Rothing was summoned to answer Margery, relict of John Somery, in a plea of trespass, wherein the latter complained that the defendant had a pit dug in her free tenement in the parish of St Michael of Wodestrete, and had it filled with filth from the privy, against the Mayor's prohibition[1], in contempt of the King and to her damage 100s. The defendant denied the offence and claimed a jury. Afterwards a jury of Gregory le Botoner and others found her guilty and assessed damages at 5 marks. Judgment for the same, and that the defendant be summoned to hear judgment as regards what was done after the Mayor's prohibition.

Walter de Canefeld, butcher, came and admitted that he took John Oseburn as his apprentice for seven years, and at the end of the first year quitclaimed the apprenticeship for 40s. A day was given to hear judgment on Monday.

Saturday after the Feast of the Annunciation B.M. [25 March]
Membr. 1 b 27 March 1305

A jury of Robert le Convers and others said on oath that Margery de Wengham did not hurt Margery, daughter of

---

[1] In accordance with the general regulations of the City as to cleansing. Cal. of Letter Book A, pp. 183, 218, 219; *Memorials of London, etc.* pp. 35, 67.

William le Mareschal, on the arm as Francis de Vilers and Agnes his wife alleged, but that the above Agnes, who was the mother of Margery, had done the hurt, and that Margery de Wengham diligently caused it to be cured; and further that the latter maintained and instructed the girl, and maintained the house and rents devised to her well and faithfully; and that the property when leased was worth 75s per annum, subject to payment of 31s 8d to the chief lords, and 6s 8d was paid for repairs per annum.

Reymund de St Clement was summoned to answer Reginald de Thonderle in a plea that he restore to him two bills of £70 15s 11d, which the plaintiff bought from William Foundepe, merchant, and which the said William entrusted to the custody of the defendant for delivery to the plaintiff. Reymund admitted receipt and detinue of the bills, and said he was willing to give them up, if the plaintiff would pay a debt of 15s 11d, and undertake to acquit him as regards the above William. The plaintiff admitted the debt. Judgment that he pay Reymund and Reymund give him the bills.

Roger de Paris, Sheriff, was summoned to answer Matthew de Arace in a plea of trespass, wherein the latter complained that although the defendant had 44 coloured and ray cloths of his, valued by oath of lawful and honest men at £167 6s 8d for payment of a certain debt of £167 4s, which William de Combemartin recovered against the plaintiff in the defendant's Court, and although the defendant caused the said cloths to be sealed by David his clerk and William de Combemartin, thus ratifying the value of them for payment of the debt, nevertheless the next day the defendant sequestrated 16 other cloths of the plaintiff. The defendant said that William de Combemartin recovered against the plaintiff £233 11s 8d and that he sequestrated the 16 cloths at the suit of the above William, who brought a writ of the King, for £66 5s.

2 April 1305   *Friday before the Feast of St Ambrose, Bishop* [*4 April*]

John de Wavendon, baker, was attached to answer Simon Geram of St Albans in a plea that he pay him 25s, due for three quarters of wheat, payable on delivery. The defendant admitted the debt, but said that several magnates of the land owed him large sums, and as soon as he received them, he would pay the plaintiff. And because it was of old ordained, and is still the custom, that bakers should pay on the spot all those who sell grain to them, under penalty of imprisonment, on account of the quarrels and actions which arose between them in past times, judgment was given that the defendant go to prison until &c. Afterwards he was mainprised by William de Ravenestone to pay before noon (*ante horam nonam*). And a day was given to him on Monday to hear judgment.

Henry de Passenham was attached to answer John Tedmar, Robert de Mocking, and their fellows, executors of the will of John le Benere, in a plea of trespass, wherein they complained that John le Benere, in his house by London Bridge, handed to the defendant a Statute Staple in which Richard le Spicer was bound to him in £20, in order that the defendant might collect that sum, and that the latter had sold it to Richard le Spicer, thus defrauding John and his executors. The defendant denied that he received or sold the Statute, and demanded to acquit himself by his law. The plaintiffs pleaded that he ought not to be admitted to his law, as they were ready to prove the receipt and sale by a jury. Afterwards the Court directed that the case be inquired into by a jury of the venue of the Bridge and Smethefeld.

Wednesday after the Feast of St Ambrose, Bishop [4 April]

Membr. 2
7 April 1305

Roger le Graunt, barber, collector of the Customs of Smethefeld[1], was attached to answer John Underwode in a plea that he pay him 42s 6d, unjustly detained for five oxen which he sold to the defendant for 47s 6d, 5s of which the latter paid on the spot, promising to pay the rest next day, but next day he refused to do so and charged the plaintiff with stealing the oxen, and had several times since refused

---

[1] Cf. *Lib. Alb.* I, p. 233.

to pay, using opprobrious words to him, to his damage and the scandal of the city. The defendant said he never bought oxen from the plaintiff, but that a certain William atte Knole....Afterwards the defendant entered into a Recognizance to pay the plaintiff 37s 6d on the morrow, and was in mercy. The money was paid to William de Hichingg, clerk, in the Chamber of Guildhall, and by him paid to Walter le Lord, attorney of the plaintiff, who gave an acquittance in the presence of Richard Poterel, then Chamberlain.

William de Foresta, smith, was attached to answer Adam de Clerkenwell, beadle of the Ward of Cornhulle, in a plea of trespass, wherein the latter complained that the defendant struck him with a stick the previous night after curfew. The defendant denied the charge and demanded a jury. He was mainprised by John de Ware, "mauncher"[1], Roger le Ferour and Roger Herand to hear the verdict. Afterwards a jury of William le Wolf and others found for the plaintiff with damages half a mark. Judgment accordingly. Subsequently a smith's whetstone (?) and a pair of bellows (*unus lapis aplar⁹ fabr⁹ et duo flabelli*), seized upon the said William, were valued by John de Elsingham, John atte Holte, John May, and Thomas de Wymbihs, smiths, at 4s, and delivered to the plaintiff in part payment of the half mark, and order was given that the defendant be distrained for the remainder.

8 April 1305 ### Thursday after the Feast of Sᵗ Ambrose, Bishop [4 April]

A jury of Cheap Ward was summoned for Saturday to say whether Geoffrey de Meldebourne beat and ill-treated John de Harwe and John, servant of John Juvenal, Serjeants of the Sheriff, and took away from them two carts with horses, requisitioned by them for the King's service.

30 April 1305 ### Friday after the Feast of Sᵗ Mark the Evangelist [25 April]

Nicholas le Batour entered into a Recognizance to pay Sir Roger de Hegham and Ysabell his wife one good and decent brass bowl at Pentecost.

[1] A maker of "maunches," or sleeves.

Odo le Goldbeter and Robert atte Forde, "seler"[1], were attached to answer William de Carleton, Serjeant of John de Lincoln, Sheriff, and the Sheriff, for refusing to allow the above William to make delivery of a supertunic belonging to Sir John de Horne, knight, which had been taken from the latter and was found in the possession of the defendant; and also for interfering with the Serjeant by keeping him in the defendant's house as a prisoner until he was liberated by the Sheriff, to his damage £10. The defendants denied the charge. Afterwards a jury of Goderonelane, consisting of William de Sinigham and others, found them not guilty. Judgment accordingly, and that the plaintiff be in mercy.

Wednesday after the Feast of the Holy Cross [3 *May*]

Membr. 2 b
5 May 1305

David de Gloucestre, clerk, offered himself against Symon Bolimer and William de Hestone, plaintiffs, in a plea of trespass. The plaintiffs did not come nor prosecute their plea. The defendant went thence without a day, and the plaintiffs were amerced.

Robert le Sauser was attached to answer Maud de Milham in a plea of trespass, wherein she complained that she bought from him three casks of wine and three silver cups for £9 19s 11½d, and entered into a Statute Merchant to him for payment, and that she had hired from him a house from Sunday in Midlent till the Easter following, and from that Feast for a year, at two marks annual rent, and had put the above wines and other goods in the house, and that on Wednesday after Midlent the defendant had expelled her from the house, and seized the goods therein to the value of £20, to her damage £30, and to the scandal of the City £100. The defendant denied the charges and offered to acquit himself by his law. The plaintiff pleaded that in so serious a matter, involving imprisonment, the defendant ought not to be admitted to his law, and she demanded judgment thereon. Afterwards the defendant offered himself against the plaintiff, and she did not come on the day given her.

---

[1] Saddler.

Judgment that she and her pledges be in mercy, and the defendant go thence without a day.

7 May 1305 ## Friday after the Feast of the Invention of the Holy Cross [3 May]

William de Ponte of Leytonebusard, attorney of the Abbess "*de Fonte Ebrudi*"[1], acknowledged that he had received from Girard Orgul £9 10s, in which Girard was bound to her, as appears by a Recognizance in the Court of Peter de Bosenham, Sheriff.

A day was given to Thomas Sely on Wednesday to bring his clerks and memoranda, in order to answer Thomas le Barber of Bredstret, who complained by petition[2].

Membr. 3
17 May 1305 ## Monday before the Feast of St Dunstan [19 May]

Adam atte Rose, "poter," was summoned to answer Alice Pas in a plea of trespass, wherein she complained that he invited her to dinner, and afterwards took her into his chamber and forced her to seal a certain document, the tenour of which she did not know, to her disinherison, as she believed. The defendant denied the sealing, and said he had no deed from her, except a quitclaim of a rent at Wytewellebech belonging to the inheritance of John Pas, his apprentice, and he demanded a jury. Afterwards a jury of the venue of Bredstret, consisting of Simon de Rokesle and others, said that Alice sealed no deed unwillingly. Judgment for the defendant. A day was given on Friday for the defendant to hear judgment as regards the deed made in disinherison of John, his apprentice.

10 June 1305 ## Thursday after Pentecost [6 June]

Further proceedings in an action by Richard Hauteyn against Geoffrey de Hengham. [See p. 141.]

[1] *Sc. Ebraldi.* Fontevrault.   [2] See p. 196, note 1.

David de Gloucestre, clerk, was attached to answer Simon de Bolimere in a plea of trespass, wherein the latter complained that David distrained him on his goods to the value of one mark, alleging a mainprise which the plaintiff never undertook. The defendant pleaded that at the suit of Sir Robert de Snoryngg, chaplain, Renter of St Paul's, London, he distrained the Abbot of Flaxele by a horse for a debt due to Sir Robert, the horse being valued at one mark by the above Simon and William de Heston, and that the horse was returned to the Abbot under mainprise of Simon and William; afterwards the Abbot eloigned himself and the horse, so that justice could not be done to Sir Robert for the debt, and accordingly, he had distrained the plaintiff to produce the horse. The plaintiff denied being mainpernor of the Abbot for the horse or the value of it, and demanded a jury. A jury of the venue round St Paul's Quay was summoned for Wednesday.

William de Parys, defendant, and William de Bray, "stockfismoggere" essoined against Michael, the Prince's tailor, in a plea of debt by Henry de Oxford.

A jury was summoned in an action between Thomas Box of Brinchesle and Roger de Queneby. The former had bought 500 quarters of coal for £20 from the latter, and had taken pledges for the delivery of the coal. He refused either to give up the pledges or pay the price until the coal was delivered; the plaintiff demanded the price and the return of the pledges before delivery.

Thomas Juvenal was attached to answer Robert le Pestour of Aldresgate in a plea of trespass, wherein the latter complained that on Monday after the Feast of St Leonard [6 Nov.] A° 28 Edw. [1300] the defendant broke into his house and took away timber &c. to his damage 100s. The defendant

came and said that as no bailiff gave evidence that he had
been summoned or attached, he demanded judgment as to
whether he was bound to answer. Nevertheless he pleaded
that he bought three parts of a house from three sisters, the
fourth part being held by the plaintiff by virtue of his wife,
who was the fourth sister, and the house was partitioned,
according to the custom of the city, by the sworn carpenters
and masons[1], and that he took the timber belonging to his
part and not that belonging to the plaintiff. Afterwards a
jury of the venue of Aldresgate, consisting of Henry de Kele
and others, found for the defendant, who went quit. Judgment that Robert be in mercy for his false claim.

William de Toulouse produced a writ directed to the Mayor
and Sheriffs, and dated at St Albans 2 May A° 33 Edw. [1305],
which recited that William had freighted in London a ship
belonging to John, son of William Aykyn, merchant and
mariner of Middelbourgh in Seland, with wines and other
goods for conveyance to the King in Scotland, when the
latter was engaged in his warlike expedition there, but the
above John had sailed for Seland, had forcibly put William
ashore at Wulpsand, and taken the ship and William's goods
to the value of 200 marks to Middelbourgh; thereupon the
King had moved the Count of Hainault, Holland and Seland
to make restitution, but as he delayed doing so, the King
directs that goods belonging to merchants of Holland and
Seland in London should be arrested to the value of William's
loss, and information thereof returned with the writ.

Accordingly Hardekyn of Hardwyk, Thedrik Swalman,
and Aldeger of the same place, merchants, were attached.
They appeared and said that they were unjustly distrained,
because they were under the authority and Hanse of Almaine.
The plaintiff maintained that they belonged to Holland and

---

[1] The sworn masons and carpenters were officials, usually four in
number, who advised the Mayor and Aldermen in disputes relating to
party-walls, encroachments, and other matters arising under Fitz Aylwin's
Assize of Building. For their oath, A.D. 1301, see *Lib. Cust.* I, p. 100; Cal.
of Letter Book C, p. 86. References to them, and their reports, continue
throughout the Middle Ages, until their office was absorbed into that of
the Sworn Viewers after the Fire of London. They are represented to-day
by the city and borough surveyors.

Seland, and demanded an inquiry by merchants and sailors; and the defendants likewise demanded a jury. Afterwards a jury of the venue around Billinggesgate, consisting of Godfrey Moof and others, said that the defendants belonged to Hardwik in the domain of the Count of Geldres [*Gerlie*] and under the dominion of the King of Almaine. Judgment that their ships and goods be delivered to them.

Reginald de Thunderle was summoned to answer Henry Rammesdong, Henry Baysetart, Henry le Wolf and Janinus le Hefene, merchants of Malines, in a plea that he pay them £81 for cloths which he had bought of them, and which by common assent had been handed over to the shearmen to be sheared and to remain with the shearmen till the price was paid. The plaintiffs said that the defendant, by virtue of his being King's Aulnager for cloth, had taken away their cloths against their will and contrary to their Charter from the King concerning the New Custom. The defendant admitted that he owed £63 18s 4d for cloths, in various proportions to the plaintiffs. A day was given to pay them, and the matter of the remaining £17 1s 8d claimed was adjourned till the morrow.

Wednesday the Vigil of the Nativity of St John the Baptist [24 *June*]

Membr. 4 b
23 June 1305

Judgment by default was given for Thomas Sely against Thomas le Barber of Fridaystrete, who complained that the former during his Shrievalty had allowed to lapse a sequestration made on William de Boys, executor of Arnold Murdak, whereby the plaintiff lost 60s owed to him by Arnold.

A jury of the venue brought in a verdict that Adam le Bedel of Alegate and Margery atte Blakelofte were not guilty of assaulting Nicholas de Ardern, chaplain, and expelling him from a house in Alegatestrete, which he rented from them. The defendants had denied the assault and pleaded that they ejected him because he could not find sufficient security for the rent on entry, as he had promised to do.

Martin de Aumbresbiry and William de Fridaystrete were attached to answer John Musard of London and Joan his wife on a charge that, during Martin's Shrievalty, when John was absent on the King's service, they dragged Joan by the feet out of her house, ill-treated her and put her into the prison of Crepelgate unjustly and against the peace. Afterwards a jury of the venue brought in a verdict that the defendant William, by Martin's order, took Joan out of her house in East Cheap and kept her in prison eight days, to the plaintiffs' damage 40s. Judgment was given that Martin and William go to prison and satisfy John and Joan for the 40s.

Henry le Taylour of the Riole was attached to answer John de Vintry, Alderman, on a charge that when the plaintiff, with the Sheriff's bailiff, made a sequestration for the money which the defendant owed to the tallage made in the City by common consent of the citizens for the gift of money to the King, Queen and magnates, the defendant broke the sequestration and slandered the Alderman, the Mayor and other aldermen, and the bailiffs of the City. The defendant admitted breaking the sequestration and was adjudged to prison, but he claimed a jury as regards the slander. He was mainprised by Hugh de Oxford, John Scharp, John of the Chamber, Thomas le Fleming, Robert de Beaulou and John de Wynton to appear on Friday to pay his fine to the King. Afterwards, on Friday, he was fined 20s for his contempt of the King, which was respited until &c.

On the above day a proclamation was made (French) to the effect that John, bishop of Cardoil[1], and his bailiff John le Bole were in Court prepared to pay a quarterly rent of 100s for the Manor of Melreth, which the Bishop had leased from Dame Margaret, widow of Sir Warin de Bassingbourne.

Membr. 5   Richard de Caumpes was summoned to answer Thomas Crodde and his wife for having, during his Shrievalty, sequestrated their doors for an unjust claim of 40s, thus forcing them to pay 20s. The defendant claimed judgment

---

[1] Carlisle.

on the ground that the wife did not prosecute. The plaintiff
Thomas was ordered to bring his wife on Wednesday, as the
Court desired further information about the plaint.

Symon de Paris, late Sheriff of London, was attached to
answer Andrew de Hengeham, who complained that Symon
had neglected to obey a writ concerning trespasses done
against the plaintiff. The defendant said that he obeyed the
writ, but that the plaintiff had lost his case because he did
not prosecute his plaint; he demanded a jury of people living
round Guildhall and of persons frequenting the Court.
A jury was summoned for Saturday.

John de Writele, John de Radewell and William de
Haukesdene were attached to answer John Miles of Cornhull
in a plea of trespass, wherein he complained that they came
to his house and took away half a wey and one clove of cheese
to the value of 16s against his will and without payment,
tally or valuation. The defendants admitted receipt of the
cheese for the King's use and to the value of 4s. Afterwards
a jury of the venue consisting of Ranulf Balle and others said
that the defendants took one wey of cheese for the King's
use, in their capacity as his servants by letters patent, and
offered the plaintiff a tally. As it was clear that the cheese
was taken for the King's use, judgment was given for the
defendants.

[Record and process of an action in the Sheriff's Court.]

Court of Simon de Paris, *Wednesday after the Feast* Membr. 6
of St Martin [11 *Nov.*] *A° 30 Edw.* [1302] *14 Nov. 1302*

Writ 26 Oct. A° 30 Edw. [1302] to the Sheriffs that they
cause Ebright le Estreys to pay to Alan de Maldon a debt
of £34 13s.

Egbrytht le Estreys was attached by virtue of the above
writ to answer Alan de Maldon in a plea of debt, wherein
the latter complained that whereas he and the defendant
traded in common, and had an account made at Wycumbe,
as the result of which Egbrytht was shown to owe the plaintiff

£34 13s, which he promised to pay in London, nevertheless
he refused to do so. Thereupon came Thetard[1] le Estreys,
Alderman of the Hanse of Almaine, and demanded his Court
as regards Egbrytht. The plaintiff pleaded that he ought not
to have his court, since Egbrytht was attached by the King's
writ. The writ being read, the defendant pleaded that no
account was held and that he owed nothing on the day and
year alleged. On this the plaintiff asked leave to produce
witnesses, Thomas and Roger, immediately, as the parties
were foreigners, which was granted. The former, Thomas,
swore that he was present at Wycumbe in the house of
William le Lung, "heyward," when the plaintiff and defendant made an account on a certain tabard hung up in the solar,
the defendant being shown to owe £33 11s 2d, and that he
and Roger Athelard, the other witness, and Thomas Corbet
were present. Being asked if they made account by tallies,
rolls or other writings, he said no, but that Alan had a
schedule. Roger gave the same evidence except that he did
not recollect any schedule. Judgment in respite till the next
Court to give the parties an opportunity of coming to an
agreement. At subsequent courts Egbrytht was represented
by William de Railee, his attorney, and judgment was respited
that the Court might be further advised. Finally, at a Court
for Foreigners held on Monday after the Feast of St Andrew
the Apostle [30 Nov.], Alan offered himself against Egbryth,
who appeared by Richard Gladewyne his attorney, and

---

[1] The name appears elsewhere in the City Records as Thetard, Thodard,
Decard, etc. A similar case where the Alderman of the Hanse claimed
his Court is to be found in the City's Plea and Memoranda Rolls, A 5,
membr. 24, A.D. 1344. The merchants of Almaine, known as the "Easter-
lings" and "men of the Emperor," had long held a favoured position in
the City. The Colognese, who had their own Guildhall at Dowgate (*Lib.
Alb.* I, pp. 241, 243) appear to have amalgamated with the other Easter-
lings towards the close of the thirteenth century. Their Charter from
Henry III, dated 8 November 1235, was confirmed by Edward I, 28
July 1290 (*Lib. Cust.* I, pp. 66, 67). The Hanse Merchants also had a
Charter from Henry III, 15 June 1260, which was confirmed by Edward I,
18 November 1281 (Rymer's *Foedera*, I, pt ii, p. 588; City's *Liber Horn.*
fo. 281; Cal. of Letter Book C, p. 41). In 1282, a composition was made
between the citizens of London and the merchants of the Hanse as to the
repair of Bishopsgate, which the German merchants had the duty of de-
fending (*Lib. Alb.* I, pp. 485–88). See also *Lib. Alb.* Introd. pp. xcvi,
241, 243; *Lib. Cust.* Introd. p. xlii; Cal. of Letter Book C, pp. 39, 41.

demanded the record and a reasonable judgment in his action. On inspection of the record, it was then found that the defendant was not indebted in the sum mentioned in the writ, since the plaintiff's witnesses stated the amount as £33 11s 2d. Judgment was given that Alan recover this sum and the defendant be in mercy, and the plaintiff also be in mercy for demanding more by the writ than his witnesses proved.

Court of J. le Blound, *Mayor, held on Saturday after the Feast of S*^t *Lucia Virgin, A*° 31 *Edw.* [13 *Dec.*]

Membr. 6 b
15 Dec. 1302

Alan de Maldone[1] was summoned to answer Egbrith de Werle of Almaine in a plea of error made in the Court of Symon de Paris, Sheriff; the error, according to the plaintiff, consisting in the fact that though Decard, Alderman of the Free Merchants of the Hanse, claimed his Court over Egbrith according to grants and charters of the Kings of England and of the citizens, nevertheless the Sheriff did not allow him his court; further, the Sheriff condemned the plaintiff in £33 11s 2d, although the above Alan had claimed £34 13s, and although the witnesses could not say out of what contract the alleged debt arose, as they should have done. A day was given to the parties to hear judgment at the next Husting.

Afterwards, at a Court of the Mayor held on Saturday after the Feast of St John the Baptist [24 June] A° 33 Edw. [1305], the plaintiff by Richard Gladewyne his attorney offered himself against the defendant, and pleaded that the error lay in the record and process, in that the witnesses did not fully prove the sum mentioned in the writ. Judgment was given that the process and proof of the witnesses be null.

26 June 1305

[Reasoned judgment (French) apparently delivered by the Mayor.]

The Court annuls the process and proof because (1) There was a difference between the sum mentioned in the writ and that in the proof. (2) The witnesses differed as to the source of the indebtedness, whereas according to the Law Merchant they ought to agree. (3) The proceedings of the Aldermen

[1] Cf. pp. 140–1, 180–3.

who examined the witnesses were not fully recorded, and thus no sufficient reasons were given for the judgment.

Friday the morrow of St John the Baptist [24 June]

Richer de Refham was attached to answer Hugh Baudri in a plea of trespass, wherein the latter complained that Richer prevented foreign merchants from going to the plaintiff's quay with their merchandise, and threatened that if they did, he would not pass them through the Customs. The defendant said that he went to Hugh's quay and passed all the merchants found there and handed to them cockets[1] as regards the New Custom and passed them. He demanded a jury, and Hugh did likewise. A jury of the venue of Billinggesgate consisting of merchants frequenting the said quay was summoned for Monday. Afterwards the parties made agreement by permission of court, on terms that Hugh quitclaims all actions against Richer, and Richer puts himself in mercy.

Simon Bolimer, William de Heston, and David the clerk made agreement by permission of Court. Simon and William were in mercy. The terms were that Simon and William pay half a mark for the mainprise of the Abbot of Flaxle, and David half a mark.

Martin de Aumbresbiry and the executors of the will of Robert Dobes[2], late Sheriff of London, offered themselves against Gilbert le Mareschal, plaintiff, in a plea of debt. As the plaintiff was in prison, the case was respited until &c.

Wednesday the morrow of the Apostles Peter and Paul [29 June]

William de Honiton appointed Master Robert de Swithelund or John de Rislee his attorney against Richard le Despenser, chaplain, and Juliana la Hoddere[3] his concubine,

---

[1] The Cocket was originally a seal, but the term was generally used to signify a document issued under seal by an officer of the Customs. *Rolls of Parliament*, II, 138 b, A.D. 1293; Madox, *Firma Burgi*, p. 9; *History of the Exchequer*, I, p. 783; *Lib. Alb.* I, p. 45.

[2] Robert Rokesley, junior, Sheriff, 1293–4.

[3] A maker of hoods or *chaperouns*. Sharpe, *Cal. Wills in Court of Husting*, p. 248, n.

William de Collecestre, chaplain, and Robert le Mire, in a plea of trespass by petitions.

Salamon le Cotiler was attached to answer Alice de Panbregge in a plea of trespass, wherein she complained that she sent six quarters of corn for sale by her reeve Eustace, and that the above Salamon seized the corn and the horse of a certain Richard Pecche, her servant, and still detains them. The defendant said the plaintiff owed him 48s on a bond, and that Eustace sold him the grain for 27s, which money Eustace then handed over to him in part payment of the debt; and he demanded a jury. As regards the horse, he demanded judgment as to whether he was bound to answer Alice, because in her petition she said that the horse belonged to Richard, who could bring his own action against him "*quo et quando*," unless the plaintiff could prove that Richard was her villein[1]. Membr. 7 *b*

Sayer le Barber was attached to answer Gunnora de la Welde in a plea of trespass, wherein she complained that she hired a house in Lymstrate from William du Mareis, attorney of the Earl of Gloucester, for one year for 50s, and that the defendant broke into her close during that term and carried away her goods to the value of 40 marks, and imprisoned her daughter and her maidservants for a day, against the peace and to her damage £40. The defendant denied the charge and claimed a jury. He was delivered to the Sheriff for his appearance at the next Court to hear the verdict. Afterwards a jury of Lymstrate, consisting of Adam le Paviloner[2] and others, said that the defendant, as bailiff of the Earl of Gloucester, removed linen and canvas from Gunnora's house for arrears of rent, and retained them to her damage one

---

[1] The defendant pleads that the servant, Richard Pecche, could sue for himself unless he were a serf or villein, in which case the lord would be the legal if not the actual owner of the horse, and the onus of suing would be upon him. This pleading does not agree with the contemporary theory of the villein's position; except in relation to his lord he was treated as a free man (Hengham Parva, c. 8, in Selden's *Fortescue: De Laudibus*). In relation to other men he might have lands and goods, property and possession and all appropriate remedies in the Courts. See Pollock and Maitland, *History of English Law*, i, pp. 419–421.

[2] A maker of pavilions or tents.

mark. As regards the imprisonment the jury could not inquire. Judgment for Gunnora for one mark damages and that Sayer be in mercy.

Richard de Chigewell was attached to answer John Bacheler in a plea of trespass, wherein the latter complained that Richard came to his house in Breggestrate and carried away salt fish to the value of £4 14s 10d. The defendant pleaded that William de Marchia, the King's Treasurer, sent his men and servants to him, as though to a sworn servant (*tanquam jurato*), and ordered him to tell them where fish could be found for stocking the King's Castle of Dover, and that these men carried away the fish for the King's use to Brokene Wharf, and there loaded it into a ship to be taken to Dover, and that he, the defendant, did not carry away the fish for his own use. The plaintiff said that the defendant and his servant John carried away the fish without any of the King's Household or any command of the Treasurer, and claimed a jury. Afterwards the defendant offered himself against the plaintiff, who did not prosecute. The plaintiff and his pledges were in mercy and the defendant went thence without a day.

Richard de Chigewell was attached to answer John Lambin in a plea of trespass, in which he was charged with carrying away John's fish called "abberdene"[1], to the value of two marks. The defendant made the same defence with the same result.

Membr. 8   Nicholas de Berkhampsted did not prosecute against John le Ku of Finkeslane in a plea of trespass. He was amerced.

Richard le Trewechapman was attached to answer William le Long, "portur," in a plea of debt, wherein the latter complained that the defendant detained 2s 10½d arrears of 4s, recovered against him in the Sheriff's Court. The defendant defended "the words of Court," and admitted the 4s debt, but said that afterwards by execution of Simon de Paris, then Sheriff, Philip de Merdele levied the debt with the exception of 10d, which Philip put in defence in his hands, until the plaintiff had satisfied the Sheriff for an

---

[1] A variety of cured fish, or stockfish. Cf. p. 195.

amercement suffered by him because he did not prosecute a plaint against the defendant. Afterwards a jury of the venue of Bredstrate, consisting of Lovekyn le Ku and others, said that the defendant paid the 4s, except 10d put in defence by John of the Chamber, late clerk of Simon de Paris. Judgment that the plaintiff take nothing by his action and be in mercy.

Thursday after the Feast of the Apostles Peter and Paul *1 July 1305*
[*29 June*]

Robert de Nedham was attached to answer Alan de Waleton in a plea of trespass, wherein the latter complained that when he, as attorney of the Abbot of St Albans, made a distraint on the house of Walter le Porter at Brokenwharf, the defendant wanted to take the distraint away from him, and threw water on him, to his damage 20s. Afterwards the plaintiff did not proscute. He was amerced and the defendant went thence without a day.

William de Bray, fishmonger (*piscator*)[1], was attached to answer Michael the Tailor of the Wardrobe of the Prince, in a plea of debt of 20 marks due on a bond. He admitted the debt, and was ordered to pay on the morrow.

William de Leyre[2] was attached to answer Roger de Broune in a plea of trespass, wherein the latter complained that he leased from Avice la Haubergere, widow of Roger Cary, for the term of her life and two years after, a tenement by the Conduit of London, which the defendant wanted to have himself, and that the latter caused Avice to eloign the plaintiff's deed, and maintained the said Avice in the Court of Roger de Paris, Sheriff, so that he could not obtain the deed from her hands by form of law, for she said she would make her law that she had received no deed from him. The

---

[1] See p. 177, where he is described as "stockfismoggere."

[2] William de Leyre was Alderman of Castle Baynard Ward and Sheriff 1290–1. He frequently presided over the Mayor's Court at this period as deputy of the Mayor, and acted as an examiner of witnesses in the Sheriff's Court. The plaintiff in this case charged him with "maintenance," and complained that he had cut short his arguments by impleading him, probably for disrespect in Court. Nothing further was heard of this action, and in due course the plaintiff secured his remedy. See p. 190.

plaintiff was ready to prove by a jury that the defendant was guilty of this maintenance, to his damage 100 marks; further, that when the plaintiff was on the King's service in Scotland and under his protection, the defendant ordered his doors to be closed and sequestrated until his wife had paid a tallage, against the above protection; and when he argued with Roger, asking for proper amends, the latter caused him to be attached before the Mayor by pledges, and kept him in a plea and vexed him for a quarter of a year, whereas the plaintiff was always ready to answer by form of law and do whatever the law demanded; moreover the defendant caused 21s to be levied from the plaintiff when the latter was in Scotland under the King's protection. The defendant, on the ground that he was not a bailiff of the city, and had distrained nobody and received money from nobody, demanded judgment as to whether he was bound to answer concerning the tallage and moneys received from the plaintiff.

William Servat came, and in the presence of the Mayor and Aldermen entered into an obligation to save harmless, against the King and all others, the mainpernors of Bernard Baran.

William de Leyre was attached to answer John Mariscelle in a plea of trespass, wherein the latter complained that though he recovered against the defendant in the Husting before Henry le Waleys, Mayor, and Richard de Gloucestre and Henry Box, Sheriffs, 10 marks for a trespass, the present Mayor and Sheriffs refused to give him execution of that judgment, although he had often brought writs "*de execucione facienda.*" The defendant acknowledged that there had been a plea of pledges[1] between them in the Husting, in which he, the defendant, had been amerced for an unjust distraint, but no damages had been adjudged, and he called to record the Rolls of the Husting. And John likewise. Afterwards, on Monday after the Feast of the Apostles Peter and Paul [29 June], the parties came, and as it was found by the Rolls of Common Pleas A° 23 Edw. [1295] that neither the above 10 marks nor any other sum was adjudged to the plaintiff, judgment was given that he gain nothing by his action.

[1] An action in the Husting to give redress for unjust distraint.

John de Dunstaple was attached to answer John de Kent in a plea of trespass, wherein the latter complained that the defendant, during his Shrievalty, took the plaintiff's horse, value 60s, and still detains it. The defendant said that a messenger from Lord Edmund, the King's brother, then overseas, came to the King, and Master William de la Marche, Treasurer of the King's Exchequer, ordered him (the defendant) to provide a horse for the messenger, whereupon he took John de Kent's horse and gave it to the messenger, and he demanded judgment whether he was bound to answer the plaintiff as regards a horse taken for the King's service and not for his own use. The plaintiff pleaded that it was for the defendant's use, and claimed a jury. Afterwards a jury from the venue of Langebourne and Candelwykstrete, consisting of James le Botiller and others, gave a verdict for the defendant. Judgment accordingly.

Monday after the Feast of the Apostles Peter and Paul *5 July 1305* [29 *June*]

Richard Hereng, chaplain, was attached to answer Robert de Bissheye in a plea of trespass, wherein the latter complained that Richard wounded him with a sword in the left arm, the head and other parts of his body, so that he was confined to his bed for half a quarter of a year. The defendant pleaded that he was coming from the house of Master John de Sencler about curfew with a servant of Master John carrying a lantern[1], and opposite the Church of Holy Trinity the Less he found about twelve men attacking the Rector of that Church with swords and other weapons, and on the Rector crying out, he asked them if they wanted to kill him, whereupon the plaintiff, who was one of the malefactors, attempted to strike the defendant on the head with a sword, and he, the defendant, turned the blow with his own sword and struck the plaintiff in defence, so that if the latter got any harm it was due to

---

[1] By the King's articles (Cal. of Letter Book C, p. 16) no one was allowed to walk the streets after curfew tolled with sword or buckler, unless he was a great lord or other respectable person of note, or their retainer bearing a light.

his own assault, and he demanded a jury. He was mainprised by John Laurence, John de Crokesle, Adam de St Albans, "ferron"[1], and Walter de Cheswyk, woolman. Afterwards a jury of the venue, consisting of Robert de Cornedale and others, said that Richard wounded the plaintiff, to his damage 20s. Judgment that he go to prison until &c., and be in mercy.

John le Botener was attached to answer Thomas de Wymondham and Maud his wife, daughter of John Elys of Collecestre[2], in a plea of covenant, wherein the latter complained that the defendant covenanted to take Thomas, son of Maud, as apprentice for 13 years on payment of 5 marks, and after two years unjustly drove him away, keeping the money. The defendant admitted the covenant, but said that the boy was so malicious and caused him so much damage that he expelled him, until Thomas and Maud should satisfy him for the damage, and that they made an agreement through mutual friends that all covenants between them should be annulled. For this he called to witness the record of the Mayor and Aldermen, who were present. As regards the money, he denied receipt and demanded a jury. A jury from St Laurence Lane and round the Church was summoned against Thursday.

William le Herneys Makere was sent to prison for assaulting William le Lameman and Cecilia his wife in Sholane.

Avice la Haubergere[3] was attached to answer Roger de Broune in a plea of trespass, wherein the latter complained that he hired from Avice a house by the Conduit for the term of her life and two years afterwards, by an indenture between them, and on her asserting that she had lost her counterpart, he delivered his counterpart to her, which she refused to restore. The defendant said that a covenant was made, and a deed drawn up, which the plaintiff delivered to her on the covenant being annulled, and that he never had seisin of the tenement by virtue of the deed, and she demanded a jury. Afterwards a jury of the venue, consisting of William de Bristol and others, gave a verdict for the plaintiff, further

---

[1] Ironmonger.   [2] See p. 192.   [3] See p. 187.

saying that Avice tore the deed, to the plaintiff's damage half
a mark. Judgment that she go to prison until &c.

William Fratre was attached to answer John le Brewer of
Billirica in a plea of trespass, wherein the latter complained
that William detained a mazer in the form of a nut, value
one mark, and a basin and a washbowl, value 3s, which the
plaintiff pledged to him, to be returned on request. The
defendant pleaded that the plaintiff sent to him asking him
to supply two quarters of malt, and that he sent the [mes-
senger] to the house of William Lambyn, who sold him two
quarters of malt for 10s 2½d, of which he paid 2s, and for
the remainder pledged the above goods to William Lambyn
by the hands of Simon de Botertunte, and he demanded
judgment as to whether he, the defendant, was bound to
answer for the pledges delivered to William. John le Brewere
said that he received the malt in his solar on Cornhill, and
handed over the pledges there, and he demanded a jury. Afterwards a jury of the venue, consisting of Thomas de Flete and
others, said that Simon Botertounte (*sic*) went with William
Fratre to the house of William Lambyn and there pledged
the cup for 8s 2½d; and as regards the basin and washbowl,
that William Fratre lent the plaintiff 4s on them. Judgment
that John gain nothing by his plaint, and be in mercy, and
that William go quit.

Petronilla, widow of Walter Wolleword, was attached to
answer William Wolleward in a plea of trespass, wherein the
latter complained that he demised to her a house for the term
of her life at an annual rent of 20s, as appears by a deed, and
that in the 25th year of the present King she seized and
carried away from the house three lead cisterns, value 20s;
three pairs of handmills, value 12s; one bed (*torallum*), value
one mark; three vats, two tuns, five kemelins[1], and other
utensils, value 40s. The defendant pleaded that the plaintiff
granted and released to herself and her husband Walter and to
the survivor of them for life the above house with all its appurtenances, and that after the death of Walter the plaintiff

---

[1] *O.E.D.* A tub for brewing, kneading and other household purposes.

released to her and her heirs and assignees all his right in the house, by a deed which she proffered in Court, and she demanded judgment whether the plaintiff could claim any thing in the house against the deed. The plaintiff did not deny the deed or impugn it. Judgment for the defendant &c.

Membr. 9 Hugh de Waletone, alias de la Marche, was attached to answer Thomas de Oxford, tailor, and Ellen his wife for having assaulted them in front of their door three years before. Afterwards a jury of the venue of Fridaystrete was summoned, but the plaintiffs withdrew from their action. They and their pledges in mercy &c.

Roger de Broune was attached to answer Avice la Haubergere, who complained that the defendant had been her tenant at will for seven years from year to year, and that she gave him notice three months ago to find other accommodation, because she heard he was claiming a free tenement in the house, and that he said he would not leave for any Justice, Mayor, or other bailiff, in consequence of which he remains in her tenement against her will.

6 July 1305 *Tuesday the Octave of the Apostles Peter and Paul [29 June]*

Afterwards (see p. 190), on Saturday before the Feast of St Margaret [20 July], a jury, consisting of Robert de Thorneye and others, said that John le Botoner received from Maud, daughter of John Elys of Colecestre, 5 marks, with Maud's son Thomas as his apprentice. Judgment that Maud recover the 5 marks.

William Servat was attached to answer Thomas Migg, master of the ship "The Welfare," in a plea that he pay 13 marks 12s arrears of 26 marks, for which the defendant chartered the ship to take wine from London to Aberdene in Scotland, and coal from Newcastle-on-Tyne to London or Southampton, the money to be paid six days after discharging the cargo. The defendant pleaded that the plaintiff discharged the wine at Berewyc and the coal at London and not at

Southampton, as he ought to have done, and that it was agreed by his supercargo (*mercator*) and the plaintiff that they should subtract from the charter-money the value of the distance between Berwick and Aberdeen, and London and Southampton. The plaintiff said that he discharged the wine at Berwick and the coal at London by order of the defendant's supercargo, James, and that there was no such agreement about deductions between them, and he was prepared to verify this by sailors and merchants. A jury of the latter was summoned. Afterwards the plaintiff withdrew from his action. He and his pledges were amerced.

Richard de Bokelande, John de Etone, John de Caustone, John de Hakeword, John de Pampesworthe, William de Dallingg, Richard de Midelbourgh, Hugh de Caustone, John de Dokesworth and William de St Albans were attached to answer William Faukoun in a plea of trespass, wherein he complained that they dragged him out of his house in St Lawrence Lane and beat and wounded him, and when his mother Roysia raised the hue and cry, the neighbours came and rescued him half alive, and his life was despaired of, to his damage £40. The defendants demanded a jury. Afterwards the plaintiff made default. He and his pledges were amerced.

John de Bottertone was attached to answer John Horn-clerk[1], in a plea of trespass, wherein the latter complained that, whereas he had two horses, value 40 marks, 36 quarters of grain, value £8, and £17 Parisian[2], value £4, at Abevyle in Ponthieu, the defendant had these goods arrested for a debt of 16 marks which the plaintiff had already paid him, and when the plaintiff said he was a clerk and would only answer before his Ordinaries, the defendant had him imprisoned for a day and a night till he was delivered by the Bishop of Amyas, and as he was thus so impoverished that he could not hire an advocate, he returned to England and so lost all his goods; further, the defendant by the King's writ of "*monstravit*" demanded an account from him as from his bailiff and receiver, and maliciously detained him in prison for a whole

[1] He appears afterwards as John Horn, clerk.
[2] The value of the *Livre Parisis* varied; apparently the rate of exchange at this period was about 4s 8½d.

year less six weeks, though a jury had found that he had
received nothing from him for which he need render account;
further, that the defendant detained fifteen gold rings, two
silver buckles, four silver spoons, one pot and one posnet of
brass, value 40s, which the plaintiff delivered to him for
custody, and also merchandise to the value of 2s, to the
plaintiff's damage £100. The defendant demanded judgment
whether he was bound to answer here for an arrest and
attachment made in the kingdom of France and likewise for
the imprisonment there. As regards those two charges he
was absolved by the Court for the present. He pleaded further
that the plaintiff, at the time when the pollard was worth
sterling, pledged to him for 60s eight gold rings, one silver
gilt ring and one brass pot, which he would have restored
on payment of the 60s, and that he never received any more
goods from him, and he demanded a jury. Afterwards a
jury of the venue of Smethefeld, consisting of Andrew le
Blader and others, said that the plaintiff pledged eight gold
rings, one silver ring, and two silver buckles, but as regards
the silver spoons and merchandise they could not inquire;
and further that the defendant had from the same John
Hornclerk one brass pot and one posnet value 4s, to the
plaintiff's damage 12d. Judgment that the plaintiff recover
these goods and damages and the defendant be in mercy.

Membr. 9 b   Richard de Chigewelle was attached to answer Robert de
Mokkyng in a plea of trespass, wherein the latter complained
that the defendant came on Saturday after the Feast of
St Nicholas [6 Dec.] A° 23 Edw. [1294], and sequestrated and
sealed the door of the plaintiff's cellar on St Botulph's Quay,
without any bailiff of the King, and kept it sequestrated until
he had received herrings to the value of £4 17s 6d, and refused to give him any tally, writing or payment for the same.
The defendant pleaded that at the time when the King was
engaged in his expedition in Wales, Master William de
Marchia, the King's Treasurer, ordered him by his fealty
to the King, to inquire and find out where fish could be
found for the service of the army and send it to the King.
Thereupon, together with the King's servants appointed for

the purpose, he took the herring, and sent it by a ship freighted at the Brokenewharf, and he demanded judgment whether he was bound to answer or pay for fish thus taken for the King's service. The plaintiff pleaded that it was taken for the defendant's own use, and demanded a jury. Afterwards a jury from the venue round St Botulph's Quay and Brokenewharf, consisting of William Hardel and others, said that the clerk and cook of Master William de la Marche took the fish, and that the defendant showed them where the fish was, but took none himself. Judgment that Robert gain nothing by his plaint, and be in mercy for his false claim and that Richard go quit.

Similar actions at the suit of Walter Gubbe, Richard Swote, William Abel, Henry Amys, son of Juliana la Jovene, Henry le Wite and John Gubbe concerning seizures of "mulvel"[1], "aberdene"[2], and "stockfis." The plaintiffs allowed the actions to go against them by default.

Simon de Parys, late Sheriff of London, was attached to answer Richard de Hatfeld, butcher, who complained that he entrusted to a certain Margery de Camerwelle a hood of "bluet" furred with "meniver," value ½ mark, a brass pot, value 3s 6d, and two "coverchefs"[3] and two "barbes"[4], value 3s, and that a certain William de Canefeld, by his own authority, and without a bailiff, took the goods away; and the plaintiff then went to the Sheriff and found pledges to prosecute William, and to prove that Margery had no property in the above goods on the day of the attachment, but the Sheriff was unwilling to attach William or to do justice, whereby the plaintiff could not have his goods through default of the Sheriff. The defendant pleaded that the action was discontinued for lack of prosecution and called his Rolls to witness. At a later Court the defendant produced his Rolls, which showed that the case was discontinued as alleged. Judgment for the defendant &c.

[1] Codfish.
[2] A kind of hard stockfish, "dimidia centena duri piscis vocati Aberdene."   [3] A head-covering or head-cloth.
[4] *O.E.D.* Part of a woman's headdress, still sometimes worn by nuns, consisting of a piece of white plaited linen, passed over or under the chin, and reaching midway to the waist.

Agnes, widow of Guy le Hurer and executrix of his will, was attached to answer John de Stratford on a charge of detaining a quitclaim of all rights of dowry, made by Lucy, widow of German Brid, to the plaintiff, with regard to a house which he had bought from German. This quitclaim he had entrusted to the late Guy le Hurer, whose widow he now charged with maliciously returning it to Lucy. The above Agnes appeared and demanded judgment whether she was bound to answer without her co-executor, John Gamel. The plaintiff pleaded that Agnes was sole administratrix, and demanded a jury. Afterwards a jury of Sivethenelane, consisting of William de Finchingfeud and others, said that Agnes was sole administratrix, as the above John and Custance his wife declared. Judgment was given that Agnes go to prison till she restore the deed.

Membr. 10
8 July 1305

Court of J. le Blound *concerning plaints and petitions*[1], *Thursday after the Feast of the Translation of the blessed Thomas the Martyr* [7 *July*]

James de Sene[1] was attached to answer Adam Godesone in a plea of trespass, wherein the latter complained that James came to his house on Tuesday before the Feast of Sᵗ Edward [18 March] A° 24 Edw. [1295–6] and entered it against his will and the King's peace, broke the chain of a lock, and took away two horses, value 40s and 30s. The defendant admitted the distraint on the two horses, which were valued at 26s before John le Bretoun, then Warden of the City, and taken for arrears of 2 marks due on an annual rent of half-a-mark. This annual rent had been demised to the defendant for 12 years by German Brid and Lucy his wife, as appeared by

---

[1] A plaint was the usual method of beginning an action in the Mayor's Court, and the trial was according to City Law and the Common Law. The equitable jurisdiction of the Mayor's Court was invoked in later times by petitions. The occurrence of the two terms thus early suggests that the Mayor already decided cases for which no ordinary legal remedy was appropriate. A similar development was taking place in the Chancery, though hardly so early. See Pollock and Maitland, I, pp. 189, 197; II, p. 671.

[2] James le Brabazun of the Society of Bonseignours of Sienna. See pp. 109, 124.

a deed produced in Court. He further denied breaking the chain etc. against the peace, and except as stated, and demanded a jury. Afterwards a jury of the venue of St Olave by the Tower, consisting of Walter le Pestour and others, said that the defendant found Adam's door closed, and went to John le Bretoun, who sent his serjeant, who opened the chain and delivered to him the two horses to pay the arrears of 2 marks, being four years' arrears of the rent. Judgment for the defendant.

John de Paris, clerk, executor of the will of Joan Goldcorn, was attached to answer Thomas Squier and Saira his wife in a plea of detinue of certain muniments, wherein they alleged that Bartholomew le Locksmyth acquired a tenement outside Ludgate and bequeathed it to Joan his wife for life, and after her death Bartholomew's daughter Saira and her husband Thomas, the plaintiff, entered and had seisin, but that the defendant detained the deeds relating to the property, and procured the Mayor and Commonalty, to wit, Nicholas Pykot and William de la Chaumbre, who unjustly disseised and ejected the plaintiffs. The defendant admitted having certain deeds in his custody as executor, but said they did not concern the plaintiffs, nor was he bound to make them any restitution; and thereupon he produced in Court a deed from Guy le Seler to Bartholomew and Joan Goldcorn relating to a tenement without Ludgate, which Joan in her widowhood sold to Henry Sprot; and another deed under the name of William de Rokeslee of Westhamme and Joan his wife, daughter of Richard le Keu, which was made to the above Bartholomew and Joan, relating to an acre of meadow in Westhamme; and further, a certain will of the above Bartholomew, which will the defendant delivered to the plaintiffs in full Court. He denied that he had any other deeds and demanded an inquiry. Thomas and Saira, who were in court, were unable to show that the defendants had any other deeds or had done any trespass against them. Judgment for the defendant.

Note, that the above Thomas and Saira came and acknowledged that they had sold their tenement outside Ludgate on the North side to Thomas de Luda, clerk.

John de Bureford, William de Frideistrate and Philip de Merdelee were attached to answer Agnes la Longe in a plea of trespass, wherein she complained that John, during his Shrievalty, with William his clerk and Philip his serjeant, at the suit of Roger le Flaoner, entered her house on Lamberhull and attached two horses of Sir Richard de Overton, and had them valued at 20s for a debt of £7 due from Sir Richard to Roger. The plaintiff, as hostess of the house, entered into a mainprise against John de Bureford to pay for the above Richard if the debt was proved against him. When it was so proved, the said Sheriff and his men carried away, in lieu of the 20s, a mantle of white cameline[1], furred with "Eremyn," value 30s, a mantle of piers blue[2] cameline lined with red "sendall"[3], value 2 marks, a supertunic of azure-blue furred with squirrel, value 15s, and a towel in which the above garments were wrapped, value 12d, and also 20s, which the Sheriff received from Agnes for delivering the pledges, which delivery he refused to make; likewise the defendants came to her house and declared that more goods and chattels of Sir Richard were attached on the day when the horses were attached, whereas none had been found or attached; and they carried away two quarters of pure grain, value one mark, and 1200 of large faggots at 5s 6d the hundred, amounting to 66s, and by other distraints 47s 8d in silver and a washbowl, value 3s, as an amercement on the above Sir Richard, unjustly and to her damage, &c. The defendants pleaded that they attached two horses, valued at 20s, and the harness of Sir Richard, which was not valued, and caused Agnes to come into Court to answer as regards the harness that it might be valued, and that she willingly bound herself to answer for Sir Richard if he were convicted of the debt, viz. £7, and that subsequently, on the debt being established by a jury, they levied the £7 from Agnes. The plaintiff pleaded that she never agreed in Court to answer for Sir Richard in the form alleged. The defendants appealed to the record of the Rolls

---

[1] *O.E.D.* Originally a kind of stuff made or supposed to be made of camel's hair.

[2] Stone-blue "de camelino perso."

[3] *O.E.D.* A thin rich silken material, but the word was also occasionally used for lawn of linen.

of the Court, which the above Sheriff was ordered to produce on Saturday. At a subsequent court came the defendant by Reginald Woleward, his attorney, and the plaintiff, and although the Mayor and Aldermen found the record and process pleaded and enrolled as was stated, yet at the instance of the plaintiff they granted that inquest be made by the servants and attorneys of the Court at Guildhall and by the neighbours of Guildhall, as to whether the plaintiff, in the Sheriff's Court, demanded an imparlance to consult with Sir Richard; and whether she joined with Sir Richard's attorney in pleading, and promised to satisfy the Court or the other party with regard to the attachment made in her lodging-house, or for the whole debt claimed, or not. Afterwards a jury, consisting of Elyas Everard and others, said that the two horses, and other goods in boxes and outside, in Agnes' house, were attached on Sir Richard de Overtone at the suit of Roger le Flanner[1] for £7, and that the horses were valued at 20s; and as regards the residue of £6, Agnes being summoned was unwilling to swear as regards the value of the remaining goods attached in her house, although Roger was willing that she should, but she demanded an imparlance of fifteen days to consult with Sir Richard as to the value of those goods and certify to the Court, and on returning to Court she was still unwilling to certify, but joined with Sir Richard's attorney and pleaded against Roger in the principal plea of the said £6. The then plaintiff Roger recovered the £6, for which she was distrained by the Sheriff until, &c. Judgment that she gain nothing by her plaint. And because she said in presence of the Mayor and Aldermen in full Court that the jury were lying, she was condemned to prison, and delivered to Roger de Parys, Sheriff.

John de Bureford, late Sheriff, was attached to answer Peter de Corb, merchant of Ferar, in a plea of trespass, wherein the latter complained that the goods of a certain Master Peter de Sancto Marico were attached at his suit in John's Court for a debt of £4, which the plaintiff recovered

Membr. 10 b

---

[1] According to Riley (*Memorials*, p. xxi) a maker of flans or flauns, a light cake once much in vogue.

against Master Peter, but the Sheriff had returned the attachment to the latter without any satisfaction to the plaintiff
beyond 24s, which the above Peter paid to him. As regards
the 56s, the defendant, who was present in Court, could not
deny the charge. He was ordered to pay the plaintiff within
the Octave, and be in mercy for his unjust detinue.

Robert de Romeseye was attached to answer Agnes, widow
of Richard de Newerk, in a plea of trespass wherein she
complained that the defendant assaulted her at her house in
Fletegate in the parish of St Bride, and carried away her
goods viz. eleven doors, three pairs of handmills, one chest
sealed with the seal of J. de Wengrave, three large vats, two
tuns, one basin, one washbowl, four tables and other goods
to the value of £20. Also she complained that whereas she
demanded against the defendant a messuage in the parish of
St Dunstan, Fletestrete, by writ of Right, and the action had
been brought to judgment, the defendant, while judgment
was pending, alienated the messuage to a certain Robert de
Hauvile, who was suing in the King's Bench to support his
injustice, to the disinherison of the plaintiff and to her
damage £100. The defendant denied the first charge and
demanded a jury. As regards the alienation, he demanded
judgment, since she admitted that the action between them
was pending, and since, until judgment was given, she could
have no legal right in the above messuage. The plaintiff did
not deny this. Accordingly nothing can be done at present.
Afterwards a jury of Henry Rofot and others said that Robert
carried away her goods, value one mark, to her damage 20s.
Judgment accordingly, and payment to be made in the
Quinzime. The defendant was mainprised for payment by
Hugh le Armurer and William de Holebourne, taverner.

Vilanus Stolde and his companions of the Society of
Perouche[1] were attached to answer Peter de Maners for
detinue of 100 marks which he entrusted to them, to be
paid out at Andvers in Brabant a week later, or failing that,
in London at Midlent, which money they now refuse to pay.

---

[1] The Peruzzi of Florence were one of the most important Italian
banking Companies, with numerous branches on the Continent.

The defendant admitted that some of his partners had received the money, but they had sent a letter to a partner, John Vyleyn, at Andvers by John de Maners, the plaintiff's brother, to pay the money, which they supposed had been done; but if the plaintiff would return the letter and prove that payment had not been made, they would satisfy him. As the plaintiff could not produce the letter and the defendants could not prove that payment had been made, a day was given to the parties to certify in Court on the above matters.

Saturday after the Feast of the Translation of 10 *July* 1305
*S*ᵗ *Thomas the Martyr* [7 *July*]

Adam de Scheftington and Maud his wife were attached to answer Adam "le Palefreour" of Sir Peter Maloure[1] and Robert de Lekke in a plea of trespass, wherein they complained that the defendants assaulted them when they were watering their lord's horses at Castle Baynard. The defendants denied the charge and claimed a jury. Afterwards an agreement was made by licence of Court, on terms that the defendants pay the plaintiffs half-a-mark. The defendants were amerced. The amercement was condoned by the Mayor at the instance of Sir Peter Malouree.

Peter le Clerk was attached to answer Thomas Seli in a plea of trespass, wherein the latter complained that Peter, being his clerk during his Shrievalty, made an attachment on Master William de Boys, executor of the will of Sir Arnold de Mordak, for 60s owed to Thomas le Barbour of Friday Street, and without the plaintiff's consent, the defendant delivered the attachment, whereupon Thomas le Barbour recovered that amount from the Sheriff. The plaintiff demanded that Peter should repay him the 60s. The defendant pleaded that he made and delivered the attachment by the plaintiff's orders, and demanded a jury. Afterwards a jury of Friday Street and Melkestrete, consisting of Robert de Gloucestre and others, said that the defendant delivered the

---

[1] Justice of Common Pleas, A.D. 1292–1309. *Cal. Patent Rolls,* 1292–1301, p. 218; *Chronicles of Edw. I and Edw. II,* I, pp. 139–42, 149.

attachment without the plaintiff's consent. Judgment accordingly.

Membr. 10 c   Jury panel in the Sheriff's Court between Simon Beauflur and John de Melan, plaintiffs, and John de Thotenham, defendant.

Membr. 10 d
10 Dec. 1304
Court of Roger de Paris, *Sheriff, on Thursday after the Conception B.M.*

John de Totenham was attached to answer John de Melan for assaulting him on the Quay of Robert Hardel in Vintry. A jury found him guilty and assessed damages at 5 marks. Judgment that the defendant go to prison till he pay the damages, and that he be amerced.

Membr. 10 e   Judgment for Simon Beauflur with £10 damages in a similar action.

Membr. 11
10 July 1305
Court of J. le Blound, *Mayor, Saturday after the Feast of the Translation of St Thomas the Martyr [7 July] A° 33 Edw. [1305]*

Simon Beauflur and John de Melan were attached to answer John de Totenham in a plea that they sued him in the Sheriff's Court for an assault, and that a packed jury, which was not sworn, found him guilty and taxed damages at 20 marks, although no wound was seen nor any effusion of blood, in consequence of which the plaintiff was adjudged to prison, where he had been for six months and more, and had spent all his goods. He demanded that the record and process in the Sheriff's Court be produced and the error therein amended. Afterwards the Sheriff sent his record, in which no error was found. Judgment was given that the plaintiff gain nothing by his action &c.

15 July 1305
Thursday before the Feast of St Margaret Virgin [20 July]

Roger de Hevere was attached to answer Walter Meriot and Alice his wife in a plea of trespass, wherein they complained that when Alice was in the brewhouse of William atte Ramme in the parish of St Mary of Wolcherchehawe, the defendant and others broke into the two doors of the house, carried her away unwillingly to Roger's house, kept her there as in a prison, and despoiled her, so that she was not liberated until Thomas Juvenal, by order of Elyas Russel, then Mayor, delivered her—to her damage £100. The defendant denied the charge and claimed a jury. Afterwards a jury of the venue of Cornhill round the Shambles, consisting of Henry de Benge and others, said that Alice was detained as alleged until she was delivered by Nicholas Pycot, chamberlain, and Thomas Juvenal, Serjeant, to her damage 10s. Judgment accordingly. Roger to go to prison until &c. Afterwards came Salamon le Cotiler, Symon le Pestour and John Dode and mainprised the defendant, Roger de Evere (*sic*), for his appearance before the Mayor on Tuesday &c.

Roger de Evere was attached to answer Walter Cote in a plea of trespass, wherein the latter complained that when he was under age and in the wardship of Roger, A° 19 Edw. [1290–1], Roger by promises and smooth words instigated and procured him to demise and grant all his houses in the parish of St Mary Wolcherchhawe for a term of years, and also made him betroth himself to Alice his daughter, then being under age, and afterwards bound his hands behind him and beat him until he made a charter of feoffment; and thirteen years later, he forced Walter to seal a quitclaim relating to the houses, to his disinherison, and likewise to bind himself by a Statute in £42, payable at £4 a year, of which he had paid 100s; and afterwards Roger enfeoffed Walter and Alice with the houses to themselves and Alice's heirs, to the disinherison of Walter and his heirs. The defendant showed an acquittance in Court under the names of Walter the plaintiff and Walter de Berdenn, quitclaiming all actions against the above Roger by reason of any charters, letters, or deeds of covenant &c. dated at London the Vigil of the Trinity [13 June] A° 33 Edw. [1305], and he demanded judgment whether the plaintiff could have any action against this acquittance. Afterwards the plaintiff craved view of this deed, and as he did not deny it, he confessed it. Judgment that he gain nothing by his action.

A jury of Fletestrete, consisting of John de Flete, "chapeler"[1], and others, brought in a verdict that Henry le Sporoner[2] did not promise to pay 100s on behalf of his brother Richard le Sporier[2] for a quitclaim made to the latter by John le Chaundeler of Flete.

<table>
<tr><td>Membr. 11 b
22 July 1305</td><td>

Court of J. le Blund, *Mayor, Thursday the Feast of* St *Mary Magdalene* [22 *July*]</td></tr>
</table>

James Cok, barber, of Cornhull was sued by John le Barber for having maliciously rented (*conduxerat*) three houses in the neighbourhood of Cornhull, one of the fee of the Prior of the New Hospital without Bishopsgate, another of the fee of Thomas le Palmere, and the third of the fee of the Rector of St Peter's Cornhill, which the plaintiff had previously rented, owing to which the plaintiff could not dwell in the bounds (*in patria*) of Cornhull, to his damage 40s. The defendant pleaded that he himself dwelt in the Prior's shop, and that Thomas le Paumer ejected the plaintiff from his house owing to the latter's malice, and as regards the third house the defendant was still living there, and that he had not let (*locavit*) the houses for malice or any other cause. The plaintiff did not deny the defendant's pleading concerning the first two houses, but asserted that the defendant had let the third house against Michaelmas to his damage and maliciously, and he demanded a jury. The defendant admitted letting the third house to a relative, and said that this was lawful on proper notice, and denied malice. Afterwards a jury of the venue, consisting of John le Fourbour[3] and others, brought in a verdict that the defendant rented two of the houses maliciously, to the plaintiff's damage 20s. Judgment accordingly. The defendant, who was mainprised for payment within the Quinzime by Thomas le Palmere and William de Laufare, cutler, subsequently paid the damages, and his pledges were returned to him.

[1] *Sc.* Fr. *chapelier*, a hat-maker.   [2] Spurrier.
[3] Furbisher.

John de Heston, carpenter, was attached to answer Alice de Evere on a complaint that he assaulted her on Monday before Pentecost [6 June] and broke her shoulder with a bar (*de una barra*), and damaged her reins (*renes suos quassavit*), and did other enormities to her damage. The defendant pleaded that an action about the same charge was pending in the Sheriff's Court, and although the plaintiff had changed the date and place, there was no action between them, or could be, except the action in the Sheriff's Court, and he demanded a jury. The plaintiff said that the trespass she complained of took place after the action was begun in the Sheriff's Court. Afterwards a jury of Alegate, consisting of Philip de Offord and others, gave a verdict that no trespass was committed after that alleged in the Sheriff's Court. Judgment that Alice gain nothing by her plaint and be in mercy.

John le Furbour of Cornhull was convicted on his confession that he practised with a stone-bow[1] on churches and houses in the City, against the public proclamation made by the Mayor, Aldermen and citizens. Judgment that he go to prison. Afterwards it was condoned on his swearing on the Gospels that he would never again practise with a stone-bow in the City.

John de Berdefeld was attached to answer John de Membr. 12 Wautham in a plea of trespass, wherein the latter complained that he lived with the defendant for eight days in order to sell his wines, and that, on an account being made between them before Geoffrey Scot, Robert Portehors, taverner, and Walter le Furmager, he remained in arrears to the defendant for 18s 7d. For this sum he found pledges, Baldechon le Chaucer and Robert Portehors, and also pledged to the defendant goods to the value of 20s. Nevertheless the defendant, by a writ of *monstravit*, caused him to be imprisoned in Newegate falsely and maliciously. The defendant denied that the plaintiff had been imprisoned at his suit, and claimed a jury. A jury of Cheap was summoned, but the plaintiff made default. Judgment was given for the defendant.

[1] *O.E.D.* A kind of cross-bow or catapult used for shooting stones.

Saturday before the Feast of St Peter ad Vincula [*1 Aug.*]

Thomas Sely[1] was attached to answer Thomas le Barber of Fridaystrete in a plea of trespass, in which the latter complained that the defendant sent him and his apprentice Wymar to Newegate at no one's prosecution and kept them there till the plaintiff produced a writ of delivery, after receiving which writ and pledges, the defendant still kept Wymar in prison for a night and a day to his damage &c. The defendant pleaded that Thomas and his men assaulted the men of John, son of the Duke of Brittany[2], and it was at the latter's suit and by order of H. de Waleyes, then Mayor, that he detained them in prison, and he claimed that the imprisonment was just. The said Sir John of Brittany sent a letter testifying to the assault and that no amends had been made as yet. A day was given till the arrival of the above Sir John.

William de Lincoln, lorimer, was attached to answer Henry de Kemesseye, and Ellen his wife, on the charge that he assaulted the latter when she was in her house by Aldrisgate in the Rents of Sir Roger de Brabazon. The defendant demanded a jury, and was mainprised to hear the verdict by Richard Horn, "feron," and Walter Cote, "*sub periculo quod incumbit.*" Afterwards the plaintiffs made default. Therefore &c.

William de Spersholte, "chaundeler," was attached to answer William Jolyf in a plea that he pay him two marks for a horse which the plaintiff lent him to try at Kensingtone, on condition that he either pay the two marks or return the horse, neither of which he had done. The defendant admitted that the plaintiff lent him a horse, value 10s, to try to Henley and back, and pleaded that the horse died by accident on the way, and he demanded a jury. The plaintiff reiterated the condition relating to the two marks. Afterwards a jury of Holebourn, consisting of Hugh de Hereford and others, said that William received the horse, value 12s, to

---

[1] Sheriff, A.D. 1298-9.   [2] Cf. p. 109, and 109 note 2.

try it, and that it died by accident. Judgment for the plaintiff for the 12s, and that the defendant be in mercy for his unjust detinue.

John de Oxford, "stremuler"[1], plaintiff, did not prosecute against Henry de Benge in a plea of trespass.

Monday the morrow of St Peter ad Vincula [1 *Aug.*]   2 *Aug. 1305*

John de Bottertone was attached to answer John Hornclerk, who complained that after he had recovered 17 marks against the defendant in the Court of Hengry de Fyngrie, then Sheriff, the defendant, in order to hinder execution of that sum, had served a writ of *monstravit* on Richard de Caumpes and the other Sheriff, and had charged the plaintiff with owing him £200, for which he ought to render account, owing to which the plaintiff was imprisoned for a year by the defendant's malice, although he was acquitted of the debt before Elias Russel, Mayor, and the Aldermen in full Husting of Common Pleas. The defendant admitted the writ and the imprisonment, and pleaded that the plaintiff had been amerced[2], on which matter he demanded judgment; and he denied having acted maliciously, and on this charge he put himself on a jury. Afterwards a jury of Smethefeld and Alegate, consisting of Hugh le Chaundeler and others, gave a verdict that the defendant did not by the writ demand a great sum maliciously, so that the plaintiff lay in prison for lack of mainprise, as alleged. Judgment for the defendant on this issue. As regards the imprisonment, the parties had a day on Monday to hear judgment.

Robert de Blakeslou, cornmerchant, was summoned to answer Philip, son of Guyco de Florence, in a plea that he restore to him three obligations of £137 15s 1d, which the plaintiff had exchanged with him for 20 marks, that sum being repaid to the defendant by the hands of Sir John de Drokenesford. The defendant said he handed over the deeds to Sir John de Drokenesford[3] by agreement of the plaintiff.

[1] The meaning of this word I have not been able to ascertain.
[2] I.e. he had been kept in prison till he paid his amercement.
[3] Keeper of the King's Wardrobe. Cal. Pat. Rolls, 1292–1301, p. 431.

and he called to witness the record of Sir John. A day was given, and the defendant was mainprised by Robert de Kelesseye. Afterwards the defendant produced letters patent of Sir John to the effect that he was willing to deliver the deeds to the plaintiff on payment of the 20 marks which he, Sir John, had paid out on his behalf. The plaintiff was advised to go to Sir John for the deeds. Judgment for the defendant.

Membr. 12 *b*   A jury of the venue of Heldefihstrete[1] summoned against Wednesday to say whether Agnes la Lunge slandered the Mayor and Court.

John le Blound, "Cirger"[2], was attached to answer William atte Watere on a charge that he produced a writ of *monstravit* maliciously against the plaintiff, whereby the latter was kept in Newegate for seven weeks, being delivered because John made default in the Husting of Common Pleas. The defendant denied the malice, and said that William was his man, hired by the day from Michaelmas to Easter, and had charge of scoops and other utensils, for which he was bound to render account. He demanded a jury. Afterwards a jury of Cordwanerestret and Candelwykestret, consisting of Matthew le Chaundeler and others, said that William was servant of John at 3s the quarter, that they could not find out that William had any goods in charge, and that John maliciously caused him to be imprisoned by the above writ, to his damage 10 marks. Judgment accordingly, and the defendant was committed to the Sheriff until &c. Afterwards came Thomas de Oxford, skinner, and John de Staundone, "chapeler," and undertook to pay the clerks of the Court 20s, which the plaintiff presented to them.

Alice de Sutton was attached to answer William de Spersholt in a plea of detinue of chattels, wherein the latter complained that the defendant had recovered in the Mayor's Court a tenement in which were certain vessels and utensils

---

[1] Old Fish Street.
[2] *O.E.D.* A cierge-bearer, one who carried a large wax candle in religious processions. More probably a cierge-maker, as he had a journeyman.

belonging to the plaintiff and that she detained them, viz. two "ʒilvates"[1], value 12s; one "masfat"[2], 4s; one "rering vat"[3], 3s; seven "cumelyngs"[4], 21d; two "seges"[5], 12d; and two "*clayes ad toreyl*"[6], 20d. The defendant pleaded that all these goods belonged to the house, and that her ancestors bought them, and that she had none of William's goods. A jury was summoned, and as the defendant made default, the verdict was given in her absence. The jury found that the plaintiff had no goods in the house except two "*crates ad torell*"[6], value 20d. Judgment was given for the plaintiff for the 20d, and that the defendant be amerced; and as regards the rest, judgment was given for the defendant and that the plaintiff be amerced.

A jury of the venue of St Antonine found Richard Harm, "bolenger"[7], not guilty of assaulting William Sothcrist.

John de Lewes was attached on a charge that he and others at curfew assaulted Robert de Arundel, who had been appointed by Nicholas de Farendon, Alderman, and the faithful men of the Ward to guard the Gate of Newgate and close it at night. The plaintiff withdrew from his plaint, and his amercement for so doing was condoned by the Mayor and J. de Wangrave[8], because he was poor.

Ivo de Fynchingfeud, butcher, and Richard le Bocher, his man, were attached to answer Richard le Forester, baker, for refusal to pay 40s in which they had been condemned in the Court of Salamon le Cotiler, Sheriff, for a trespass against him. The defendants admitted the conviction, but said that they had satisfied the plaintiff by the hands of Ralph de Finchingfeud and Geoffrey de Finchingfeud, their main-pernors, and other friends, and they asked that inquest be made. The plaintiff demanded judgment because the defendants brought no proof of the payment and did not dispute

[1] "ʒilvates," *sc.* yilvates, alevats.
[2] A mashing or brewing vat. [3] A raising or yeast vat.
[4] *Sc.* kemelins, kimnels, a brewing tub. [5] Seats, stools.
[6] "Clayes" and "crates" were hurdles, placed on a framework to make a bed. Toreyl, *sc. torellum, torallum*, diminutive from Latin *torus*, a bed.
[7] Fr. *boulanger*. Low Latin *bolengarius, bolendegarius*, a baker.
[8] The City's Recorder.

the record of the conviction. On these grounds the Court ordered the above Salamon to send his record to the present Sheriffs, and that the latter should make execution on the goods and chattels of the defendants for the 40s, according to the judgment in Salamon's Court. The defendants were amerced.

Robert le Brokettour and Maud his wife were attached to answer Thomas Dogget in a complaint that whereas the plaintiff handed to Maud a cloth[1] of thread of wool (*une leyne de fillaz de leyne*) value 12s 6d, that she might sell it for that price, she sold the cloth and retained the money, and afterwards she and her husband went to the plaintiff's house and by false suggestion made to the latter's wife Alice, demanded and carried away half a cloth of thread of wool (*dimidium filacium lane*), value ½ mark. The defendants admitted the debt of 12s 6d, which they were ordered to pay within the Quinzime; but as regards the half-cloth, they said they took it away for sale by the plaintiff's orders, and demanded a jury. Afterwards a jury of the venue round the Church of St Margaret atte Patines, consisting of Nicholas de Hadlee and others, said that Maud took the half-cloth by fraud. Judgment that Thomas recover the half-mark from Robert and Maud. And Maud was delivered to the Sheriff by Richard de Croftone until &c.

Membr. 13[2]
7 *Aug.* 1305

John Goys, smith, was attached to answer Robert de Wedon, carpenter, in a plea of trespass, wherein the latter complained that when he, the plaintiff, had begged Geoffrey de Blyd, Master James, the King's smith, Henry le Poter, Robert de Alegate, "poter," Geoffrey le Poter, Salamon le Poter, Michael de Wymbys, Gilbert de la Marche and his brother, and Gilbert atte Herst in the Church of St Mary Wolcherchawe to arrange an agreement and peace between the defendant and William de Northampton, late his servant—the defendant, with a band of unknown persons armed with swords and bucklers, assaulted the plaintiff, took him by the

---

[1] A "cloth" denoted a number of ells or yards, which varied according to the material and the district where it was woven.

[2] Membranes 13 and 14 are transposed in the Roll.

nose and tried to drag him out of the Church, and threatened and still threaten him in life and limb, against the peace and to his damage £20. Afterwards a jury of the venue, consisting of Geoffrey de Nottingham and others, said that the defendant did not commit a trespass against the plaintiff to the value of 4d. Judgment for the defendant.

The Prior of Holy Trinity, London, Walter de Burgo and Robert de St Martin, his canons, Norman, John le Pestour, John the clerk, John le Porter, and Simon le Clerk, servants of the Prior, were summoned to answer Richard atte Nax, "bokeler," in a plea of trespass wherein the latter complained that between Prime and Tierce they crossed his walls by the Prior's curtilage, and broke and carried away his doors and windows into the Prior's close. The Prior and the others said a presentment was made before the Alderman in his Wardmote, by the oath of good men, that prostitutes dwelt in the plaintiff's houses[1], whereupon the Beadle of the Ward was ordered to gather to himself the neighbours, and after warning given to Richard for removing the prostitutes, to take away the doors. As the plaintiff did not comply, the Beadle gathered the neighbours, including the Prior &c., and removed the doors and windows. They demanded a jury. Afterwards a jury of the venue round the Church of St Mary atte Nax, consisting of Gilbert Schep and others, found for the defendants. Judgment accordingly. And order was given to the Inquest Jury to go to the house and remove the prostitutes, as the jury said they were still there.

Simon le Palefreour[2], Richard le Despenser, Simon the cook and Maddok, servants of William de Trente, were attached to answer Thomas de Wautham on a charge of assaulting the latter and taking his goods, to wit, four writs under the King's seal and a tally of 19s, and 6s 11d cash, a gown, value 6d, a hood of burnet[3], value 8d, a purse, value 4d,

---

[1] By the Assize of Gregory de Rokesle, mayor, A.D. 1276–8, women of evil character were not allowed to dwell in the City. Cf. Cal. of Letter Book A, p. 218; *Lib. Alb.* I, pp. 275, 283, 332, 591–2.

[2] Groom to palfreys.

[3] Burnet: a superior cloth originally of a dark-brown colour.

and a pair of tables[1] with a comb, value 4d, and that they did
so by order of William de Trente, and were abetted by John
Storremonthe, to his damage £100. The defendants Simon,
Richard and Maddok pleaded that the plaintiff and eight
others assaulted them, and such harm as they received was
their own fault, and demanded a jury. The bailiff reported
that Simon the cook was dead. William and John demanded
judgment whether they need answer as to the order and
abbetting until the defendants were convicted of the fact.
They went quit for the present. Afterwards a jury of Roger
de Lenne and others said that Maddok assaulted the plaintiff
without provocation, to his damage one mark. Judgment
that he go to prison until &c. Simon and Richard were
acquitted. The jury said further that William and John
knew nothing of the matter. They were acquitted, and the
plaintiff was amerced for his false claim.

John de Harewe, Serjeant, was attached to answer William
Cok, butcher, for detinue of five boxes, value 12s, four vats,
value 11s, three barrels and two kemelins, value 2s 6d, two
rainwater cisterns, value 12s, firewood, value 20s, one lantern,
value 4s, one "houche"[2] and one carpet, value 4s, and 9s 6d
which he received from John Fuatard for the hire of a shop;
also 6s due to the plaintiff from two chaplains for rent in
Yvilane, and four cushions (*auricular*⁰) and four little costers
(*costerellis*), value 6s, and one hair-blanket for a bed (*cilicium
ad torellum*) value 4s 6d, one coat of "Morre"[3], value 2s, and
"rocheres"[4] and mortars and other small vessels, value 5s,
and two handmills, which he took from the plaintiff, to a
sum total of 104s 6d. The defendant pleaded that he took
one box, value 4s, and one "cheker"[5], value 18d, and 100 of
firewood, value 2s 4d, and 18d in money from the chaplains
for a quarter's rent, and from John Fuatard for the same, for
arrears of 20s rent due from the plaintiff to Margery de
Gysorrs and her sister, daughters of Anketin le Mercer, and
for a certain leaden vessel in an oven (*pro quodam plumbo in
fornace stante*) removed by the plaintiff; and as regards the

---

[1] Writing tablets.   [2] *Sc.* hutch: a chest or coffer.
[3] Murrey—coloured cloth.   [4] Probably some kind of stone vessel.
[5] A chequered table for accounts.

four vats, four barrels, two kemelins, and two handmills, they belonged to a house bought by his father and descended to him, and were never the property of the plaintiff. Subsequently the plaintiff made default and the defendant went thence without a day.

Roger de Lauvare, cordwainer, was attached to answer John de Gaytone, cordwainer, in a plea of trespass wherein the latter complained that he hired a room (*placea*) in Roger's house in the parish of St Sepulchre to sleep in at night, and that Roger came in the middle of the night to his bed and assaulted him and drove him out of the house, and took from him a coat party-furred with lambswool, one carpet, two towels and one "houce"[1], value ½ mark, and threatened him in life and limb, so that he did not dare to return to the neighbourhood until he had agreed to pay the defendant 3s, of which he had paid 6d, to his damage 100s. Afterwards a jury of Stephen de Hereford and others said that John did not hire the room, but was himself the hired servant of the defendant, who beat him and took away his clothes, because he was unwilling to go to Croydone with him, the clothes being valued by the jury at 2s 6d, and the damage at 6d. Judgment accordingly for these amounts.

William de Rothewelle, clerk, William de Cornewale, clerk, dwelling in the parish of St Sepulchre, Roger, servant of Sir Robert Chivaler, Agnes de Newerk, Adam Wade, "wodemogger"[2], and Roger Wyndwawe, "tapicer"[3], were attached to answer Robert de Romeseye in a plea of trespass, wherein the latter complained that they broke into his house and took away goods to the value of £40, to his damage £100. All the defendants except Roger Wyndwawe were attached for their appearance, the latter being present and pleading that he had been acquitted of that charge before Sir Ralph de Sandwych and the other Justices at Newegate. The plaintiff said the trespass took place after the above acquittal. Afterwards a jury of Flete Strete came together and was sworn, but the plaintiff then left the Court and withdrew from his plea. He and his pledges were amerced &c.

[1] *Sc.* houche, hutch.   [2] Woodmonger.   [3] Tapestry-maker.

Monday the Vigil of St Laurence [10 *Aug.*]

Walter de Walepol, goldsmith, was attached to answer Henry de Gloucestre in a plea of trespass, wherein the latter complained that Walter came to his shop in the Goldsmith's quarter[1], and assaulted his servant William de Walepol, and broke a marble piece fitted for precious stones, and a dish in which were rubies and "esmeraged," so that the stones were scattered through the house and some were lost, to his damage £20. The defendant admitted the charge and was committed to prison until &c.

Judgments by default. William de Harwode, plaintiff against Gervase le Frend; Alan de St Albans and Margaret his wife, plaintiffs against Roger de Evere, John de Haleford, Edmund his servant, Walter de Waldegrave, "smeremogger"[2], and Hamond le Barber &c.

Peter le Latoner and Juliana his wife were attached to answer Gilbert le Bracer of Hiengham for entering his house in St Botulph's Lane by Billinggesgate and assaulting Gilbert, who hid for his life in a room, and for beating and stamping on his servant Margaret and carrying away the plaintiff's goods. A jury of Walter Pykeman and others said that Peter did nothing, but Juliana beat Margery, and that no harm was done to Gilbert. Judgment for the defendants.

John le Heymogger[3] and Mabel his wife were summoned to answer Gilbert le Brasour of Hiengham for a debt of 13s 10d for beer which Mabel took in Gilbert's house in Wodestrete. Mabel came and said that as John her husband was not mentioned by name in the charge she could not and ought not to answer. The plaintiff said she took the beer without her husband's knowledge, and that she kept an inn, received guests and traded "sole"[4]. On this issue the parties

---

[1] *In Aurifabria*, in the west portion of Cheap.
[2] Grease-merchant.   [3] Hay-monger.
[4] *Laws and Customs of London*, A.D. 1765, p. 111. "If a *feme couvert*, the wife of a freeman, trades by herself in a trade, with which her husband does not intermeddle, she may sue and be sued as a *feme sole*, and the husband shall be named only for conformity; and if judgment be given against them, she only shall be taken in execution." Cf. *Lib. Alb.* I, p. 204. Pulling, *Laws, Customs, etc., of the City and Port of London*, A.D. 1842, pp. 179, 484–5, where a full list of authorities and cases is given.

went to a jury of the venue of Wodestret and round the Brewhouse of St Paul's, who said that Mabel traded "sole" in hay and oats and kept an inn. John le Heymogger did not come. Order was given to attach him to appear at the next Court to hear his judgment, and a day was given to Mabel and the plaintiff.

A jury of the venue round St Antonin's Church, consisting of Roger de Balsham and others, found for the defendant Richard Harm, who was sued by his late servant, Stephen de Dillewyss, for assaulting and imprisoning him. *Membr. 14 2 Aug. 1305*

Wednesday after the Feast of St Peter ad Vincula [1 Aug.] *4 Aug. 1305*

William Passemer was attached to answer Robert de Romesseye in a plea that though all the parties were free of the City, William caused Robert and Margery his wife to be attached before the Steward and Marshal at Westminster[1] in prejudice of the City's liberties and to Robert's damage £20. The defendant said that a certain Hugh de Badborouham, John Marie and William Gomage of the King's Household were lodging at his house, in which the plaintiff, Walter de Hormede and others assaulted them, whereupon Hugh and his fellows caused the plaintiff and his wife Margery to be attached before the Steward and Marshal, and had the defendant's name inserted in the plaint, but that he, the defendant, did not cause them to be attached or prosecute them there; and he was willing to verify his pleading as the Court should direct. Robert demanded a jury on the issue that the attachment was at William's suit. The latter said that a jury could have no knowledge of what happened in the other Court, and especially before the King's Steward and Marshal, which were naturally matters of record, and he willingly granted to the plaintiff to demand the record. The latter refused, and demanded judgment. Afterwards the plaintiff made default, and judgment was given for the defendant.

[1] By the Charter of Henry I to London it was granted that no citizen should plead without the walls of London for any plea. Henry II added: "except only pleas of foreign tenure, our moneyers and ministers excepted." This liberty was repeatedly confirmed by later kings.

John de Wrytele, "furmager"[1], and Isabel his wife were
attached to answer Cristian le Foundour in a plea of trespass,
wherein he complained that they dragged him inside their
seld in Cheap, closed the door, and beat him. A jury of
Westchepe, consisting of John Poyntel and others, said that
John did not, but Isabel did assault Cristian, to his damage
40d. Judgment that Cristian recover that amount against
John and Isabel, and that they be in mercy.

Bennet de Burgo was attached to answer Godfrey de
Loveyne in a plea of trespass, wherein the latter complained
that he bought from Bennet two barrels of ashes of good
and faithful woad (*duos barillos cinerum wisde*)[2], of which one
barrel was mixed with earth and the other almost all false,
and Bennet refused to make amends as he was bound to do,
because he had sold the ashes as good, and on the plaintiff's
warning had recovered damages against the merchants who
sold them to him. The defendant denied receiving damages
from the merchants, and said that they had gone abroad
before the fraud was known to him, and he demanded a jury.
Afterwards a jury of Candelwykstrate, consisting of woad-
merchants and dyers, came in the persons of Richard Wolmar
and others, who said that at the suit and warning of the
plaintiff, the defendant had recovery of his damage (*habuit
suum recuperare de dampnis suis*), to wit, 60s for nine barrels.
A day was given for hearing judgment, when the plaintiff
made default. He and his pledges were amerced and the
defendant went thence without a day.

6 Aug. 1305   *Friday after the above Feast.*

A jury of Walebrok, consisting of William Tovy and others,
found John Cotoun, skinner, not guilty of a charge of slandering the Mayor and John de Dunstaple, alderman, when the
latter went round his Ward to collect money for a courtesy-
gift to the King and other magnates, for the benefit of the

---

[1] Furmager: a cheesemonger.
[2] Ashes were used in dyeing in the Middle Ages, apparently mixed
with the dyes. Cf. *Trans. Hunter. Arch. Soc.* II, p. 69, where the dyers
of Chesterfield are mentioned as buying wood-ashes for their trade in
A.D. 1441.

City. The collectors, William de Red, Thomas de Waledene and William de Caxtone were summoned to give evidence.

William de Stalham, taverner, and Peter le Taverner, were Membr. 14 b charged with slandering the collectors of the tallage for a courtesy-gift to the King and Queen and other magnates, against their oath, so that others taking an example from them were unwilling to do anything for the honour of the City. Richard Horn, fishmonger, William Lambyn, John de Wymondham and William de Braye, the collectors, appeared on summons. The defendant Peter admitted breaking a sequestration, and was committed to prison. A jury of the venue of the Bridge round Estchep found the other defendant guilty of the same, and a *Capias* was issued against him.

John de la Marche of Alegate put himself on the Mayor's mercy for insulting the collectors in Alegate Ward, Robert de Campedene and Robert Lorchoun. He was ordered to come up for judgment on Monday.

John le Cu, "brasour"[1], was attached to answer Ysabel de Estre in a plea of trespass, wherein the latter complained that John hired a brewhouse in the parish of All Hallows Stanigne-church for 3½ marks per annum, and took away goods from it to the value of 46s 1½d, viz. for rent 11s 8d; half a tun of beer, 15d; a spade, 8d; 3 kemelins, 15d; 5 pieces of tables (*pecias tabularum*), 4s; timber, value 8d; one standard, one hair-sieve for clarifying beer (*unum saitum ad coland⁹ cervis⁹*), one "malre"[2] and one basket, value 2s 9d; one pair of handmills, value 3s 6d; and a dog with a chain, value 20s 4d. John admitted hiring the house, and said that Ysabel ejected him long before the end of his term, so that it was not his fault if he owed her any part of the rent; as for the dog, he understood that she gave it to him, but she could have it back if she would pay for its feed; all he removed was a pair of handmills belonging to himself. A jury of the venue of Blaunchapelton was summoned, but Ysabel did not prosecute her plea. She was amerced, and the defendant went thence without a day.

Edmund le Taylour of Alegate was attached to answer Cristina, daughter of William de Suffolk, in a plea of trespass,

[1] Brewer.   [2] Maul, hammer.

wherein she complained that she impleaded the Abbot and
Convent of Sibertone as regards a tenement which she claimed
by inheritance, and that she recovered part by judgment, and
judgment on the other part was pending undecided. The
defendant, she said, took the capital messuage of the tenement
from the Abbot to hold part thereof in order to sustain and
maintain his plea and to eloign the plaintiff, who is under
age, from her rights; and moreover, as regards her part of
the tenement which she recovered, she could not take or
have profits and esplees on account of the estrepement and
threats and violence done by Edmund to the tenants thereof,
against the peace and to her damage £10. The defendant
said that he took the tenement, which Cristina claimed, from
the Abbot a year before she obtained her writ, for the
lifetimes of himself and his wife, that he was the Abbot's
bailiff to collect the latter's rents, and that he made a distraint
for arrears, lawfully and not maliciously; and he demanded
a jury. Afterwards a jury of Alegate, of Walter le Taylour
and others, said that the defendant took the house after the
obtaining of the writ, maliciously in champerty[1], to the
damage of Cristina 10s. Judgment accordingly, and that
Edmund go to prison &c.

7 *Aug. 1305* *Saturday after the above Feast*

Thomas, late Vicar of the Church of St Sepulchre without
Newgate, and John le Copersmyth were attached to answer
William Cok, butcher, on a charge that they came to his
houses in Cokkes Lane before Christmas A° 29 Edw. [1300]
and entered them and tore away eleven doors and five
windows with hammers and chisels, against the precept of
the Mayor and Alderman of the Ward, who ordered the
defendants to restore them. The defendants pleaded that
the plaintiff was presented before the Wardmote for harbouring prostitutes, and that the Beadle, after due warning to

[1] Jacob, *Law Dict.* A bargain with the plaintiff or defendant in a suit
to have part of the land, debt or other thing sued for, if the party that
undertakes it prevails therein. It was repeatedly forbidden by statute.
3 Edw. I, c. 25; 13 Edw. I, c. 49; 20 Edw. I, *de Conspiratoribus*; 28 Edw. I,
c. 11; 33 Edw. I, etc.

remove them, gathered the neighbours, among whom were the defendants, and carried away the doors &c. as was lawful. Subsequently a jury of the venue round Cokkes Lane came, but the plaintiff did not prosecute his plea. Therefore &c.

A jury of Bradestrete found Richard le Barber not guilty of abusing the Alderman and collectors of the tallage, against his oath as a freeman. Salamon le Cotiller, the Alderman, and Robert de Asshendon, Simon the baker and Thomas Perceval, the collectors, were present in Court.

Wednesday the morrow of St Bartholomew the Apostle [24 *Aug.*] Membr. 15 *25 Aug. 1305*

John Orpedman was attached to answer the Master of the Hospital of St Giles, who complained that when he went to John's house in Briggestrete to make a distraint for one mark, annual rent, then two years in arrears, the defendant, in the presence of Thomas de Kent, the Mayor's Serjeant, refused the distress and assaulted the plaintiff. On a later occasion the defendant admitted the plaintiff and his men, and then closed the doors behind them, so that the Master with difficulty escaped into the shop in front. The defendant sent the Master's men after him, kicking and ill-treating them, and when the plaintiff raised the hue and cry, the defendant took him by the neck and pushed him out of the shop-door and ill-treated him, to his damage £40. The defendant demanded a jury. Subsequently a jury of Roger de Bury and others said they could not find out whether John ill-treated the plaintiff, but that he denied to him a pledge in the presence of John de Kent, the Serjeant, when the Master took up a fish on his stall (as a pledge); and further, the defendant refused entry to the Master, to his damage 2s. A day was given to hear judgment on this matter. They said also that the defendant did not imprison the plaintiff's men nor do him any other harm. Judgment was given that the plaintiff be in mercy, and that the defendant be quit as regards this charge.

John, son of Henry le Bole, was attached to answer the Mayor and bailiffs of the City for breaking the sequestration made on him for the King's money. The defendant demanded a jury, and was mainprised by Richard de Hadlee, fishmonger, and Ralph de Bury, cordwainer. A jury of the venue of Martelane, consisting of Adam Honteman and others, found him guilty. A *Capias* was issued against him to hear judgment.

Hugh de Wautham, and Robert, servant of Gocelin, the Serjeant of Roger de Paris, Sheriff, were attached to answer Roger de Southcote, "paternostrer"[1], in a plea of trespass, wherein the latter complained that when he went into the road on the North of St Michael at Corn to look at the head of William le Waleys[2], the above Robert took him to the Sheriff's house and there detained him in prison by Hugh's order. The defendant Hugh said that he found Roger making a disturbance, and behaving as one against the King's peace towards Robert the Sheriff's servant, who had custody of a prisoner by the Sheriff's command. Robert pleaded that he was taking a man attached by the order of the Justices, when the plaintiff assaulted him, so that the prisoner nearly escaped, and accordingly he attached the plaintiff. He demanded a jury. A jury of the venue round the Church of St Michael at Corn was summoned.

Walter Diry and Alice his wife were attached to answer Nicholas Turgis in a plea that whereas it was agreed that Alice should go to the Husting to acknowledge and confirm the sale of a house in Marcelane in the parish of St Olave by the Tower, which she had sold to the plaintiff, and whereas ten marks had been put in the hands of Richard Pykeman for

---

[1] A maker of paternosters, or prayer-beads.

[2] On the previous day, 24 August 1305, Sir William Wallace, the Scottish patriot and hero, was executed. He was brought to London on 22 August, and lodged in the house of William de Leyre in the parish of All Hallows at Hay. The next day he was taken on horseback to Westminster and there tried before John de Segrave, Peter Malory, Ralph de Sandwych, John de Bacwelle, and John le Blound, Mayor of London, as Justices of Gaol Delivery. He was sentenced to be taken to the Elms at Smithfield and be there hanged, beheaded, disembowelled, drawn and quartered. His head was set up on London Bridge. These events appear to have been the occasion of some disorder in the City. See *Chronicles of Edw. I and Edw. II*, Rolls Series, I, pp. 139–42.

delivery to Alice after the confirmation, the defendant now refused to confirm the sale, wherefore the plaintiff demands repayment of the ten marks. The defendant Walter acknowledged the agreement, but Alice pleaded that she never agreed to it and would not carry it out. Judgment was given that Nicholas recover the ten marks. The defendants were amerced. And because Walter insulted and abused the plaintiff in full Court in the presence of the Mayor and Aldermen, he was adjudged to prison and delivered to the Sheriff through Gocelin, his Serjeant. Afterwards he was mainprised by Adam Hunteman, John de Hamme, Matthew de Hakeneye and John Cook for his appearance on Saturday to hear judgment on his contempt and for keeping the peace with Nicholas.

James le Reve, Roger de Parys, Sheriff, and Hugh de Wautham, clerk, were attached to answer Gerard de Waldericham, master of the ship called "Gronewold," Ludekyn de Waldericham, master of the ship called "Welefare," Wilebrand de Waldericham, master of the ship called "Gronewold," Reyner de Waldericham, master of the ship called "Lythfot," Reyner de Waldericham, master of the ship called "Blytheleved," and Adam de Waldericham, master of the ship called "Blycheyleved" (*sic*), in a plea of trespass wherein they complained that Roger and Hugh, at the suit of James, unjustly attached their ships and goods. Roger and Hugh pleaded that James delivered to them a writ for attaching all ships, and goods therein, which seemed to them to belong to the men of Holand, Zeland and Frigia, and to be under the dominion of the Lady Katherine de Vorne. The plaintiffs denied that they belonged to the dominion or power of the above Count[1] or Katherine, and demanded a jury of merchants trading in those parts. Afterwards a jury of Billiggesgate and of foreign merchants, consisting of Stephen de Prestone and others, said that the plaintiffs were not of the dominion of the Counts of Holand, Zeland and Frigia, nor of Katherine de Vorne, but of the dominion of the Bishop of Outrich, who holds from the King of Almaine. A day was given on Monday to hear judgment.

[1] Of Holland, etc.

Membr. 15 *b*
27 *Aug. 1305*

Court of J. le Blound *held by* John de Wengrave *on Friday after the above Feast*

John de Breydeston and Robert de Breydeston were attached to answer William de Raveneston in a plea of trespass, wherein he complained that the defendants harboured his apprentice, William de Breideston, who left his service against his will, and carried away his goods, to the value of 40s. The defendants came by Richard Horn, ironmonger, their attorney, and said that the plaintiff beat the apprentice and drove him out naked, and that they did not harbour him with the plaintiff's goods. A jury of the parishes of St Michael Wodestrete and St John Zacarias was summoned against Monday.

Action by the above apprentice against his master, on the ground that the latter drove him away, and did not instruct him, and find him in woollen and linen clothes.

1 Sept. 1305

Wednesday after the Feast of the Decollation of St John the Baptist [29 Aug.]

A jury of the venue of Graschurch was summoned to say whether Peter le Taverner abused and insulted the Earl of Athol[1], as the Mayor was given to understand.

2 Sept. 1305

Thursday after the above Feast

Judgments by default of plaintiffs:—Thomas de la Rye, "aparailour[2] de Forcos," plaintiff against Ivo de Wyttelee; William de Hengeham, "bracer"[3], plaintiff against Andrew de Hengeham, tailor, and Agatha his wife; Cok Willem, plaintiff against Robert de Abbyndon and Maud de Cauntebregg.

Edward de Fremelingham, Clerk of the Arches (*de Arcubus*)[4], was attached to answer Emma, relict of Nicholas le Taylour,

---

[1] John, Earl of Athol, who was afterwards brought to London and executed. *Chron. Edw. I and Edw. II*, I, pp. 149–50.
[2] Probably a tailor.
[3] Brewer.
[4] The Court of the Arches was held at St Mary le Bow Church.

for assaulting her in Tower Street, and breaking her left arm &c. A jury of the venue of the Tower, consisting of Thomas Pourte and others, said that Edward was guilty of the assault, except breaking the arm. Judgment for the plaintiff for 5s damages.

John de Rokeslee, dyer, of London, was attached to answer Adam Godesone in a plea of debt of 9s due from John to Adam for a thousand of firewood called "bilets." The defendant admitted purchasing the wood at the price, but said that a certain Edmund le Marny, who married the plaintiff's daughter, owed him that sum, and that he, the defendant, asked him, the plaintiff, if he would undertake to discharge Edmund's debt, and it was under this agreement that the plaintiff sold him the wood. The plaintiff said he never agreed to receive payment for the wood from Edmund. The plaintiff was ordered to make his law, and did so. Judgment was given that Adam recover the 9s from the defendant, and that the latter be in mercy for his unjust detinue.

Friday after the Decollation of St John the Baptist [29 *Aug.*]

Membr. 16
3 Sept. 1305

William Pykeman, Thomas de Colingham and Richard Pykeman were attached to answer John de Stratford, William de Stratford, and Richard de Hadlee in a plea that they pay the plaintiffs a moiety of a ship value £10, and goods therein value £20, which foundered at the mouth of the Thames by collision with the ship of the defendants, which ran over it; on the ground that it was immemorial usage both at sea and in the Thames[1] that if ships or boats collided by accident

[1] In maritime disputes the City Courts appear to have been guided by the Law of Oleron, a copy of which is to be found in the City's *Liber Memorandorum*, fos. 103 b–110 b. There is no judgment in the City's Law of Oleron relating to collisions when both vessels were under sail, but only when one vessel was moored. *Lib. Mem.* fo. 107 b. But apparently rules applicable to the present case were known in the City, and were similar to those in other and later compilations of sea-law. Thus in the *Black Book of the Admiralty* (Rolls Series), I, pp. 37, 38, it is ruled that any ship entering a port which through obstinacy, hatred, or envy of the sea damaged another, should pay the whole of the damage, but if the collision were by reason of storm or otherwise unwillingly, the master

or in any other way, whereby one sank with its goods, the surviving ship or boat should make good the half of the ship and goods thus sunk—which half the defendants refused to pay &c. The defendants pleaded that their ship entered the mouth of the Thames with lowered sail (*velo sublato*) because of the danger of the sands, and the sailors in the plaintiffs' ship sailed under full sail, and with malice aforethought collided with the defendants' ship which was crossing into the mouth of the river, intending to overturn it, but stove in their own ship, so that it sank from the water rushing into the breach; and when the sailors in the defendants' ship saw it, they launched their boat and with difficulty saved the sailors of the plaintiffs' ship. The defendants demanded judgment whether they were bound to make any restitution for the loss of a ship and goods thus lost by the malice of the plaintiffs' crew. The plaintiffs pleaded that the ship was lost by the malice of the defendants' crew, and demanded a jury of merchants trading by sea and sailors, which was summoned. The defendants appointed John de Cornhulle their attorney, and their ship was delivered to them on their acting as mainpernors to each other. Subsequently they made an agreement by permission of Court, on terms that the plaintiffs quitclaim all actions against the defendants, and that the defendants pay the plaintiffs 10 marks sterling, entering into a Recognizance for payment, and that the defendants be in mercy. Afterwards the defendants paid the money in the Chamber and were quit.

Avice la Haubergere, who was delivered out of prison on mainprise because of sickness, came before the Mayor and acknowledged that she tore the deed delivered to her by Roger de Brunne. Judgment was given that she be delivered to prison as before.

should pay and make amends for half the damage. The compilation in which this rule occurs is dated by the Editor of the *Black Book* (I, Introd. pp. xxxii–xxxiv) as between A.D. 1360 and 1369, but, as he justly observes, much of the matter was far earlier in origin. Similar rules are found in the Gotland Sea Laws (*ibid.* IV, p. 125; Introd. pp. xxii–xxvi) and the Laws of Wisbury (p. 284; Introd. pp. xxvi–xxxvi), which appear to have been earlier in date. In the present instance the plaintiff claimed entire damages on the ground of malice, but the agreement suggests that half damages were paid according to the rule.

Two counterpanes, two covers of catskin (*cooperture mure-legorum*), two barber's basins, and two red serges, taken upon James le Barber at the suit of John de Benham for 20s which the latter recovered against him in the Mayor's Court, were valued by oath of Thomas de Oxford, Simon de Brouchtone, William de Laufare, Roger the beadle of Candelwykstrete and William de Reyle at 18s 4d. Afterwards he received the goods on paying that amount.

Saturday after the Nativity B.M. [8 Sept.] *11 Sept. 1305*

The good men of the Ward of Chepe, viz. Thomas de Northwiz, Robert de la Daunce, John Goyz, Roberd (*sic*) de Farneberghe, John de Greneford, John Snow, William de Hamptone, Adam de Bouthone, William le Coffrer, John Herm, Robert de Paddinton and Peter de Hungerford, came to this Court and complained against Master Stephen the surgeon in a plea of trespass. The Sheriffs were ordered to produce him at the next Court.

Tuesday the Vigil of St Michael [29 Sept.] *28 Sept. 1305*

Martin de Dullingham and Gilbert, his son, and David de Dullingham were attached to answer Thomas de Kent, Serjeant of the Mayor, in a plea that when he wished to attach the defendant Gilbert at the suit of Walter, marshal of the household of Sir John Botetourte, plaintiff in a plea of trespass, Gilbert would not allow himself to be attached or find pledges, whereupon the Serjeant delivered him to the Sheriff, and the others then abused and insulted the plaintiff[1] in contempt of the King and his bailiffs. A jury of the venue round St Mildred's Church, was summoned. Afterwards the parties made agreement by permission of Court on terms that the plaintiff remit all actions, and the defendants deliver to the plaintiff a tun of wine, which was put in respite till one of them should be convicted of an offence against the bailiffs of the City. The defendants agreed that each of them was bound to pay the tun, and they put themselves in mercy.

[1] *Ipsum insultarunt verbis deformis.*

Tuesday after the above Feast.

Henry Scof was summoned to answer Reginald de Thunderle, Sheriff, in a complaint that whereas Henry was Reginald's tenant-at-will of a house called "la Coppedhalle"[1], and had received notice at Christmas, he refused to give up the house, whereby the plaintiff, his clerks and servants, were dispossessed. The defendant denied receiving notice, and the plaintiff replied that he had witnesses. A day was given on Thursday.

21 Oct. 1305 *Thursday after the Feast of St Luke the Evangelist [18 Oct.]*

Richard de Bolnhirst, called "Godard," pepperer, acknowledged that he impleaded the executors of the will of William de Beton before the Official of the Archdeacon of London, after prohibition made to him by the Mayor. Judgment that he go to prison until &c. Afterwards he was mainprised by Simon de Guldeford, Simon Gut, Peter Adrian, and William de Bydik to be in Court on the morrow to receive whatever the Court should adjudge.

Roger Blaket, apprentice of Adam de Horsham, was found this day to have assaulted Gilbert de Horsham in the King's highway with a drawn falchion. And because he carried a sword and falchion against the King's proclamation, judgment was given that he go to prison.

Because it was testified that Arnold Waxemot of Almaine struck the King's Beam loaded with wax, thrice with a large cowlstaff (*tinulo*), in contempt of the King and to the breaking of the beam, Reginald de Thunderle, Sheriff, was ordered

---

[1] This was the "Coppedehalle" on Dowgate Hill, which subsequently became Skinners Hall [Husting Rolls 18 (6), 40 (12) (13)], etc. Its descent can be traced in the deeds enrolled in the Husting. Reginald de Thunderle conveyed it to Margery de Wyleghby in 1311. See Stow (Kingsford), I, p. 230; II, p. 318. Harbin's *Dictionary of London*, p. 170. There was a building of the same name in the parish of St Mary Axe [H.R. 8 (23)] and a Copdonhall in the parish of St Dunstan in the East [H.R. 160 (18)]. Harbin suggests that it had a flat or "copped" roof.

to attach him by his body for his appearance before the Mayor and Aldermen.

Friday after the above Feast   *22 Oct. 1305*

As an order was given as above, and neither did Arnold Waxemot appear, nor Reginald de Thunderle answer for his body, the other Sheriff, William Cosin, was ordered to summon Reginald to answer why he had not obeyed the King's orders, and also to attach the above Arnold for his appearance on the morrow.

ROLL H

Court of J. le Blound, *Mayor, on Thursday after the Feast of St Andrew the Apostle* [30 *Nov.*] *A° 34 Edw.* [1305]

Geoffrey de Gernemuhe was summoned to answer the Commonalty and Richer de Refham, collector of the Murage of London, in a plea that he render an account of his receipt of murage[1], issuing from corn within and without Neugate, from 6 Sept. last till the day of St Luke the Evangelist [18 Oct.]—he having received during that time £16 and having paid over only 75s, and refused to pay the remainder. The defendant pleaded that he had paid over to Richer all he had received. The plaintiff answered that some days the defendant had received murage from 240 carts, at other times 220, sometimes more or less, and demanded a jury. A jury of the venue towards Neugate and round St Nicholas at Shambles was summoned. Afterwards, since Geoffrey had acknowledged that he was a receiver of murage, he was ordered to render an account, and Walter de Finchingfeld and Thomas Romeyn were appointed auditors. On an account being made, it was found that Geoffrey had received five marks more than he had paid in to Richer. He was delivered to the Sheriff until &c.

Adam de Fulham, Richard Aleyn, John Aleyn, Walter Pykeman, Thomas de Colingham, Walter Mounde, John de

---

[1] Murage was a toll taken from every cart and horse coming laden through a city or town, for the building or repairing of the walls, and was due either to grant or prescription. Edward I seems to have taken the theory that it was always a matter of grant (*Statute Westminster*, 1, 3 Edw. I, c. 31). In 1276 (City's *Liber Horn.* fo. 284) and again in 1279, grants of murage were made to London, in the latter case for three years in order to rebuild the wall by Ludgate, a schedule of tolls being given (Cal. of Letter Book A, pp. 222–4). An extension was given in 1284 for two years, for building the wall near the Preaching or Black Friars towards the Thames (Cal. of Letter Book B, pp. 55–6). From this time onwards murage appears to have been taken continuously. Collectors and a receiver were appointed in 1302. In 1305 Richer de Refham was put in charge of the issues (Cal. of Letter Book C, p. 107). Three years later the right of collecting murage was put to farm (*ibid.* pp. 161–3, 166–7), and on many subsequent occasions. As the City was itself exempt by Charter from paying murage in other towns (*Lib. Alb.* 1, p. 141), it is not surprising that the latter complained, and that many of them secured exemption in London, also on the ground of chartered right. See Letter Books, *passim*.

Croydone, Robert Turk, William Cros le Bole, John Lambyn of Colecestre, Adam de Tindale, Walter le Benere, Robert Baudry, William Frere, Pynnefoul, Robert le Portier, Homfrey, journeyman of Adam de Foleham, Robert de Mokkingg, Hugh Frohs, John Pyfre, Roger Bacheler, Richard Brith, John Baldewyne, John de Wodeforth, John de Boys, William le Reve, Walter Miles, Adam Hospinel, Simon Morival, fishmongers of Bridge Street, and Robert de Ely, Richard, journeyman of Walter de Hakeneye, Roger de Bernes, John Pardome, Henry Matefrey, Thomas Matefrey, Stephen le Bakere, William le Lung, Simon his man, William Flinchard, Alan Flinchard, John his man, John Flinchard, Simon Fiz Robert, Matthew de Ely, Alan, journeyman of Geoffrey Scot, junior, William Monamy, Robert Scot, William his brother, John de Tornham, Simon de Tornham, John de Guldeford, John de Stratford, Henry de Fingrie, William Pardome, and Adam de Ely, fishmongers of Old Fish Street, were summoned to answer the Mayor and Commonalty and John de Ely, who prosecuted for the King, on a charge of forestalling fish coming to the City by land and water against the Statute of their aforesaid trade, to the damage of the King, the magnates of England, the whole commonalty of London, and the people resorting to the city. The defendants pleaded not guilty and demanded to acquit themselves by their law. The prosecutors pleaded that as the offence was against the King &c. they could not so acquit themselves. The defendants were ordered to inform the Court whether they wished to acquit themselves in any other way, whereupon they demanded a jury. Subsequently the cases were dealt with by three juries of William de Lutone, John Dode, Richard le Barbere of Bredstrete and others, who found the majority of the defendants not guilty. William Cros le Bole, Robert Turk and Henry Graspeys were found guilty of buying a boatload of fish and each selling to the other, thus enhancing the price. Robert Baudry was found guilty of hiding his own fish to the scarcity and damage of the people, and adjudged to prison &c.; Adam de Fulham was found guilty of taking more lampreys and fish for the King's use than he delivered to the King, thus making a profit.

Friday after the Feast of St Nicholas [6 Dec.]

William Passemer was summoned to answer Peter de Neuport in a plea of trespass, wherein the latter complained that when he wanted to repair his houses in the parish of St Andrew Holebourne and to roof them, by hanging his ladder on the house, the defendant drove away the tiler by force and arms, and would not allow the tiling to proceed for 2½ years, whereby the timber and walls were rotted. Afterwards an agreement was made by permission of Court, on terms that the plaintiff quitclaim all actions, and the defendant pay an amercement of 20d through the Mayor, which amercement was afterward paid to the Chamberlain, R. Poterel.

Wednesday after the above Feast

Peter Adrian was attached to answer the Master of the Hospital of St Giles without London in a plea of trespass, wherein the latter complained that when he went to Peter's house in Sopereslane and took a pledge of a piece of wax weighing 20 lbs, for 16s arrears due on an annual rent of 8s, the defendant took the wax away from him, against the peace and to his damage 100s. The defendant pleaded that the house in which the plaintiff made the distraint was not held from the plaintiff, and the annual rent of 8s was not chargeable upon it. A jury of the venue was summoned.

William de Londoneston, who was attached to answer William de Lyndesseye in a plea of trespass, came and said that he was discharged without a day before Sir Roger de Hegham, the King's Justice. The plaintiff could not deny it, and the defendant went thence without a day.

A jury of butchers was summoned for Friday to say whether Godfrey le Webbe bought 500 sheep at Thotenham[1] on their way to London, as Richer de Refham alleged.

Roger de Rokesle, senior, was attached to answer Thomas de Frowyk and Alice his wife for entering the house of Alice at Ebbegate with eighteen other men, when she was living

---

[1] Thus forestalling them.

apart from her husband (*dum a viro fuit soluta*), assaulting her and ejecting her into the street, where she raised the hue and cry, breaking open her cupboards, "forcers"[1] and coffers and taking away gold and silver jewels to the value of 20 marks, to her damage £40. The defendant was mainprised by Peter Berneval and Richard de Brompfeld. Afterwards the parties made agreement on terms that the plaintiffs pardon the offence and the defendant pay 46s 8d, which was done. The defendant was amerced.

Martin de Ambresbury, late Sheriff of London, was attached to answer Gilbert le Mareschal in a plea that he pay him 12 marks, because the defendant and Robert Dobes[2], during their Shrievalty, allowed Richard Gentilcors to go at liberty, although he had been delivered to them by the Stewards and Marshals to keep in custody until he had paid the plaintiff 12 marks, acknowledged by him as due to the plaintiff. Martin pleaded that he never received the body of Richard as the plaintiff alleged.

Simon del Eldestrete, Golding de Crepelgate, John de Bumstede, Osebert Wildegos, Geoffrey Giffard, Robert le Holer, William Maners of Hundsdich, Richard le Wilde, John de Badbourham, Robert Dosing and his wife, Holilde and Felice their daughters, Richard Priour, John son of John de Alegate, Mabel de Pelham atte Nax, John atte Barre, Alexander of ʒe helde, John Botis, John de Canterbiry, Alice de Haliwelle, Robert Wedhok, John de Redbourne, John Burel, Roger le Longe, John Seward and Adam Russel, poulterers, were attached to answer the Mayor, Aldermen and Commonalty, on a charge that they bought and forestalled by day and night all kinds of poultry both coming to the City and within the City, to the grave damage of all the people of the City and those resorting there, unjustly and against the ordinances and statutes of the City. The defendants demanded a jury. A jury of the Poultry and Cornhill was summoned for Wednesday. The defendants mainprised each other for their appearance to hear the verdict &c.

---

[1] Chests.   [2] Robert Rokesley, junior.

Membr. 2
16 Dec. 1305

Thursday after the Feast of St Lucia Virgin [13 *Dec.*]
before J. de Wengrave

Roger de Sprengwelle and William Cros Muriele, executors of the will of John de Midelborou, were attached to answer the Mayor and Commonalty as regards the wardship of Juliana and Alice, daughters of John de Midelborou, which wardship was devised to them by John, as it is said. Roger appeared, and was ordered to bring the will and the children on the morrow. Order was given to distrain William for his appearance.

It was ordered that Roger de Rokesle and Joan his wife be attached to bring John and Alice, the children of Robert Lambyn, with their goods into Court on the morrow.

17 Dec. 1305 *Friday after the above Feast*

Roger de Sprengwell and William Cros Muriele, executors of the will of John de Midelborou, were attached to answer the Mayor and Commonalty as regards the wardship of Juliana and Alice &c. and to render account of the goods devised to them. The defendants admitted the wardship of the children and £90 of goods. John de Wengrave, Richer de Refham, Simon de Paris and Nicholas Pycot were appointed auditors for an account. After making default, the defendants appeared and said they were unwilling to show the will or render an account. They were delivered to the Sheriff[1] until they should be willing.

20 Dec. 1305 *Monday, the Vigil of St Thomas the Apostle* [21 *Dec.*]

John, son of Henry le Bole, was attached to answer Reginald de Thunderle, Sheriff of London, in a plea that whereas the Sheriff wished to attach a certain man in the house of John de Romeneye, the defendant warned him, so that the attachment could not be made, and he (the man?) thrust out the Sheriff and abused him. A jury of Billingesgate was summoned. Afterwards the plaintiff made default, and the defendant went without a day.

[1] I.e. to prison.

Geoffrey de Horsham, butcher, who was attached to answer Richard le Baumere[1] of Kynemeretone in a plea of trespass, did not come. He and his pledges were in mercy. And as it was testified that he had no lands, tenements or goods by which he might be distrained, order was given to attach him by his body against Wednesday.

Monday after the Epiphany [6 *Jan.*] *A° 34 Edw.* [1305–6]

10 Jan.
1305–6

Robert Turk, Geoffrey de Lyre, John de Fulham, Edmund Lambyn and Robert de Mokking were summoned to answer Richard de Farmberwe on a charge that they took his fish and held it in forfeit until he paid a fine, to his damage 20s. The defendants said they were sworn before the Sheriffs and bailiffs of the City to take the paniers of all people coming to the City, which they found to be less than a bushel and of worse quality below than above, in order that the fish might be forfeited to the King and his bailiffs[2].

The Sheriff was ordered to take security from John de Ely to appear before the Mayor on Wednesday after the Feast of St Hilary, to hear the verdict of the jury as to whether he received divers moneys from divers persons for the suit which he prosecuted on behalf of the King. Afterwards a jury of Alexander Pik and others said that John de Ely received from William Pykeman 40s, and from William Flinchard 10s, for wrongfully withdrawing his prosecution against them. Judgment that he go to prison until &c.

Schedule. Mainprise for John de Ely taken by William de Carletone at the Exchequer, at the Purification of the Blessed Mary [2 Feb.] A° 35 Edw. [1305–6]—John de Radewell, William de Esthalle, Edmund, Keeper of the Gaol of Flete, William de Bretevill of co. Kent, Peter Chyld and Robert Dyvelyn.

[1] Probably embalmer. Cf. verb "balm," *N.E.D.*
[2] The practice of "dubbing" fish baskets, by putting the best fish on top and the inferior below, was strictly forbidden under penalty of forfeiture in the Ordinances for the Fishmongers, made by the Mayor and Aldermen A° 8 Edward I (1279–1280). See *Lib. Alb.* I, p. 381. This prohibition was repeated in the following reign (*ibid.* p. 377; City's *Liber Memorandorum*, fo. 169).

Because Isabel, wife of Nicholas de Tenete, bought hens and capons coming towards the City, a jury of the venue of Bridge was summoned to say whether she was a common forestaller of victuals for the profit of her husband. The jury of William le Chapeller and others said that she went to meet poultry at Suthwirk and bought it before it could come to the City. She was committed to prison, and was mainprised by Robert de Rye, John le Chapeler, Stephen le Taverner and William le Chapeler. Afterwards she paid 40d fine to Richard Poterel, Chamberlain.

Membr. 2 b   A jury of the venue of Fletestrete was summoned to say whether Richard le Barber of Fletestrete raised the hue and cry, after knocking down Brother Peter, the Renter of the Hospital of Sᵗ Katherine, in the presence of Joce the bailiff, who was sent with the Brother by the Mayor in order to keep the peace. Afterwards a jury of Richard Leueson and others said that the defendant did no harm to the plaintiff, but as he did not know him, he raised the hue and cry over him. Judgment for the defendant.

This day it was ordered by the Mayor and Aldermen that the fishmongers of Bridge Street and Old Fish Street should allow the free fishmongers of the City standing at the Stalls, to deal with them and to obtain their share of the wares bought, as was right and just and as the liberty of the City required[1].

5 Feb.   *Saturday after the Feast of the Purification B.M.*
1305–6   *[2 Feb.]*

John Orpedman, guardian of Henry and Hugh, the children being under age of Thomas Orpedman, offered himself against Margery Cros, Thomas Cros and William Lambyn, executors of the will of Thomas Cros, in a plea that they pay to the said orphans, chattels to the value of £50. Thomas and William came, but not Margery. Order was given to distrain her against the next Court.

[1] Cf. *Lib. Cust.* I, pp. 120, 404. The Stalls were at the Stocks market. The claim was that the Stocks fishmongers should be "at lot" with the others, i.e. have their share in fish brought into the Thames and sold wholesale.

Master Geoffrey Hengeham, clerk, was attached to answer Richard Hauteyn for impleading the latter against the Mayor's prohibition in a matter of chattels and debts before the Official of the Archdeacon of London and his Commissary. The defendant denied the charge and demanded to acquit himself by his law. He was mainprised by William de Norhampton and Thomas de Salloppia to make his law on Friday. Afterwards the plaintiff made default and did not prosecute his plea. Judgment for the defendant.

Thomas le Kyng, butcher, was attached to answer John le Messer[1] of the Prioress of Clerkenwell in a plea of trespass, wherein the latter complained that when he had to impound 20 sheep found in his mistress's corn and pasture, the defendants and others rescued them and beat him, to his damage 40s. The defendant denied the charge and was adjudged to make his law. Afterwards on Saturday before the Feast of St Peter in Cathedra [22 Feb.] the defendant made his law and was acquitted. The plaintiff was amerced.

Roger de Rokeslee was attached to answer William Lambyn and Edmund Lambyn, executors of the will of Robert Lambyn, and the Mayor and Aldermen, to whom belongs the custody of orphans under age, in a plea of account, wherein they complained that Roger received £40 sterling devised to Alice and John, children of Robert Lambyn, and £62 of the issues of their rents. The defendant came and said that Alice was of full age and had her rent and received it, and that John had no rent, and he refused to render account. And since Roger did not deny receipt of £40, but tacitly admitted it, as well as the receipt of the rent of Alice before she was of age, as was charged against him, he was delivered to the Sheriff, William Cosyn, until &c.

Wednesday the Octave of the Purification B.M. [2 Feb.]   Membr. 3
9 Feb.
1305–6

Thomas Cros, Margery Cros, and William Lambyn, executors of the will of Thomas Cros, were summoned to answer Hugh and Henry, sons of Thomas Orpedman, deceased, in a

---

[1] Reaper.

plea that they pay them £38, also 20 marks, being the third part
of the value of a ship, and 40s in gold, which the late Thomas
Cros received by legacy from Thomas Orpedman for the use
of the latter's children. The defendant William pleaded that
he never administered his father's will, and Thomas and
Margery said that a certain Edward de Wycumbe was their
co-executor, and his executor was a certain John de Essex,
without whom they were not bound to answer. The latter
appeared on summons and said that he never administered
Edward de Wycumbe's goods, and so was not bound to
answer. Thomas and Margery Cros said that it was unjust
to demand the money from them, because the children remained in the custody of their mother Custance, together
with their goods, and she delivered to Thomas de Kent £40
of their property, and they demanded a jury on that point.
The children answered that the goods were in the custody of
Thomas Cros, senior, on the day of his death, and afterwards
came into the hands of the defendants Thomas and Margery,
his executors, and they were ready to prove by a jury that
Thomas and Margery had never paid them. Afterwards the
parties came to an agreement by permission of the Court on
terms that the defendants pay the plaintiffs £40, from which
the defendants claimed an allowance for the sustenance of
the plaintiffs during four and a half years. Subsequently on
Monday after the Feast of St Barnabas [11 June] the same
year, the Mayor and Aldermen gave judgment that the
children were then of full age to receive their goods, and
ordered that the defendants be distrained by all their goods
to pay them the said £40.

11 Feb. 1305 **Friday after the Octave of the Purification B.M.**
[2 Feb.]

William de Lyndesseye complained that he had brought
pledges before William de Londoneston, Undersheriff, for
prosecuting an action relating to certain goods, value £20,
which his wife Alice had eloigned into the houses of William
de Wynchelsee, and the Undersheriff had put these goods
under a sequestration, but afterwards he had delayed the

action for three months, by which time a divorce (*divorcium*)[1] between himself and Alice had been celebrated in the face of the Church (*celebratum in facie ecclesie*], and then the Undersheriff had delivered the goods to Alice, to the plaintiff's damage £30. The defendant denied having done so and put himself on his country. A jury of the venue round Colman-strete brought in a verdict that the Undersheriff never received the plaint, nor did he attach or deliver the goods. Judgment was given accordingly.

Friday before the Feast of St Peter in Cathedra [*22 Feb.*] *18 Feb.* *1305-6*

Robert Dru, butcher, was attached to answer William Andreu of Bernflete in a plea that he pay him 7s 6d arrears due on a sale of 60 lambs at 6¼d each. The defendant admitted the purchase, and that so far he had only paid 5d for each lamb. And because the Statute of the City[2] directs that a butcher should pay for the animals he buys before he kills them, and the defendant had not so paid, judgment was given that he go to prison till he should pay &c.

A jury of Henry le Brewere and others say that William Passemer did not find fault with his fellow jurors in the inquest made about the robbery at the Carmelite Friars, to the persons who were indicted, as he was accused of doing by Hugh le Armurer and others. He was acquitted.

John, son of Luke de Ware, was summoned to answer Elyas de Salle in a plea of account, wherein the latter complained that the above John as his apprentice received goods to the value of £10, to render account thereof, but wasted them

---

[1] Divorce in the modern sense was extremely rare at this period. Apparently absolute divorce *a vinculo matrimonii* could only be given by the Church on the ground that the union was unlawful. The ordinary divorce *a mensa et toro*, while it discharged the husband and wife from the duty of living together, left them husband and wife. It was granted for misconduct and was equivalent to a judicial separation. Pollock and Maitland tell us that *divortium* standing by itself generally pointed to a divorce *a vinculo*. In the present case it seems to be used of a separation due to misconduct. Pollock and Maitland, II, pp. 394–6.

[2] Cf. *Lib. Alb.* I, p. 263; *Lib. Cust.* fo. 201. This Ordinance, among others, is undated, but was evidently made before A.D. 1306.

and fled into hiding. The defendant denied receipt of the goods and put himself on his country. Afterwards a jury of the venue round Sᵗ Michael at Corn, consisting of Andrew Mel and others, said that John accompanied Elyas to the Fair of Sᵗ Botulph, and Elyas sent him to his wife, who delivered to him goods which were in his shop, and that John traded with them well for fifteen days, and afterwards fell ill, whereupon Elyas on his return from the Fair had him taken to his father's house; for these goods he ought to render account, but the jury did not know the value of them. Judgment was given that he render an account, and William de Leyre and Walter de Finchinfeld were appointed auditors. The defendant was mainprised by his father Luke de Ware. Afterwards the parties accounted, and it was found by a jury of Robert le Convers and others, taken before the auditors, that John remained indebted to Elyas in 40s. Judgment that he go to prison until &c.

Membr. 3 b
24 Feb.
1305–6

Thursday the Feast of Sᵗ Matthias the Apostle

Nicholas le Keu of Fridaystrete was attached to answer Simon Guth, John de Guldeford, William de Bidik, William de Helmeton and the other pepperers of Soperuslane in a plea of trespass, wherein they complained that he, by his journeyman who was at Sandwych, made an agreement with William Motoun and Robert Noldin, burgesses of Sandwich, that they should buy almonds, figs and raisins at Sandwich, and he would pay them for the goods, thus forestalling and enhancing these goods to the damage of the merchants and the whole City. The defendant pleaded that he bought from William Motoun two baskets (? *buillones*)[1] of almonds faithfully and without fraud or forestalling, and offered to make proof as the Court should direct. A day was given that the Court might be certified. Afterwards the parties made agreement by permission of Court.

---

[1] *Buillones* is possibly a mis-spelling for *bulliones*. A bullion was used of a boiling of salt, or of a mass of metal. The *O.E.D.* gives no instance of its application to produce. *Buillot* is an old French term used of a basket.

Nicholas, Edward, William, and Thomas, sons of Hamo le Paumere, deceased, came by John de Paris, "corder"[1], and Thomas le Paumer, executors of Hamo's will, and demanded against Nicholas le Lung, William de Caustone, Geoffrey de Langele and Laurence, son of Nicholas le Lung, executors of the will of Edith la Paumere, £200 which Edith gave to them during her lifetime, and prayed that the money be put into safe custody for their benefit, inasmuch as the Mayor and Aldermen are guardians of the orphans of the City. The defendant pleaded that neither the Mayor and Aldermen nor any other persons had any standing in that matter, because the above Edith gave to the six children £200 on condition that if any of them died before he came of age (*cetera desunt*).

Court of J. le Blound *held by* J. de Wengrave, W. de Leyre *and the other Aldermen on Wednesday after the Feast of S*^{t} *Mathias the Apostle* [24 *Feb.*] 2 *March* 1305–6

A jury of Henry de Harewe and others said that William de Hoggenortone threw down John de Lincoln, so that he fell in the mud and turned over three times before he could rise, and that the defendant also took John's sword and wanted to strike him with it, raising a tumult in which the neighbours joined. Judgment that he go to prison &c.

A jury of Robert Sterre and others said that Thomas le Tapicer is good and loyal, and that Thomas de Blendesowe goes to the tavern at night, gets drunk and is quarrelsome, and is a nuisance to the neighbours. Judgment that the latter do not remain in the Ward. Afterwards he was main-prised by Adam de Rokesle for his good behaviour.

Saturday after the Octave of St *Matthias the Apostle* 5 *March* 1305–6

Geoffrey de Gernemue was attached to answer Geoffrey de Garscherche in a plea that, being the plaintiff's receiver of moneys coming from the King's Custom on corn entering the City during two years, he refused to render account. The defendant admitted receiving the Custom for 12d salary, and

---

[1] *Sc.* roper. See Cal. of Letter Book C, p. 17.

said he rendered account every Saturday and paid over all moneys received. A jury was summoned, but the plaintiff made default. Judgment for the defendant.

Membr. 4   John de Lincoln, late Sheriff of London, was summoned to answer John le Botoner on a complaint that he took six pieces of sendal[1], value 6 marks, to the plaintiff's damage &c. The defendant admitted taking the sendal as a distress in connection with the forfeiture of two tuns of new wine, which the plaintiff had harboured among his old wines against the ordinances of the City. The plaintiff said he had paid 20s for the forfeiture, to which the defendant replied that he had produced no proof of the payment. Afterwards the latter admitted receiving 20s, but only in part payment of the forfeiture, and demanded a jury on that issue. A jury of Queenhithe of the Parish of Holy Trinity the Less was summoned.

10 March
1305-6   *Thursday before the Feast of St Gregory* [12 *March*]

John de Lincoln was summoned to answer Reginald de Walsingham who complained that Peter Ogger of Bourths, who owed him 19s 6d for board, pledged to him a horse, which the Sheriff had taken to the Guildhall by his clerk Richard and his son Reymund for valuation, after which the Sheriff had taken the animal to his own house and detained it. The defendant said he was always willing to restore the horse to the plaintiff. As the defendant's attorney did not deny this, judgment was given that the plaintiff receive his horse and be in mercy for a false claim.

Thomas de Wrotham was summoned to answer Stephen le Bakere, fishmonger, in a plea of trespass, wherein the latter complained that the defendant caused him to be imprisoned for a month and two days, by maliciously suing him as his bailiff on a writ of *monstravit*, and that afterwards a jury acquitted him. The defendant, on the ground of the plaintiff's allegation that he was acquitted and the defendant amerced, demanded judgment as to whether he ought to be twice punished for one offence.

[1] A thin fine material of silk, or linen.

Thursday after the above Feast

William le Plater complained that William Cosyn, Sheriff, who had attached, by his Serjeant William Sallok, the goods of Sir John de Engayn to the value of £7, viz. a palfrey, value 100s, and a robe, value 40s, at the plaintiff's suit against Sir John for a debt of 5 marks 6s 4d, afterwards delivered the attachment without the plaintiff's consent and to his damage. As the defendant said that he could not answer without the Serjeant, who was mentioned in the petition, he was ordered to bring him on Saturday.

Wednesday after the Octave of Easter [3 April]

Reginald de Thunderle, Sheriff of London, was summoned to answer Richard Priour, Osebert le Poleter, John de Bumpstede, Richard le Wilde, Golding le Poleter, Margaret la Buttermonggere, John de Alegate, Alice de Dunstaple, John de Wautham, Alice de Haliwelle and Felicia, daughter of Hughelyng, poulterers, in a plea of trespass wherein they complained that he took from them 51 pigeons, 7 hens, 6 capons, 8 pullets, and two and a half hundred of eggs and 5 cheeses. The defendant said that he took the above goods lawfully as forfeitures to the Sheriff, because the plaintiffs were common forestallers who forestalled poultry both in the lodgings of poulterers and by meeting foreigners coming to the City. Afterwards a jury of Cornhull gave a verdict for the defendant. Judgment was given that the plaintiffs be committed to prison[1] until &c. and that the poultry be forfeited to the Sheriff.

Anianius de Peyssoun had a day on Thursday after the Feast of the Invention of the Holy Cross [3 May] to give evidence that Ralph de Honilane was debtor on a Statute Merchant, and did not come. He was summoned for the morrow.

---

[1] As defendants, a position into which they had been thrown by the Sheriff's accusation.

Membr. 4 c   [Record and Process of an action in the Sheriff's Court.]

17 Nov. 1305 *Court of* Reginald de Thunderle, *Sheriff, Wednesday before the Feast of St Edmund King* [20 Nov.] *A° 33 Edw.* [1305]

Michael de Pistorie was attached to answer John de Eton in a plea of covenant, wherein the latter complained that a certain Mone le Lumbard came to his house and bought from him a "morel"[1] horse for £10 for the use of the defendant, and afterwards the latter came and was satisfied with the horse, but not with the price, whereupon they settled on a price of 12 marks, but the defendant had not paid this sum and so had hindered the plaintiff from selling the horse, which he might often have done for a higher price. The defendant denied the whole transaction and offered to make his law. The plaintiff said that he had two witnesses, who were present, and could be produced to prove that the defendant agreed to pay the same day. Afterwards the plaintiff produced his witnesses, and the defendant did not show any cause why they should not be examined. The first witness, Salamon, being sworn and examined before the Sheriff and Richer de Refham, Alderman, said that the defendant came to Marcellus *de Novo Mercato*[2] at Wolle-chirchagwe and met John de Etone, with whom he made a bargain about the horse that he would pay twelve marks before sunset, and in order to clinch it, he took a penny from the lining of his shirt [*de birra camisie sue*] and gave it to the plaintiff. In answer to questions, he said this was immediately after noon struck, and that the defendant was wearing a green supertunic, and that Bartholomew de Redyngg and others were present. Bartholomew gave similar evidence. Judgment was given for the plaintiff with damages, which damages were afterwards taxed both by the Court and a jury at 8 marks.

dorso   Michael de Pistorie alleged error in that the plaintiff claimed £10 and only proved 12 marks; and that the Court caused the jury to tax damages instead of taxing them itself.

[1] Dark-coloured.   [2] Newmarket.

On Thursday after the Feast of St Gregory [12 March] A° 34 Edw. [1305–6] the parties and the Sheriff came before the Mayor and Aldermen, who inspected the record, in which they found no error, and confirmed the judgment, except that they mitigated the damages by 40s.

[Record and Process of an action in the Sheriff's Court.]   Membr. 5

Court of Reginald de Thunderle, *Friday after the*   4 March
Octave of St Mathias the Apostle [24 Feb.] A° 34 Edw.   1305–6
[1305–6]

Richard de Fersdene and John de Ely were summoned to answer John Jacob, master of the "Edmund" of Brith-lingeseye, in a plea of debt, wherein the latter complained that they freighted his ship at Bordeaux with 68 casks and 3 pipes of wine, of which Richard loaded 58 casks and 3 pipes, at 21 to the 20, and the three pipes makeweight (*de avantagio*), at 10s the cask to London, the freight amounting thus to £27 10s, and John loaded 10 casks at 100s freight; and that this money should have been paid twenty-one days after the cargo had been disembarked, in proof of which he produced the charter. The defendants admitted freighting the wine according to the charter, but pleaded that they were not bound to answer the plaintiff, because the charter contained a proviso that he should take the wine to London to be dis-embarked, and he anchored at Sandwich and there left the ship, whereby it fell into danger, and the men of Sandwich and Mergate received 13 casks of wine for salvaging it by his default, and the bailiff of Sandwich one cask, and the master himself received four casks in part payment of his freight at Sandwich; and after the wines had thus been salvaged, they hired another master and mariners at Sandwich to take the ship to London at a cost of £11. They demanded judgment whether they were bound to answer the plaintiff. The plaintiff pleaded that being tossed about by contrary winds and tempest he anchored in the port of Wynchelse in order to save the men and cargo, and being unfamiliar with the course from thence to London, he and the merchants in the ship, to wit, Emeric Salmer and Walter and Gerard Pedyn, hired a certain Simon Carnon, their lodesman[1], to take the ship to the Thames at the expense and responsibility of the merchants, according to the custom of sailors[2], and that Simon took the ship to a port of safety before Sandwich; and since he, the master, was entirely lacking in money and victuals, and anticipated that they could not set sail on account of the uncertainty of the weather, he set out for his home in order to find money and victuals[3], giving orders to all in the ship that they were not to depart before his return. But the merchants in the ship, Walter and Gerard, together with Simon their lodesman, taking no notice of his orders, continued their journey, whereby they ran into danger, so that if the merchants suffered any damage or expenses, it could not be imputed to the plaintiff and did not arise from any default of his. To this the defendants answered that Emeric was not in the ship, and that Walter and Gerard were under age, and were not merchants, nor were they acting for the merchants in the ship. The plaintiff pleaded that they were merchants, and that they and the lodesman took the ship out of port against his orders, and he offered to prove this by a jury of merchants and mariners. Afterwards on Wednesday before the Feast of St Gregory, Pope [12 March], came the parties and a jury, which the defendants challenged without giving any ground for their challenge. And as the plaintiff was a foreigner, four good and lawful men were chosen and sworn to examine the challenge, to wit:—Adam Wade, John de Parys, "corder," John Paul and John de

---

[1] Pilot.

[2] No reference to the expense of the merchants is to be found in the Law of Oleron as copied into the City books (*Liber Horn.* fos. 355 *b*–360; *Liber Memorandorum*, fos. 103 *b*–110 *b*), this being the maritime law used in the City Courts. It is implied, however, in one of the ten additional customs given in the *Black Book of the Admiralty* (Rolls Series), I, p. 127, Rule 33, where it is laid down, that the pilot and not the master is responsible to the merchants for loss.

[3] According to the Law of Oleron (*Lib. Mem.* fo. 109 *b*; *Lib. Horn.* fo. 359 *b*), if a ship tarried in a haven so long that money failed, the master could send in haste to his country for money, but he ought not to waste time; for if he did, he was bound to redress the damages of the merchants. He was entitled to take the merchants' wine and goods, in order to sell them to replenish the ship's stores; and on arrival, the wine so taken was to be valued at the market price. The master was entitled to his freight on such wine as well as on the rest of the cargo.

Rokesle, who said upon oath that Alexander Pyk, Thomas Cros, Adam Lutekyn and Adam Ballard were not of the affinity of the plaintiff; after which they and the others were sworn in the panel which is annexed to this record. The jury gave a verdict that Walter and Gerard were merchants and regarded as merchants in the ship, and that they, together with their lodesman, set sail from Sandwich against the master's orders, so that if the defendants sustained any loss, it was not to be imputed to the master, according to the law and custom of mariners. Judgment that the plaintiff recover the sums claimed, and the defendants be in mercy for unjust detinue.

Court of J. le Blound, *Thursday before the Feast of* S*t* *Barnabas the Apostle* [11 *June*]

Membr. 6
9 *June 1306*

Thomas, Rector of the Church of S*t* Mary Wollechirchehawe, Guy le Clerk, and Richard le Coffrer, executors of the will of Thomas le Fleming, were summoned to answer Ralph de Wottone in a plea that they return to him one "gambeson"[1], one "aketoun," one "corset"[2] and one "banere," pledged with them for a loan of 13 marks, for which the plaintiff had paid 2 marks and a gambeson, value £10. Guy appeared and said he could not answer without his co-executors. Order was given to distrain them against the next Court.

Thursday after the above Feast

16 *June 1306*

A jury of Robert de Norhampton and others said that Richard le Barber of Cornhill bought timber coming to Cheap, before it was on sale, and put the timber in foreign carts so that the buyers were deceived, and that he had done this at Chinggeston[3] and Souwer[4] and elsewhere, and that he forestalled all things relating to his trade. Judgment that he go to prison, and only be liberated by special precept of the Mayor. Afterwards he was released on mainprise for his appearance on Monday to hear judgment.

---

[1] The "gambeson" and "aketoun," otherwise "acton" or "haketon," were padded or leather jackets worn under armour.
[2] A piece of body-armour.   [3] Kingston.   [4] Southwark.

Saturday after the Feast of St Lawrence [10 *Aug.*]

Elias Renaud of Gascony appointed Katherine Bompuz his attorney to receive from Richard de Burgh, goldsmith, his gold ring with a sapphire in it.

31 Aug. 1306 *Wednesday after the Feast of the Decollation of St John the Baptist* [29 *Aug.*] *before* John de Wengrave, *deputy of the Mayor*

John de Coppedok, Geoffrey Giffard, John Brid, John de Rodbourne, and Hamo atte Barre, poulterers, were attached to answer the Commonalty, for buying poultry within the City to sell it outside, as though they were freemen, thus producing a scarcity of poultry to the damage of the citizens. The defendants pleaded that they bought poultry in the markets of Kyngeston, Berkingg, St Albans and other places far and near, paying custom there, and brought it to the City and sold it there to the profit of the City, and that they paid the bailiffs murage and other customs; and they demanded a jury. Afterwards John de Redbourne (*sic*) and Hamo atte Barre paid a fine to the Commonalty to have the freedom, and went quit. A jury of John Burel and others gave a verdict in accordance with the defendants' pleading. They were main-prised by John de Sabrichesworth, John atte Barre, John Burel and Roger Prior, poulterers, to hear judgment on Saturday. Afterwards the defendants made satisfaction to the Commonalty and were admitted and sworn to the freedom of the City.

Maud Fattyng was summoned to answer Warin Page, her apprentice, for unjust dismissal. She pleaded that the plaintiff beat her, her daughter, and her household, despised his food, tore his linen clothes, and lent the money, which she had entrusted to him to trade therewith, to others against her will to the amount of 69s 4d, and also she had paid for him 13s for a mayhem[1] done by him on Alice Martyn, and accordingly she had dismissed him till he should pay the above debts. The plaintiff denied these charges and demanded a jury. After-

---

[1] Maiming, bodily injury.

wards a jury of John le Loung and others said that the plaintiff did not beat the defendant, despise his food, or tear his clothes. A day was given to hear judgment. Afterwards the parties made agreement by permission of Court on terms that Maud quitclaim all actions against the plaintiff, for which the plaintiff pay her 102s 8d. Maud was in mercy, which was condoned for 2s 8d, which she paid to Richard Poterel the Chamberlain.

Friday after the Feast of the Decollation of St John the Baptist [29 *Aug.*] 2 *Sept.* 1306

John de Bluntesham, taverner, was attached to answer William de Wynchelse and his fellows, collectors of the present tallage in the Ward of Cheap, in a plea of trespass, wherein they complained that when they demanded from Richard de Bluntesham, brother and landlord of the defendant, 2s, being his assessment, the defendant violently abused and cursed them, to their damage 100s. The defendant denied that he abused or cursed them, but acknowledged saying, "let those who thus assessed him be cursed and hanged by the devil." And since he cursed the collectors in the presence of the Mayor, judgment was given that he go to prison until &c. Afterwards he was mainprised by Salamon le Cotiller and William de Lauvare to come to the next Court and pay a fine.

John le Spencer, spicer, was attached to answer William de Prestone in a plea of fraud, wherein the latter complained that the defendant bought from him a cask of wine for 36s 8d, and asked him either to come or send some one with him to fetch the money. The plaintiff thereupon sent his servant William, and the defendant had the wine carried to Bredstrate and caused it to be . . . . there, and told the servant to follow him, which the latter did through various streets until they came to London Bridge, when the defendant told the servant to wait for him while he went into the privy there. The servant did so, but the defendant left the privy by another entrance . . . . [remainder of the membrane mutilated].

Membr. 7
5 Sept. 1306

Monday before the Feast of the Nativity B.M. [8 *Sept.*]

Alan le Baker, who was attached to answer the Mayor and Commonalty for breaking the sequestration made on him for his share of the tallage levied for the gift to the Prince of Wales, came and said that Thomas Juvenal gave him permission to break the sequestration in order to pay the collectors of Cheap Ward 2 marks. He admitted that he still owed 2s 8d, and he abused the collectors in the presence of the Mayor and Court. Judgment that he go to prison until &c. Afterwards he was mainprised by Walter de Bardeneye, William de Laufare, Adam de Auntioche and John de Lincoln, cordwainer, to appear on the morrow to pay a fine.

Nicholas de Herdewyk was attached to answer Thomas le Parmenter of Baudak in a plea of detinue of chattels, wherein the latter complained that when he deposited five sacks of wool in the house of Peter de Coumbe towards the Tower, the defendant had them removed to an unknown place, took away the plaintiff's seal and put another on, and afterwards delivered to him three sacks, but retained two, to his damage £10. The defendant pleaded that the detinue was just, because the plaintiff had pledged the sacks to him for £10 in which he, the defendant, had stood surety for him, i.e. for the sum of 13 marks in which the plaintiff had been convicted by the Justices of Traylebaston in an action of trespass against him at the suit of Walter le Parmenter, and for an amercement of 2 marks. He said further that the plaintiff, on delivery of the three sacks, begged him in the presence of the Sheriff and others to retain the two sacks till the plaintiff had paid the £10. The plaintiff denied this, and demanded to acquit himself by his law. The defendant said that this was an unjust defence[1], because he could produce witnesses, Peter and William. After taking an oath that he would not produce others than those named, and that he would not suborn them nor cause them to speak anything but the truth, he produced Peter de Cornwall, and caused the other witness

---

[1] I.e., against the defendant's allegation, which put the plaintiff, as it were, into the position of a defendant.

William to be essoined by John de Ware. The plaintiff demanded judgment against him as to whether an essoin lay,
on the ground that the defendant was a foreigner, and according to the custom and law of the City, he ought to have
his suit ready in Court. The defendant pleaded that after
he had one witness ready in Court, according to the custom
and law of the City, the other could be essoined. A day was
given to hear judgment at the next Court. After three post-
ponements that the Court might be certified, judgment was
given for the plaintiff, on the ground that according to the
laws and custom of the City an essoin did not lie.

Friday the morrow of the Nativity B.M. [8 Sept.]

Membr. 7 b
9 Sept. 1306

Stephen le Barber of London was attached to answer
Robert le Barber of Graschirche and Maud his wife, in a plea
of trespass, wherein they complained that Stephen came to
their house with a woman and asked to see the solar and to
drink there, and when Maud heard them making a noise she
ascended to the solar and found Stephen pulling on his
breeches, and he struck her on the head with a quart pot and
kicked her, to her damage £20. The defendant pleaded that
he went only to drink and buy wine, and that the plaintiff
assaulted him first. Afterwards a jury of Grascherche, consisting of William Wastel and others, found for the plaintiff,
with damages 10 marks. Judgment was given for that amount,
and that the defendant go to prison.

Saturday after the above Feast

10 Sept. 1306

Robert le Barbur of Graschirch and Maud, his wife, were
summoned to answer Stephen le Barbur in a plea of trespass,
wherein he complained that when he went to Robert's house
to drink, Maud and her maidservant assaulted him, and tore
out his eye (*oculum suum eruerunt*) while he was in the custody
of Thomas Juvenal the bailiff. A jury of the venue, consisting of John Laurens and others, found for the defendants.
Judgment accordingly.

Monday after the above Feast before John de Wengrave, *deputy of the Mayor*

The jury between Joan, relict of John de Armenters, and the Mayor and Aldermen, who sued on behalf of John's orphans, came in the persons of Richard de Wandelesford and others, and said that Joan had no goods belonging to John de Armenters, except what he devised to her and what was delivered to her by the executors. Judgment that her goods, which were sequestrated, be delivered to her.

Monday after the Feast of the Exaltation of the Holy Cross [14 *Sept.*]

A jury of the venue of Neugate was summoned to say by whom dung was cast into the ditches of the City.

John de Troys was attached to answer Gocelin the Serjeant on a charge of assaulting the latter in Grascherche Street and tearing his hood. The defendant admitted the charge, and prayed leave to make agreement. This was granted, on terms that Gocelin pardon the trespass and John pay him a tun of wine to be taken at his will. A day was given to hear judgment.

Thursday after the Feast of St Michael [29 *Sept.*]

Robert de Armenters, John Tedmar, Peter de Armenters and John de Northampton, chaplain, executors of the will of John de Armenters, were attached to answer Henry Scof in a plea of debt, wherein the latter complained that the late John de Armenters by his son John and Peter de Armenters, his merchants, bought cloth from him at the Fair of Westminster to the value of £50, A° 26 Edw. [1297–8], for which payment was to be made, half at Christmas and the rest at the Purification, and that £22 was paid, leaving a debt of £28. The defendants denied the transaction, and demanded a jury. Afterwards a jury of William de Parys, draper, and others said that the plaintiff sold £50 worth of drapery to John, son of John de Armenters, and Peter de Armenters, and that the latter paid £22 by an agreement under their names, but that the cloth never came into the hands or to the profit of John de Armenters, senior. Judgment was given for the executors, Robert, John and John. Peter de Armenters did not appear.

Saturday after the Feast of St Edward [13 Oct.]   *15 Oct. 1306*

Robert de Berkyng, goldsmith, was summoned to answer William de Helmeton for having sued the latter in the King's Court, and there charged the plaintiff with prosecuting a sentence of excommunication against him[1] contrary to the King's prohibition. The plaintiff pleaded that such an action in the King's Court was against the Liberties of the City. The defendant admitted having sued the plaintiff, and said it was lawful to do so. The Mayor and Aldermen forbade the defendant to prosecute his plea any further in the King's Court, as such action was against the Liberties of the City.

Friday after the Feast of St Luke the Evangelist [18 Oct.]   Membr. 8 b
21 Oct. 1306

A jury of the venue of Cornell and round the House of the Friars Minors was summoned for the morrow to say on oath whether John de Offington, mason, threatened the King's masons and carpenters, who were brought to London by Master Walter de Herford, mason, for the Queen's work, telling them that if they accepted less wages than the other masons of the City, they would be beaten; in consequence of which the Queen's work was unfinished.

Saturday after the above Feast   *22 Oct. 1306*

William de Leycestre, "fevere"[2], was found guilty of striking Stephen le Barber over the left eye, by a jury of All Hallows, Garscherche, and St Bennets, which assessed damages at 1 mark.

[1] I.e. in the Court Christian.   [2] Smith.

Court of J. le Blound, *Mayor, on Saturday after the Feast of St Martin* [11 *Nov.*]

Thomas Brok and Robert Pickard were attached to answer Nicholas de Cantebrig and his fellows, who were impanelled as a jury between Matthew de Essex and Baudewyn le Chaucer, for having said that the plaintiffs spoke falsely in the inquest and were perjured, to the damage of the latter 40s. A jury of Westchep and Cordwanerstret was summoned. Afterwards the parties came to an agreement without permission of the Court. They were amerced, but their amercement was condoned by the Mayor.

ROLL I

Court of J. le Blound *held on Wednesday the Feast of
St Andrew the Apostle* [*30 Nov.*] *A° 35 Edw.* [1306]

John le Flemeng, "verrer"[1], and William de Chichestre, verrer, who threatened the Beadle and guardians of the peace of Basseshawe Ward and Adam de Ordeby, "brazour"[2], were attached, and afterwards mainprised by Thomas le Verrer, Nicholas le Verrer, Richard de Sarum, verrer, John Aleyn, William de Seint Need, and Hugh de Tichemersh, mason, for their good behaviour.

Robert de Wych, taverner, and Ellen his wife, Robert, Thomas and John, their men, were attached to answer Henry de Scheleford in a plea of trespass, wherein he complained that they assaulted him and his friends at their tavern, because they offered to pay 3¾d for a gallon and a quart of wine according to the proclamation, and not 4d per gallon as demanded, and also that they imprisoned him till the middle of the night, to his damage £40. A jury was summoned between the parties.

Henry de Scheleford was attached to answer the above Robert on a charge that he and others drank a gallon and a quart of wine and ate a halfpenny loaf and were unwilling to pay for them, and assaulted Robert, his wife and his maidservant, to their damage 100s. Afterwards a jury of the venue round the Church of St Michael at Corn, consisting of Thomas de Kent, saddler, and others, said that the plaintiffs and the defendant assaulted each other, and that the latter took the plaintiff's supertunic off him and threw it down, and kept the plaintiff in his house until William Sallok, the Sheriff's Serjeant, ejected him. They assessed the plaintiff's damages at one mark. Judgment for that amount.

Friday after the Feast of St Lucia Virgin [*13 Dec.*]

John Bonde was attached to answer Peter Berneval in a plea of trespass, wherein the latter complained that when an

---

[1] Glazier.   [2] Brewer.

action between them in the Court of William Combe Martin in the Guildhall had come to a jury, the defendant assaulted him, to the hindrance of justice, and to his damage £40. Afterwards a jury of Reginald de Undle and others in full Husting brought in a verdict that both parties abused and insulted each other. Judgment was given for the defendant, and that the plaintiff be amerced.

1 Feb. *Wednesday the Vigil of the Purification B.M.* [2 *Feb.*]
1306-7 *A° 35 Edw.* [1306-7]

Richard Costentyn was attached to answer Peter Berneval on a charge of assaulting him in the Guildhall. A jury round the Guildhall [*patria circa Gialdam*] was summoned. Afterwards in full Husting came the parties and a jury of Reginald de Undle and others, who said that after the session of the Sheriff's Court the parties abused each other at the door of the Guildhall, and the defendant would have struck the plaintiff, but was prevented, and only touched him with his fingers, to his damage 12d. As it seemed to the Mayor and Aldermen that the damages were too small, they taxed them at half-a-mark, and inasmuch as the assault took place within the Guildhall, judgment was given that the defendant go to prison till he had satisfied the King for the contempt and the plaintiff for the damages. The half-mark was paid by the hands of Roger le Barber, Serjeant.

A jury of Langebourn was summoned to say whether Gilbert le Marischal and William Amiz had in hand 42s 4d of the tallage of £1048 made to acquit the purprestures and Sheriff's debts, as was charged against them by William de Hikling, clerk, who sued for the Commonalty. Afterwards a jury of William le Fullere and others said that 4s 4d remained in the hands of Gilbert, and that the rest was still owed. Judgment was given that Gilbert pay the 4s 4d, and that he and William be quit of the remainder.

Membr. 2 *Friday after the Feast of St Ambrose, Bishop* [4 *April*]
7 April 1307

Peter le Taverner and Richard de Mauncestre complained of error in the Court of Geoffrey de Conduit, Sheriff, in an action of debt brought against them by Peter Bolom. The record was read and confirmed and the Sheriff was ordered to give execution. The record remains in the Bag of Common Pleas among the writs of the thirty-fifth year of King Edward.

Wednesday after[1] *the Feast of St Leo, Pope* [19 *April*]   ? *12 April*
1307

A jury of the venue of the Ward of Nicholas de Farndon round the Church of St Michael at Corn and Ludgate was summoned to say whether John Bogeys insulted and cursed the Mayor, Aldermen and collectors of the Twentieth. Afterwards a jury of John Huberd and others said that the defendant did not curse the Mayor and Aldermen, but used abusive words to the collectors, and the collectors did the same to him. Judgment for the defendant.

Thursday after the Feast of St Mark the Evangelist 27 *April 1307*
[25 *April*]

Walter . . . . and John, his servant, were summoned to answer Thomas Scott, groom of the Prince, on a charge that when he wanted to relieve himself in . . . . Lane, they assaulted him and struck him with a knife, to his damage 100s. The defendants pleaded that they told the plaintiff that it would be more decent to go to the common privies of the City to relieve himself, whereupon the plaintiff wanted to kill Walter, and he in fear of his life defended himself, and that he did the plaintiff no other damage. A jury was summoned, but afterwards the plaintiff did not prosecute. He was amerced.

Monday after the Feast of St John before the Latin Membr. 2 b
Gate [*May* 6]   8 *May 1307*

Stephen de Uptone was in mercy for his many defaults.

The same Stephen was attached to answer Nicholas de Farndon, Alderman, and Andrew Mel and his fellows, collectors of the Twentieth in the Ward of Nicholas, for failing to pay his contribution to the Twentieth, and breaking the sequestration made upon him and carrying away the seques-

[1] Query: before the Feast of St Leo?

trated goods. Stephen pleaded that at the time of the sequestration he was in Norfolk, and the sequestration was not broken by him or with his knowledge. A jury of the venue of Paternosterstrete was summoned. And as Stephen acknowledged that in his absence his wife unknowingly broke the sequestration, it was ordered that she be attached against Wednesday. Afterwards a jury of John de Writele and others said that Stephen's wife broke the sequestration. Judgment was given that she go to prison &c. She was delivered to the Sheriff through William de Londoneston.

Walter de Dunstaple, called "*de Templo*," was attached to answer Roger de Brunne in a plea of trespass, wherein the latter complained that he found two men quarrelling at the Conduit, and was attempting to separate them and compose the quarrel, when the defendant assaulted him. The defendant pleaded that he found Walter and the others quarrelling, and went to stop the dispute, and that he did him no harm. Afterwards a jury of the venue said that when the plaintiff was stopping the dispute, the defendant took him maliciously by the hood, and kept him until he was delivered by the guardians of the peace. Judgment that Walter go to prison until &c.

24 May 1307 ### Wednesday after the Feast of Holy Trinity [21 May]

William de Conduit, taverner, essoined against William de Beauchaump, John Mautravers, knight, Hugh his groom, and Philip atte Beche, by W. de Reyle; Adam atte Bowe essoined against the same by the same. And the defendants came and said that the essoins were faulty, as the plaintiffs prosecuted jointly and essoined separately. Judgment was given that William and Adam gain nothing by their plea and be in mercy for a false claim, and that William, John, Hugh and Philip go quit.

Membr. 3
6 March
1306–7
Monday before the Feast of St Gregory, Pope [12 March] A° 35 Edw. [1306–7] in full Husting of Pleas of Land

Simon Bolet, Sheriff of London, was summoned to answer Nicholas le Pesshoner in a plea of trespass, wherein the latter complained that when he, as free of the City, bought from a certain merchant 301 fresh congers for 6 marks, immediately satisfying the merchant for the same, the defendant came and took the congers and detained them, to his damage £20. The defendant pleaded that John de Moking, William Lambyn, Richard Horn, Robert Turk and many other fishmongers of Bridge Street and Old Fish Street gave him to understand that the plaintiff bought the congers from a foreign merchant by night on the Thames, thus forestalling them against the regulations and the Liberties of the City, and accordingly he took the fish justly as a forfeiture. The plaintiff answered that the ship which brought the congers lay at the quay bound with a cable, and that the merchant exposed the fish for sale for a night and a day, and that John and the other fishmongers several times affeered them and sorted them in the casks (*in tendlos*[1] *sorciebantur*[2]), and he, the plaintiff, afterwards bought them from the merchant legitimately by day, the ship being tied up by the cable at the proper place, and that he granted a share of them to the others. He demanded a jury. The defendants repeated that the plaintiff bought the fish by night in the middle of the river, at an unlawful place, and the ship was not then tied up by a cable. A jury of the venue round " Fihswarf " was summoned. After several adjournments, owing to the fact that the Mayor could not attend, that the jurors made default and the plaintiff challenged some of them, a jury of John de Wymondham and others gave a verdict that the ship was tied up by the cable to the quay for three tides before Nicholas affeered the conger, and that Nicholas at vespers caused the master of the ship to move her from the quay, and then bought the fish at the Chapel of St Thomas on the Bridge, paying God's penny there[3]. A day was given to hear judgment on the Wednesday.

---

[1] *Tendlos*, perhaps for *tenellos*. Cf. Du Cange, *Obturaculum oris dolii*. The word appears in the City's Records, *Lib. Alb.*, *Lib. Cust.* and *Lib. Horn.* in different forms: *tandles*, *tendells*, *tandeles*, etc. Riley, *Lib. Alb.* Glossary, suggests a measure, and points out that a whelk-boat usually carried five tandles. The tandle was probably a cask of a certain fixed content.

[2] *Sorciebantur*, sc. *sortiebantur*, to sort or examine.

[3] The Ordinances of the Fishmongers, *temp.* Gregory de Rokesle, A.D. 1280, are given in *Lib. Alb.* I, pp. 379–386. It was ordered that no one

Afterwards an adjournment was made, and the jury was summoned to certify the Court as regards damages. They taxed damages at one mark. And as it seemed to the Court that too small damages were taxed, a day was given to hear judgment, in order that meanwhile the Court might be certified. Finally, on the ground that the ship lay at the quay for three tides with the congers exposed for sale before Nicholas bought them, and therefore the congers were not liable to forfeiture, and as they were detained for a long time and cost six marks, judgment was given that the plaintiff recover against Simon the price of the congers and 4 marks for his expenses and damages.

Membr. 4
26 May 1307

Friday after the Feast of Holy Trinity [21 May]

Simon de Rokesle and John de Fincham, goldsmiths, mainprised Roger Seyer, goldsmith, to restore to the Chaplain of the Abbess of Ancerwyk four cups of mazer, value 2 marks, when they were repaired, as agreed between the Chaplain and Roger.

16 June 1307

Friday after the Feast of St Barnabas the Apostle [11 June]

Adam de Ely was mainprised by Walter de Hakeneye and William Flinchard to hear judgment concerning putrid fish sold to Robert le Benere of the Stalls. The above Adam testified that Robert was accustomed to buy putrid fish and sell it again.

Richard de Braye of Bredstrete admitted that he cursed Robert de Gloucestre and Simon de Rokesle, collectors of the Twentieth in Bredstrate Ward, by calling a curse on those who assessed him. Judgment was given that he go to prison until &c.

Membr. 4 b
23 June 1307

Robert Box was attached to answer Hugh de Wautham, the Sheriff's clerk, in a plea of trespass, wherein the latter

should go to meet fish in order to forestall it, or should buy fish in a ship until the vessel had been moored to the land by a cable, or in any case before sunrise.

complained that when he went by order of the Court, together with the Chamberlain's clerk and Serjeant, to the corner of St Antonin's churchyard, in order to deliver to Peter Andreu and his partners, merchants of Montpelers, seisin of half the lands and tenements of the defendant in payment of the sum of £48 due to them on a bond, the defendant made a premeditated attack on him, and threatened that if he entered any of the houses he would lose his head, to his damage 100s. A jury was summoned against Wednesday.

Writ of attorney to the effect that Nigel le Brun, executor of the will of Robert de Bree, being in Ireland, had appointed Richard de Mortone and William FitzHugh his attorneys for a year or until his return. Witness the King at Lanercost, 1 March A° 35 Edw. [1306–7].

Wednesday the Vigil of the Apostles Peter and Paul [29 *June*]   Membr. 5
                                                                    28 June 1307

The jury between Hugh de Wautham, plaintiff, and Robert Box, "peverer" [1], defendant, respited.

William de Kent, tailor, and Richard Levesone, executor of the will of Walter le Sergaunt of St Paul's, were summoned to answer Nicholas le Archer for detinue of certain deeds which the plaintiff entrusted to the testator. The defendants said they had a co-executor, Henry de Neubiry, taverner, without whom they could not answer, and they demanded judgment thereon. Order was given to summon the above Henry.

Wednesday the morrow of St James the Apostle [25 *July*]   26 *July 1307*
by J. de Wengrave, *deputy of the Mayor, and other Aldermen*

John Deveneys was attached to answer John de Frysingfeld, knight, in a plea that the defendant, being the plaintiff's servant, and receiving his clothing in pay, at the plaintiff's request A° 23 Edw. [1294–5], had to obtain credit for him for carrying out certain duties ordered by the King, and that

---

[1] Pepperer.

he did so obtain £19 16s from certain creditors, and together
with the plaintiff entered into an obligation to pay those
creditors. Afterwards, when the plaintiff was setting out for
Ireland on the King's service, he, at the defendant's request,
bound himself to the latter by a Statute of £40, on condition
that the defendant would not demand more from him than
the above sum of £19 16s and any damages the defendant
might sustain owing to the non-payment of that sum at the
proper dates. And although the defendant received from the
plaintiff in Ireland A° 24 Edw. [1296] the sum of £9, and 9
marks on two other occasions for satisfying the creditors, he
had not paid the creditors, but kept the money, and had sued
the plaintiff on the Statute and obtained seisin of a manor
belonging to the plaintiff of an annual value of £26, by an
extent of £14, and had kept it for five years, to his damage
100 marks. The defendant pleaded that he did not belong
to the plaintiff's household, and that he never bound himself
with the plaintiff to pay any creditor, except a sum of 9½ marks
to Fulc de St Edmunds, which he had paid and for which
he now had the obligation, and that as regards the rest of
the money in the Statute of £40, that concerned the defendant's own property which he had delivered to the plaintiff
in the form of money, victuals, hay and corn. The plaintiff
replied that as regards the £40 in the Statute, he had not
received from the defendant more than the £19 16s originally
borrowed, and he offered to verify it by a jury. The defendant
pleaded that the Statute was a judgment in itself and ought
not to be annulled by a jury, and that he could not be ejected
from his free tenement to which he had entry by judgment,
and he demanded judgment on the ground that the plaintiff
had not produced any special deed exonerating him from the
£40. Afterwards the plaintiff failed to prosecute his suit.
Judgment was given that he and his pledges be amerced, and
that the defendant go thence without a day.

Membr. 5 b   William de Conele was attached to answer John de Trum-
peshale in a plea of trespass, wherein the latter complained
that he and the defendant were partners trading with the
goods of the children of William de Herforth, deceased, and

that on Sunday before the Feast of St James the Apostle
last [25 July] they began to render account before Thomas
Romeyn and their other auditors, and on account of noon
supervening, the closing of the account was adjourned till
the next morning, when the above William refused to
come, maliciously retaining the paper of memoranda of the
accounts; and when the plaintiff went to him at the Cold-
hakber[1] in the parish of All Hallows at Hay, and was asking
him in a friendly way about his absence in the morning, &c.,
the defendant and his servant assaulted him, to his damage
£20. The defendant pleaded that the paper was in the hands
of Thomas de Norhampton, as common friend, by mutual consent, and that John received no harm from him. Afterwards
a jury of John de Paris, "corder," and others said that the
defendant assaulted the plaintiff, to his damage 40s. The defendant was distrained to come on Saturday to hear judgment.

Wednesday the morrow of St Peter ad Vincula [1 *Aug.*]   *2 Aug. 1307*

A jury of the venue of Cornhull was summoned to say
whether Thomas de Flete, pheliper[2], derided the Mayor,
Aldermen and guardians of the peace, when they were riding
by, by neighing like a horse, and using other abusive words, in
contempt of the Mayor and Aldermen, as was charged against
him.

[Record and Process of an action in the Sheriff's Court,   Membr. 6
endorsed "*istud Recordum affirmatur.*"]

Court of Simon Belet, *Sheriff of London, on Friday before*   *21 April 1307*
the Feast of St George [23 *April*] *A° 25 Edw.* [1307]

John de Kent, tailor, was attached to answer John, servant
of Richard le Barber, in a plea of trespass; pledges of prose-

---

[1] Coldharbour was a capital messuage. It was leased for ten years by
Robert, son of William de Hereford, to Sir John Abel in A.D. 1317 [H.R.
46 (6)], together with easements on his wharf. It was purchased by Sir
John de Pulteney, four times Mayor of London, and was known as
Poultneys Inn. For the history of this house see "Sir John de Pulteny
and his two Residences in London," by Philip Norman, *Archaeologia*,
LVII, pp. 257–84. Kingsford's *Stow's Survey*, I, pp. 236–7; II, pp. 321–2;
Letter Books E, pp. 108–9; F, p. 158; Husting Rolls *passim*.
[2] Fripperer, or dealer in old clothes and furniture. Cf. *Lib. Alb.* I,
pp. 718–19; *ibid*. Glossary.

cution, Richard de Kelleneden and John Sayer. The plaintiff charged the defendant with an assault. A jury of the venue, consisting of Henry de Somersete and others, gave a verdict for the plaintiff, with damages ½ mark. Judgment accordingly. The defendant found pledges for the ½ mark, Hugh Absolon and Thomas le Barber.

Membr. 7 [Record and Process of an action in the Sheriff's Court endorsed "*Recordum placiti inter Petrum le Taverner & Ricardum de Mauncestre....*"]

Peter Bolom, merchant, was attached against Richard de Mauncestre and Peter le Taverner of Garscherch in a plea of covenant. Pledges of prosecution, John Laurenz and Simon the tailor of Garschirche.

21 April 1305 The plaintiffs essoined by Walter de Ebbegate. Subsequently the parties appeared, and the plaintiffs complained that they bought from the defendant 12 casks of wine for £24, paying £6 down, and finding security for the payment of the remainder; and at that time the wine was so dense and impure that it could not be recognised by sight or taste, but the defendant promised that it was good, and of good proof and short assize, and that it would draw well to the end. Thereupon the plaintiffs agreed that it should remain in the defendant's custody for a week, after which they met in London. The defendant then agreed that the plaintiffs should take the wine at his risk, declaring that the wine was good and merchantable, and that otherwise he would make the wine good and indemnify them in full against any loss. On this agreement the plaintiffs received the wine and kept it for a fortnight, when it was found to be putrid and corrupt, whereupon they went to the defendant and asked him to take it back or make it good, according to the agreement, which he refused to do. Afterwards the wine was found by the City's Scrutineers to be putrid, so that the casks were broken and the wine condemned, and again the defendant refused to make good the loss. The defendant pleaded that no answer need be given to the plaint. He admitted the sale, but said that the plaintiffs did not pay the residue of £18 at the stated time, and that he had sued them for that amount

in the Court of Geoffrey de Conduit, then Sheriff. The plaintiffs had tried to exclude him from his action by saying that he sold them the wine under pledge, and that it was found to be other than stated, and they had claimed judgment on that issue. But this exception had not been allowed by the Court, which gave judgment in his favour; and this judgment had been confirmed in the Mayor's Court. He now demanded judgment whether he need answer as to the covenant.

The plaintiffs replied that the defendant admitted the sale, and the payment of £6, and the time of the sale, and that he recovered the remainder of the purchase price, and they pleaded that they made the covenant with him eight days and more after the sale. They said also that the present action was a plea of account in which they were movers, and that a plea of account had to be finished otherwise than a plea of debt. They offered to prove the covenant in any way that the Court might direct, and to prove that it was subsequent to the sale, and as the defendant had put in no answer to that statement, they demanded judgment as in an undefended action.

After several adjournments for consultation, the Court had the record inspected, and because it was found that the defendant had received payment, that the covenant was of later date than the sale, and that the wine was found to be unsound, and as the defendant made no answer to this, judgment was given for the plaintiffs as in an undefended action.

[Record and Process of an action in the Sheriff's Court endorsed "*Recordum placiti inter Walterum de Merlawe et Thomam Pourte.*"]

Court of Simon Bolet *held on....*[1] *after the Feast of* Membr. 8
All Hallows [1 *Nov.*]

Henry de Merlawe complained that Thomas Pourte sold him a messuage in the Parish of St Dunstan by the Tower, on payment of 2 marks yearly to the defendant during the latter's lifetime, and that he paid the defendant the God's penny and 20s earnest money, but the defendant refused to fulfil the sale and agreement. The defendant denied the plaint,

[1] Probably Friday, i.e. 4 Nov. 1306.

and offered to defend himself by his law. The plaintiff said that Henry unjustly defended, since he had two good and lawful men, John and William, who were present when the covenant was made and when the God's penny and 20s were paid. He was sworn to produce them at the Quinzime. Afterwards the parties came, and John, the first witness, being sworn and examined in the presence of Salamon le Cotiler and Nicholas Picot, Aldermen, said he was present in the tavern of Peter le Taverner of Grascherch at Vesper hour with William, his fellow-witness, and David, the Sheriff's clerk, and others, when the covenant was made, and that the defendant made this covenant with the plaintiff because the latter had betrothed himself to his daughter, and he said the messuage would be safer in the hands of Henry and his daughter than in any other's. William gave the same evidence in the same words. Judgment that the plaintiff recover the 20s and his damages. A day was given to the defendant to pay the 20s, and also damages if he thought fit. As the defendant did not pay either, the plaintiff came and demanded that the damages be taxed by the Court, and the defendant came by his attorney to hear the taxing. The record and process were then read and recited and understood by Thomas Romayn, Richer de Refham, Richard de Gloucestre, Salamon le Cotiler, Nicholas Picot, Aldermen, Ralph de Alegate, William de Grafton, Reginald de Oundle, Andrew de Staunford, John de Waltham, Richard Gladewyne, John le Botoner, Roger le Viroler, Ralph Rattespray and others in Court, and the damages were taxed, including the 20s and God's penny, altogether at 100s. Judgment was given for the plaintiff for this sum, and that the defendant be in mercy.

End of Early Mayor's Court Rolls

INDEX OF SUBJECTS

BAKERS, forbidden to buy grain on credit, 173
— list of those hiring bakehouses, 155
— punishment of fraudulent, 67, xx
— seals for bread, 152
BANKERS, Lumbard, 94
BARDI, Society of the, of Florence, 32, 32 n.
BATOURS, complaints of the Girdlers against the Mistery of, 65
BEAM, charge of breaking the King's, 226
— action by the weigher of the King's, 93
— charge of weighing with a private, 160
BEQUEST, for construction of pavement of Bishopsgate Within, 151
BERMEN (porters), Society of the, 41
BILLINGSGATE, Wardenship of, 4
BISHOPSGATE, Hanse merchants charged with the repair of, 182 n.
— bequest for pavement of, 151
BLACK BOOK OF THE ADMIRALTY, 223 n. 1, 244 n. 2
BLACKFRIARS, murage taken for rebuilding the Wall by, 228 n. 1
BLADERS, acquitted of a charge of selling dearer after the Proclamation about Pollards, 63–4
BONUS SYSTEM, among the cordwainers, 148–9
BREAD, price of, actions relating to, 57–8, 67, 152, 153
BREADSTREET WARD, brewhouse-keepers of, 19
BRIDGE WARD, Collectors of, 38
BROKERS, the Sworn, 8
— persons charged with acting as unlicensed, 7–9, 28, 30, 32–3, 33 n. 2, 37
BUCKLER-PLAY, forbidden, 86, 86 n.
BURELLERS, complaints of, against the Weavers, 53–5
— action of, against the Weavers for ceasing work, 106, 107
BURGLARY, man caught in, committed to Newgate, 120
BUTCHERS, enhancing of prices by, 65
— ordinance as to cash-payment by, 237

CANDLES, Assize of, 67
CARMELITE FRIARS, the robbery at the, 237
CARPENTERS, alleged confederacy of, to disobey an ordinance touching their craft and wages, 25

CHAMBER OF THE GUILDHALL, 174
CHAMBERLAIN, Pleas in the Court of the, 46–8
CHAMPERTY, charge of taking a house unlawfully in, 218, 218 n. 1; see Maintenance
CHANDLERS, charged with enhancing prices, 59
— Craft of the, 67
CHEAP, presentment by the Ward of, 225
"CITY LAW," description of the Mayor's Court in, xxvi–xxvii
CITY OFFICERS, charge of resistance to, 258–9
CLERGY, Writ of Delivery in favour of a clerk unlawfully imprisoned in Newgate, 36
CLOTH, Assize of, 54
— prices for weaving, 54
COAL, Sea-Coal, bought at Retheresgate, 3–4
— price of, 177
— sent from Newcastle-on-Tyne, 192
— unhealthiness of, 34
COAL METER, the, 4
COBBLERS, accused of bad work, 4
COCKET, meaning of, 184, 184 n.
COIN, base and counterfeit, cases relating to, 39, 42, 86
COKEDONII, COKEDENI, COCODONES, base money, 149
COLLISION AT SEA, action relating to, 223, 223 n.
COLOGNESE, Guildhall of, 43 n., 182 n.
COMMISSION, sales by, 64
COMMONALTY, prosecutions by, for unlawful brokerage, forestalling and harbouring foreigners, 7–9, 12–3; retail trading by foreigners, 16, 35, 49; avowry of foreign bargains, 32–3, 37–8; unlawful confederacies, 1–2, 25, 33–4, 52, 157–8; forestalling, 46, 228–9, 231; unlawful ordinances by the Weavers, 53–4; refusing pollards, 58; neglecting to repair the bridge over Walbrook, 80–1; assault on City officers, 113–4
COMPURGATION, see Law, Wager of
CONDUIT, gift for building the, 112
CONFEDERACY, charge of unlawful, against the Coopers, 1–2, 16; Carpenters, 25; Fruiterers, 157–8; Skinners, 154; Smiths, 33–4

CONTEMPT OF THE KING, by defiant words against him, 58
— by breaking the King's Beam, 226
CONTRACT, breach of, for tiling houses, 40–1; for roofing a chapel, 82
— — to acknowledge and confirm the sale of a house, 220–1; to sell a house, 263–4
— — decisory oath of plaintiff in, 14, 14 n. 1
COOPERS, charged with suing a cooper in the Court Christian, 1
— — making an ordinance enhancing prices, 1–2
— fines paid by, on conviction, 16
CORDWAINERS, ordinances relating to apprentices, 170 n. 2
— accused of bad work, 4
— charged with enhancing prices, 62–3
— complaints of journeymen against masters, 148–9
— and·cobblers, Scrutiny of, 4
CORN, metage of, at Queenhithe, 3–4, 102–3
CORONER, of the City of London, 7, 102, xviii
COURT CHRISTIAN, charges of impleading in, 1, 12, 28, 33, 44, 52, 88, 141, 156, 226, 235, 251
— King's prohibition against, 28, 88, 251
— Mayor's precept against, 12, 28, 141, 226
— action in 1292 relating to, xx
COURTESY-GIFT, to the King, Queen and other magnates, 180, 216–7
COVENANT, actions relating to, 55–6, 81, 84, 93, 96–7, 99, 102, 123, 125, 158–9, 168–9, 190, 242, 259–60, 262–3
CURFEW, prohibition of nightwalking after, 189
CURRIERS, charged with enhancing prices, 61
— complaints of the Skinners against, 92–3
CUSTOM OF THE CITY, in essoins, 249
— foreign attachment, 17 n. 1
— gavelet, 75, 75 n. 1
CUSTOMS, actions relating to the collection of, 7–11, 16, 39, 41, 42, 71, 79, 85–6, 114, 161, 184, 184 n. 1, 239–40
— the King's, 16
— of wools and hides in Ireland, Rolls of, 132

CUSTOMS, for metage of corn at Queenhithe sanctioned by Mayor, Aldermen, and four men of each Ward, 150
CUSTOMS AND SERVICES, writ of, in action of Gavelet, 75, 75 n.
— pleas of, in the Husting, xiv
Custumals, of the City of London, viii

DAMAGE, caused by interference with a tiler, action relating to, 230
— charges of wilful, 113–4, 127, 214
DAMAGES, complaint that a jury taxed, 243
— a day given for defendant to pay, if he thought fit, 264
— mitigation of, 243
— taxed by Court, 243, 264
— taxed by jury, increased by Court, 254, 258
— taxed in Sheriff's Court, action for payment of, 209
DE ARESTO FACTO, writ of, 178
DEBT, ACTIONS OF, 104, 105, 109, 122, 126, 146, 173–4, 177, 179, 187, 192–3, 214–5, 223, 227
— against executors, 13–4, 184, 250–1
— by writ, 26–8
— removed into the Sheriff's Court, 29
— submitted to arbitration, 43
— against an official for allowing a debtor to escape, 48–9, 231
— in the Sheriff's Court, 101–2, 117, 118, 243
— by writ in the Sheriff's Court, 69–70, 181
— against Sheriff for refusing to execute a judgment, 100
— against a foreigner who makes his law with the seventh hand, 74
— Court of the Weavers allowed in, 96
— for detinue of a horse, 114
— against a father as debtor for his son, 138
— for detinue of money recovered in the Sheriff's Court, 186
— in the Husting and Mayor's Court, xxii
DEFAMATION, action of, in the King's and local Courts, 147 n.
— — for opprobrious words to a citizen, 20; an employer, 41
— — for defaming the Earl of Athol, 222; the Forest Justiciar,

INDEX OF NAMES AND PLACES

Assh, Robert de, 5
Asshendon, Robert de, Collector of Bradestrete Ward, 219
— Roger de, 19
— William de, goldsmith, 2
Asshewell, Thomas de, of St Anthony, 13
Athelard, Roger, 182
Athol, John, Earl of, 222, 222 n. 1
Attecherch, Adam, "batour," 65
— Katherine, 47
— — Thomas, son of, 47
Atteloke, Robert, 64
Atterderne, Ralph de, merchant of Almaine, 9
Atteweld, William, "batour," 65
Auberkyn, Reginald, 97
Aulyn, Beringer, 165
Aunore, Alan, fishmonger, 63
Auntioche, Adam de, 248
Aveswote, 12
Aykyn, John, son of William, merchant and mariner of Middelbourgh in Seland, 178

Bacheler, John, fishmonger, 63, 186
— Roger, fishmonger, 229
Bacwell, Baukwell, Bauquelle, John de, 26, 75
— — Justice of Gaol Delivery, 220 n. 2
Badborouham, Hugh de, of the King's Household, 215
— John de, poulterer, 231
Bailiff, Joce the, 234; see Sergaunt, Gocelin le
Baker, Bakere, Adam le, fishmonger, 63
— Alan le, 248
— Robert the, boatman of Serre, 79
— Simon the, Collector of Bradestrete Ward, 219
— Stephen le, fishmonger, 229, 240
Baldewin, Baldewyne, John, fishmonger, 131, 229
Ballard, Adam, blader, 63, 245
— Colouth, 9, 11
Balle, Ralph, 181
— Ranulph, 98, 118
— — Isabella, wife of, 98, 118
— Yvo, 64
Balsham, Roger de, 215
— William, tanner, 60
Baman, William, 115 n. 2
Barage, Ernald, 101
Baran, Bernard, 188

Barber, Barbour, etc., Gilbert le, 30, 42
— Hamond le, 214
— James le, 225
— John le, 42, 134, 135, 139, 162
— Manettus, son of William le, 124
— Reginald, Renaud le, of Vintry, wine-merchant, 39, 43, 101
— Richard le, 121, 122, 219, 229, 261-2
— — brewer of Dowgate, 19, 81
— — of Fletestrete, 42, 234
— — of Cornhill, 245
— — cook, 51
— — beadle of Walebrok, 86, 124
— — blader, 63
— Robert le, of Ewelleshalle, 59
— — of Garscherch, 23, 249
— — — Maud, wife of, 23, 249
— Roger le, serjeant, 254
— Saer le, 23, 42, 185
— Stephen le, 249, 251
— Thomas le, 176, 262
— — of Fridaystrete, 179, 201, 206
— William le, 110, 124
Bardeneye, Walter de, 248
Bardi, the Society of, of Florence, 116 n. 3
Bardolf, Sir Hugh, 34
Bare, Ralph de la, goldsmith, 146
Bareth, Walter, 40
Barlack, Guy, 101
Baroun, John, "batour," 65, 124
Barre, Hamo atte, poulterer, 246
— John atte, poulterer, 231, 246
— John de la, 81
Barres, the, of the Suburbs, 103
Barton, William de, fishmonger, 63
Basing, Basinge, Basinges, John de, 20
— Thomas de, 50
— William de, 139
Basseshawe Ward, the Beadle and Watch of, 253
Bassingbourne, Dame Margaret, widow of Sir Warin de, 180
Batour, Hugh le, 65
— Nicholas le, 174
— Ralph le, 65
— Roger le, 147
— William le, 65
Batricheseye, John de, cordwainer, 62
Baudechun, Richard, 83
Baudri, Baudry, Adam, tanner, 60
— Hugh, 97, 184
— John, tanner, of the Moor, 60, 161
— Robert, fishmonger, 63, 229

BAUMERE, Richard le, of Kyne-
meretone, 233
BAUNBER, John, 153
BAYSETART, Henry, merchant of
Malines, 179
BEAUBLET, BEAUBELET, Nicholas,
spurrier, 52, 168, 170
BEAUCHAMP, Sir Walter de, Steward
of the King's Household, 31,
36
— William de, 256
BEAUFIZ, Richard, 16
BEAUFLOUR, BEAUFLUR, John, 13
— Simon, 202, xxv n.
— Thomas, 81
BEAULOU, Robert de, 180
BEBLE, Geoffrey, chaplain, 94,
94 n. 2
BECHE, Philip atte, 256
BECHESWORTHE, John de, journey-
man cordwainer, 148
BECLES, John de, 5
BEDEFORD, John de, 70
— Thomas de, 152, 153
BEDEFUNTE, John de, "kisser," 61
— Walter de, "kisser," 61
BEDEL, Adam le, of Alegate, 179
— Robert le, 29
BEDLEEM, Brother Thomas de; see
Donecastre, Thomas de
BEFALD, John de, 64
BELET, BOLET, Simon, Sheriff, 256,
261
BELHOUS, Walter atte, 59
— William atte, 59
BELLEHOUS, Henry de, 63
BELLERYTERYSLANE (Billiter Lane),
74
BENERE, John le, fishmonger, 63,
76, 84, 93, 110, 133, 143, 173
— — Warden of London Bridge,
110
— Robert le, fishmonger, 63, 258
— Walter le, fishmonger, 229
BENETELE, Adam de, 158
BENGE, Henry de, 203, 207
BENHAM, John de, 225
BERCHENERESLANE, on Cornhulle,
103
BERDEFELD, John de, 205
BERDENN, Walter de, 203
BEREFORD, BEREFORTH, Richard de,
King's Treasurer in Ireland, 142
— William de, King's Justice, 153,
153 n.
BEREGHOLTE, Robert de, 7
BEREWYC (Berwick), 192-3
BERKHAMSTED, BERHAMSTEAD,
Nicholas de, 186
— William de, "batour," 65

BERKING, BERKYNG, Andrew de, 84
— John de, 154
BERKINGG, market at, 246
BERLEE, Adam de, 138
BERMINGHAM, Richard de, fruiterer,
157-8
BERNARD, Adam, 42
— Stephen, 107
BERNERS, James de, 112
BERNES, Richard de, fishmonger, 63
— Roger de, fishmonger, 229
BERNEVAL, Peter, 146,165,231,253-4
BERNHAM, Richard de, currier of
Crepelgate Without, 60
BERTAND, Guy, 50
BERTON, Walter de, 42
— William, clears himself by the
Great Law, xxxi
BETELY, James, 9
BETON, BETOYNE, BETTOYN, William
de, Willyem de, Alderman, 102,
109, 226
BEVERLEE, BEVERLEY, William de,
wine-merchant, 101, 166
— — Thomas, son of, 166
BEYNIN, William, 82
BIDIK, BYDIK, William de, pepperer
of "Soperuslane," 226, 238
BIGOT, Hugh, King's Justice at
Guildhall in 1258, xv
BILLINGESGATE, 103
— juries of, 49, 162, 179, 184, 221,
232
— Wardenship of, 4
BISHOPSGATE, Hanse merchants
charged with the repair of, 182 n.
— Within, bequest for pavement of,
151
BISSHEYE, Robert de, 189
BITTERLE, BITTRELE, John de, 112
BLACKFRIARS, murage taken for re-
building the Wall by, 228 n. 1
BLADER, Andrew le, 194
BLAKELOFT, Margaret atte, 149
— Margery atte, 179
BLAKENEYE, Peter de, 87
— Stephen de, 97
BLAKESLON, Robert de, cornmer-
chant, 207
BLAKET, Roger, apprentice, 226
BLAUNCHAPELTON, a jury of, 217
BLECHINGLEE, Robert de, 97
BLOUND, BLOUNT, BLUND, etc.,
Alice la, 81
— Henry le, stockfishmonger, 154,
165
— John le, 20, 141, 202
— — Mayor, 119, 135, 139, 165,
170, 204, 228, 239, 252, 253
— dominus John le, Mayor, 123,131

GAYTONE, John de, cordwainer, 213
— William de, 20
GEFFARD, GIFFARD, Geoffrey, 58
— — poulterer, 231, 246
GELDERE, John le, 2
GELDRES, Count of, 179
GENTILCORS, Richard, 231
GENUE, Gylenzon de, 160
GERAM, Simon, of St Albans, 172
GERARD, Brachius, 86
— Elys, 39
GERARDINI, Philip, *alias* Philip de Spine, 115 n. 2
GERARDOUN, GERAUNDON, Reymund, 166, 167, 168
GERMIN, Reginald, 110
GERNEMUE (Yarmouth), 162
GERNEMUHE (Yarmouth), Geoffrey de, 63, 228, 239
GERYN, John, 64
GILBERD, John, 64
GILINGHAM, GUILLINGHAM, Adam de, 5
GISORS, John de, falsifies the City's books in order to mainprise a man accused of felony, xxix
GLADEWYN, Richard, "sokenreve" of St Paul's, 81
— — attorney, 126, 130, 182, 264
GLOUCESTER, the Earl of, 185
GLOUCESTRE, David de, clerk, 175, 177
— Henry de, 50
— — alderman, 127, 264
— Richard de, 83, 112
— — Sheriff, 188
— Robert de, 79, 201, 258
— William de, cobbler, 2
GODALE, Geoffrey, at Flete, 63
— William, 64
GODARD, Simon, 112, 147
— — Alice, widow of, 147
— Thomas, 9, 99
GODCHEP, Ralph, 16, 167
GODERONELANE, a jury of, 175
GODESNAME, Richard, 10
GODESONE, Adam, 196, 223
GODMAN, Agnes, cook, 51
GOLDBETER, Odo le, 175
GOLDCORN, Joan, widow of Bartholomew le Locksmyth, 197
GOLDSMITH, William, 56
GOLY, Guy de, 88
GOMAGE, William, of the King's Household, 215
GORRE, William, cook, 51
GORYNGG, William de, 59
"GOTE, John the," 112
GOUS, Robert, 103
GOYS, GOYZ, John, smith, 210, 225

GRAFTON, William de, 264
GRAHAM, Simon de, 161
GRANDISONE, Sir William de, 53
GRAS, Gilbert le, 59
— — John, son of, 59; *see* Gros
GRASCHERCHE, GARSCHERCH, etc., juries of, 14, 222, 249, 251
GRASCHIRCHESTRATE, etc., 125, 250
GRASPEYS, Henry, fishmonger, 229
GRAUNT, Roger le, 148
— — barber, 173
GRAVESENDE, Cristina de, 14
GREENWICH, Roger de, 5
GRENE, Boidinus de, butcher, 58, 65
GRENEFORD, John de, 225
GRENEWYCH, 39
GREYLAND, GREYLAUND, Agnes, 97
— William, fishmonger, 63
GRIGORI, John, 70
"GRONEWOLD," the Ship called, 221
GROS, John le, clerk, 31
GUBBE, John, 63, 195
— Walter, 63
— William, fishmonger, 63, 64
GUIDICCIONI, Ricardo, 111 n. 2; *see* Gydechoun
GUILDHALL, the, 10, 15, 19, 44, 55, 87, 128, 152, 160, 163 n., 170 n. 2, 174, 181, 199, 240, 254
GULDEFORD, GILDEFORD, John de, cordwainer, 62
— — fishmonger, 229
— — pepperer of "Soperuslane," 238
— Simon de, 226
GUMBARD, John, 28, 29
GURDELERE, Robert le, Master Cornmeter at Queenhithe, 103
GUT, GUTH, Simon, 226
— — pepperer of "Soperuslane," 238
Guyppewyco (Ipswich), John *de*, smith, 33
GY, GUY, Gydotty, partner of Brachius Gerard, 86
GYDECHON, GYDECHOUN, Thomasyn, 97
— Thomas, of Lucca, 111, 111 n. 2
Gyhalda Teutonicorum, 43; *see* Hanse (Index of Subjects)

HABER, William, "hostermongere," 58
HACKENEYE, HAKENEYE, Adam de, "kisser," 61
— Matthew de, 221
— Richard de, 109
— Walter de, fishmonger, 63, 106, 107, 229, 258

For EU product safety concerns, contact us at Calle de José Abascal, 56–1°,
28003 Madrid, Spain or eugpsr@cambridge.org.

www.ingramcontent.com/pod-product-compliance
Ingram Content Group UK Ltd.
Pitfield, Milton Keynes, MK11 3LW, UK
UKHW030858150625
459647UK00021B/2745